DIRECT BEHAVIOR RATING

Also Available

Evaluating Educational Interventions:
Single-Case Design for Measuring Response to Intervention
T. Chris Riley-Tillman and Matthew K. Burns

The Guilford Practical Intervention in the Schools Series
Edited by T. Chris Riley-Tillman

Interventions for Reading Problems:
Designing and Evaluating Effective Strategies, Second Edition
Edward J. Daly III, Sabina Neugebauer, Sandra M. Chafouleas, and Christopher H. Skinner

RTI Applications, Volume 1:
Academic and Behavioral Interventions
Matthew K. Burns, T. Chris Riley-Tillman, and Amanda M. VanDerHeyden

RTI Applications, Volume 2:
Assessment, Analysis, and Decision Making
T. Chris Riley-Tillman, Matthew K. Burns, and Kimberly Gibbons

School-Based Behavioral Assessment:
Informing Intervention and Instruction
Sandra M. Chafouleas, T. Chris Riley-Tillman, and George Sugai

DIRECT BEHAVIOR RATING

Linking Assessment, Communication, and Intervention

Amy M. Briesch
Sandra M. Chafouleas
T. Chris Riley-Tillman
and Contributors

THE GUILFORD PRESS
New York London

A Division of Guilford Publications, Inc.
370 Seventh Avenue, Suite 1200, New York, NY 10001
www.guilford.com

Printed in the United States of America

This book is printed on acid-free paper.

Last digit is print number: 9 8 7 6 5 4 3 2 1

Library of Congress Cataloging-in-Publication Data

Names: Briesch, Amy M.
Title: Direct behavior rating : linking assessment, communication, and intervention / Amy M. Briesch, Sandra M. Chafouleas, T. Chris Riley-Tillman.
Description: New York, NY : The Guilford Press, 2016. | Includes bibliographical references and index.
Identifiers: LCCN 2016013968| ISBN 9781462525836 (paperback) | ISBN 9781462525843 (hardcover)
Subjects: LCSH: Attention-deficit-disordered children—Education. | Attention-deficit-disordered children—Behavior modification. | Attention-deficit hyperactivity disorder—Treatment. | Behavioral assessment. | BISAC: PSYCHOLOGY / Psychotherapy / Child & Adolescent. | SOCIAL SCIENCE / Social Work.
Classification: LCC LC4713.2 .D57 2016 | DDC 371.94—dc23
LC record available at *https://lccn.loc.gov/2016013968*

To my father, John Briesch,
who never failed to ask about what I was working on
and always listened patiently to my lengthy replies.
I will always cherish the support and encouragement he gave me
in work and life.

—A. M. B.

To my family, especially my husband, E. J.,
who have never refused to serve as willing participants
in providing critical and positive feedback
since DBR began and continues forward.

—S. M. C.

To my family,
whose support and encouragement
have been essential throughout my professional career.

—T. C. R.-T.

About the Authors

Amy M. Briesch, PhD, is Associate Professor in the Department of Applied Psychology at Northeastern University. Her primary research interests include the role of student involvement in intervention design and implementation, and the development of feasible and psychometrically sound measures for the assessment of student behavior in multi-tiered systems of support. Dr. Briesch is Associate Editor of the *Journal of School Psychology* and a recipient of the Lightner Witmer Award for early-career scholarship in school psychology from Division 16 of the American Psychological Association (APA). She has authored over 40 peer-reviewed journal articles.

Sandra M. Chafouleas, PhD, is Professor in the Department of Educational Psychology at the Neag School of Education, University of Connecticut. Her research focuses on school-based behavior assessment and intervention and school mental health. Dr. Chafouleas is a member of the Society for the Study of School Psychology and a Fellow of both the APA and the Association for Psychological Science. She has authored over 150 articles, book chapters, and books.

T. Chris Riley-Tillman, PhD, is Professor and Associate Division Director in the Department of Educational, School, and Counseling Psychology at the University of Missouri. He is Associate Editor of *School Psychology Quarterly* and *Assessment for Effective Intervention*. His research interests include the development and validation of assessment and intervention methodologies, single-case design, and consultation. The author of five books and over 100 articles and book chapters, Dr. Riley-Tillman is a member of the Society for the Study of School Psychology and a Fellow of the APA. He is Series Editor of The Guilford Practical Intervention in the Schools Series.

Contributors

Kaitlin Bundock, PhD, is an instructor in the Department of Special Education at The University of Utah and a high school special education teacher at Cottonwood High School in Murray, Utah. Her research interests include Tier 2 academic and behavioral interventions. She focuses primarily on interventions for students struggling in mathematics at the secondary level, Tier 2 behavioral interventions, and functional behavioral assessment in secondary schools. Dr. Bundock has helped to implement check-in/check-out in high schools and middle schools, and has trained special and general education co-teaching pairs in effective methods for teaching mathematics to students with disabilities in inclusive settings.

Ruth Chaffee, MEd, is a doctoral candidate in the School of Psychology at Northeastern University, where she is a graduate research assistant at the Center for Research in School-Based Prevention. She earned her BA in American Studies from Wesleyan University and her MEd in Learning and Behavior Disorders from the University of Louisville. Ms. Chaffee's research interests include feasible classwide/Tier 1 interventions, use of technology in interventions, and addressing schoolwide climate.

Nicholas J. Crovello, BA, is a doctoral candidate in the School Psychology Program at the University of Connecticut. He earned his BA in Psychology from Siena College. Mr. Crovello served as a research assistant on Project VIABLE-II, which investigated the unified validation of Direct Behavior Rating in a problem-solving model. His research interests focus primarily on behavior assessment and intervention.

Gregory A. Fabiano, PhD, is Professor of Counseling, School, and Educational Psychology in the Graduate School of Education at the University at Buffalo. His interests are in the area of evidence-based assessment and treatment for children with attention-deficit/hyperactivity disorder. He is author or coauthor of many peer-reviewed publications and book chapters. Dr. Fabiano's work has been funded by the Administration for Children and Families, the Centers for Disease Control and Prevention, the National Institutes of Health, and the Department of Education. In 2007, he received the Presidential Early Career Award for Scientists and Engineers, the nation's highest honor for early-career investigators.

Leanne S. Hawken, PhD, BCBA, is Professor in the Department of Special Education at The University of Utah. Her research interests are in the area of positive behavior support, particularly the implementation and evaluation of the Tier 2 behavior intervention check-in/check-out.

Rose Iovannone, PhD, BCBA-D, is a faculty member in the Florida Center for Inclusive Communities and College of Behavioral and Community Sciences at the University of South Florida. She is Director of the USF–Interdisciplinary Center for Evaluation and Intervention and the co-principal investigator of a recently funded Institute of Education Sciences development grant, Students with Autism Accessing General Education Model. Dr. Iovannone previously served as the director of the Prevent–Teach–Reinforce project, a 5-year randomized controlled trial of a standardized functional behavior assessment model; as Assistant Director of the Center for Autism and Related Disabilities; and as a co-principal investigator in the Professional Development in Autism project.

Austin H. Johnson, PhD, is Assistant Professor in the School Psychology Program at the University of California, Riverside. Dr. Johnson's research interests focus on the identification of evidence-based behavior support practices and the evaluation of observationally based behavior assessment methodologies. Before joining Riverside, he was a postdoctoral research fellow with a 3-year grant project funded by the Institute for Education Sciences examining national practices in social, emotional, and behavioral screening.

Stephen P. Kilgus, PhD, is Assistant Professor in the School Psychology Program within the College of Education at the University of Missouri. Dr. Kilgus's primary research interests include the development and validation of emotional and behavior assessment tools, including those related to universal screening, progress monitoring, and problem analysis. He is particularly interested in the effect of assessment on intervention outcomes and the evaluation of Tier 2 targeted emotional and behavior interventions. Dr. Kilgus serves as Associate Editor for the *Journal of School Psychology* and *Assessment for Effective Intervention*. He is also an editorial board member for *School Psychology Review* and *School Psychology Quarterly*.

Faith G. Miller, PhD, is Assistant Professor of Educational Psychology within the School Psychology Program at the University of Minnesota. She is a licensed psychologist and nationally certified school psychologist. Dr. Miller's research interests pertain to the implementation of evidence-based practices in schools, particularly as it relates to improving outcomes for children who experience social, emotional, and behavioral difficulties. As an applied researcher, she works to bridge the research-to-practice gap in order to improve outcomes for this population.

Amy L. Reschly, PhD, is Professor of Educational Psychology and Director of the School Psychology Program at the University of Georgia. Her research focuses on assessment of and interventions for student engagement and school completion, including working with families and schools. Along with Sandra L. Christenson and Cathy Wylie, Dr. Reschly was a coeditor of the *Handbook of Research on Student Engagement* and is Editor of *School Psychology Review*.

Preface

Direct Behavior Rating (DBR) represents a broad category of tools that have been popularly used over time in both practice and research in order to communicate information about behavior so as to improve student performance (e.g., home–school notes, daily report cards, check-in/check-out). Within the past decade, however, DBR use has expanded to also serve an important role in behavior assessment. In particular, DBR has been touted as providing an efficient mechanism to communicate information about behavior—information that is needed to make decisions about appropriate intervention supports. Although a great deal of interest has been generated by the development and use of DBR for different purposes, this book is the first unified text to offer a comprehensive overview of its use across applications.

The book is divided into four primary sections. Within the first section, we aim to establish the foundations of DBR. The three chapters introduce key terms and defining features of DBR, review the literature related to relevant target behaviors, and illustrate how DBR can be used to facilitate communication across contexts. The second section describes the use of DBR in assessment. These four chapters lay the foundations for DBR in assessment, illustrate specific applications of DBR in progress monitoring and screening assessment, and review issues related to training raters using DBR accurately and reliably. In the third section, we illustrate the flexibility of DBR application in intervention planning across a diverse range of possibilities. Specifically, the three chapters in this section provide an overview of how DBR tools can be used in targeted, individualized, and student-directed interventions. Finally, the fourth section brings together content related to the use of DBR for communication purposes by linking assessment and intervention. These three chapters (1) illustrate how to summarize DBR data for use in interpretation and decision making, (2) review information related to how technology can be used to facilitate such summarization and interpretation, and (3) describe how DBR can be used along with other data sources to create a comprehensive process for assessing and intervening with student behavior at the individual, class, and school levels.

Our goal in writing this book is to disseminate state-of-the-art research knowledge related to the use of DBR; however, we have also aimed to maintain a focus on applied utility. As such, you will find hypothetical case study examples woven throughout the book to demonstrate use across different settings (e.g., regular classroom, transition, home) and populations (e.g., preschool, high school). Each chapter also includes an implementation blueprint that clearly delineates the steps for using DBR across different purposes. We hope that these features will help to enable direct application to your own practice setting.

We are indebted to many individuals who helped to make this book possible. First and foremost, we would like to express our gratitude to the many talented individuals who made important contributions to this book. Austin Johnson, Stephen Kilgus, and Faith Miller have served as partners in this line of work over the years and served as coauthors across multiple chapters. We also greatly appreciate the contributions of our colleagues who have been conducting critical work in related areas: Kaitlin Bundock, Ruth Chaffee, Nick Crovello, Gregory Fabiano, Leanne Hawken, Rose Iovannone, and Amy Reschly. Thanks are also extended to the many mentors, colleagues, and students who have helped to shape our thinking and practices over the years. Finally, we are grateful to the individuals at The Guilford Press who helped to bring our ideas into print, including Acquisitions Editor Natalie Graham and Editorial Assistant Katherine Sommer.

Contents

PART III. DBR Applications: Intervention

PART IV. DBR Communication: Linking Assessment and Intervention

Purchasers of this book can download and print enlarged versions of select materials at *www.guilford.com/briesch-forms* for personal use or use with individual students.

PART I

Foundations of Direct Behavior Rating

CHAPTER 1

Conceptual Foundations of Direct Behavior Rating

Amy M. Briesch, Sandra M. Chafouleas, and T. Chris Riley-Tillman

School-based professionals have long relied on the rating of student behavior in order to communicate information about student functioning and promote behavioral change. Despite this history of use across purposes, attention within the literature has not captured the wide-ranging uses of such ratings in relation to facilitating student success. In an era of increased data-based and outcomes-oriented decision making for all students, capitalizing on the efficiency and effectiveness with which these types of ratings can be used across purposes simply makes sense for busy school-based professionals. This is particularly true given that educators have important responsibilities for conducting behavioral assessments, analyzing behavioral data, developing behavioral interventions based on their analyses, monitoring intervention implementation impact, and modifying interventions based on their formative evaluations across a range of problem behaviors, settings, and populations. Across the chapters of this book, we therefore aim to demonstrate the potential of Direct Behavior Rating (DBR) to serve as a tool with utility across assessment, intervention, and communication purposes. In particular, DBR serves as a critical link across these applications, each of which can be relevant for promoting child success across settings (e.g., home, school).

In this first chapter, we begin by providing an understanding of the historical and conceptual foundations of DBR before discussing specific practical applications across assessment, intervention, and communication purposes. We first outline the history of DBR from its origins in intervention to more contemporary applications in assessment and communication.

Historical Foundations of DBR in Intervention

The origins of DBR can be traced to the late 1960s. Although token economy interventions (using candy and trinkets) had recently been introduced into classroom settings as a way to reinforce students for the performance of appropriate behaviors (e.g., Birnbrauer & Lawler, 1964), a school psychologist by the name of Calvin Edlund (1969) was interested in finding a way to increase the saliency of reinforcement. He described an intervention in which the classroom teacher would first explain what acceptable social behavior looks like to the student and then rate the student's behavior accordingly at the end of each instructional block (e.g., reading, arithmetic). If the student demonstrated appropriate behavior during the specified time period, the teacher made a checkmark on the student's rating form. At the end of the school day, the form was reviewed and sent home with the student. Instead of using classroom rewards, the student's parents were charged with responsibility for administering rewards based upon the number of checkmarks earned during the school day, which ranged from free time to fishing trips! Edlund noted anecdotally that both parents and teachers found the procedures simple to follow and that desirable changes in student behavior were typically observed within a week.

In subsequent years, several additional studies were conducted using similar intervention procedures. In large part, the focus of this literature at that time was on establishing a more feasible way in which to deliver reinforcement based upon appropriate behavior. As Sluyter and Hawkins (1972) wrote, "Teachers often have too many demands upon their time to be able to systematically observe and reinforce the behavior of problem children during school hours" (p. 17). Shifting responsibility for reinforcement to the home setting was seen as an effective way of reducing demands on the classroom teacher and increasing the power of reinforcement. Over the next decade, several different names were used to describe this intervention approach, including *daily report card* (Bailey, Wolf, & Phillips, 1970), *good behavior letter* (Ayllon, Garber, & Pisor, 1975), *brag sheet* (Lahey et al., 1977), *praise note* (Imber, Imber, & Rothstein, 1979), and *home–school notes* (Kelley, 1990). These studies found that parents required only brief instructions for the intervention to be successful (Barth, 1979; Karraker, 1972) and that home-based reinforcement was more effective than praise alone (e.g., Schumaker, Hovell, & Sherman, 1977; Sluyter & Hawkins, 1972). Although some research suggested that positive effects were possible if the report card was sent home once at the end of the week (Dougherty & Dougherty, 1977), parents expressed a preference for receiving notes on a daily basis (Lahey et al., 1977). In light of the relatively low resource and time demands involved in a daily report card intervention, such an approach quickly came to be viewed as an important first step in classroom management before more intensive strategies are applied (Dougherty & Dougherty, 1977) (see Table 1.1 for examples of studies that have incorporated DBR).

TABLE 1.1. Examples of Empirical Studies Incorporating DBR as a Component in Intervention

Topic	Authors
Daily report card used to improve "rest time" behavior of kindergarten students	Lahey et al. (1977)
"Good news note" used to improve math work completion in elementary school students	Blechman, Taylor, & Schrader (1981)
"Brag sheet" used to decrease the number of inappropriate verbalizations in middle school students with learning disabilities	Burkwist, Mabee, & McLaughlin (1987)
Self-management intervention used to teach and promote social interactions between children with autism spectrum disorder	Sainato, Goldstein, & Strain (1992)
"Home–school note" used to improve on-task behavior of elementary students struggling with inattention, work completion, and disruptive behavior	McCain & Kelley (1993)
Behavior education program used to decrease number of office discipline referrals in an urban elementary school	Hawken, MacLeod, & Rawlings (2007)
Daily report card used to improve classroom functioning in students with ADHD	Fabiano et al. (2010)

Much of the research conducted over the last two decades, however, has focused on the use of DBR-like tools as part of a targeted intervention. As discussed in Chapter 8, the daily progress report (DPR) serves as a critical component in a check-in/check-out intervention (see also Crone, Hawken, & Horner, 2010). Typically, an intervention coordinator discusses the behavioral expectations outlined on the DPR with students at the beginning of the day and then students receive feedback regarding how well they met the expectations on the DPR at the end of each period. Rewards are then administered based upon the number of points earned throughout the school day. To date, positive effects of check-in/check-out have been noted across a wide range of students, with stronger effect sizes noted in elementary than in secondary settings (Hawken, Bundock, Kladis, O'Keeffe, & Barrett, 2014).

Additionally, there exists a robust literature involving the use of daily report card procedures specifically with students with attention-deficit/hyperactivity disorder (ADHD). Significant improvement in on-task behavior has been documented when home–school notes have been used with preschoolers (McCain & Kelley, 1993) as well as with low-income minority students diagnosed with ADHD (e.g., Jurbergs, Palcic, & Kelley, 2007; Palcic, Jurbergs, & Kelley, 2009). Frequently, daily report cards (DRCs) have also been used as part of a multicomponent intervention package involving strategies such as the posting of classroom rules, use of point systems, and administration of social reinforcement (e.g., Fabiano et al., 2007; Pelham et al., 1993). Studies have shown that the use of behavioral modification procedures such as the DRC may result in improvements to classroom behaviors that are comparable to the effects seen in medication conditions (Fabiano et al., 2007). The utility of the DRC in targeted intervention is discussed in greater detail in Chapter 8.

In 2010, Vannest, Davis, Davis, Mason, and Burke conducted a meta-analysis of those studies conducted between 1970 and 2007 involving a daily behavior report card (DBRC) intervention. The 17 studies reviewed were fairly split across primary and secondary settings, and were typically used to target either on-task or disruptive behavior. Results suggested a mean improvement rate of 61% from baseline to intervention; however, a wide range of effect sizes was noted. Moderator analyses were subsequently conducted in order to determine whether DBRC interventions were differentially effective based on either characteristics of the student or the intervention. No differences in effectiveness were identified in relation to the age of the student (i.e., elementary, secondary) or the target behavior (i.e., on-task, disruptive); however, larger effect sizes were found for those studies in which the intervention was implemented throughout the day (rather than during one specific time period), and higher levels of home–school collaboration (e.g., extent of home training, parent participation in reinforcement selection) were noted.

In addition to the use of teacher-generated ratings to provide students with behavioral feedback, an extensive literature base exists with regard to use of DBR in self-management interventions (see Chapter 10). Self-ratings are commonly used to increase the likelihood that a desired target behavior will occur without immediate external prompting (Shapiro & Cole, 1994). For example, a student might complete the rating independently, and then later meet with an adult to evaluate the target behavior and receive feedback (e.g., Briesch, Hemphill, & Daniels, 2013; Gureasko-Moore, DuPaul, & White, 2007). When students have utilized DBR-like forms to make self-ratings, positive effects have been identified at both the individual (e.g., Dalton, Martella, & Marchand-Martella, 1999) and classroom (e.g., Chafouleas, Sanetti, Jaffery, & Fallon, 2012) levels. Additionally, research has indicated that students as young as the elementary level can be trained to make accurate self-evaluations, thereby confirming the usefulness and reliability of information provided by children and adolescents (Ardoin & Martens, 2004).

Establishing the Psychometric Evidence Base for DBR in Assessment

Although much of the research on DBR-like tools over the past 40 years has incorporated DBR as the independent variable (i.e., within the context of intervention), researchers have frequently used DBR as both an intervention *and* as a means of monitoring student progress (e.g., Schumaker et al., 1977). Work conducted by Pelham and colleagues with regard to ADHD intervention monitoring, for example, has long referenced support for this type of behavior rating as both a piece of the behavioral intervention and as a sensitive and feasible data source (e.g., Pelham, 1993; Pelham, Fabiano, & Massetti, 2005). Additionally, results from a survey of classroom teachers indicated that over 60% of respondents viewed the use of DBR as both an intervention tool and as a way to measure behavior as highly acceptable (Chafouleas, Riley-Tillman, & Sassu, 2006). Unfortunately, although reference to use of DBR-like ratings in assessment has been made for many years, most often such statements were made informally or anecdotally, and the psychometric defensibility of DBR as a data source received little attention.

In recent years, however, the need for efficient sources of school-based assessment data, such as DBR, has become not only a desirable feature but also a critical one. The advent and popularity of positive behavior support and multi-tiered models of service delivery require the development and refinement of improved assessments. From 2007 to 2011, the percentage of K–12 district administrators reporting implementation of a multi-tiered model of supports rose dramatically from 24 to 94% (Spectrum K12, 2011). Unfortunately, however, developments with regard to appropriate assessment technologies have not kept pace, causing educators to struggle with how to efficiently and effectively make decisions regarding student behavior. Assessments within a multi-tiered model of service delivery must be sufficiently flexible and dynamic to yield data that are useful at the system, group, and individual level, and although a great deal of literature exists surrounding these substantive issues with regard to academic assessment (e.g., curriculum-based measurement), a similar statement cannot be made with regard to the assessment of social behavior. The argument has been made, however, that DBR holds particular promise as a viable method for use in emerging assessment contexts, given both the current popular use of nonstandard versions among educators (Chafouleas et al., 2006) and the speed at which the empirical base supporting use of standard versions has grown (Christ, Riley-Tillman, & Chafouleas, 2009).

When conceptualized as an assessment tool, procedures under the domain of DBR have been said to combine the characteristics of both systematic direct observation and behavior rating scales (Chafouleas, Riley-Tillman, & Sugai, 2007). Systematic direct observation typically involves having an independent observer evaluate a child's behavior using a coding system to record the presence of prespecified behaviors. Given that the level of inference is reduced through the direct measurement of behavior, systematic direct observation is often considered the gold standard of behavioral assessment procedures. The feasibility of this approach, however, can become a substantial concern as the number of students or observations increases. In contrast, indirect behavior rating scales (e.g., Behavior Assessment System for Children, Third Edition [BASC-3]; Reynolds & Kamphaus, 2015) consist of ratings that are usually marked at a time that is temporally removed from the actual behavioral event. For example, a teacher might be asked to rate how often a student appeared sad over the past month. Although behavior rating scales are simple to complete—thus enhancing feasibility—the fact that they require highly inferential interpretations to discern the target behavior may limit the validity of the data obtained.

DBR represents a hybrid tool, combining the strengths of a rating scale and the benefits of direct observation. Like indirect behavior rating scales, using DBR requires rating target behavior on a scale. For example, a teacher might monitor and rate the degree to which "Jesse" was actively engaged (0 = *not at all engaged*, 10 = *completely engaged*) within a given 60-minute interval. However, DBR is also similar to systematic direct observation, in that rating occurs under specific and similar conditions (e.g., 45-minute morning independent seatwork), is in close proximity to the target behavior and requires minimal inference to discern the target of measurement, given the use of operational definitions. Thus, although the rating process may be similar to a traditional behavior rating scale, the fact that the rating follows a specified shorter period of time increases the directness of assessment.

Much work has been conducted over the past decade to better understand the psychometric defensibility of using DBR as a behavioral assessment tool. A comprehensive research line funded by the U.S. Department of Education was initiated in 2006 to develop and evaluate single-item scale versions of DBR (Chafouleas, Riley-Tillman, Christ, & Sugai, 2009; Project VIABLE: R324B060014). In addition to exploring issues related to target behavior selection and scale design, this line of research investigated the interrater reliability, temporal stability, convergent validity, and sensitivity to change of DBR ratings. In addition, a more recent, federally funded line of investigation (Chafouleas, Riley-Tillman, Fabiano, Welsh, & Swaminathan, 2011; Project VIABLE-II: R324A110017) has explored the use of DBR within a problem-solving model to identify at-risk students (i.e., behavioral screening) as well as to monitor their progress in response to intervention. Research within this line has begun to provide guidance with regard to behavioral screening decision points, such as the use of appropriate cut scores and optimal frequency of screening assessments. Across both projects, studies have been conducted in order to understand the degree of training required to conduct accurate DBR ratings, given concerns related to potential rater bias. Individual studies are outlined in Table 1.2, and research evidence accumulated to date is discussed in greater detail throughout the chapters on the foundations of assessment (Chapter 4), progress monitoring (Chapter 5), screening (Chapter 6), and rater training (Chapter 7).

Additionally, recent research conducted by several authors has demonstrated the potential role that DBR-like tools may play in intensive intervention. Because behavioral intervention plans at the intensive level are individualized to address unique student needs, greater customization may be needed when it comes to assessment tools than is typically afforded by a standard DBR form consisting of the same items considered as core behavioral competencies for all students (e.g.,

TABLE 1.2. Empirical Studies of DBR-SIS Use for Assessment Purposes

Topic	Citation
Target behavior selection	
Item wording (positive vs. negative), level of behavior (low, medium, high) for AE, DB, RS	Chafouleas, Jaffrey, Riley-Tillman, Christ, & Sen (2013)
Item wording (positive vs. negative) of multiple target behaviors	Christ, Riley-Tillman, Chafouleas, & Jaffery (2011)
Item wording (positive vs. negative, specific vs. global) of AE, DB, CO	Riley-Tillman, Chafouleas, Christ, Briesch, & LeBel (2009)
Scale design	
Scale gradients (5 vs. 10), scale length (50 vs. 100 mm), scale type (discrete vs. continuous) for AE, DB	Briesch, Kilgus, Chafouleas, Riley-Tillman, & Christ (2012)
Scale gradients (6- vs. 10- vs. 14-point scale) when assessing active manipulation of objects and visually distracted behavior	Chafouleas, Christ, & Riley-Tillman (2009)
Observation length	
Scaling (proportional vs. absolute), observation length (5, 10, 20 minutes) when assessing AE and DB	Riley-Tillman, Christ, Chafouleas, Boice, & Briesch (2010)
Reliability	
Across raters and occasions when assessing AE	Briesch, Chafouleas, & Riley-Tillman (2010)
Across raters and occasions when assessing social behavior of preschool students	Chafouleas, Christ, Riley-Tillman, Briesch, & Chanese (2007)
Across raters and occasions when assessing AE and DB	Chafouleas, Briesch, et al. (2010)
Across raters and occasions when assessing active manipulation of objects and visually distracted behavior	Christ, Riley-Tillman, Chafouleas, & Boice (2010)
Concurrent validity	
Of AE ratings in comparison to systematic direct observation	Briesch et al. (2010)
Of screening assessments of AE and DB in relation to SSRS	Chafouleas, Kilgus, & Hernandez (2009)
Of on-task ratings in comparison to systematic direct observation	Chafouleas, McDougal, Riley-Tillman, Panahon, & Hilt (2005)
Of on-task ratings in comparison to systematic direct observation	Chafouleas, Riley-Tillman, Sassu, LaFrance, & Patwa (2007)
Of on-task and DB ratings in comparison to systematic direct observation	Riley-Tillman, Chafouleas, Sassu, Chanese, & Glazer (2008)

(continued)

TABLE 1.2. *(continued)*

Topic	Citation
Sensitivity to change	
In response to a daily report card intervention when assessing AE, DB, RS	Chafouleas, Sanetti, Kilgus, & Maggin (2012)
In response to a silent reading intervention intervention when assessing AE, DB	Riley-Tillman, Methe, & Weegar (2009)
Classification accuracy	
Of AE, DB, and RS ratings in comparison to scores on the BESS and SRSS	Chafouleas, Kilgus, et al. (2013)
Of AE, DB, and CO ratings in comparison to scores on the BESS and SSIS	Kilgus, Chafouleas, Riley-Tillman, & Welsh (2012)
Of AE, DB, and RS ratings in comparison to scores on the BESS and SSIS	Kilgus, Riley-Tillman, Chafouleas, Christ, & Welsh (2014)
Of AE, DB, and RS ratings in comparison to ODRs, nomination methods, scores on the BESS, and scores on the SSIS	Miller, Welsh, Chafouleas, Riley-Tillman, & Fabiano (2015)

Note. AE, academic engagement; BESS, Behavioral and Emotional Screening System; CO, compliance; DB, disruptive behavior; ODR, office discipline referral; RS, respectful behavior; SRSS, Student Risk Screening Scale; SSIS, Social Skills Improvement System; SSRS, Social Skills Rating Scale.

academically engaged, nondisruptive, respectful). One approach has been to create a summated DBR consisting of three to five targets selected from a student's individualized education program (IEP; Fabiano et al., 2010). Other researchers have advocated for creating brief rating scales (e.g., 10 items) by selecting target items from comprehensive behavior rating scales based on high defensibility (e.g., Volpe, Gadow, Blom-Hoffman, & Feinberg, 2009). Furthermore, as is discussed in Chapter 9, the Individualized Behavior Rating Scale Tool (IBRST) was designed to maximize feasibility while allowing for customization. Although the target behavior and rating anchors (i.e., what is considered to represent a *good day*) are individually determined for each student, all ratings are conducted using the same 5-point Likert scale ranging from *very bad day* to *great day*. Preliminary research has demonstrated high levels of interrater agreement when using the IBRST to rate the behavior of students in grades K through 8 (Iovannone et al., 2014b).

Linking Assessment and Intervention to Improve Communication

Although the dual role of DBR within intervention and assessment has become fairly well established, in this book we also aim to emphasize a third role of DBR:

that of promoting communication. DBR represents both an effective and efficient way of communicating information about student behavior across a variety of individuals. As is discussed in Chapter 3, feedback can be shared collaboratively with multiple stakeholders, including professionals within the school (e.g., in-school support providers), those working in community systems (e.g., physicians, mental health counselors), families, and the students themselves.

In the past, effective communication of assessment results depended on the practitioner's ability to describe and interpret the results of standardized assessments in a way that could be easily understood by a range of stakeholders during a one-time meeting. Although this type of communication continues to have a place in schools, we argue that the importance of communication has increased substantially with the shift to multi-tiered models of service delivery. Within a multi-tiered model, proactive efforts are made to identify struggling students early and to provide those students with intervention supports that are aligned with their level of need. If student behavior is not responsive to the implemented supports and strategies, new and potentially more intensive services are considered. Because decisions regarding intervention effectiveness are made based upon student progress data, regular communication about student behavior is essential to making timely decisions about appropriate intervention supports. In order for information about student behavior to be effectively utilized, however, it needs to be both easily interpretable by professionals, easily understood by all stakeholders, and efficient to use. Accurate interpretation of data is critical to good decision making. School professionals can collect all of the data in the world, but if they do not know what the data mean or how they can be used to improve student performance, the numbers alone have no value. One of the challenges in shifting to a multi-tiered approach is that the interpretation of data requires a new and different skill set than was needed in the past. Traditionally, most school personnel were trained in the interpretation of either criterion- or norm-referenced assessment data. That is, a test score would either be compared to a predetermined criterion (e.g., a score above *X* represents mastery) or to peer performance (e.g., a score at the 75th percentile indicates that the student is performing at or above typical peers) in order to make a judgment about performance. In contrast, progress monitoring requires one to collect an ongoing stream of data, which is then evaluated systematically and routinely. We provide guidance regarding the summarization, presentation, and interpretation of DBR data to inform decision making across assessment and intervention tiers in Chapter 11.

Another factor that is critical to making timely, student-centered decisions is the efficiency of data collection, storage, and summarization procedures because those data that are the easiest to collect, access, interpret, and understand are those that are most likely to be used. Although paper-and-pencil systems of data collection and storage may be reasonable for managing the information of a small group of students, the need for data at universal, targeted, and intensive tiers necessitates more feasible and integrated systems. In recent years, electronic data systems have increased both in number and in popularity. Such systems not only reduce the amount of time needed for scoring and summarization, but also allow multiple users to easily access and share information about student performance. In Chapter 12, we review information related to how technology such as existing and emerging computer applications can be used to facilitate DBR data summarization and interpretation. We acknowledge that in order for widespread dissemination and use of DBR to occur, it is essential that commensurate advancements in technology occur to make data use relevant, efficient, and durable.

Contemporary Conceptualization of DBR

Nearly half a century of research across intervention and assessment domains has led us to the contemporary conceptualization of what we now know as DBR. In this section, we describe the defining characteristics of DBR and highlight how the flexibility, defensibility, efficiency, and repeatability of DBR make it particularly attractive for use across contemporary assessment and intervention purposes.

Defining Characteristics

Across all potential applications, DBR is characterized by a diverse and flexible set of procedures and instrumentation. At its core, however, the term *DBR* incorporates the defining characteristics of *directness* of observation, observation of specific *behaviors*, and evaluation of *ratings* (Christ et al., 2009).

Directness of Observation

When we talk about directness of observation, we are referring to how close or removed in time an assessment is to the actual occurrence of the behavior (Cone, 1978). At one end of the continuum are judgments that are highly indirect, in that behavior is considered retrospectively, long after it actually occurred. These types of judgments are often relatively simple to make; however, we know that the more time that elapses between an event and our recollection of that event, the more likely it is that our memory of the event will become clouded. An extreme example of this would be asking a teacher in May to describe how well one student interacted with his or her peers in October. The resulting judgment inevitably reflects an individual's perception of the problem more so than the actual occurrence of behavior. At the other end of the continuum are assessments that are highly direct, in that behavior is noted at the exact time and place at which it occurs. Highly direct assessments introduce far less error because judgments are made based on observed behavior; however, they are much more time and resource intensive. The most extreme example of direct assessment would be recording a target student's behavior on a second-by-second basis. Although this approach would provide the teacher with a highly accurate depiction of the student's behavior, it would also constitute a full-time job for whoever was observing the student!

Within the context of assessment, the direct feature of DBR means that rating should occur "in close proximity to the time and place of a . . . relatively short observation interval" in order to ensure the most direct assessment of behavior possible (Chafouleas, 2011, p. 579). Although an optimal observation length has not been specified, the length of an observation interval will inevitably influence the reliability and accuracy of the obtained data. An observation interval that is too short can be problematic if there is a low likelihood that the target behavior will be observed. A low sampling rate means that the rater has less information about the behavior, and raises the risk of using information gained outside of the observation period to generate ratings (Edelbrock, 1983). On the other hand, an observation interval that is too long can also be problematic in that there is a greater likelihood of rater bias. As the time between a behavioral occurrence and behavioral recording increases, so too does the chance of rater error including halo (*overall impression of person influences rating of behavior*) and recency (*rating across an observation period influenced by most recent behavior*) effects (Edelbrock, 1983). Given these concerns, the use of DBR within an assessment context has most often relied upon observation periods that correspond with natural breaks in instruction in the elementary school classroom (e.g., Briesch, Chafouleas, & Riley-Tillman, 2010) or classroom periods at the secondary level (e.g., Chafouleas, Briesch, et al., 2010).

Although directness is most often emphasized within the context of assessment, it is also important when it comes to delivering behavioral feedback in the context of intervention. Timing is an important feature of feedback, with the distinction often being made between whether feedback is immediate or delayed. Within an academic context, students who receive immediate feedback know what errors they may have made and can take action to correct them. When students receive delayed feedback, however, the concern is that they may continue to practice errors during the time period before they receive the feedback. The importance of immediate feedback has been emphasized in studies of classroom learning (Kulik & Kulik, 1988; More, 1969) and computer-based instruction (Azevedo & Bernard, 1995). Although typically considered in academic domains, this concept can certainly be extended to the treatment of behavioral problems as well. That is, whereas the provision of intermittent behavioral feedback (e.g., overall rating of green, yellow, or red for the day; performance ratings on a progress report) may be sufficient for the average student in a classroom, those students with more defined behavioral needs may require more immediate feedback about their performance. The use of a DBR-based intervention, such as a DRC, thus permits students to receive regular feedback throughout the day, which can be used to make ongoing adjustments to behavior.

Observation of Specific Behaviors

The second defining characteristic of DBR is a focus on the observation of specific behaviors. Whereas the focus of traditional personality assessment was on the measurement of underlying traits (e.g., conscientiousness, empathy) in order to predict future behavior, behavioral assessment approaches (1) focus on what an individual does and (2) view behavior as situationally specific (Goldfried & Kent, 1972). Cone (1978) categorized behaviors as motoric, physiological, or cognitive. *Motor behaviors* are those that involve movement, ranging from raising one's hand to answer a question to kicking a neighboring peer in line. These behaviors are generally easy to observe, and reliable measurements are possible without the aid of sophisticated equipment. In contrast, *physiological behaviors* must often be measured using specialized instruments. Measuring heart rate via a monitor or sweating via galvanic skin response, for example, can provide physiological indicators of arousal. Finally, cognitive behaviors are those private events that occur within one's head, including thoughts, feelings, and wishes. Cognitive-behavioral therapy, for example, aims to replace client's faulty cognitions with more adaptive ones. The commonality shared is that each type of behavior can be observed and assessed by a rater, and can be expected to vary to some degree across assessment occasions.

As opposed to traits that are considered to be more stable and difficult to modify (e.g., intelligence, personality), appropriate behavioral targets selected for use as DBR items should be those that are likely to respond to school-based intervention. Furthermore, whether within the context of intervention or assessment, DBR is best used to target those behaviors that are both observable and measurable. By focusing on observable, measurable behaviors, we avoid the need for inferences. High-inference judgments both introduce unwanted error in the context of assessment and increase the probability of disagreements in the context of intervention.

Rating of Behavior

The final defining characteristic of DBR is the use of ratings to quantify a person's perception of behavior (Christ et al., 2009). That is, rather than keeping a frequency count or directly timing the duration of a behavior, ratings provide an estimate of the chosen behavior—whether it be frequency, duration, and/or intensity of display. As is outlined throughout this book, ratings can serve one or more purposes depending on the context in which they are used. Let's imagine, for example, that "Mrs. Smith" rates "Johnny's" level of disruptive behavior during math class using a scale from 0 (no disruption) to 10 (high disruption). Within the context of intervention, this rating might be shared with Johnny to provide him feedback about his behavior, with the goal of his receiving a rating of less than 2 in order to earn a reward. Although Mrs. Smith could file the ratings away at the end of each day, she could also choose to send them home at the end of the day. In this way, the ratings might be used to facilitate communication between home and school and keep Johnny's parents informed regarding his behavior in the classroom. Finally, these ratings can be used as a form of assessment data. If Mrs. Smith graphs her rating each day, these data could be used to determine whether Johnny is making progress over time or whether another intervention approach is warranted. This example demonstrates how it is possible to use this one tool to link intervention, communication, and assessment applications.

Strengths in Contemporary Assessment, Intervention, and Communication

As we have begun to highlight in this chapter, one of the major selling points of DBR is the fact that one tool can serve multiple purposes within school settings. That is, DBR can be used to communicate information about the assessment of, and intervention with, student behavior. However, across these purposes, DBR also offers unique strengths with regard to the flexibility, defensibility, efficiency, and repeatability of the tool (see Figure 1.1).

Flexibility

One of the key strengths across intervention and assessment contexts is the fact that DBR is flexible enough to meet the demands of different situations. As summarized by Chafouleas, Riley-Tillman, and McDougal (2002), DBRs can vary according to the behavior or behavioral attribute to be rated (e.g., academic or social, increase or decrease in target behavior), type of rating system (e.g., checklist, scale), rating frequency (e.g., once daily, throughout the day), rater (e.g., child, teacher), and frequency with which information is shared (e.g., daily, weekly) (see Table 1.3). For example, a teacher-completed DBR involving a Likert-type scale might be used to rate disruptive behavior during science instruction, whereas a high school student might complete a classroom readiness checklist at the beginning of each classroom period. Furthermore, DBR has been shown to be appropriate across multiple levels of intervention focus (universal, targeted, intensive), settings, and populations. DBR-like tools have been used successfully in preschool (e.g., LeBel, Chafouleas, Britner, & Simonsen, 2013) through secondary school (e.g., Schumaker et al., 1977) to target a wide range of behaviors (e.g., assignment completion, physical aggression) across students with (e.g., Fabiano et al., 2010) and without (e.g., Hawken et al.,

FIGURE 1.1. Among the strengths of a DBR approach are its flexibility, defensibility, efficiency, and repeatability.

2014) disabilities at the individual (e.g., Burkwist, Mabee, & McLaughlin, 1987) and group (e.g., Chafouleas, Sanetti, Jaffery, & Fallon, 2012) levels.

Defensibility

Another key strength of DBR is the fact that it is a defensible choice within both assessment and intervention. An assessment tool is *defensible* if it produces data that are accurate, reliable, and valid for its intended purpose. As previously mentioned, many studies have been conducted over the past decade in order to build the psychometric evidence base in support of the use of DBR single-item scales (DBR-SIS) within progress monitoring and targeted screening (see Table 1.2). In addition, ongoing work continues to be carried out in order to improve our understanding of the use of different types of DBR scales with different populations. However, defensibility is also important within the context of intervention. That is, we want to ensure that the interventions we employ in schools have a sufficient evidence base to support their use. Selecting an evidence-based intervention serves to increase our confidence that what we have chosen to try will likely have the intended effect (Erchul & Martens, 2010). The results of both systematic and meta-analytic reviews of the literature have identified strong effects for the use of both teacher- (Vannest et al., 2010) and student-completed (Maggin, Briesch, & Chafouleas, 2013) ratings in improving classroom behavior.

TABLE 1.3. Considerations and Options in Designing a DBR

Consideration	Options	Example Study
Desired change in behavior	Increase in [appropriate] behavior	Karraker (1972)
	Decrease in [inappropriate] behavior	LeBel, Chafouleas, Britner, & Simonsen (2013)
Number of behaviors	One	Davies & McLaughlin (1989)
	Multiple (e.g., punctuality, preparedness)	Schumaker, Hovell, & Sherman (1977)
Frequency of data collection	At least once a day	Blechman, Schrader, & Taylor (1981)
	Less than once a day	Bailey, Wolf, & Phillips (1970)
Rater	Teacher	Dougherty & Dougherty (1977)
	Self	Dalton, Martella, & Marchand-Martella (1999)
Rating system	Checklist	Gureasko-Moore, DuPaul, & White (2007)
	Scale	Kelley & McCain (1995)
Focus of rating	Individual	Burkwist, Mabee, & McLaughlin (1987)
	Classwide	Chafouleas, Sanetti, Jaffery, & Fallon (2012)
Setting of consequence delivery	School	Hawken, MacLeod, & Rawlings (2007)
	Home	Fabiano et al. (2010)

Note. Adapted from Chafouleas, Riley-Tillman, and McDougal (2002). Copyright 2002 by John Wiley & Sons, Inc. Adapted by permission.

Efficiency

In the busy world of schools, where time and resources are at a premium, efficiency is always an important consideration. Models of consumer acceptability, for example, have emphasized that the less time and effort that a new technology requires, the more likely teachers will be to use it (Reimers, Wacker, & Koeppl, 1987). DBR represents a highly efficient assessment tool because those individuals who are already present in the target setting can complete it in a matter of a few seconds. Furthermore, DBR also represents an efficient intervention approach, in that the intervention requires minimal resources, can be carried out in a short period of time, and can be implemented without substantial external supports.

Repeatability

Finally, DBR offers an advantage over other tools within a multi-tiered system of supports (MTSS) in that it is repeatable. That is, it can be used in an ongoing fashion over time. Within a multi-tiered model, assessment tools that can be administered repeatedly are needed in order to produce time-series data. Such streams of data are necessary to assess the level, trend, and variability of behavior within and across baseline and intervention phases (Christ et al., 2009). Within the context of intervention, repeatability is more directly linked to efficiency. That is, because a DBR-based intervention requires small amounts of time and resources for implementation, it can easily be implemented across multiple contexts and times of day. Check-in/check-out, for example, requires the student to receive feedback periodically over the course of an entire school day. The repeatability of DBR interventions therefore means that students receive ongoing rather than isolated behavior supports.

Conclusions

Our goal in this first chapter was to highlight the important function that DBR can serve within contemporary models of school-based service delivery. Although DBR has long been regarded as an effective tool within the context of classroom intervention, much research has been conducted over the past decade to establish its utility as an evidence-based assessment. Furthermore, DBR serves to link assessment with intervention by providing an efficient way to communicate with stakeholders about student behavior. We continue to lay the foundations for use of DBR within the next two chapters before shifting to more thoroughly discuss specific applications across assessment, intervention, and communication purposes.

CHAPTER 2

Identifying and Selecting Behaviors for Use in DBR Items

Amy M. Briesch and Sandra M. Chafouleas

As outlined in Chapter 1, DBR is similar to a behavior rating scale in that a rater is asked to quantify his or her perception of a student's behavior using a numbered scale (e.g., 0–10). However, whereas items on traditional rating scales are generally fixed and thus might not capture behaviors that are of most interest to a specific context (Hosp, Howell, & Hosp, 2003), a signature strength of DBR is its flexibility in assessing a wide range of possible behaviors (Christ et al., 2009). That is, DBR can be tailored to assess either a specific observable behavior (e.g., hitting) or a larger constellation of behaviors (e.g., aggressive behavior; Riley-Tillman, Chafouleas, & Briesch, 2007). Additionally, the focus of assessment might be an individual student with specific needs or an entire class with regard to core classroom behaviors. Although flexibility in DBR item selection can be a strength given the wide range of possible applications, this flexibility also can present difficulty, given that the list of possible items is virtually limitless and several different avenues exist by which to decide which behavior(s) to target. The goals of this chapter are therefore to (1) review the literature related to behaviors relevant to student success, (2) discuss options for selecting target behaviors across different contexts, and (3) describe the rationale behind the selection of DBR's core behavioral competencies.

General Guidelines for Selecting Behavioral Targets

Selecting a target behavior may appear to be a relatively simple process at first glance; however, it is in fact relatively complex and multifaceted (Barnett, Bauer, Ehrhardt, Lentz, & Stollar, 1996; Wilson & Evans, 1983). To assist in untangling the complexity of selecting behavioral targets, we begin by providing general guidelines for this task as borrowed from the larger behavioral assessment literature involving direct observation and rating scales (see Table 2.1).

Step 1: Determine the Appropriate Level of Assessment or Intervention

The first consideration in selecting target behaviors is determining the level at which assessment or intervention will take place. Within a MTSS, emphasis has shifted from the remediation of existing problems to prevention and early intervention efforts. Services are believed to exist along a continuum, wherein both intervention and assessment efforts require increasingly greater effort and individualization as one moves from addressing the needs of the general population (i.e., universal level) to providing more targeted and individualized supports (i.e., secondary and tertiary

TABLE 2.1. DBR Blueprint for Selecting Behavior Targets

☐ 1. Determine the appropriate level of assessment or intervention.

The scope and specificity of behavioral targets will vary depending on the level of interest. Global indicators may be most appropriate at the universal level, whereas individualized targets should be selected at the intensive level.

☐ 2. Determine the appropriate level of behavioral molarity.

DBR can be used to target global constructs (e.g., disruptive behavior, social competence) or specific indicators (e.g., calling out, expressing frustration appropriately).

☐ 3. Ensure that behavior can be reliably measured.

DBR is best used to target those behaviors that can be directly observed by the rater and do not require a high degree of inference.

☐ 4. Ensure that behavior is socially valid.

Target behaviors should be considered important to stakeholders within a particular context and relevant to both instruction and intervention planning.

☐ 5. Consider inclusion of positive behavior targets.

If the goal of intervention is to both reduce negative behaviors and to increase positive behaviors, it is important to ensure that the DBR includes these replacement behaviors.

levels). It is therefore important to consider the level at which assessment and intervention will take place in order to select the target behavior(s) that will provide the most appropriate scope of information.

Assessment and intervention at the universal level (Tier 1) include all students in a given population (e.g., classroom, school). Given the broad scope of efforts conducted at the universal level, it is necessary to target variables that demonstrate broad applicability to a range of students and can be measured quickly. Universal-level assessment has been compared to the medical process of taking one's vital signs (e.g., blood pressure, temperature) to determine whether follow-up assessment and care are needed. Knowing a person's vital signs provides a global indication of whether something is wrong, but does not necessarily provide information about what the specific problem may be. Within the academic domain, general outcome measures (GOMs) have long been used to provide a similar global indication of risk (Hosp, Hosp, & Howell, 2016). For example, by measuring the number of correct words read per minute (i.e., oral reading fluency) or the number of correct digits per minute (i.e., curriculum-based measurement—math) using brief assessment probes, teachers are able to identify those students who may benefit from additional instructional supports. Although the same model can be extended to behavioral assessment and intervention, there has been less consensus as to which behaviors may serve as the best behavioral GOMs (Chafouleas, Volpe, Gresham, & Cook, 2010). Chapter 6 provides one example of universal screening utilizing DBR, wherein all students are rated across three single-item scales designed to provide a global indication of core school-based behavioral competencies (i.e., academically engaged, nondisruptive, respectful). At the targeted level (Tier 2), intervention and assessment are more narrowly focused on those students who have been identified as at risk or in need of additional supports. Most often, supports are provided for small groups of students who have been identified as having similar needs; therefore, the target behaviors selected should be tailored to these groups. Given that intervention at the targeted level is typically focused on a more specific area of functioning, target behaviors are likely to be more closely linked to a particular intervention. The chosen behaviors for those students who are participating in a check-in/check-out intervention (see Chapter 8), for example, would be linked to the schoolwide behavioral expectations (e.g., be safe, be responsible, be respectful).

The select, or most intensive, level (Tier 3) is differentiated from the previous tiers due to the degree of individualization (National Center for Intensive Intervention, 2013). Problem identification is therefore narrowly focused on those unique behaviors that are believed to be most detrimental to the student's functioning (Kratochwill & Bergan, 1990). Given that intensive-level interventions are designed to address individualized problem behaviors, selected target behaviors may be much more discrete in nature. Although core behavioral competencies likely continue to be important, there may be additional benefit to individualizing the target items. The IBRST (see Chapter 9), for example, was designed to assess the specific problem and replacement behaviors targeted through a functionally based intervention plan.

Step 2: Determine the Appropriate Level of Behavioral Molarity

In conjunction with determining the appropriate level of assessment or intervention, we must also consider the level of behavioral molarity. Hawkins, Barnett, Morrison, and Musti-Rao (2009) likened this process to using the "zoom" feature on a camera. If we zoom out, our focus shifts to constructs (e.g., disruptive behavior, social competence) or global indicators of behavioral functioning. If we zoom in, our focus shifts to the specific skills or indicators that comprise the larger behavioral constructs. For example, the broader construct of *disruptive behavior* encompasses the specific target behaviors of *calling out*, *talking to peers*, *making noises*, and *leaving one's seat*. As outlined in Step 1, the decision of molar versus molecular may be based upon the intended level of intervention or assessment. That is, molar behaviors with broad relevance to many students are often targeted at the universal level, whereas individualized, molecular behaviors are often most appropriate at the intensive level.

In those situations in which the molar versus molecular decision is less obvious, however, it is important to consider both advantages and disadvantages of each approach. One argument for focusing on specific indicators is that more molecular behaviors are often easier to measure than more global constructs (Noell, 2009). For example, assessing the *frequency with which a student is out of his or her seat* is a much more straightforward a task than assessing the frequency with which a student's behavior is *disruptive* to the classroom. At the same time, however, if the behaviors we target are overly specific, we risk narrowing our focus to those behaviors that are not clinically meaningful. Molar behaviors (e.g., social competence, disruptive behavior), on the other hand, are more likely to capture and reflect global behavioral changes. One limitation, however, is that global ratings can reflect a broad range of specific behaviors (Edelbrock, 1983). For example, one student's "highly disruptive" behavior may involve tapping a pencil on a desk, whereas another student might be judged as "highly disruptive" for yelling and throwing items across the classroom. Researchers have therefore recommended the use of a funneled approach to assessment, wherein broad, molar behaviors are targeted initially. If, however, it is found that the chosen behavioral targets either cannot be measured reliably or are not predictive of meaningful outcomes, it may be necessary to move to a more fine-grained level of analysis (Hawkins et al., 2009; Noell, 2009).

Step 3: Ensure That Behavior Can Be Reliably Measured

Once a target behavior has been globally identified, we must ensure that it can be rated reliably. Hosp and colleagues (2003) have argued that appropriate target behaviors should pass the "dead man" test, meaning that they are both observable and involve movement (i.e., behaviors that a dead man could not exhibit). This is because target behaviors that do not involve action can only tell us what a student is *not* doing rather than what he or she *is* doing. If the identified behavior is not one that can be directly observed by the rater or requires a high degree of inference, an assessment option involving observation and rating such as a DBR may not offer the best choice. Generally speaking, the more explicit and thorough the operational definition, the more reliable the rating should be. Judging a student's "enthusiasm for learning," for example, requires the rater to make several assumptions based on the student's observed behavior and therefore makes the assessment less direct. Although internalizing behaviors (e.g., self-esteem) should not be assessed by an external rater for the same reasons, such behaviors may be more appropriately assessed by the individual him- or herself, such as within the context of a self-management intervention (see Chapter 10).

Step 4: Ensure That the Target Behavior Is Socially Valid

Assuming that the target behavior can be rated reliably, it is next important to consider whether it is generally believed to be important, or socially valid, for the specific case at hand. Hosp and colleagues (2003) suggested that those behaviors that are believed to be important and socially valid can be said to pass a "so-what" test. Because *importance* is determined subjectively, it may be that those behaviors deemed important or socially valid in one context (e.g., classroom) may not be so in the next (e.g., afterschool activity).

Although selecting items with empirical support and broad applicability across a range of students is certainly good practice, it can sometimes be important to also consider those concerns or problems that are more idiographic in nature (i.e., unique to the individual) or to consider an individual's behavior in relation to his or her environment (e.g., degree of impairment) (Kazdin, 2005). These behaviors need not have proven clinical significance or utility as long as they are deemed important to the individuals who best know the student. Take the example of picking one's nose. On a general level, there is no research to suggest that occasional nose picking will lead to any serious negative outcomes for either the student or her peers. Within a particular classroom context, however, it may be that the student exhibiting this behavior has begun to elicit feedback from peers that is potentially hurtful and socially isolating. Given these conditions, the student's teacher may view nose picking to be an important target for intervention and assessment, whereas a teacher in the classroom next door may view the same behavior as relatively minor and inconsequential.

There are a number of approaches for determining targets with high social validity for idiographic purposes. Kazdin (2005), for example, suggested that those items that are most relevant to the individual could be selected from a standardized rating scale and used to monitor more specific, individualized progress. Therefore, one approach to selecting target behaviors may be to administer a comprehensive behavior rating scale, identify those items with the highest (i.e., most problematic) ratings, and include these items within an individualized DBR (Volpe, Briesch, & Chafouleas, 2010; Volpe & Gadow, 2010). Preliminary research has suggested that a dependable estimate of disruptive behavior can be obtained fairly quickly (i.e., in approximately 1 week) when using a DBR consisting of an individualized composite of items (Volpe & Briesch, 2015). An alternative approach is to directly create items that are most closely linked with the client's presenting concerns, such as has been the focus of goal attainment scaling (Kiresuk, Smith, & Cardillo, 1994). Given the decision making regarding individualization, the idiographic selection of target behaviors would most likely be reserved for those students demonstrating the greatest level of behavioral need (i.e., Tier 3).

Step 5: Consider Inclusion of Positive Behavioral Targets

Next, it is important to consider the inclusion of intended *positive behavioral targets*, also referred to as *replacement behaviors*. Although a primary focus has often been placed on the reduction of problem behaviors because of their saliency, it has been suggested that one "should not propose to reduce a problem behavior without also identifying alternative, desired behaviors the person should perform instead of the problem behavior" (O'Neill et al., 1997, p. 71). Therefore, if the goal of an intervention is to increase the degree to which a student exhibits a positive replacement behavior (e.g., raising a hand instead of calling out), it is important to ensure that the DBR includes positive behaviors. We often assume that decreasing a problem behavior will automatically increase desired behaviors; however, this is not always true. Hosp et al. (2003) use the example of a student whose previous hyperactive behavior is replaced by a depressed mood and lethargy. An assessment that focused exclusively on hyperactive symptoms would suggest that the student's functioning had improved when this was not the case in actuality. As Hosp and colleagues (2003) note, "The absence of a certain negative behavior does not automatically equate to the presence of a positive behavior" (p. 204).

In summary, the guidelines presented here offer good practice in selecting targets for any behavioral assessment, yet are particularly relevant for DBR item selection given the characteristics of *direct* and *rating*. Next, we turn to a review of different options for selecting among possible items, using a lens for options as derived from policy-, practice-, or research-based considerations.

Frameworks for Choosing among Options for DBR Item Selection

Although the previous section provides some guidance in terms of general considerations when selecting a target behavior for use in DBR, the options may still seem limitless. Many choices must be made when it comes to selecting an appropriate target behavior, and in most situations, there is no one right answer. In this section, we frame decisions regarding target behavior selection across three possible paths: (1) policy-based, (2) practice-based, and (3) research-based. We have chosen to organize discussion across these pathways in order to illustrate how item selection often is driven by the reason or purpose for the assessment. Although we certainly acknowledge overlap in potential items across the three options, we hope that framing discussion across these paths can facilitate decision making regarding the *why* behind *which* items are chosen.

Policy-Based Options

The first pathway for selecting DBR items is linked to local or state policy, and appears to be gaining momentum in recent years. State learning standards have long been used to describe what students should have learned and what they should be able to do at different stages in their education. Until recently, however, these standards have been focused exclusively on academic domains (e.g., English language arts, math). Social–emotional learning (SEL), on the other hand, focuses on "the capacity to recognize and manage emotions, solve problems effectively, and establish positive relationships with others, competencies that clearly are essential for all students" (Zins & Elias, 2007, p. 1). It has been argued that SEL is critical to academic achievement because learning occurs in the context of relationships, and those students who interact positively with both peers and adults are more likely to experience success in schools (Macklem, 2014). Standards related to social–emotional and behavioral competencies are relatively new; however, there is longstanding evidence in the literature linking mastery of social–emotional competencies to both academic performance and general well-being (Caprara, Barbaranelli, Pastorelli, Bandura, & Zimbardo, 2000; Durlak, Weissberg, Dymnicki, Taylor, & Schellinger, 2011; Payton et al., 2008).

A recent review of state SEL standards conducted by the Collaborative for Academic, Social, and Emotional Learning (CASEL; Dusenbury, Weissberg, Goren, &

Domitrovich, 2014) found that although 49 states had SEL standards for use at the preschool level, only three states (Illinois, Kansas, Pennsylvania) had adopted standards that include developmental benchmarks at the K–12 level. In Illinois, the first state to have adopted SEL standards in 2004, standards focus on three central goal areas: (1) developing self-awareness and self-management skills to achieve school and life success; (2) using social awareness and interpersonal skills to establish and maintain positive relationships; and (3) demonstrating decision-making skills and responsible behaviors in personal, school, and community contexts (Illinois State Board of Education, 2004). In Table 2.2, we present a summary of the CASEL Framework for SEL Standards, along with examples of state-specific competencies.

One option for creating the DBR items may therefore be targeting specific competency standards. In a study by Chafouleas, Christ, Riley-Tillman, Briesch, and Chanese (2007), for example, target behaviors were selected from Connecticut's preschool assessment framework, a tool designed by the state to assess the learning of preschool students across four domains of development: personal and social, physical, cognitive, and creative (Connecticut State Department of Education, 1999). Preschool teachers then rated their students across two DBR items: "works to resolve conflicts" and "interacts cooperatively with peers." State standards can be used in this way to select important behavioral indices for use in the universal screening of all students in a given school or to monitor student response to targeted supports (e.g., a conflict resolution group).

Practice-Based Options

DBR items can also be selected based upon the priorities in local practice. Implementation of a schoolwide positive behavior supports framework, for example, requires that school staff first engage in a process to determine which behaviors they deem most relevant and important for all students to demonstrate. Consequently, it may be most relevant and of interest in a school implementing positive behavior supports to map DBR items to the chosen schoolwide expectations for student behavior. In Chapter 8, examples of the use of a check-in/check-out intervention are provided to illustrate this option. That is, the behaviors selected for inclusion on the DPR (e.g., be safe, be respectful, be responsible) are typically aligned with the schoolwide expectations.

Items can also be created to measure those behaviors that are judged to be most problematic locally. Although the prevalence of specific problem behaviors will inevitably vary from one system to the next, a larger literature regarding teacher expectations and perceptions related to student behavior does exist. Among those behaviors identified as being of critical importance to teachers are those related to classroom conduct and control, including following classroom rules, listening

TABLE 2.2. CASEL Framework for Social–Emotional Learning Standards

CASEL core competencies	Definition	Examples of state-specific competencies
Self-awareness	• Recognizing own emotions and thoughts • Assessing own strengths and limitations	• Identify and describe basic emotions (KS; K–2) • Describe a range of emotions and the situations that cause them (IL; late elementary) • Analyze impact of a variety of personal traits on relationships and achievement throughout life (PA; 6–8)
Self-management	• Regulating own emotions, thoughts, and behaviors	• Examine the impact of emotions and responses on view of self and interactions with others (PA; 1–5) • Predict possible outcomes to behavioral choices (KS; 3–5) • Set a postsecondary goal with action steps, time frames, and criteria for evaluating achievement (IL; late high school)
Social awareness	• Showing understanding and empathy for others from diverse backgrounds • Recognizing resources and supports	• Identify similarities and differences between self and others (PA; PreK–K) • Use listening skills to identify the feelings and perspectives of others (IL; early elementary) • Discern nonverbal cues in others' behaviors (KS; 6–8)
Relationship skills	• Establishing and maintaining positive relationships	• Practice and evaluate good manners (KS; 3–5) • Analyze ways to establish positive relationships with others (IL; middle school) • Use communication skills to effectively interact with others (PA; 9–12)
Responsible decision making	• Making constructive, ethical choices about personal and social behavior	• Demonstrate knowledge of how social norms affect decision making and behavior (PA; 1–5) • Evaluate strategies for resisting pressures to engage in unsafe or unethical activities (IL; middle school) • Assess lessons learned from experiences and mistakes (KS; 9–12)

Note. Based on Illinois State Department of Education (2004), Kansas State Department of Education (2012), Pennsylvania Department of Education (2012), and Weissberg and Cascarino (2013).

to directions, and complying with teacher requests (Kauffman, Lloyd, & McGee, 1989; Walker & Rankin, 1983). In contrast to these "teacher pleaser" behaviors, failure or refusal to comply with requests (i.e., noncompliance) is seen as a challenge to the teacher's authority and often to his or her value system. It is therefore unsurprising that surveys of both classroom teachers and school psychologists have repeatedly identified noncompliance as one of the most common reasons for referral to a school-based team (Bramlett, Murphy, Johnson, Wallingsford, & Hall, 2002; Briesch, Ferguson, Volpe, & Briesch, 2013; Lane, Mahdavi, & Borthwick-Duffy, 2003).

In addition, studies have been conducted to determine the actual prevalence of particular challenging behaviors in school settings. Reviews of office discipline referral data at both the district (Kaufman et al., 2010) and national (Spaulding et al., 2010) levels have suggested that the most common problem behaviors tend to vary by grade level. Whereas aggressive behaviors have been shown to be most prevalent at the elementary level, the most significant problems at the middle and high school levels have been shown to be disruptive, disrespectful behavior and attendance (i.e., tardiness, truancy), respectively. In contrast, more consistent results were found across grade levels when analyzing the data from Behavior Assessment Scale for Children, Second Edition (BASC-2) rating scales completed for 3,600 students nationally (Harrison, Vannest, Davis, & Reynolds, 2012). Across child and adolescent populations, the most frequently endorsed items were those related to distractibility, overactivity, and following directions. Taken together, these results suggest that although some target behaviors may have broad relevance across K–12 populations, others may be best suited for use with particular age and grade levels.

Although selecting items via practice-based considerations (e.g., teacher preference) is one potential option, one caution is worth noting. Concerns have been raised regarding the errors of inference that teachers may make when selecting particular behaviors to target (Barnett et al., 1996). One of the central problems highlighted by Wilson and Evans (1983) is that students rarely demonstrate a single problem behavior. Rather, the decision of which behavior to target must often be made from among several presenting problems (Wittlieb, Eifer, Wilson, & Evans, 1978), and, interestingly, the reliability of target selection has been found to be weak. When Wilson and Evans (1983) presented participants (i.e., doctoral-level behavioral clinicians) with a case vignette involving a child struggling with social, emotional, and behavioral concerns and asked them to prioritize targets for intervention, the mean percentage of agreement for priority target behaviors was found to be very low ($M = 38\%$). Compounding this issue is the fact that individual teachers differ greatly in their tolerance for and expectations of student behavior (Walker & Rankin, 1983). The concern therefore arises that if individuals are left to identify particular target behaviors on their own, potentially important concerns may be overlooked.

Research-Based Options

The final path for basing decisions regarding DBR item selection comes from the empirical literature. Again, choices based on this path are not considered mutually exclusive from selection that is policy- or practice-based. Rather, in this section, we summarize information regarding domains that have been identified as important indicators of student functioning within the literature. For example, in school-based settings, the ultimate goal for use of any assessment relates to its impact on student achievement. Thus, identification of those behavioral indicators of academic success is relevant and tied to DBR item selection. Before continuing, however, we should preface this discussion by noting that this literature is vast and diverse across disciplines. Thus, the examples we highlight next are intended to illustrate bigger points related to the information that might be extracted when using a research-based approach to DBR item selection. For simplicity, we have organized our review within two main categories of focus: (1) intraindividual and (2) ecological systems.

Intraindividual Focus

One literature from which relevant DBR items might be drawn involves those studies that have examined outcomes for children who display particular behaviors. As one example, a very large body of literature exists with regard to aggressive behavior in children, suggesting that this might be a relevant and significant domain to consider when selecting DBR targets. Crick (1996), for example, found that peer ratings of physical and verbal aggression at the beginning of the school year significantly predicted future rejection from peers. Although aggression can be either physical or verbal, much of the extant research has focused on identifying the trajectories of children demonstrating physically aggressive behavior (e.g., hitting, kicking, biting, fighting, bullying others). Tremblay and colleagues (2004) assessed physical aggression in a sample of young children from the ages of 3 years 6 months to 5 years. These authors found that the majority of children demonstrated either modest (58% of the children) or high (14% of the children) levels of physical aggression toward others (e.g., peers, adults) before entering preschool. However, whereas most children will learn to use more socially acceptable alternative strategies as they progress through the preschool years, those students who continue to demonstrate physical aggression into elementary school have been shown to be at greater risk for future adjustment problems (Bongers, Koot, van der Ende, & Verhulst, 2004; Tremblay et al., 2004). Aggressive behavior during elementary school has also been found to be a significant predictor of externalizing problems in secondary school (Lochman, 1995) as well as future delinquency (Loeber, 1990). Furthermore, physical aggression has been found to predict a range of negative outcomes in adulthood, including violent behavior, substance abuse, and criminal activity (Kellam, Rebok, Ialongo, & Mayer, 1994).

As noted previously, another domain that has received substantial attention in the literature is that of prosocial behavior. The class of prosocial behavior generally includes those behaviors that benefit either individuals or groups of individuals, including helping, sharing, and comforting (Eagly, 2009). Although the links between prosocial behavior and constructs such as *bullying* (e.g., Gini, Albiero, Benelli, & Altoe, 2007) and *peer acceptance* (e.g., Wentzel & Erdley, 1993) are not altogether unexpected, research has also demonstrated a significant relationship between prosocial behavior and other important variables. Studies have shown that prosocial behavior may serve as a protective factor against both school-based disciplinary action (Horner, Fireman, & Wang, 2010) and later delinquency and antisocial behavior (Morrison, Robertson, Laurie, & Kelly, 2002). Interpersonal skills (e.g., demonstrating humor, empathy) have also been shown to moderate intervention effectiveness with adolescents who have serious emotional disturbance (Vance, Bowen, Fernandez, & Thompson, 2002). Finally, links have even been found between prosocial behavior and academic achievement. As one example, Caprara and colleagues (2000) investigated the contributions of early prosocial behavior on academic and social trajectories. Using a longitudinal design, their results supported the finding that prosocial behaviors (e.g., cooperating, helping, sharing, consoling) but not aggressive behaviors (both verbal and physical) rated in the early elementary grades had a strong influence on academic achievement and peer preference in adolescence.

A third important domain relates to internalizing behaviors, or those potential problems characterized by the fact that they are directed inward and therefore not easily observable (Achenbach & Rescorla, 2001). The four clusters of internalizing disorders include depression, anxiety, social withdrawal, and somatic problems (Levitt & Merrell, 2009). Although survey studies have found that substantially fewer referrals are made for internalizing problems (Bramlett et al., 2002; Briesch et al., 2013), the potential outcomes for internalizing problems that go untreated are of great concern. Internalizing problems experienced in childhood have the potential to negatively influence peer relations, as well as to increase risk of drug use and suicide attempts (Levitt & Merrell, 2009). Some studies have also identified a significant relationship between internalizing problems and both academic achievement (Rapport, Denney, Chung, & Hustace, 2001) and high school completion (e.g., Duchesne, Vitaro, Larose, & Tremblay, 2008). Although these findings suggest that internalizing behaviors should certainly be considered when selecting DBR targets, it is important to keep in mind that it may be difficult for external raters (e.g., teachers) to both detect and differentiate between internalizing problems (Lonigan, Carey, & Finch, 1994). Because studies have shown that teachers report significantly fewer internalizing problems than their students (e.g., Stanger & Lewis, 1993), the argument has been made that internalizing behaviors are best assessed by the student him- or herself (Merrell, McClun, Kempf, & Lund, 2002).

Ecological Systems Focus

Another area of rich literature from which DBR items might be drawn uses an ecological systems focus in which risk and protective factors within the student and surrounding systems are targeted in assessment and early intervention efforts. Risk and protective factors are those variables that have been shown to increase or decrease the probability of negative outcomes, respectively (Crews et al., 2007). These factors can exist at either the individual (e.g., empathy, problem-solving ability) or environmental (e.g., parental support, school climate) levels, and it has been argued that targeting generic risk factors may have a more widespread impact on a range of outcomes than trying to target any one particular problem (Coie et al., 1993). Although no one risk or protective factor can be used to predict students' emotional and behavioral adjustment, it has been suggested that risk factors may have an additive effect, in that the more risk factors are present, the more likely the risk of emotional or behavioral disorders (Crews et al., 2007). Given both the sheer number of potential risk factors, and the fact that many risk factors can be temporary in nature, it has been argued that schools should use developmental theory to identify those factors most important at a particular age (Severson, Walker, Hope-Doolittle, Kratochwill, & Gresham, 2007) and should focus on those factors with the greatest empirical support (Hawkins et al., 2009).

Coie and colleagues (1993) highlighted seven generic categories of risk factors that have been shown to predict several different types of disorders: *family characteristics* (e.g., family structure, relationships with parents), *emotional difficulties* (e.g., self-concept, emotional regulation), *school problems* (e.g., academic achievement), *environmental circumstances* (e.g., socioeconomic status, neighborhood safety), *constitutional handicaps* (perinatal problems, physical disabilities), *interpersonal problems* (e.g., peer relations), and *skill development delays* (e.g., cognitive ability, learning disabilities). It has been suggested that the most useful behavioral markers in school-based assessment are those that are potentially modifiable by school-based personnel (e.g., emotional difficulties, interpersonal problems) rather than stable or external factors such as temperament or parental discipline practices (Lochman, 1995). However, given evidence that protective factors may serve to buffer against the negative effects of existing risk factors (Luthar, Cicchetti, & Becker, 2000), the argument could also be made that simply understanding the degree of risk with which a student enters school may help to inform the scope of intervention needed.

Crews and colleagues (2007) conducted a mega-analysis of 18 meta-analyses examining risk and protective factors in children living in the United States. Of the risk factors examined across studies, the highest correlations with externalizing disorders were found for lack of bonding to school (.86), delinquent peers (.49), and internalizing comorbidity (.47), whereas the highest correlations with internalizing disorders were found for having a chronically ill sibling (.76) and having comorbid externalizing symptoms (.49). In contrast, the protective factors that were found to correlate most strongly with externalizing disorders included age at first juvenile justice commitment (.34), academic performance (.33), and peer play activity (.26), whereas having a popular sociometric status (.40) and an internal attributional style (.37) correlated most strongly with internalizing disorders. Taken together, the findings of this ecological systems focus are consistent with the intraindividual literature, revealing that indicators such as academic and prosocial behaviors, peer relationships, and school engagement may be potentially relevant options for DBR items.

Establishing DBR Core Behavioral Competencies

As has been highlighted throughout the chapter thus far, many options are afforded when it comes to selecting appropriate target behaviors for use in DBR. Nonetheless, much of the research on DBR to date has focused on identifying core student behavioral competencies. In this section, we provide history regarding the decisions and research associated with selecting three primary targets for DBR to represent core student behavioral competencies. Over the years, decisions regarding directions for this research line integrated considerations from policy, practice, and research frameworks. In addition, decisions were guided by a keystone approach to target behavior selection, in which priority in assessment and intervention is given to those "keystone variables" (e.g., compliance, social skills, on-task skills, communication skills) most likely to have positive ripple effects across multiple behaviors (Barnett et al., 1996; Ducharme & Schechter, 2011).

In the DBR literature, three constructs were chosen as the keystone contributors to the academic success for all students: academically engaged, nondisruptive, and respectful behaviors (Chafouleas, 2011; see Figure 2.1). In Table 2.3, we present operational definitions of these constructs, including examples and nonexamples of behaviors falling within each domain. In brief, students who are respectful and nondisruptive experience more positive relationships with peers and adults, and student learning is maximized when students are engaged and nondisruptive (Chafouleas, 2011). Next, we expand our review of literature to encompass each of the "big three" competencies, drawing together information across policy, practice, and research arenas.

Academically Engaged

Inattention and distractibility have been noted as a primary concern of teachers across studies (Briesch et al., 2013; Harrison et al., 2012). Although students who exhibit disruptive behavior tend to be the focus of classroom management

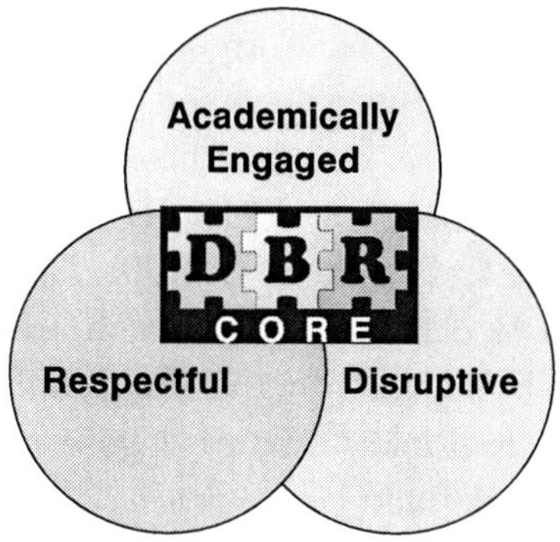

FIGURE 2.1. The "big three" DBR core behavioral competencies/barriers: academic engagement, nondisruptive behavior, and/or respectful behavior.

TABLE 2.3. Core Behavioral Competencies/Barriers: Definitions and Examples

Core behavioral competency	Examples
Academically engaged Actively or passively participating in the classroom activity	*Examples:* writing, raising his or her hand, answering a question, talking about a lesson, listening to the teacher, reading silently, or looking at instructional materials *Nonexamples:* doodling, looking around the room, staring, aimless flipping through materials, activity unrelated to instructional task
Disruptive Action that interrupts regular school or classroom activity	*Examples:* out of seat, fidgeting, calling out, talking/yelling about things that are unrelated to classroom instruction, acting aggressively, playing with objects *Nonexamples:* staying in seat, raising hand, waiting to be called upon before responding, keeping hands/feet to self, using objects appropriately, working quietly
Respectful Compliant and polite behavior in response to adult directions and/or interactions with peers and adults	*Examples:* follows teacher directions, prosocial interaction with peers, positive response to adult request, verbal or physical disruption without a negative tone/connotation *Nonexamples:* refusal to follow teacher directions, talking back, eye rolling, inappropriate gesture, inappropriate language and/or social interactions, disruption with negative tone/connotation

interventions and strategies, it has been argued that those students who quietly demonstrate inattentive or unengaged behavior may be of greater concern (Finn, Pannozzo, & Voelkl, 1995). This is because the amount of time a student spends actively thinking about or working on academic content is a strong determinant of achievement (Gettinger & Callan Stoiber, 1999). Therefore, those students who are chronically unengaged in classroom instruction are less likely to develop the academic skills necessary to succeed in the classroom. Note here that although we acknowledge there are multiple forms of engagement (academic, psychological, behavioral, cognitive) as defined by Appleton, Christenson, Kim, and Reschly (2006), our definition focuses on academic engagement, which is represented by behaviors such as time on-task and work completion.

Over a half century ago, Carroll (1963) proposed a theoretical model of engagement and learning, in which the degree of learning that occurs in the classroom is equal to the time spent learning divided by the time needed to learn. Given that time spent not attending to task would diminish the amount of time an individual spends learning, the link between academic engagement and academic achievement has generally been assumed. This relationship has, however, also been confirmed across a small number of empirical investigations. In developing a theoretical model to explain the effects of alterable instructional variables on academic achievement, Greenwood, Terry, Marquis, and Walker (1994) found the relationship between instruction and academic achievement to be significantly mediated by student engagement. Rabiner and Coie (2000) later followed nearly 400 children from kindergarten to fifth grade and found attention to task to be a significant predictor of reading achievement even when controlling for cognitive and other behavioral variables. In fact, over one-third of those students who demonstrated average reading achievement at the start of first grade despite high levels of inattention were performing significantly below their peers in reading by the fifth grade.

Furthermore, studies have shown that inattention may have a greater effect on school success than externalizing behavior problems. A longitudinal study conducted by Vitaro, Brendgen, Larose, and Tremblay (2005) found that hyperactive/inattentive behaviors exhibited in kindergarten helped to predict high school noncompletion, whereas aggressive/oppositional behaviors did not demonstrate the same predictive power. Additional research has shown that significant relationships between academic achievement and conduct problems (Frick et al., 1991), aggressive/delinquent behavior (Barriga et al., 2002), and internalizing problems (Breslau et al., 2009) could be explained by comorbid problems with inattention. Taken together, literature examining the influence of engagement in academic activities for both the general student population and those students identified as at risk provides strong support for inclusion within a framework defining core student behavioral competencies.

Nondisruptive

Disruptive behavior is generally defined as any behavior that causes an interruption in a class or activity, and may include such behaviors as sustained loud talk, yelling, or screaming; noise with materials; horseplay or roughhousing; and/or sustained out-of-seat behavior (Todd, Horner, & Tobin, 2005). Returning to Carroll's (1963) model of student learning, disruptive behavior also reduces the amount of time spent learning by either distracting classmates or diverting the teacher's instruction (Gettinger & Ball, 2008). Additionally, disruptive behavior can also have a contagion effect, whereby one instance of disruptive behavior begets the next (Finn et al., 1995). A poll of the American Federation of Teachers found that 36% of teachers reported losing between 2 and more than 4 hours of instruction per week due to disruptive behavior. It has been suggested that because disruptive behavior interferes with the overall welfare of the classroom, teachers find it to be among the least acceptable of problem behaviors (Safran & Safran, 1985). Interestingly, however, the effects of disruptive behavior on individual student performance are less clear. Swift and Spivack (1968), for example, identified a statistically significant relationship between classroom disturbance and academic achievement; however, the strength of this relationship was found to be in the small to medium range (range of *r*'s = .22–.40). It has been suggested that students demonstrating disruptive behavior may experience fewer academic setbacks because these students are more likely to solicit attention from teachers and to be directed back to a task than their inattentive yet nondisruptive counterparts (Finn et al., 1995).

Disruptive behavior represents a significant concern among teachers, and thus it is important to fully understand the implications (and potential unintended consequences) of defining, measuring, and providing supports around disruptive behavior. One of the potential issues, for example, is the fact that what is considered *disruptive* can be somewhat subjective across persons. Consequently, emerging analyses continue to reveal concerns related to racial disproportionality and claims of disruptive behavior. In a recent study, Skiba and colleagues (2011) documented that black students were nearly four times as likely at the elementary level and five times as likely at the middle school level to receive office discipline referrals specifically for disruptive behavior. As such, although the relevance of nondisruptive behavior as a core student behavioral competency is established, caveats are given to acknowledge that supports may be needed to identify intended, and mediate unintended, consequences. For example, inclusion of disruptive behavior as a core behavioral competency establishes that opportunity to provide adult training around definitions of disruptive behavior, including relevance of identification and early remediation of potential difficulties before reactive consequences are applied, such as office referrals leading to suspension.

Respectful

Although there are multiple influences on school learning that range from individual to contextual (e.g., classroom, school, community) factors, a comprehensive literature review by Wang, Haertel, and Walberg (1993) found that among those variables with the greatest influence on student learning was the quality of student–teacher interactions. In fact, positive student–teacher relationships have been linked to a number of positive outcomes, including engagement in school (Zimmer-Gembeck, Chipuer, Hanisch, Creed, & McGregor, 2006) and psychological well-being (Herrero, Estevez, & Musitu, 2006).

A critical component defining the quality of student–teacher interactions can be linked to whether teachers perceive their students as demonstrating respectful, rather than noncompliant or defiant, behavior. For example, in examining data collected through an inventory of teacher social–behavioral standards and expectations, the behaviors considered to be the most maladaptive included those that conflict with teacher value systems and/or challenge the teacher's authority (Walker, 1985). These findings appear to be consistent with continuing trends as revealed within the School-Wide Information System (SWIS), the electronic system used within systems of schoolwide positive behavior support for documenting office discipline referrals. Specifically, in grades K–6, the category of defiance is the second most referred major problem behavior and is ranked within the top three minor problem behaviors as documented by SWIS (Spaulding, Irvin, Horner, May, Emeldi, et al., 2010). In addition to externalizing behaviors such as aggression and disruption, defiant behaviors contribute to overwhelming teachers, disrupting learning, threatening safety, and impacting the student's chance of success in schools (Walker, Ramsey, & Gresham, 2003–2004). Taken together, a domain related to respectful and compliant behavior therefore appears relevant as a core student behavioral competency.

Admittedly, our early attempts to capture this construct were not entirely successful. One challenge lies in settling on a best definition of the construct that broadly represents "teacher-pleasing" behavior. Our initial definition focused on compliance, such as initiating and/or completing a requested response within 5 seconds in a socially acceptable manner. Results from the initial studies, however, did not support sound technical adequacy (e.g., Riley-Tillman, Chafouleas, Christ, Briesch, & LeBel, 2009), to the point that our later studies dropped the competency and focused solely on academically engaged and disruptive constructs. However, a practice-related issue subsequently arose, in that teachers in our intervention studies consistently commented that rating those two constructs did not adequately capture what was happening in their classroom. Simply put, dropping a competency that included respect lost sight of the importance of relationships in the classroom, most centrally, the student–teacher but also student–student relationships. Thus, we shifted terminology in our later work to *respectful*, and incorporated defining elements around compliant and polite behaviors as related to both adult and student relationships. As our assessment work in progress monitoring continued and transitioned to also include screening applications, we acknowledge that although respectful as a standalone competency is not highly effective, it does offer contributions within a composite that includes disruptive and academically engaged.

Conclusions

In this chapter, we have attempted to organize presentation of the many complexities associated with selecting behavioral assessment and intervention targets. More specifically, we have provided various frameworks for decision making, leading to a history of our rationale for focusing on core student behavior competencies including academically engaged, disruptive, and respectful behaviors. The bottom line message is that when designing or selecting a specific assessment tool and determining a course of action related to intervention supports, it is important to first step back and think about what the desired behavioral outcome(s) might be (McIntosh, Reinke, & Herman, 2009), understanding the lens that frames the rationale or justification for the decisions. For example, although an initial discussion might be specifically concerned with decreasing the number of side conversations that a student is having with his or her peers, why is this behavior problematic? Likely it is a problem because the student is less engaged in ongoing classroom instruction as a result. The decision must therefore be made as to whether targets would be more appropriately focused on the discrete behavior of talking to peers or a more general constellation of behavioral competencies, such as focus on academically engaged behavior. There are certainly justifications for either focus, or a combination of both, depending on the situation at hand and chosen framework for considering options.

There is no doubt that target behavior selection is critically important. Bergan and Tombari (1976), for example, found that initial problem identification was one of the best predictors of actual plan implementation. Unfortunately, however, the heavy lifting is not over once the target behaviors have been selected. As is outlined throughout the next several chapters, identifying target behaviors is the first of several steps necessary to appropriately develop and effectively implement DBR.

CHAPTER 3

Using DBR to Communicate across Contexts

Sandra M. Chafouleas, Amy L. Reschly, Ruth Chaffee, and Amy M. Briesch

DBR holds particular promise for promoting communication among important stakeholders in the lives of children and adolescents. Timely, relevant, and positively framed communication across the many contexts within which students are situated can be an important contributor to student outcomes. Although we acknowledge communication as multifaceted and multidirectional, in this chapter we focus specifically on promoting communication between teachers and both students and families as a way of facilitating these important relationships. We begin by reviewing the broader literature related to the critical need for positive relationships in promoting student development, before discussing how DBR specifically can be used to promote effective communication among different parties. Finally, we illustrate the practical considerations to be made in using DBR to promote communication, using case examples involving home–school and teacher–student collaborations.

The Student as Situated within Multiple Contexts

The relative influence of nature (genes) and nurture (environment) has been debated throughout history. This classic debate has given way to a more nuanced view of development—that it is not one or the other, but the interaction between individual characteristics and the environment over time that best characterizes development. Longitudinal research has suggested, for example, that life outcomes may be predicted by the interaction between individual protective factors and the presence of external resources, ranging from primary caregivers to informal supports in the community (Werner, 2005).

Bronfenbrenner's ecological systems theory serves as the cornerstone of current child theoretical models and research in development, education, and psychology (e.g., Christenson & Reschly, 2010; Gutkin, 2012; Pianta & Walsh, 1996; Tudge, 2008). Bronfenbrenner (1979, 1992) underscored the importance of viewing children (i.e., their behavior, achievement, outcomes) within a context. He proposed that individuals are embedded within a set of environmental systems that interact with one another. These systems range in proximity and influence, from those with which the child has direct contact (i.e., microsystem; e.g., homes, schools, churches) to those that are further removed from the child (i.e., exosystem; e.g., a parent's workplace; public policy; broad cultural values, beliefs, and practices), and are often represented graphically as a series of nesting dolls or embedded circles (see Figure 3.1). Because children are active in their own development, they both affect, and are affected by, these environmental systems.

Despite widespread acceptance of Bronfenbrenner's theory, it has been noted that there is a tendency to view students and outcomes of interest (e.g., graduation rate, substance use, reading achievement) as a function of a single context (e.g.,

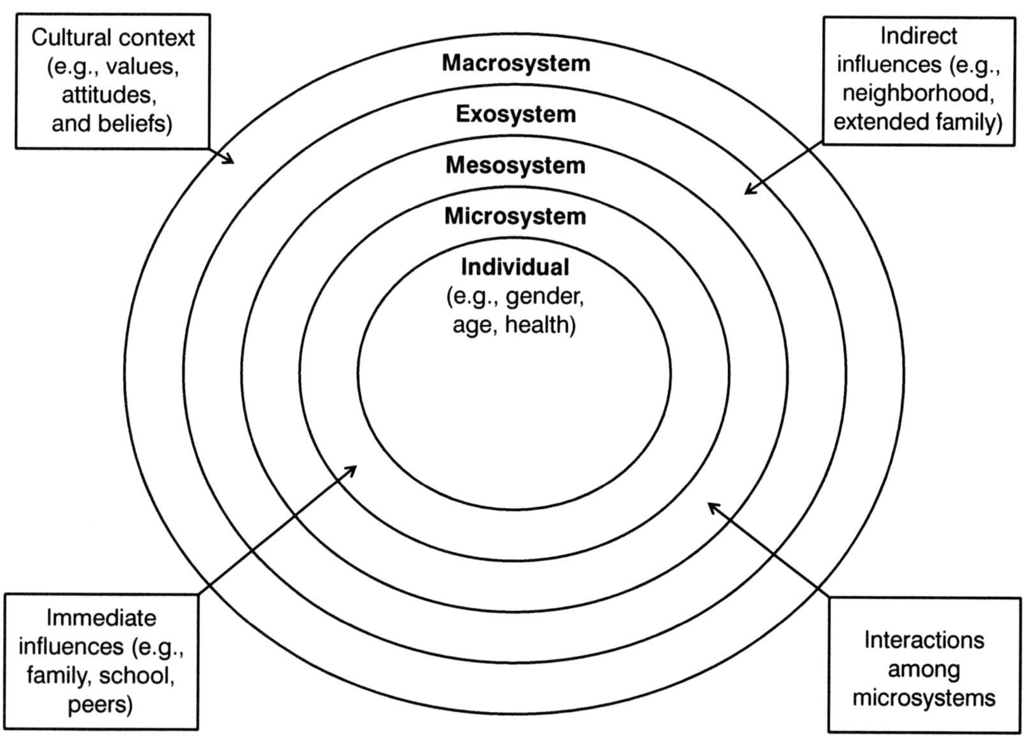

FIGURE 3.1. Bronfenbrenner's ecological model.

family). Policies that seek to hold teachers solely accountable for student performance are one such example. Attributing student failure to family or student characteristics (e.g., socioeconomic status, ethnicity, marital status, home language) is another. This "single location discourse" (Pianta & Walsh, 1996, p. 47) is too narrow and simplistic, however, to capture the complexity of interactions among children, family members, teachers, and others across contextual systems and time. Because, however, it would be impractical to attempt to discuss and account for all developmental systems and interactions within the context of this chapter, we turn our focus to the two systems in which students spend the majority of their time: school and home.

The Teacher–Student Relationship

The first level of Bronfenbrenner's (1979) model (i.e., the microsystem) focuses on the immediate environments that influence an individual's development. In the case of children, primary environments of interest include the home, school, and neighborhood. There is no doubt that caregivers within the home substantially influence children's development. Parent–child relationship quality has been shown to affect a wide range of outcomes, including school readiness (e.g., Parker, Boak, Griffin, Ripple, & Peay, 1999) and peer relationships (e.g., Russell, Pettit, & Mize, 1998). There is also research, however, to suggest that teacher–student relationship variables can significantly influence children's outcomes as well.

As one example, teacher–student conflict has been found to mediate the relationship between individual variables (e.g., socioeconomic status, gender, temperament) and risk-taking behavior in adolescence (Rudasill, Reio, Stipanovic, & Taylor, 2010). That is, students who demonstrated more conflictual relationships with their teachers were found to exhibit more risk-taking behaviors than their peers who did not have conflictual relationships with their teachers. In fact, positive teacher–student relationships have been linked to a number of positive outcomes, including student learning (Wang et al., 1993), engagement in school (e.g., Wentzel & Erdley, 1993; Zimmer-Gembeck et al., 2006), and psychological well-being (e.g., Herrero et al., 2006). As noted by Masten and Reed (2002), "The best documented asset of resilient children is a strong bond to a competent and caring adult, which need not be a parent" (p. 83).

Teacher–Student Communication

One critical piece in promoting positive teacher–student relationships is ensuring that communications are clear, consistent, and positive in nature. First, teachers' expectations for student behavior should be clearly communicated from the time that students first enter the classroom. In reviewing the literature base on prevention and intervention strategies to promote positive student behavior, an Institute of Education Sciences panel (Epstein, Atkins, Cullinan, Kutash, & Weaver, 2008) identified strong (i.e., consistent and generalizable) evidence in support of the teaching and reinforcement of skills in improving student behavior. That is, expected behaviors and skills should be taught in the same explicit manner as academic content. However, because one-time teaching of skills is insufficient to ensure meaningful behavioral change, providing positive reinforcement contingent upon students' demonstration of these learned skills is critical to ensuring their maintenance (Epstein et al., 2008).

Second, the way in which teachers communicate with their students on a daily basis is also important to consider. Over nearly half a century, researchers have documented the effects of teacher expectancies on a range of student outcome variables (Raudenbush, 1984). Collectively, this research suggests that even the subtle ways in which teachers communicate their expectations to students can have notable effects on students' learning and engagement in school. Teachers can communicate their support of students both verbally and through nonverbal means. There is longstanding evidence, for example, to suggest that teacher delivery of either verbal praise (e.g., Rosenshine, 1976) or criticism (e.g., Brophy & Evertson, 1974) can significantly influence student behavior. Even the act of individually greeting students as they enter the classroom has been shown to improve student engagement (Allday & Pakurar, 2007). At the same time, however, nonverbal signals (e.g., facial expressions, vocal intonation, proximity) can communicate equally powerful messages to students regarding how their teachers perceive them (Miller, 1988).

Although positive communication is critically important to building healthy teacher–student relationships, there are several barriers that may prevent effective communication. One is the fact that teacher-to-student ratios have increased over the past three decades. In 2008, the average class size in the United States was 20 students at the elementary level and 23 students at the secondary level (U.S. Department of Education, 2010). As the size of classrooms increases, it becomes more difficult for teachers to provide the individualized attention and feedback that students may need. Another potential barrier relates to the lack of time in a day. The popular media is brimming with quotes from classroom teachers expressing their frustration that there is not enough time in the day to cover anything beyond the required academic curriculum. A number of different factors, from classroom management to high-stakes testing, have been blamed for this time drain; however, it is clear that finding time to engage in nonacademic relationship-building conversations with students has become increasingly difficult. Finally, it can be easy, particularly when dealing with students who exhibit behavioral problems, to fall into negative patterns of communication that are then difficult to reverse. Students who exhibit noncompliance, for example, can quickly elicit negative, confrontational responses from teachers who are attempting to maintain control. Although research has suggested that making small changes, such as altering the manner in which teacher commands are given (i.e., ensure that commands are direct, specific, positive, and developmentally appropriate), can improve student compliance and academic engagement (Matheson & Shriver, 2005), changing behavioral responses that have become ingrained can be quite difficult.

The School–Family Relationship

The interactions between families and schools reside in the second level of Bronfenbrenner's model, termed the *mesosystem* (Bronfenbrenner, 1979). Pianta and Walsh (1996) underscored the importance of the history and pattern of relationships and interactions across families and school personnel. Their work highlighted that there is increased risk for negative outcomes when relationships between schools and families are poor, and youth receive different messages regarding expectations, behavior, and priorities across settings. At the same time, however, research has shown that partnerships between schools and families can lead to meaningful academic gains (Henderson & Mapp, 2002). The mesosystem of home and school is therefore a social system that can, and should, be harnessed to facilitate student development and success.

Many terms have been used to describe the interactions between families and school systems, including *parent involvement*, *family engagement*, *family–school collaboration*, and *family–school partnership*. Over time, these terms have evolved with increasing recognition of the myriad ways in which families support student learning. Whereas the word *involvement* can be used to describe isolated unidirectional activities such as contributing to a fundraiser or volunteering in the classroom (Reschly & Christenson, 2009), the words *collaboration*, *relationship*, and *partnership* are frequently used to signify an interactive, mutually supportive relationship that focuses on student learning (Hoover-Dempsey, Whitaker, & Ice, 2010). For example, Clarke, Sheridan, and Woods (2010) defined a family–school relationship as "a child-centered connection between individuals in the home and school settings who share responsibility for supporting the growth and development of children" (p. 61). Such a conceptualization emphasizes the bidirectional and cooperative nature of the work done by schools and families to enhance student academic, behavioral, and social–emotional outcomes. It is collaborative partnerships of this nature that have been noted by a number of scholars as being a key to addressing educational disparities (Reschly & Christenson, 2012; Rothstein, 2004; Tolan & Woo, 2010), improving outcomes for all students (Christenson & Reschly, 2010), and serving as a protective factor for those students most at risk (Christenson & Sheridan, 2001). For these reasons, school–family relationships have increasingly been the focus of school and district efforts to work with families to enhance outcomes for all youth (Christenson & Reschly, 2010).

Although home–school partnerships are inarguably important, they cannot be developed or maintained without concerted efforts. Building relationships takes time, effort, and significant leadership. In addition, Clarke et al. (2010) suggested that healthy family–school relationships must be built upon the interpersonal aspects of trust, sensitivity, and equality. First, *trust* is defined as the confidence that the school will act in a manner that benefits the relationship and achieves positive outcomes for the student. Research has suggested that trust itself is composed of respect, competence, personal regard for others, and integrity (Bryk & Schneider, 2002; Minke, 2006). Parents with higher trust in the parent–teacher relationship are more likely to value their involvement in schools and demonstrate a greater willingness to forgive occasional negative events. Second, *sensitivity* is defined as an acknowledgment of and respect for the diverse social, cultural, historical, and linguistic experiences of students and families. The diversity of public schools has been steadily increasing, with the percentage of minority students rising from 40 to 48% from 2001 to 2011 and the percent of English language learners (ELLs) on the rise (National Center for Education Statistics, 2014). Educators must develop multicultural awareness and sensitivity to work with families from diverse backgrounds and to support student achievement. Lastly, *equality* is defined as "the opportunity to acknowledge and value the expertise of the other as being equal to their own" (Clarke et al., 2010, p. 69). The family–school relationship is often imbalanced, with educators holding research and professional opinions and families often lacking the social capital and resources to exert their opinions (Lareau & McNamara-Horvat, 1999). Thus, the responsibility falls to schools to engage with families in a manner that avoids power struggles and allows families to access their own expertise (i.e., by exhibiting the value of equality).

Family–School Communication

Effective communication between home and school is one key action or mechanism through which healthy relationships are developed and maintained (Clarke et al., 2010). Communication allows both parties to understand each other's context and goals, and can extend the relationship into a true partnership with shared goals, contributions, and accountability (Fantuzzo, Tighe, & Childs, 2000). For many years, the predominant model of family–school communication has been unidirectional, with information concerning academic or student behavior typically sent from school to home when a problem arises. Family–school communication is most effective, however, if it is *bidirectional* in nature, such that families and schools can share responsibility for communication (Christenson & Sheridan, 2001). Current technology allows for the easy exchange of information across home and school settings. For example, e-mail can be used to send information regarding ongoing student performance or to share strategies for addressing concerns. It is also important for teachers to be positive and proactive when communicating with parents. Rather than waiting to contact families until students have fallen significantly behind, teachers should aim to make positive phone calls home and to contact parents at the first sign of concern. By focusing on the first sign of a concern, teachers can work collaboratively with parents in a "win–win" orientation focused on mutually defined goals. Inclusive pronouns, such as *we* and *our* as opposed to *you* and *yours*, can be used to invoke the collaborative nature of the relationship and to focus on the family's ability to help.

Though we are beginning to understand the steps needed to build strong communication between schools and families, many barriers to effective communication remain. For one, parents are significantly influenced by their past experiences with schools and other agencies with authority (Bermudez & Marquez, 1996) and may be suspicious and unresponsive to a school's communications. Research has also indicated that teachers may hold negative or stereotypical attitudes about people from certain cultures and may set a hostile or insensitive tone (Bermudez & Marquez, 1996). Logistical demands may also impede communication, such as access to a phone or the scheduling of employment. Finally, the quality of the communication from schools can also be a barrier to effective communication. Educator jargon can be difficult for parents to understand, especially those who may have had less formal education or for whom English is not their first language. As discussed above, communication that focuses on inappropriate behavior or a child's inadequacies may create distrust and is not sensitive to the family role. Similarly, many families do not respond positively when educators employ an authoritarian tone (Christenson & Sheridan, 2001). Well-intentioned educators may undermine effective communication by sending home a prescriptive note or informing a family of an intervention, rather than giving options or collaboratively developing solutions.

Concluding Thoughts Regarding Communication across Contexts

Whether between teachers and students or home and school, the evidence is clear that relationships are critical to student success, and that communication is an essential part of establishing and maintaining effective relationships. Strong lines of communication do not, however, appear overnight; rather, dedicated efforts are needed by both parties in order to build these connections over time. DBR is one tool that can be used in this building process; thus, next we turn to a discussion of the role that DBR can play in promoting effective communication across different parties.

Using DBR to Facilitate Effective Communication

Despite acknowledgment that communication is a key ingredient in the development and maintenance of healthy relationships between students, their teachers, and their families, this is often much easier said than done. The demands placed on busy classroom teachers, families, and students themselves can make it difficult to find the time and/or to remember to initiate the communication that we know is so important. Fortunately, DBR offers one potential mechanism for enhancing communication—and hence relationships—via multiple avenues.

The sharing of information across different parties has long been a key characteristic of DBR within intervention applications (Chafouleas et al., 2002). As described in Chapter 1, the earliest studies involving DBR emphasized family participation in light of the increased feasibility and saliency of using home-based rewards for students. That is, the classroom teacher would rate the student's performance throughout the school day, but then families would bear responsibility for administering rewards that were seen as more attractive (e.g., extra time outside, special outing) than those that could be provided in the school (e.g., stickers, small tangibles). Over time, however, emphasis was increasingly placed on the ability of the DBR to promote dialogue between different stakeholders. In the 1980s and 1990s, for example, researchers embraced the name school–home notes as a way to emphasize the lines of communication that could be opened using a DBR (e.g., Kelley, 1990; Kelley & McCain, 1995). Rather than viewing the intervention as school-based and simply supplemented at home, the importance of family participation both in designing and implementing the intervention was increasingly stressed. This emphasis was supported by the findings of a meta-analysis, which identified high levels of home–school collaboration as among the most significant moderators of intervention effectiveness (Vannest et al., 2010). Specifically, stronger effects were noted when parents were involved not only in the administration of feedback and rewards but also in decision making related to plan implementation and reinforcement planning, in particular.

There are several potential benefits of using DBR to communicate across parties. First, whether used to intervene or simply to assess, DBR can be used to promote bidirectional communication that is frequent, predictable, and positive (Kelley & McCain, 1995). As previously noted, unfortunately, communication in schools has often been characterized as unidirectional, sporadic, and negative. Descriptive studies have shown that teachers tend to provide a greater number of reprimands than praise for social behavior (Merrett & Wheldall, 1992; Harrop & Swinson, 2000), and parents of children who demonstrate behavioral problems often only hear from teachers when something has gone wrong. DBR, however, is intended not only to document problem behaviors but also, more importantly, to acknowledge and reinforce appropriate behaviors as well. For example, training in DRC procedures (see Chapter 8) emphasizes the importance of focusing on what the child has done correctly while acknowledging undesirable behavior matter-of-factly. By opening the lines of communication to share both positive and constructive feedback on a daily basis, teachers' conversations with both students and their families can assume a more positive and supportive tone.

Second, because it can be both simple to use and interpret DBR, information about student behavior can be more quickly and easily shared across parties. With the recent shift to multi-tiered models of service delivery, there is increased pressure to communicate frequently about student behavior in order to facilitate timely decisions about appropriate intervention supports. Simply put, the longer and more complex an assessment procedure is, the less likely it is to be carried out with integrity. The fact that DBR requires a minimal time commitment therefore increases the likelihood that ratings will be completed with the regularity that formative decision making requires (see Chapter 5 for an in-depth discussion of progress monitoring). Furthermore, because interpretation of DBR data does not require highly specialized skills or knowledge (see Chapter 11 for discussion of summarizing and interpreting DBR data), information can be shared across multiple parties and used to inform decision making more quickly than may be true of more traditional assessment procedures (e.g., norm-referenced behavior rating scales).

Third, the sharing of information across multiple parties may help to promote stronger generalization of treatment effects. Given the multiple spheres of influence within a student's life, behavior supports put in place solely during the school day are inevitably less effective than those that are consistent across settings (Esler, Godber, & Christenson, 2008). Communication across systems enhances efficacy because it allows the student to predictably understand the expected behaviors as well as the consequences for violating those expectations. Because the expectations for behavior are clearly outlined on the DBR, both teachers and families are equipped to use consistent language and reinforce shared expectations across settings. For example, a student involved in a check-in/check-out intervention (see Chapter 8) may receive feedback based on how well he or she meets the schoolwide expectation of being responsible (e.g., arriving at class on time, putting trash in trashcans, keeping desk tidy) on a DPR. This expectation could then be further supported at home by providing the student with positive feedback for doing things such as keeping his or her room clean and completing assigned chores before going outside.

Now that we have discussed the importance of communication and broadly reviewed the benefits of using DBR to communicate across parties, we outline the specific considerations that should be made in order to promote effective communication when using DBR (see Table 3.1).

TABLE 3.1. DBR Blueprint for Promoting Effective Communication

☐ 1. Identify target behavior(s) collaboratively.

Target behaviors should be identified collaboratively to ensure initial buy-in and sustained commitment to the intervention or assessment.

☐ 2. Establish shared goals.

Meaningful, realistic performance goals should be established using baseline data but may be modified using feedback from families/students.

☐ 3. Determine with whom information will be shared.

When DBR is used as an intervention, data must be shared with the student but may or may not be shared with families as well. Within the context of assessment, DBR data may be shared with a range of individuals within and outside of the school setting.

☐ 4. Determine how and how often information will be shared.

Although DBR intervention data should be shared with students in close proximity to the observation period, there exists greater latitude in determining how (e.g., via e-mail, paper) and how often (e.g., each day, end of each week) data are shared with families.

☐ 5. Schedule a meeting with relevant stakeholders.

All parties should provide feedback on the proposed plan and understanding of each individual's role should be ensured.

☐ 6. Monitor effectiveness of the communication.

After plan implementation begins, reassess the communication system to determine if changes (e.g., frequency or manner of communication) need to be made.

Step 1: Identify Target Behavior(s) Collaboratively

The first step in using DBR is to select the behavior(s) that will be targeted for intervention or assessment. Engaging parents and families in the determination of target behaviors is a way to stress the importance of family–educator relationships and the identification of shared goals. Likewise, soliciting the input of students at this initial stage can be important, given that increased participation in intervention decision making is believed to increase one's motivation to engage in behavior change (Kanfer & Gaelick-Buys, 1991). If target behaviors are identified entirely in-house (i.e., by school personnel only), we risk missing important targets for intervention and failing to gain buy-in for the intervention. If, on the other hand, all parties agree upon and genuinely value the behaviors identified, the likelihood of both initial buy-in and sustained implementation is enhanced (Kelley, 1990).

In identifying appropriate target behaviors, two important questions should be asked. The first question is whether concerns about this behavior have been previously communicated to the other party. In the case of teacher–parent relationships, the teacher should have a strong ongoing communication system with students' families, especially around conveying academic and social–emotional strengths and concerns. Whether through conferences, report card comments, or letters home, parents should be informed about the targeted behaviors before intervention occurs. These expectations for teacher–parent communication apply to teacher–student communication as well. The first discussion regarding problem behavior should not take place when a formal intervention is being introduced. Rather, implementation of a structured intervention should follow from proactive, informal conversations between relevant parties, with first steps to foster positive communication directed toward problem solving.

The second question that should be asked is how changing this behavior will improve conditions for the student. Any behavior selected for intervention should be socially valid, meaning that addressing that particular behavior will result in significant improvements in social and behavioral functioning. It is important to keep in mind that hierarchies of target behaviors may differ across individuals. For example, a teacher may be most interested in decreasing a student's calling-out behavior because it is disrupting the entire classroom environment, whereas a parent may prioritize increasing the same student's completion of assignments. If competing priorities are identified, they should be collaboratively discussed and a decision made as a team. Acknowledging the student and/or family's perspective is fundamental to improving overall buy-in for the intervention.

Step 2: Establish Shared Goals

Once the target behaviors have been collaboratively identified, the next step is to establish performance goals for the student. Baseline data should be collected and used to inform the development of performance goals that are both meaningful and realistically attainable for the student. Although there can be a tendency to want to set the goal at the level of behavior that is ultimately desired (e.g., zero instances of talking out in class), it is important to ensure that the criterion is not so stringent that the student will have great difficulty meeting it (Kelley, 1990). Feedback should therefore be solicited from the family and/or student (if developmentally appropriate) regarding both the meaningfulness (e.g., will a reduction of 10% make a difference in the home?) and reasonableness (e.g., is it realistic to assume that a 40% reduction could be achieved?) of the goals.

Step 3: Determine with Whom Information Will Be Shared

After identifying and defining the target behavior(s), the next step is to determine with whom the DBR ratings will be shared. When DBR is being used as an intervention tool, these data must be shared with the student as a way of providing behavioral feedback. It is optional, however, whether these intervention data are also sent home to the student's family. Certain DBR interventions, such as the DRC (see Chapter 8), typically require daily communication of the ratings so that the family can provide home-based rewards. In contrast, implementation of a self-management intervention (see Chapter 10) does not automatically require that ratings be shared with the student's family. In some cases, the decision as to whether information should be shared between school and home may also be based on knowledge of family dynamics. For example, if the classroom teacher was aware that a student's parents had a particularly punitive orientation, it might be in the child's best interest not to send ratings home so as to avoid eliciting negative feedback.

When DBR is being used as an assessment tool, the options for the sharing of data increase substantially beyond students and families alone. Within the school, it may be beneficial to share DBR data with other in-school support providers, such as the speech–language therapist, occupational therapist, paraprofessionals, or social workers/adjustment counselors. This sharing of information can be particularly important for special education students with IEPs. Information collected via DBR can provide feedback for annual reviews of progress toward IEP goals and can inform adjustments to the IEP. Outside of the school, data may also be shared with other systems that interact with the student. Relevant personnel may include community-based providers (e.g., physicians, social worker/mental health counselors), Department of Child and Family Services, or even extracurricular coaches. Clear cross-system communication enhances consistency across settings and may help inform the care provided to students, thus serving a critically important function for facilitating positive child outcomes. For example, DBR data regarding academic engagement would be particularly helpful to a primary care physician managing medication dosage for an attention disorder. Before sharing information with anyone outside of the school, however, it is important to ensure that the appropriate permissions are obtained.

Step 4: Determine How and How Often Information Will Be Shared

Although DBR is defined by at least daily ratings, the team must determine how and how often to share these data. As is discussed in Chapters 8–10, within the context of intervention DBR is believed to be effective in improving student behavior largely because students receive ongoing, specific feedback regarding their performance. For this reason, it is important for teachers to provide students with feedback in close proximity to when the behavior actually occurs. Brief meetings are therefore typically set up between teachers and students periodically during the school day (e.g., during transitions, at the end of the school day) to share and discuss DBR ratings.

There is greater latitude, however, in determining how and how often ratings are shared between home and school. Although information has most typically been sent to families at the end of each day, some research has suggested that positive behavior change may occur if a summary report of performance is sent home only at the end of each week (Dougherty & Dougherty, 1977). Furthermore, DBRs have traditionally been sent home with the student (e.g., in a backpack or folder), but other modes of communication may be more appropriate. For example, if the student encounters difficulty in successfully bringing the DBR home, it may be necessary to communicate with parents via e-mail or phone. Sending DBR data via e-mail may also increase the ease with which information is shared and create an electronic record of ongoing communications.

One additional consideration that should be made is how to establish a feedback loop between home and school so that communication is not unidirectional. Most typically, family members have been asked to review and sign the DBR so as to confirm that it was received; however, families may also be asked to complete their own ratings or provide qualitative behavioral feedback in order to keep the classroom teacher aware of how the student is performing at home. It is important to keep in mind that different family contexts necessitate different approaches and considerations. Some families may not be available to review DBR data each night, but may find the system feasible if DBR feedback is sent home weekly. In other cases, families may wish to engage in more frequent bidirectional communication via e-mail. Communication schedules should therefore be determined collaboratively in order to improve the chances of the plan being implemented with fidelity.

Step 5: Schedule a Meeting with Relevant Stakeholders

Once the intervention or assessment plan has been drafted, it is critical that a meeting is scheduled with the relevant stakeholders before implementation begins. Bringing multiple stakeholders into a unified meeting also demonstrates to the student that the significant forces in his or her life (e.g., school, family) are in a partnership to support him or her. Furthermore, having all parties in the same room helps to ensure that the student will receive a consistent message across home and school settings. The goal of the meeting should be twofold. First, it is important to gather feedback from all parties regarding the practicality of the plan. If concerns are raised regarding the ability of one party to carry out the plan as it has been described, it is important to identify what the potential barriers to implementation are and to problem-solve how the plan might be adapted to avoid any stumbling blocks. Once the plan is agreed upon, it is then important to ensure that everyone involved in the plan has a clear understanding both of how it will be implemented and what their specific role will be.

Step 6: Monitor Effectiveness of Communication

After the plan has been in place for a few days, it is important to reassess the communication system to determine if any changes need to be made. Specifically, the frequency or manner of communication may need to be modified. Some students, for example, may require more frequent behavioral feedback in order to be successful. Families may also identify potential clogs in the system for information sharing that need to be addressed, such as when paper forms mysteriously disappear from the student's backpack! Taking the time to reevaluate and adjust these aspects of a communication system may have a dramatic effect on the efficacy of an intervention.

Putting It All Together: Case Examples

Now that we have outlined the considerations that should be made in using DBR to promote communication, we illustrate these points using two case examples involving students from different grade levels. The first example focuses on the development and use of a school–home note to address the aggressive behaviors of a preschool student. In the second example, we illustrate how teachers and students can work together to implement a self-management intervention at the high school level.

Example 1: Home–School Communication (Preschool)

"Mr. Pilli" utilizes a number of universal prevention strategies in his preschool classroom to support all students, including strong classroom management skills, a child-focused environment, clear expectations, and positive behavioral strategies. Most students are experiencing behavioral success; however, he has been particularly concerned about "Taron" since the beginning of the school year. Taron has been exhibiting severe behavior problems in the classroom, including yelling, hitting, throwing items, and frequently refusing to comply with his directions. Mr. Pilli has been in regular contact with Taron's mother, "Ms. Wallace," about these behaviors, but he now feels that a more structured intervention is warranted. They set up a phone call to discuss the behaviors that are being seen at home and at school, and agree that Taron's aggressive behaviors involving hitting and throwing things are of greatest shared concern. Both agree to keep a record of how often these behaviors occur over the course of the week and then to meet in person to share what they found and to consider next steps. Mr. Pilli works with Ms. Wallace to find a time to meet that will work for the both of them. Because Ms. Wallace works during the day and is a single parent, it is important that she is able to find child care for Taron. They agree to meet right before school in order to accommodate Ms. Wallace's work schedule, and so that Mr. Pilli's assistant teacher can supervise Taron.

After reviewing the baseline data, Mr. Pilli and Ms. Wallace find that Taron has been hitting four times a day and throwing objects seven times a day, on average. They spend some time talking about what a meaningful, yet attainable, goal might be for Taron. Although Ms. Wallace says that she does not want Taron to be hitting at all, Mr. Pilli acknowledges that going from four hitting episodes to none might not be realistic initially. Together, they decide that two hitting episodes and four episodes of throwing objects might be an appropriate initial goal. Next, they work together to develop a school–home note targeting these aggressive behaviors. They decide to word the two goals positively (Taron will keep his hands to himself at school, Taron will play with objects nicely), and they create an age-appropriate 3-point scale with smiley face icons to represent possible observed behavior (*all the time*, *sometimes*, *rarely*) (see Figure 3.2). Together, they decide that Mr. Pilli will rate Taron's behavior two times a day (morning, afternoon), providing feedback by either praising Taron for an "all the time" rating or reviewing the expectations if lower ratings were earned. At the end of the day, Mr. Pilli will send the note home for Ms. Wallace to review with Taron.

When Ms. Wallace expressed being nervous about how to review the behavioral expectations if he did not earn an "all the time" rating, Mr. Pilli and Ms. Wallace practiced what she would say to Taron and created a sample script to ease her concerns. A significant portion of the meeting was then used to establish the home-based incentive system. They determined that if Taron earned two of four "all the time" ratings, he would earn a reward. Because Ms. Wallace was concerned that she couldn't financially afford to buy Taron big rewards every day, Mr. Pilli and Ms. Wallace brainstormed rewards that would be easily available in the home, such as getting to choose a game to play with Mom, special art project time, or playing an educational game on Mom's phone for 10 minutes.

After collaboratively establishing the target behaviors, goals, and rewards, they begin to implement the plan. At the end of the first week, Mr. Pilli calls Ms. Wallace to see if she has run into any problems. Both agree that the system seems to be working and are pleased that the school–home note has made it home in Taron's backpack each day. Within a couple of weeks, Mr. Pilli sees a dramatic reduction in Taron's aggressive behavior and hears Taron talk proudly about earning screen time. Mr. Pilli sends home a graph of Taron's progress, showing that the intervention has been effective at reducing Taron's aggressive/hitting behavior. He then follows

Morning		Keep hands to self	☺	😐	☹
		Play with objects nicely	☺	😐	☹
Afternoon	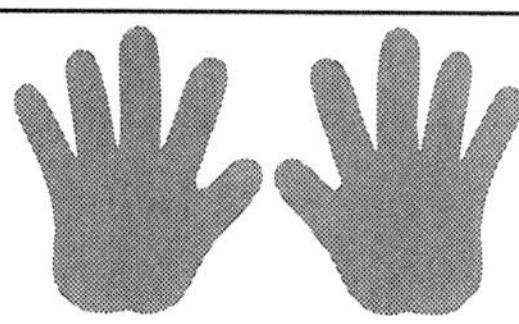	Keep hands to self	☺	😐	☹
		Play with objects nicely	☺	😐	☹

Tonight, ____

____

____

____

FIGURE 3.2. Sample of home–school note.

up with Ms. Wallace to see how Taron has been behaving at home. She reports a decrease in his aggressive behavior at home as well and hopes to continue using the school–home note system throughout the remaining weeks of the year.

Example 2: Teacher–Student Communication (High School)

"Violet" is a ninth-grade student in "Ms. Vincent's" third-period math class. At the end of the first marking period, Violet received a D in math due to a combination of missing homework assignments and incomplete classwork. Ms. Vincent wants to intervene early to ensure that Violet is able to pass the class for the semester, and asks Violet to stop by her classroom afterschool on Friday. During this meeting, Ms. Vincent expresses her concerns regarding the first quarter grade and asks Violet to reflect on what she feels has been keeping her from being successful. After some prompting, Violet admits that she has been spending lots of time talking to her friends in class rather than working on her problem sets. In addition, when she gets home she often realizes that she either did not write down the homework assignment, or is unsure how to complete the problems because she was not paying attention in class.

After some conversation, Ms. Vincent and Violet come to agreement that there are two important behaviors that seem to be standing in the way of her success in math: talking to peers in class and completing her homework assignments. Together, they design a self-management intervention plan to address these concerns. First, they develop a rating card that can be used to monitor these two behaviors (see Figure 3.3). Each time that Violet talks to her friends in class, she is instructed to make a tally mark in the first column of the form. The second column of the form then provides her with a space to write the homework assignment at the end of class. Because Ms. Vincent did not collect any baseline data on her talking to peers before discussing the concern with Violet, she asks Violet to estimate how many times she talks in class each day; Violet estimates six or seven times. Ms. Vincent then takes out her grade book and they see that over the past couple of weeks, Violet has turned in 40% of her homework assignments. Together, they decide that if, at the end of the week, Violet has less than five talking tally marks per day and has turned in 60% of her homework assignments, she will earn a reward.

In discussing what a motivating reward might be, Ms. Vincent encourages Violet to think about ways in which she could reward herself as a way of promoting independence. Violet decides that if she meets her goal at the end of the first week, she will reward herself by going to the mall with her friends. Having identified a motivating yet feasible reward, the final issues to resolve are how, how often, and with whom Violet will share her ratings. Ms. Vincent suggests that they meet at the end of each class to review her ratings; however, Violet expresses some resistance because she needs to stop at her locker before fourth period. They agree to meet

	Make a tally mark each time that you talk to friends in class	Homework assignment
Monday		
Tuesday		
Wednesday		
Thursday		
Friday		

FIGURE 3.3. Sample of self-monitoring card.

once at the end of each week initially and then to make adjustments to the plan from there if necessary.

At the end of the first week, Ms. Vincent and Violet sit down to review the self-management DBR. Although Violet has made the tally marks consistently, Ms. Vincent notes that she missed writing down two homework assignments. Ms. Vincent suggests that they continue to meet at the end of the week to discuss how the week went, but that Violet also stop by her desk at the end of each period to quickly show her the completed form. Violet agrees to try it out and they decide to start the new plan on Monday.

Conclusions

Although there is often a tendency to reduce explanations for student behavior to a single source (e.g., individual, family, school, or community characteristics), in reality, student development is influenced by the highly complex interactions among multiple spheres of influence. We also know that students are likely to experience more positive outcomes when these different systems are working together rather than in parallel with—or in opposition to—one another. It is for this reason, for example, that mandates to strengthen home–school collaboration have been made increasingly strong within federal legislation over time (Carlson & Christenson, 2005). Positive, regular, and bidirectional communication is key in promoting partnerships, and research evidence has shown that communication can improve the efficacy of behavioral interventions as well. This chapter has illustrated how DBR can be used to strengthen lines of communication between both students and teachers and schools and families, broadly speaking. In the following chapters, we discuss the use of DBR within specific assessment and intervention contexts.

PART II

DBR Applications

Assessment

CHAPTER 4

Foundations of DBR in Assessment

Amy M. Briesch, T. Chris Riley-Tillman, and Sandra M. Chafouleas

Although DBR-like tools have long been used within the context of behavioral intervention, it is only within the past decade that attention has been paid to the development and use of DBR within an assessment context. Given that DBR is a fairly new kid on the behavioral assessment block, we expect that potential consumers will have questions as to the quality of the tool and the resultant data. As Glover and Albers (2007) noted, the quality of an assessment tool must be judged in relation to the assessment's purpose. That is, different assessment purposes will necessitate different considerations and requirements. Although psychometric standards (e.g., reliability, validity) are certainly one means by which tools should be judged, it is also important to consider factors such as acceptability, feasibility, and relevance (Kazdin, 2005). In the next section, we review the central purposes of assessment within a problem-solving framework and both psychometric indicators and practical considerations most relevant to each. We then lay out the historical context for the use of DBR in assessment, offering guidance for local development of DBR based on existing empirical evidence. Finally, we provide current and future directions for research and development in this area.

Purposes of Assessment within a Problem-Solving Model

Twenty years ago, the assessment of student behavior was essentially synonymous with comprehensive diagnostic testing that required multiple measures and sources in order to arrive at the most accurate understanding of a student's level of functioning. Given the high stakes of the decisions that would be made based on these data (e.g., diagnosis, special education eligibility), primary emphasis was placed on ensuring that measures received the highest level of psychometric scrutiny. The quality of an assessment tool was therefore judged largely by its psychometric properties. As an increasing number of schools have begun to adopt a problem-solving approach to identifying and addressing student needs, however, the criteria by which the quality of an assessment tool should be judged has begun to change. Within a problem-solving model, there are four questions that guide decision making: (1) whether there is a problem (and if so, what the problem is); (2) why it is occurring; (3) what we should do about the problem; and (4) whether what we did worked (Tilly, 2008). These questions correspond to the four purposes of assessment (i.e., screening, evaluation, diagnosis, progress monitoring; Salvia, Ysseldyke, & Bolt, 2012; see Figure 4.1.) Although each assessment purpose involves different considerations and requirements for validation, four features have been identified as critical to the utility of an assessment tool within a problem-solving framework: defensibility (i.e., psychometric adequacy), efficiency (i.e., minimal time and resources required), flexibility (i.e., able to be used across different contexts), and repeatability (i.e., able to be administered on multiple occasions) (Christ et al., 2009). We discuss each assessment purpose next, emphasizing defining features and relevant validation criteria.

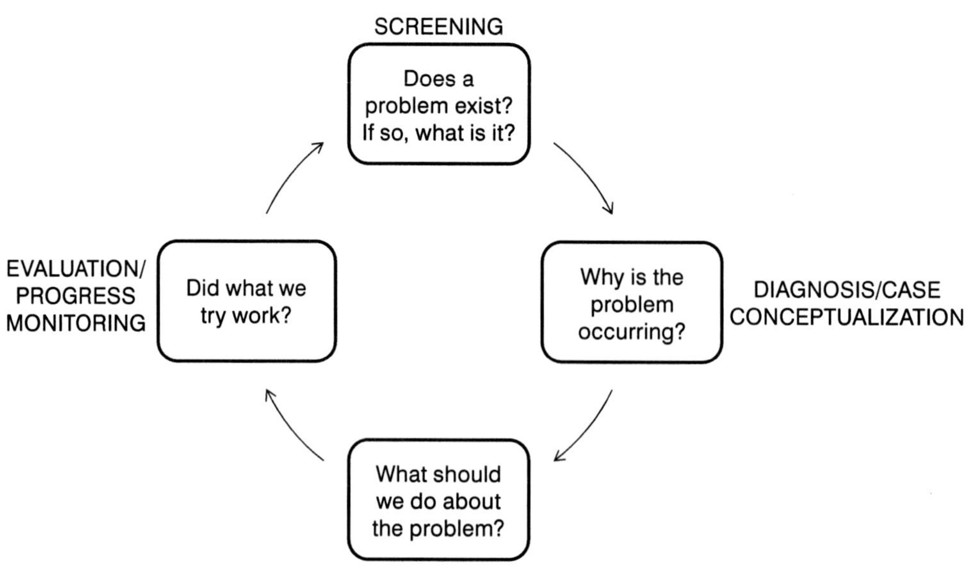

FIGURE 4.1. Purposes of assessment within a problem-solving framework.

TABLE 4.1. DBR Blueprint for Assessing Student Behavior

- ☐ 1. Determine the appropriateness of DBR.

  Although use of DBR is supported in screening and progress monitoring contexts, high-stakes decision making necessitates the use of supplemental measures.

- ☐ 2. Identify target behavior(s).

  Single- or multi-item scales can be used to assess target behaviors that require minimal inference on the part of the rater. Attention should be paid to the wording of target behaviors, given that changes may differentially influence rating accuracy.

- ☐ 3. Develop an operational definition for each target behavior.

  Strong operational definitions describe the target behavior in observable, measurable terms and pass the "stranger test," meaning that the definition should be clearly understandable to someone who has no familiarity with the student or the problem.

- ☐ 4. Determine who will conduct ratings.

  The individual best suited to conduct DBR ratings is the one who has sufficient opportunity to observe the target behavior(s). This may be the classroom teacher, an instructional aide, or even the student him- or herself.

- ☐ 5. Determine where, when, and how often ratings will occur.

  Ratings can be limited to one particular setting/time of day or conducted across multiple contexts, depending on data collection needs and the number of opportunities available for data collection.

- ☐ 6. Determine the appropriate scale and develop the DBR form.

  Although most work to date has focused on the use of an 11-point Likert-type scale, additional options include use of dichotomous ratings, categorical scales, and behaviorally anchored scales.

- ☐ 7. Conduct rater training.

  Training should review behavioral definitions, model how rating should be conducted, and allow for practice and immediate feedback.

Screening

Within a problem-solving model, the first question of whether a problem exists can be answered using universal screening. In the past, problems came to the attention of school-based teams or mental health professionals once the problems exceeded the threshold of teacher tolerability. The problem with a "wait until things get sufficiently bad" approach is that problems often become more crystallized and intense in the absence of intervention (Bradley, Doolittle, & Bartolotta, 2008). A more proactive alternative involves the use of screening to identify those students who may be at risk. Within a screening approach, all students in a given population are assessed using the same instrument, and those students exceeding a particular threshold undergo additional assessment and/or intervention. Because every student undergoes screening assessment, it is imperative that the assessment be fairly brief, inexpensive, and easy to administer. In order to ensure this level of feasibility, however, it may be necessary to sacrifice some degree of psychometric adequacy (Briesch & Volpe, 2007). The information obtained from the use of a screening instrument is not intended to provide a detailed diagnosis of the problem; rather, it is meant to provide a general indicator of student risk.

Criteria

Glover and Albers (2007) emphasized three critical features of screening measures: contextual relevance, technical defensibility, and usability. First, given that different screening measures may be designed for use with particular populations (e.g., adults, clinical populations) or may target different constructs (e.g., diagnostic symptoms, risk and resilience factors), it is important to assess the contextual fit of the instrument. A screening measure that was developed to identify anxious symptomology in clinically referred adolescents, for example, would not be appropriate if looking to facilitate early identification of students who are at risk within a general school population.

Second, the technical adequacy of the measure must be considered, including the adequacy (i.e., representativeness, size, recency) of the normative sample, the reliability of measurement, and the accuracy of classification (Glover & Albers, 2007). Traditional indicators of reliability, such as test–retest and interscorer reliability, must be considered to ensure that assessment results are not specific to a particular rater or assessment occasion. Furthermore, if the screening instrument is comprised of multiple items designed to assess the same construct (e.g., antisocial behavior, internalizing problems), the internal consistency of the measure should also be considered. The most important aspect of validity when evaluating screening measures, however, is predictive validity. That is, we want to ensure the validity of the cutoff scores that are used to identify those students potentially at risk. A strong screening instrument will ideally have a low proportion of false positives (i.e., of students identified as at risk whose behavior is actually not of concern), but more importantly should have a low proportion of false negatives (i.e., students identified as not at risk whose behavior actually *is* of concern). Criterion-related validity can be evaluated using four indicators. *Positive predictive power* tells us the probability that a student identified as at risk using a screening instrument is actually at risk, whereas *negative predictive power* tells us the probability that a student not identified as at risk is actually not at risk. Sensitivity tells us the proportion of the population that has been correctly identified as having a problem whereas specificity tells us the proportion of the population that has been correctly identified as not having a problem (American Educational Research Association [AERA], American Psychological Association [APA], & National Council on Measurement in Education [NCME], 1999). Typically, sensitivity, specificity, and positive predictive power values above 80% are considered to be adequate (Glover & Albers, 2007).

Finally, the usability of the screening measure must also be assessed. As highlighted by Glover and Albers (2007), usability can be assessed by considering such factors as the costs incurred, feasibility of administration, consumer acceptability, resources needed for data management, flexibility to assess different populations of interest, and the utility of data in treatment planning.

Diagnosis/Case Conceptualization

Within the second purpose of assessment, diagnosis and/or case conceptualization, one aims to describe the unique strengths and areas of need of a particular individual. Historically, the goal of diagnostic assessment has been to determine eligibility for special education services by identifying underlying sources of observed dysfunction. Within case conceptualization more broadly, both individual (e.g., biological, cultural) and environmental (e.g., physical, social) variables are considered in order to arrive at an informed hypothesis regarding both the causes and maintaining influences of problem behaviors.

The question of what the problem is and why it is occurring requires an assessment approach that is person-focused, or idiographic, in nature (Kazdin, 2005). In collecting assessment data, we hope to better understand the unique ways in which an individual's problems (as well as strengths) manifest themselves. Two students may demonstrate the same general problem behavior; however, both the topography and function of the behavior may look very different. Take, for example, two students who were referred to the problem-solving team for problems with "aggressive behavior." One student may call his classmates inappropriate names as a way to get attention from peers, whereas another student may kick her classmates in order to be left alone on the playground. To ensure that the most appropriate intervention is selected and put into place ("What should be done about the problem?"), it is necessary to collect idiographic data that consider both the student's unique pattern of behavior and the environment in which these behaviors occur. By using these data, we are then able to make intervention decisions based on conceptual relevance rather than a trial-and-error approach (Chafouleas, Riley-Tillman, & Sugai, 2007).

Criteria

When evaluating tools in the context of diagnostic decision making, it is most important that the obtained data demonstrate technical adequacy in terms of both reliability and validity. As with screening instruments, internal consistency should be examined when the diagnostic tool is comprised of multi-item scales (e.g., behavior rating scales). Test–retest reliability may also be important to consider when the underlying assumption is that the target construct is stable and not expected to change over time. High test–retest reliability would be expected, for example, when measuring a theoretically stable trait such as intelligence or personality. On the other hand, we would not necessarily expect to find high temporal stability for context-dependent behaviors such as those that may be examined within a functional assessment. Finally, interscorer reliability may be more or less important depending on the specific assessment instrument. When conducting a systematic direct observation using a well-defined code, for example, we would expect two independent observers to be highly consistent in their assessment of a target behavior. In contrast, research has shown that the agreement between two different informants (e.g., teacher, parent) completing a behavior rating scale tends to be much lower than agreement between similar informants (e.g., two parents; Achenbach, McConaughy, & Howell, 1987).

Given that important treatment decisions will be made based upon diagnostic assessment data, it is also important to consider test validity, or the degree to which the tool is measuring what it purports to measure. *Construct validity* tells us whether the assessment measures the intended construct. For example, we want to ensure that a test that was designed to measure symptoms of ADHD does not measure symptoms of other disorders as well. *Concurrent validity* assesses the degree to which results of one assessment tool are consistent with results from an established measure. If we were developing a novel measure of anxiety, we might look for evidence of concurrent validity by correlating scores on the new measure with scores on the Revised Children's Manifest Anxiety Scale—Second Edition (RCMAS-2; Reynolds & Richmond, 2008). Finally, *predictive validity* looks at the degree to which assessment results predict some later outcome (e.g., future achievement, dysfunction). Colleges, for example, have placed emphasis on scores from the Scholastic Aptitude Test (SAT) due to the strong validity of the test for predicting undergraduate academic performance.

Within diagnostic assessment, the *acceptability* of the assessment tool continues to be important because we know that the less accepting the consumer is of an assessment tool, the less likely he or she is to use it as intended (Eckert, Hintze, & Shapiro, 1999). *Feasibility*, however, in terms of both time and resources needed to conduct the assessment, becomes less pressing, given the limited scope of assessment. That is, because diagnostic assessment is typically conducted at one point in time with a limited number of students, feasibility considerations need not drive decision making.

Evaluation and Progress Monitoring

The question of whether an intervention worked can be answered using two different types of assessment. Historically, schools have answered this question using summative, or evaluative, assessment. This is akin to pre–post assessment, in which the student's behavior is evaluated first in the absence of intervention (i.e., baseline) and then once more at the conclusion of intervention implementation. Because the assessment is only conducted at two points in time, the focus is on ensuring that the obtained data meet a high level of psychometric adequacy rather than maximizing feasibility. The problem with a one-time, summative assessment, however, is that we must wait until implementation is complete to find out whether or not the intervention is successful. As a result, any potential mismatch between the student and the selected intervention may go unidentified for several weeks or even months.

Formative assessment, or *progress monitoring*, refers to a process of collecting and analyzing information regarding student behavior in order to assist in guiding instruction or intervention (Thorndike, 2005). Formative assessment is particularly crucial in the context of a MTSS. In this model, it is proposed that once a student has been identified as in need of academic or social–behavioral supports, one or more interventions are put into place in an attempt to bring student functioning up to an appropriate level. If student behavior proves unresponsive to empirically based intervention strategies, a student may then be referred for more intensive services that include, but are not limited to, special education.

Criteria

Whereas feasibility is paramount in screening and psychometric adequacy is the key consideration in diagnostic assessment, selecting an appropriate progress monitoring tool is about striking the right balance between measurement and usability considerations (Briesch & Volpe, 2007). Given that important decisions are being made regarding the effectiveness of intervention supports, progress monitoring data should be sufficiently reliable and valid. At the same time, however, feasibility becomes a primary concern in the context of progress monitoring. That is, measures should be able to be completed quickly and easily, given the frequency with which data are being collected (e.g., every week, biweekly). Furthermore, it is crucial that progress monitoring measures are repeatable, in that they can be administered on multiple occasions to create data streams. These data streams then become the unit of analysis in determining students' responsiveness to intervention.

Although the reliability and validity indicators discussed in previous sections must be considered in the context of progress monitoring as well, one unique psychometric criterion is the *responsiveness* of a scale (Centers for Disease Control and Prevention, 2000). Because progress monitoring measures are designed to assess response to intervention, it is crucial that they are capable of detecting change in the measured construct or behavior over time. Scale responsiveness is determined both by sensitivity to change (i.e., ability to detect an actual effect) and specificity to change (i.e., stability of the measure in the absence of an effect). Whereas specificity to change is easily determined by examining test–retest reliability in the absence of intervention, several different approaches to assessing sensitivity to change have been suggested (see Gresham et al., 2010; Meier, McDougal, & Bardos, 2008).

Summary of Purposes of Assessment

As outlined in this section, assessment is necessary within a problem-solving model to help answer the questions of whether a potential problem exists (i.e., screening), what the problem is and why it is occurring (i.e., diagnosis, case conceptualization), and whether what we did worked (i.e., evaluation, progress monitoring). Although the importance of defensible, flexible, and repeatable tools has been emphasized within a problem-solving framework (Christ et al., 2009), it is clear that the relative importance of these criteria will shift depending on the purpose of assessment. The one important feature of assessment tools that we have not yet discussed, however, is that of flexibility. Given the multiple assessment purposes within a problem-solving model, any tool that can be used across different contexts would be particularly desirable. Although the promise of DBR to inform screening and progress monitoring decision making is discussed later in this book (see Chapters 5 and 6), we first broadly describe the use of DBR within a contemporary assessment context.

Using DBR to Assess Student Behavior

As discussed in Chapter 1, use of DBR-like tools in intervention extends back several decades, encompassing the literatures on DRCs (Lahey et al., 1977), home–school notes (Kelley, 1990), and DPRs (McCurdy, Kunsch, & Reibstein, 2007). In contrast, research on the use of DBR as a defensible assessment tool has a much shorter history. In 1993 Pelham first suggested that DRC ratings might be used not only to provide students with behavioral feedback, but also to monitor the effects of medication on students with ADHD. Although he stressed that target behaviors should be operationally defined, monitored closely, and graphed to determine progress toward established goals, the goal of the paper was to provide a practical illustration rather than to delve into the defensibility of report card ratings.

Nearly a decade later, Chafouleas et al. (2002) proposed that the data from a DBRC might be used to assess a wider range of classroom behaviors, given the flexibility of the method. For example, the DBRC could be used to assess student behavior using either a checklist (e.g., Did the student disrupt class?) or a scale (e.g., To what degree did the student disrupt class on a scale from 1 to 5?) and could be administered once or more each day. Over time, this assessment method came to be known as DBR. As discussed in Chapter 1, DBR requires raters to conduct brief ratings of behavior (akin to rating scales) at the time and place that the behavior occurs (akin to direct observation). Furthermore, the use of participant observers (i.e., teachers) who maintain a constant presence in the classroom not only reduces resource demands and the potential for reactivity, but also increases the likelihood that instances of behavior will be observed (Chafouleas, Kilgus, et al., 2012). The defining features of this assessment approach were thus developed to include (1) the directness of assessment (i.e., at least daily), (2) targeting of operationally defined behaviors, and (3) use of ratings to quantify individual raters' perceptions (Christ et al., 2009).

Beyond these general criteria, however, DBR affords much flexibility in terms of scale development and procedures for implementation. In the remainder of this chapter, we use the extant literature to outline general considerations that should be made when using DBR in assessment (see Table 4.1) and then highlight areas for future research and exploration.

Step 1: Determine the Appropriateness of DBR

When considering whether the use of DBR is appropriate, the assessment purpose must be taken into consideration. Because DBR is based on a rater's perception of a target behavior rather than a more objective assessment, these data should not be used alone in the context of high-stakes decision making (i.e., diagnosis, eligibility determination). DBR data have great potential utility, however, in identifying the presence of a problem and determining whether the plan worked. As is discussed later in this book, much work has been done to support the use of DBR for the purposes of screening (i.e., identification) and progress monitoring (i.e., assessing plan effectiveness). That is, those students exceeding an established DBR cutoff may be identified for further assessment and/or intervention, or DBR scores can be plotted over time in order to assess response to intervention. However, because DBR is used to rate a particular dimension of behavior and not the context in which it is situated, the resultant data cannot be used to determine the causes of a behavior or what can be done to address it. In these cases, additional information would need to be collected using more contextually sensitive assessment methods, such as through the use of classroom observations or interviews with relevant stakeholders (see Chapter 13).

Step 2: Identify Target Behavior(s)

DBR can be constructed to measure one or more behaviors. The optimal DBR target behavior is one that requires minimal inference such that the rater can confidently identify occurrences and nonoccurrences. A behavior such as "demonstrates motivation to learn," for example, requires a much greater level of inference than "raises hand to answer questions." Efforts should therefore be made to select target behaviors that can be rated as objectively as possible. Because a participant observer completes the DBR, however, it is well suited for the assessment of lower-frequency behaviors such as tantrums or defiance.

To date, the overwhelming majority of research has focused on the use of DBR-single item scales (DBR-SIS), which involve rating a single behavioral construct (e.g., academic engagement). Ratings are conducted over multiple occasions, with each rating serving as a data point on a time-series graph. Although multiple DBR-SIS might be used to assess the same target student, data from each SIS are interpreted independently rather than being summated. Aggregation therefore occurs across repeated occasions (i.e., time) rather than across items, in order to analyze level, trend, and variability (Tawney & Gast, 1984). As discussed in Chapter 2, much of the work related to DBR-SIS has focused on the "big three" constructs of academic engagement, disruptive behavior, and respectful. These three behaviors are believed to serve as either barriers or facilitators to academic success, which are broadly applicable to all students. That is, students who engage in behavior that is respectful and nondisruptive are more likely to develop positive relationships with adults and peers, and students who demonstrate high levels of engagement and low levels of disruption are more likely to access the curriculum and engage in higher levels of learning (Chafouleas, 2011). Results of a series of studies focused on the wording of these scales suggested that greater rating accuracy could be obtained when rating the global construct (e.g., academic engagement) rather than a specific indicator (e.g., raising hand) (Chafouleas, Jaffery, Riley-Tillman, Christ, & Sen, 2013; Christ, Riley-Tillman, Chafouleas, & Jaffery, 2011; Riley-Tillman, Chafouleas, et al., 2009). In addition, consideration should be paid to the phrasing of behavioral targets, given that using either positive (e.g., nondisruptive behavior) or negative (e.g., disruptive behavior) terminology may differentially influence rating accuracy, depending on the specific behavior at hand (Chafouleas, 2011).

In contrast, DBR-multi-item scales (DBR-MIS) require a rater to rate several specific indicators of a broader behavioral construct (Christ et al., 2009). Volpe and Briesch (2012), for example, created five-item DBR-MIS for academic engagement and disruptive behavior using specific indicators of the larger construct. That is, five individual items were used to assess both academic engagement (e.g., *finishes work on time, actively participates in class, raises hand when appropriate, works hard, stays on task*) and disruptive behavior (e.g., *calls out, noisy, clowns around, talks to classmates when inappropriate, out of seat/area*). These individual ratings were then combined to create an aggregated score for the scale. One potential advantage to the use of a multi-item scale is that the scale can be tailored to address individual student concerns. For example, disruptive behavior on the part of a high school student may involve talking to peers, turning around in his or her seat, and using inappropriate language, whereas an elementary student may be more likely to call out answers, drum on the desk, and make funny noises. In these cases, unique DBR-MIS disruptive behavior scales can be created to address these individualized concerns.

Step 3: Develop an Operational Definition for Each Target Behavior

Once the appropriate target behaviors have been identified, the next step is to create an operational definition for each. An *operational definition* describes the target behavior in observable, measurable terms that specify what the behavior looks like. A good operational definition needs to pass a "stranger test," meaning that the definition should be clearly understandable to someone who has no familiarity with the student or problem. A behavioral description that we often hear thrown around in schools is *noncompliant.* If we asked 10 teachers to describe what noncompliant behavior looks like, chances are we would receive several different answers. One teacher might recall the student who responded to requests with profanity, whereas another teacher might immediately envision the student who passively sat with his head on the desk while his classmates began working. It is therefore important to create a clear and comprehensive definition of the target behavior and to list it at the top of the DBR form. Providing examples and non-examples of the target behavior can also help the rater gain a clearer sense of the behavior to be evaluated.

Step 4: Determine Who Will Conduct the Ratings

As noted previously, a central advantage of DBR is that ratings can be conducted by participant observers, who are able to maintain a constant presence in the assessment context, rather than requiring the use of external observers or raters.

Typically, ratings are conducted by the classroom teacher, who is the most familiar with the target student's behavior. Because teachers are likely to bring background knowledge and subjective opinions into their ratings, some authors have argued that the effectiveness of behavioral interventions might be best judged by assessing how an observer's perception of a problem changes (e.g., Gresham, 2005). Moderate correlations have been identified between DBRs completed by classroom teachers and systematic direct observations conducted by external observers (Chafouleas, McDougal, Riley-Tillman, Panahon, & Hilt, 2005; Riley-Tillman, Chafouleas, Sassu, Chanese, & Glazer, 2008); however, studies have also highlighted the fact that the rating patterns of some teachers may be more stringent than others, suggesting that ratings obtained from different raters cannot be considered interchangeable (Briesch et al., 2010; Chafouleas, Briesch, et al., 2010). The most appropriate rater should therefore be determined prior to data collection, and data should then be collected and interpreted based on this individual's ratings.

In some cases, however, the classroom teacher may not be the individual best suited to conduct DBRs. One of the criteria for conducting DBRs is that the rater needs to have had sufficient opportunity to observe the student's behavior. If the student-to-teacher ratio is particularly high in a classroom, or a teacher does not feel that he or she can accurately estimate one student's behavior while instructing and managing the larger class, another adult (e.g., classroom aide) may be called upon to conduct ratings instead. When external raters have been utilized to complete DBRs, rating profiles were found to be similar to those of teachers who have much greater familiarity with the students (Chafouleas, Briesch, et al., 2010). This finding suggests that as long as the target behaviors are observable and measurable, adults with different roles and responsibilities can be called upon to assist with assessment. Furthermore, if the target behavior is one that is not outwardly observable or is best assessed via self-report, responsibility for ratings may shift to the student, him- or herself. The use of student-completed DBRs is referred to as *self-monitoring* and is discussed further in Chapter 10.

Step 5: Determine Where, When, and How Often Ratings Will Occur

The decision of where to conduct ratings should be made based on consideration of the problem behavior. That is, if the problem behavior has been identified solely within a particular setting (e.g., literacy instruction), or has been noted to be most problematic in this setting, data collection may be limited to one part of the school day. However, if the problem behavior knows no boundaries, conducting ratings across multiple settings may provide valuable information regarding either the consistency or variability of the behavior.

Whereas rating scales are typically used to assess behavior over a considerable period of time (e.g., 1 month, 6 weeks), DBR was intended to be completed at the end of a short period of time in order to maintain the directness of assessment. One question that therefore arises is how short a "short period of time" should be. Riley-Tillman, Christ, Chafouleas, Boice, and Briesch (2010) examined the influence of observation duration on the accuracy of data by asking participants to complete DBR-SIS ratings on two target behaviors (i.e., academic engagement, disruptive behavior) following 5-minute, 10-minute, and 20-minute observations. Findings suggested that overestimation of disruptive behavior increased as the observation duration increased, whereas the accuracy of academic engagement ratings was not influenced by duration. Other research, however, has suggested that conducting a single rating at the end of a common activity (e.g., literacy instruction) may be sufficient rather than needing to conduct more frequent ratings within the time block (Briesch et al., 2010; Chafouleas, Briesch, et al., 2010). Pending additional inquiry, the determination of how frequently ratings will occur should be made based on both data collection needs (e.g., Are data needed at particular times?) and the number of opportunities available for data collection (e.g., Does the teacher see the student throughout the day or on a more limited basis?) (Christ et al., 2009). Regardless of the rating period selected, however, it has been recommended that ratings be conducted as soon as the designated period has ended. If ratings cannot be conducted immediately, it is recommended that the rater wait until the next rating period to conduct ratings (Christ et al., 2009).

Step 6: Determine the Appropriate Scale and Develop the DBR Form

As previously noted, long before DBR became an assessment tool, DRCs were used as a way to intervene with problem student behavior. Most typically, DRCs require teachers to complete a yes/no checklist to indicate whether the student engaged in a desired behavior (e.g., completed work, followed directions, stayed in seat) during a specified period of time (Lahey et al., 1977; Rosen, Gabardi, Miller, & Miller, 1990; Schumaker et al., 1977). The percentage of yeses is then divided by the total number of ratings in order to obtain an overall percentage of goal attainment (see Figure 4.2). Although this level of feedback has been shown to be effective in promoting behavior change (see Chapter 8), limited research has been conducted to investigate the psychometric adequacy of DRC data. Studies have demonstrated moderate to high temporal stability and internal consistency for individualized DRCs (Fabiano, Vujnovic, Naylor, Pariseau, & Robins, 2009; Pelham et al., 2005); however, additional research is needed to better understand the psychometric properties of DBR involving dichotomous (i.e., yes/no) ratings.

Child's Name: ______________________________ Date: ______________

Target Behavior

1. Entered room quietly Y/N

2. Remained seated at desk Y/N

3. Followed teacher's instructions Y/N

4. Completed all of his/her work Y/N

5. Got along with his/her classmates Y/N

Total number of Y = _____/5 = ____% of goals met

Comments:

FIGURE 4.2. Sample of daily behavior report card.

Although dichotomously scored items can be fairly simple to complete, one potential disadvantage is the fact that the scale does not allow for much behavioral differentiation. That is, a student who comes very close to meeting the goal (e.g., stayed seated for most of the period) would receive the same rating (i.e., 0) as a student who misses the goal by a long shot (e.g., spent most of the time wandering around the room talking to neighbors). Given that we are often interested not only in whether a student performed a particular behavior, but also how well, quickly, or often he did so, greater attention has been paid to the use of a DBR scale on which the rater is asked to assess the degree to which a particular behavior was observed (e.g., from *never disruptive* to *always disruptive*). Although the decision was made to focus on this type of scale within DBR assessment work, many questions needed to be answered with regard to what the scale would look like.

Much of the early work related to the evaluation of DBR as an assessment tool therefore focused on issues of scale design, such as the number of gradients or qualitative anchors needed and what behavioral dimension should be rated (e.g., frequency, duration). Generally, this research found that neither the length of the scale nor the number of scale gradients utilized significantly influenced rating accuracy (Briesch, Kilgus, Chafouleas, Riley-Tillman, & Christ, 2012; Chafouleas, Christ, & Riley-Tillman, 2009; Christ, Chafouleas, & Riley-Tillman, 2007); however, it was determined that using fewer than 6 scale points would make it difficult to detect intraindividual changes in behavior over time (Christ et al., 2009). Given findings that a DBR scale comprised of 10 categorical regions produced a similar visual profile to data collected using a continuous scale (Chafouleas, Riley-Tillman, Christ, & Briesch, 2008), an 11-point scale was ultimately adopted. The DBR-SIS Standard Form (Chafouleas, Riley-Tillman, Christ, & Sugai, 2009) thus consists of a visual line marked by 0–10 scale gradients and a few qualitative anchors (e.g., *never, sometimes, always*) on which raters indicate the proportion of time during which the target behavior was displayed (see Figure 4.3).

Although attention has been focused on the use of a 0–10 scale, Christ and Boice (2009) reviewed several other scaling approaches that might be investigated. Likert-type scales, in which items are rated using a 5- to 7-point categorical scale (e.g., *strongly agree, agree*), have a long history of use in attitudinal research. This type of scale has also been used in recent investigations of DBR multi-item scales (e.g., Volpe & Briesch, 2012; see Figure 4.4), with raters asked to indicate whether the target behavior occurred *never, rarely, sometimes, often, very often*, or *always*. Interpretation of such a Likert-type scale takes place at the scale rather than the item level (i.e., individual item scores are summed to form an overall scale score).

Another example of a type of rating scale with potential relevance to DBR is the Behaviorally Anchored Rating Scale (BARS; Cain-Smith & Kendall, 1973) (see Figure 4.5). The BARS is a categorical scale that uses unambiguous, explicit behaviors within item descriptions and anchors to reduce the level of inference needed to conduct ratings (Christ & Boice, 2009). Descriptions of what behaviors would look like at a particular rating level can be provided at each scale point or intermittently throughout the scale. Undesirable behaviors are listed at the bottom of the scale whereas desirable behaviors are listed at the top, and raters are asked to select the scale point that most accurately reflects the student's level of performance (Christ & Boice, 2009).

Date: M T W Th F	Student: Rater:	Activity Description:
Observation Time: Start: _____ End: _____ ☐ Check if no observation today	Behavior Descriptions: **Academically engaged** is defined as actively or passively participating in the classroom activity. For example: writing, raising hand, answering a question, talking about a lesson, listening to the teacher, reading silently, or looking at instructional materials. **Respectful** is defined as compliant and polite behavior in response to adult direction and/or interactions with peers and adults. For example: follows teacher's direction, prosocial interaction with peers, positive response to adult request, verbal or physical disruption without a negative tone/ connotation. **Disruptive** is defined as student action that interrupts regular school or classroom activity. For exampvle: out of seat, fidgeting, playing with objects, acting aggressively, talking/yelling about things that are unrelated to classroom instruction.	

Directions: Place a mark along the line that best reflects *the percentage of total time* the student exhibited each target behavior. Note that the percentages do not need to total 100% across behaviors, since some behaviors may co-occur.

Academically Engaged

% of Total Time: 0 1 2 3 4 5 6 7 8 9 10

0% Never — 50% Sometimes — 100% Always

Respectful

% of Total Time: 0 1 2 3 4 5 6 7 8 9 10

0% Never — 50% Sometimes — 100% Always

Disruptive*

% of Total Time: 0 1 2 3 4 5 6 7 8 9 10

0% Never — 50% Sometimes — 100% Always

*Remember that a lower score for "Disruptive" is more desirable.

FIGURE 4.3. DBR-SIS Standard Form (Chafouleas, Riley-Tillman, Christ, & Sugai, 2009).

Directions: Below is a list of behaviors that students may demonstrate in the classroom. Please read each item and rate how the child behaved during the observation period.

Circle **N** if the behavior did not occur.

Circle **R** if the behavior rarely occurred or for a slight or ambiguous occurrence.

Circle **S** if the behavior occurred sometimes.

Circle **O** if the behavior occurred often.

Circle **V** if the behavior occurred very often.

Circle **A** if the behavior occurred always during the observation period.

1. ***Finishes work on time.***

   N R S O V A

2. ***Actively participates in class.***

   N R S O V A

3. ***Raises hand when appropriate.***

   N R S O V A

4. ***Works hard.***

   N R S O V A

5. ***Stays on task.***

   N R S O V A

FIGURE 4.4. Sample of a DBR-MIS for academic engagement. Adapted from Volpe and Briesch (2012). Copyright © 2012 the National Association of School Psychologists, Bethesda, MD. Adapted with permission of the publisher. *www.nasponline.org.*

Step 7: Conduct Rater Training

Finally, given findings that DBRs may vary notably across different raters, empirical attention has been directed toward understanding the degree of training needed to conduct reliable and accurate ratings. Although the topic of rater training is handled more thoroughly in Chapter 7, in brief, studies have found that a short, direct training that (1) provides a review of behavioral definitions, (2) models the rating process, and (3) allows for practice and immediate feedback using behavioral examples that span low, medium, and high ends of the DBR scale can improve the reliability and

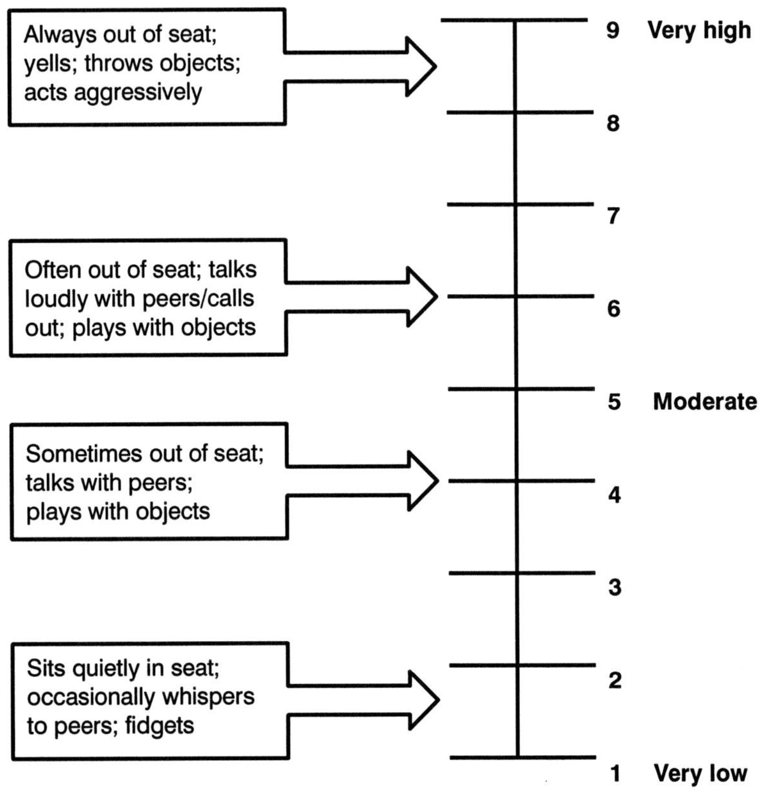

FIGURE 4.5. Sample of Behaviorally Anchored Rating Scale for disruptive behavior.

accuracy of ratings (Chafouleas, Kilgus, Riley-Tillman, Jaffery, & Harrison, 2012; LeBel, Kilgus, Briesch, & Chafouleas, 2010; Schlientz, Riley-Tillman, Briesch, Walcott, & Chafouleas, 2009).

Conclusions

Much research has been conducted over the past decade in order to better understand how DBR can best be used in the assessment of student behavior; however, additional work is still needed. In this final section, we outline areas for additional investigation in order to expand potential uses of DBR and build the existing evidence base.

First, research conducted to date has helped us understand how to best utilize teachers as DBR raters, but has not explored the use of other rater types such as parents and students. Home–school interventions, in which information is shared reciprocally between teachers and families, have been shown to be particularly effective in improving school-based outcomes for students (Cox, 2005; see Chapter 3). Student-completed DBRs have also been used for many years within the context of self-management interventions (see Chapter 10); however, the psychometric adequacy of self-report DBRs has not yet been examined. Moving forward, attention should therefore be directed toward understanding both the usability and defensibility of ratings completed by a broader range of raters, including parents and students.

Second, although DBR could theoretically be used to measure any observable behavior of interest (Chafouleas, Riley-Tillman, & Sugai, 2007), primary focus to date has been on the DBR Standard Form target behaviors of academic engagement, disruptive behavior, and respectful behavior. Because research has demonstrated that the psychometric properties of one scale cannot be assumed to apply to other scales (Riley-Tillman, Chafouleas, et al., 2009), continued analysis of other behaviors is needed. Scales can be developed to assess additional behaviors of interest to classroom teachers, such as study skills, aggressive behavior, or interpersonal skills. However, DBR also has the potential to monitor a range of less observable behaviors (e.g., anxiety, suicidality) if older students are provided with sufficient training. As one example, attention has been directed recently to the development of a DBR Social Competence (DBR-SC) scale in order to assess target behaviors most relevant to children with high-functioning autism (Riley-Tillman, Stichter, Kilgus, Schoemann, & Owens, 2015). The DBR-SC scale uses the core DBR-SIS items plus two additional items designed to specifically target social competence.

Finally, it has been noted that "DBR is not defined by a single scale, form, or number of rating items; rather, it is likely that lines of research will (and should) investigate multiple versions and applications of DBR as a method of assessment" (Chafouleas, Riley-Tillman, & Christ, 2009, p. 196). The majority of research to date has focused on the evaluation of single-item scales; however, investigation of alternative scales may be warranted. DBR-MIS, for example, requires a rater to rate several specific indicators of a broader behavioral construct (Christ et al., 2009). Results of a study by Volpe and Briesch (2012) suggested that decision making within a formative assessment context may be accelerated when using a multiple-item scale. It is notable, however, that a greater proportion of variance was also attributable to changes in student behavior over time when using the DBR-SIS, which may suggest that the SIS is more sensitive to change over time. Additional work should therefore be conducted to determine whether different instrumentation is needed to move from the assessment of global to more specific behavioral targets (Christ et al., 2009). Research is also needed to further understand the psychometric properties of DRCs, given limited exploration in this area (e.g., Fabiano et al., 2009).

CHAPTER 5

Use of DBR in Progress Monitoring

Faith G. Miller, T. Chris Riley-Tillman, and Sandra M. Chafouleas

Growing interest in the implementation of MTSS has focused greater attention on data-based decision making within educational settings. Implementation of these frameworks requires problem solving to promote early identification and intervention in academic and behavioral domains, as well as a continuum of supports designed to meet students' current needs and to promote student success. One central component of data-based decision making in MTSS involves evaluating student progress in response to intervention. Reliable and valid data are needed in order to guide decisions surrounding student supports, such as whether an intervention should be continued or whether a student requires more intensive supports. In academic domains, student progress is typically evaluated using curriculum-based assessments, which are designed to evaluate specific student skills related to the curriculum and inform learning objectives. For example, oral reading fluency probes may be administered once per week in order to evaluate a student's response to a small-group phonics intervention. Although greater attention has been paid to the development and evaluation of academic progress monitoring tools, it is critical to have assessment options that can function in a similar role within the behavioral domain. DBR is one tool that has been used by educators to monitor student progress and assess student response to social–emotional and behavioral interventions. In this chapter, we review applications for DBR as a progress monitoring method within MTSS.

What Is Progress Monitoring?

Within MTSS, data are collected for two primary purposes: to identify students in need of additional support (i.e., screening; see Chapter 6) and to evaluate student response to intervention (i.e., progress monitoring). Although emphasis is placed on the use of evidence-based interventions, we know that even those interventions with the strongest research support behind them will not be an appropriate match for every student. Therefore, the only way to know for sure whether an intervention is working for a particular student is to collect and analyze progress monitoring data. Here, we define progress monitoring broadly as the collection of information on a frequent and repeated basis in order to support timely, data-based decision making. Progress monitoring data provide important information about current student performance relative to his or her educational program, which educators can then use to inform whether student supports need to be intensified, modified, or reduced. It is therefore essential that progress monitoring assessments exhibit a few key characteristics. Specifically, the assessment should (1) function as a reliable and valid indicator of student performance, (2) allow for direct and repeated measures of student performance, and (3) demonstrate sensitivity to change in order to detect changes in the target behavior (Fuchs, Fuchs, Hamlett, Walz, & Germann, 1993). Note that it is essential that progress monitoring tools demonstrate each of these characteristics. For example, a valid and reliable method of assessment that can be administered repeatedly but is not sensitive to change will have no real utility in informing student supports.

Why Is Progress Monitoring Important?

Assessing student progress is a central component of responsive service delivery and accountability. By collecting and reviewing progress monitoring data on a routine basis, students' needs can be met by evaluating their performance and proactively modifying supports in order to enhance their success. Let's imagine, for example, that a classroom teacher decided to implement a response–cost intervention in an attempt to reduce the number of inappropriate verbalizations one of the students was making. If progress monitoring data suggest that the intervention is not resulting in the expected reduction in the frequency of the student's disruptive behavior, then modifications to the current intervention, or even a different intervention, may be needed. In this way, progress monitoring data not only support student success, but also help to ensure that resources within the school system are utilized in an optimal manner. In the absence of progress monitoring data, decisions about student supports can be made in a haphazard, trial-and-error way, which consumes valuable time and strains resources. As school systems and personnel face increased limitations with regard to available time and resources, the importance of utilizing and allocating resources in a way that maximizes efficiency cannot be overemphasized. For instance, timely data collection and review ensure that only students in need of more intensive supports are provided with those supports, thereby preventing an unnecessary allocation of resources to students with less intensive needs. Further, frequent progress monitoring ensures that time and personnel do not continue to be allocated toward interventions that are not effective for a particular student.

Historically, progress monitoring assessments were used primarily to measure student progress in academic domains. With the development of MTSS initiatives, options related to academic progress monitoring expanded greatly, primarily out of a need to determine if students were making adequate progress, or "responding," to an intervention. A number of beneficial outcomes have been associated with the process of monitoring the progress of student academic performance. In particular, progress monitoring has been associated with improved instruction and documentation, better communication in both school settings and in home–school partnerships, higher expectations, and fewer referrals (National Center on Student Progress Monitoring, n.d.). More recently, behavioral progress monitoring has received increased attention as a valued and necessary practice within MTSS as well (Malecki & Demaray, 2007; Riley-Tillman, Burns, & Gibbons, 2013). As evidenced by the recent release of technical reviews of systematic behavioral progress monitoring assessments by the National Center on Intensive Intervention (n.d.), there is a growing awareness regarding the need for evidence-based behavioral progress monitoring practices.

Progress Monitoring within MTSS

As discussed throughout this book, MTSS typically involve a continuum of at least three tiers of support (i.e., universal, supplemental, intensive). As shown in Figure 5.1, progress monitoring can occur at each tier of the system, and the unit of analysis (group or individual) can vary as well. However, both the intensity of support and frequency of data collection must increase at each tier because more comprehensive information is needed as part of the problem-solving process. A more detailed assessment of behavior can be conducted by increasing the level of specificity from a small group of students to an individual student, or by capturing information at the individual level across multiple settings or on a more frequent basis. Next, we review the strengths of DBR within a progress monitoring context and then describe specific procedures for developing a DBR progress monitoring plan at each tier of support.

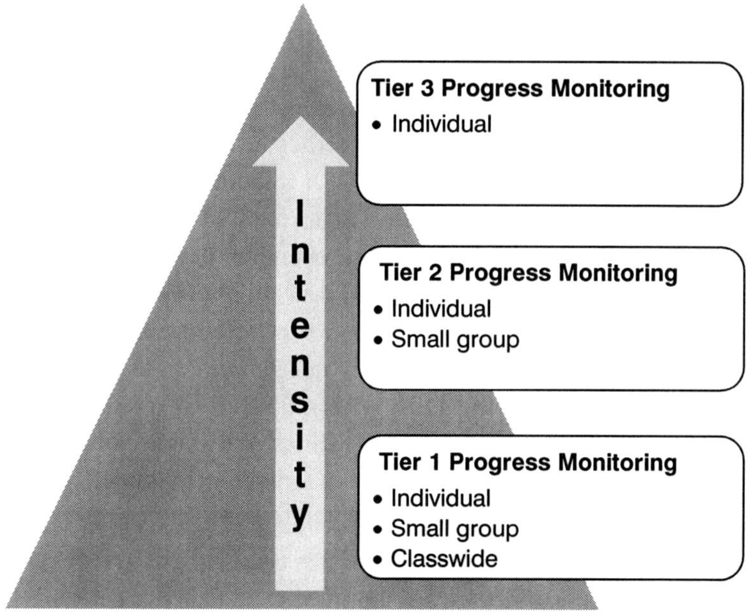

FIGURE 5.1. Progress monitoring within a multi-tiered system of supports.

DBR as a Progress Monitoring Tool

DBR is attractive for the purpose of monitoring progress in student behavior because of the efficiency in data collection and the fact that DBRs can be administered repeatedly, whether across or within days. Because individuals can complete DBRs in the natural environment (e.g., teachers) in a matter of a few seconds, modifications to teachers' typical routines are also minimized. Surveys have found that both teachers (Chafouleas et al., 2006) and school psychologists (Riley-Tillman, Chafouleas, Briesch, & Eckert, 2008) are generally accepting of DBR as a progress monitoring tool and believe it to be a feasible method of formative assessment. When surveyed about their perceptions of DBR, teachers generally agreed that they (1) liked the procedures involved in using DBR, (2) thought the assessment was a good way to manage a child's behavior, and (3) thought the assessment was beneficial to the child (Chafouleas et al., 2006).

Although efficiency and repeatability are certainly important requirements of progress monitoring tools, there are additional critical features that must be considered as well. First, progress monitoring tools must be flexible to guide a variety of assessment questions and situations. DBR is highly flexible, in that standard forms can be used (see Chapter 4) or forms can be tailored to assess additional behaviors (e.g., peer engagement) or specific dimensions of behavior (e.g., intensity). DBR can therefore be structured to align well with behavioral goals, and forms and procedures can be tailored to fit a variety of assessment needs or contexts (e.g., math instruction, recess).

Progress monitoring tools must also be defensible to produce reliable and valid outcomes. To date, a number of empirical studies have provided support for DBR as a progress monitoring method. Because *DBR* refers to a category of assessments, however, the possibility exists that different formats of DBR would demonstrate differing degrees of technical adequacy. For example, it is likely that a DBR with a 3-point scale would have less sensitivity to detect behavioral change than a DBR with an 11-point scale. Therefore, it is important to keep in mind that research conducted on specific versions of DBR may not generalize to other versions. The majority of work to date involving DBR within a progress monitoring context has focused on the use of DBR-SIS, for which ratings of a single behavioral construct (e.g., academic engagement) are interpreted independently.

Psychometric Adequacy

Within the context of progress monitoring, defensibility is judged based on both traditional indicators of psychometric adequacy (i.e., reliability, validity) and scale responsiveness. Perhaps the most tacit support of the defensibility of DBR-SIS is its inclusion on the National Center on Intensive Intervention's (2014) technical chart for behavioral progress monitoring tools. All tools submitted to the National Center are reviewed by a technical panel and rated in relation to progress monitoring standards, psychometric standards, and usability. Readers are directed to *www.intensiveintervention.org* for more information about the review process and the posted ratings of DBR-SIS; here we provide a brief review of the accumulated evidence base.

The earliest studies to investigate the use of DBR as an assessment method examined concurrent validity by comparing data obtained using DBR-SIS to established assessment methods such as systematic direct observation. Student behavior was assessed using both measures and plotted visually over time. Across these studies, moderate to high correlations were identified between data obtained using DBR and data obtained via systematic direct observation and behavior rating scales (Chafouleas, Riley-Tillman, Sassu, LaFrance, & Patwa, 2007; Chafouleas, Sanetti, Jaffery, & Fallon, 2012; Riley-Tillman, Chafouleas, Sassu, et al., 2008). It has also been demonstrated that similar decisions can be made regarding intervention effectiveness whether data are obtained using direct observation or DBR (Riley-Tillman, Chafouleas, Briesch, & Eckert, 2008).

Another aspect of interest in the validation of DBR as a defensible progress monitoring tool relates to the reliability and generalizability of the ratings. To date, the consistency of DBR-SIS data across time, raters, and items has been examined primarily through the application of generalizability theory. Whereas classical test theory only allows us to look at one source of rating variance at a time, generalizability theory enables the simultaneous examination of all sources of variance that are of interest (Brennan, 2001; Shavelson & Webb, 1991). With regard to temporal stability, studies have found that anywhere from 0 to 15% of the variance in DBR ratings are attributable to changes in student behavior across days, with greater fluctuations noted for students referred for challenging behaviors (Chafouleas, Christ, Riley-Tillman, Briesch, & Chanese, 2007; Chafouleas, Briesch, et al., 2010). Psychometric investigations have therefore suggested that a student's general level of behavior can be dependably estimated using 7–10 DBR-SIS ratings (Chafouleas, Christ, et al., 2009). Studies reporting on the test–retest reliability of DBRC ratings have identified moderate (Pelham et al., 2005) to high correlations (Fabiano et al., 2009) across days, suggesting that the percentage of goals met may be more stable over time than DBR-SIS ratings.

With regard to consistency across raters, studies have shown that some teachers may be more stringent in their DBR-SIS ratings, whether across individuals (Chafouleas, Briesch, Riley-Tillman, Christ, Black, et al., 2010) or when rating particular students (Briesch et al., 2010). As noted previously, these findings suggest that multiple raters should not be used when progress monitoring, as their ratings cannot necessarily be considered interchangeable. One caveat, however, is that these discrepancies across raters have been noted in the absence of rater training. Although research has found that rater training involving instruction, modeling, practice, and feedback may improve the accuracy of DBR ratings (e.g., Chafouleas, Kilgus, et al., 2012; Chafouleas, Riley-Tillman, Jaffery, Miller, & Harrison, 2015), additional research is needed to specifically examine the effect of training on interrater reliability of teachers using both SIS and MIS approaches. Finally, although not a relevant consideration in the context of SIS, consistency across items is an important consideration in the development of MIS. Future research is needed in this area, as no studies have examined this question to date.

As discussed in Chapter 4, scale responsiveness is determined by both sensitivity to change (i.e., ability to detect an actual effect) and specificity to change (i.e., stability of the measure in the absence of an effect). Recent research has investigated whether DBR scales demonstrate the sensitivity needed to detect behavioral change. In one study (Chafouleas, Sanetti, Kilgus, & Maggin, 2012), DBR-SIS evidenced sensitivity to detecting changes in behavior following implementation of an evidence-based DBRC intervention across 20 teacher–student dyads. Sensitivity to change has been also demonstrated when implementing interventions at the classwide level (Chafouleas, Sanetti, Kilgus, & Maggin, 2012; Riley-Tillman, Methe, & Weegar, 2009). These findings provide support for the utility of DBR-SIS for progress monitoring at both the individual student and classwide level—which makes DBR-SIS a beneficial tool for use within tiered service delivery frameworks. Future research is needed to investigate sensitivity and specificity to change for various DBR formats outside of the DBR-SIS Standard Form. For example, examinations should extend to various target behaviors and various dimensions of interest (e.g., intensity).

In summary, a growing body of research has examined applications of DBR-SIS as a progress monitoring method. Together, these studies suggest that DBR-SIS can be flexibly structured in a variety of formats to reliably measure student behavior. Deciding *how* to structure DBR-SIS for progress monitoring purposes, however, involves a number of interrelated considerations. Next, we review those considerations in greater detail.

Using DBR to Monitor Progress in Student Behavior

The first step in developing any progress monitoring plan involves determining why progress monitoring data are needed and developing a problem statement. When developing a problem statement, it is important to think about the context of the problem in relation to the level of support currently provided within the MTSS. As discussed previously, the intensity of data collection depends on the intensity of support currently provided to the student(s). For example, consider the following problem statement:

> *Devon is a fifth-grade student who frequently exhibits disruptive behavior. In particular, Devon's behavior often interrupts instruction throughout the school day. He is currently receiving small-group behavior support in a Tier-2 intervention designed to reduce disruptive behavior, and progress monitoring data are needed to determine if Devon is making sufficient progress.*

By formulating a problem statement, circumstances surrounding the need to progress monitor can be understood. In particular, the statement provides a description of the level of current support (i.e., Tier 1, Tier 2, or Tier 3) as well as a broad description of the behavior of interest (i.e., disruptive behavior). With a problem statement developed, we can then consider if DBR would be a viable method to collect data for the specified purpose. A problem statement will set the foundation for how progress monitoring data might be collected (e.g., how often, how much), and will frame the scope of the assessment. In order to develop a progress monitoring system using DBR, several decisions must be made that will help shape the process of data collection. Here, we outline the steps involved in using DBR as a progress monitoring method (see Table 5.1).

Step 1: Determine Who Will Be the Focus of Rating

The first step in establishing a DBR progress monitoring plan is to determine who will be the focus of ratings. Progress monitoring data can be collected on individual students, small groups, or large groups such as classrooms. If we want to know if a specific student is progressing as intended, the student will be the unit of analysis.

TABLE 5.1. DBR Blueprint for Progress Monitoring

- ☐ 1. Determine who will be the focus of rating.

  Progress monitoring data can be collected for individual students, small groups, or large groups (e.g., classrooms).

- ☐ 2. Identify target behavior(s).

  Target behaviors can be assessed at the global (e.g., disruptive) or specific (e.g., out of seat) level. Regardless, it is important that they be observable, measurable, amenable to change, and socially valid.

- ☐ 3. Develop an operational definition for each target behavior.

  If DBR-SIS Standard Form definitions do not accurately capture the behavior(s) of concern, alternate operational definitions should be developed.

- ☐ 4. Determine who will conduct the ratings.

  It is necessary to determine who is in the best position to rate the target behavior(s). Regardless of who is selected (e.g., teacher, aide, student), raters should remain consistent within and across observation periods.

- ☐ 5. Determine when, where, and how often ratings will occur.

  Rating frequency should be determined in consideration of the tier of support, with data collected once a day at minimum. The appropriate setting and time frame for rating should be informed by the problem statement; however, all ratings must be conducted in close proximity to the observation period.

- ☐ 6. Determine the appropriate scale and develop the DBR form.

  The DBR scale (e.g., checklist, 0–100 scale) should be tailored to the behavior of interest and developmental level of the student. It is also essential that the scale accurately reflect behavior and is able to detect changes in behavior over time.

- ☐ 7. Conduct rater training.

  Rater training should focus on promoting rating accuracy. An online training module is available for the three DBR-SIS Standard Form behaviors.

- ☐ 8. Collect baseline data, set intervention goals, and begin intervention.

  A minimum of three to five baseline data points should be collected before implementing intervention supports. It is crucial that data collection procedures remain consistent across baseline and intervention phases.

- ☐ 9. Use data to inform intervention(s), strategies, and supports.

  Summarized data should be used to determine whether behavior has improved, become worse, or is unchanged, and to develop a subsequent course of action.

If we want to know if a small-group intervention is effective for a group of students, the group can be the unit of analysis. Another possibility is to determine the effectiveness of a classwide support by collecting progress monitoring data with the class as the unit of analysis. For example, Riley-Tillman, Methe, and Weegar (2009) examined the influence of teacher modeling on the engagement of students during sustained silent reading. As one measure in the study, the teacher completed a single classwide rating of overall engagement using DBR-SIS (e.g., *Overall, how engaged was the whole class today during silent reading?*). DBRs can be flexibly formatted to provide information at multiple levels, depending on the purpose of the assessment. Once the focus of the rating has been determined, the next step is to identify the target behavior(s).

Step 2: Identify Target Behavior(s)

When selecting what should be progress monitored, three primary questions should be asked:

1. What level of behavioral specificity are we interested in assessing?
2. Is the behavior observable, measurable, and amenable to change?
3. How will changing this behavior improve conditions for the student?

In our previous example, Devon is the focus of the rating and the problem statement describes disruptive behavior. In response to the first question, we know that Devon is disruptive, but at what level are we interested in assessing this behavior? Are we generally interested in understanding the degree to which his behavior interferes with instruction? Or are there specific disruptive behaviors that Devon frequently exhibits (e.g., out of seat, talking to peers, making noises) that we wish to assess? Whereas an SIS utilizes one item to collect information relative to a domain (e.g., disruptive behavior), an MIS uses several items to measure specific behaviors within a domain (see Figure 5.2). The question of whether to use a single- or multi-item scale can be made based on the behavior(s) of interest and the goals of the intervention. That is, if goals are developed regarding specific behaviors such as completing work on time and volunteering to answer questions, then the progress monitoring data will need to reflect that level of specificity. However, if the intervention is concerned with improving engagement more globally, then single-item scales would be well-suited for that purpose. It is important to note, however, that the bulk of the research on DBR to date has focused on DBR-SIS and therefore the single-item approach remains the most defensible to date.

Once we have identified the target behavior(s), we must determine whether the behavior meets the criteria of question 2. In the case of Devon, because we believe that disruptive behavior can be observed and measured and is amenable to change, DBR is thus appropriate. Finally, in response to the third question, we posit that

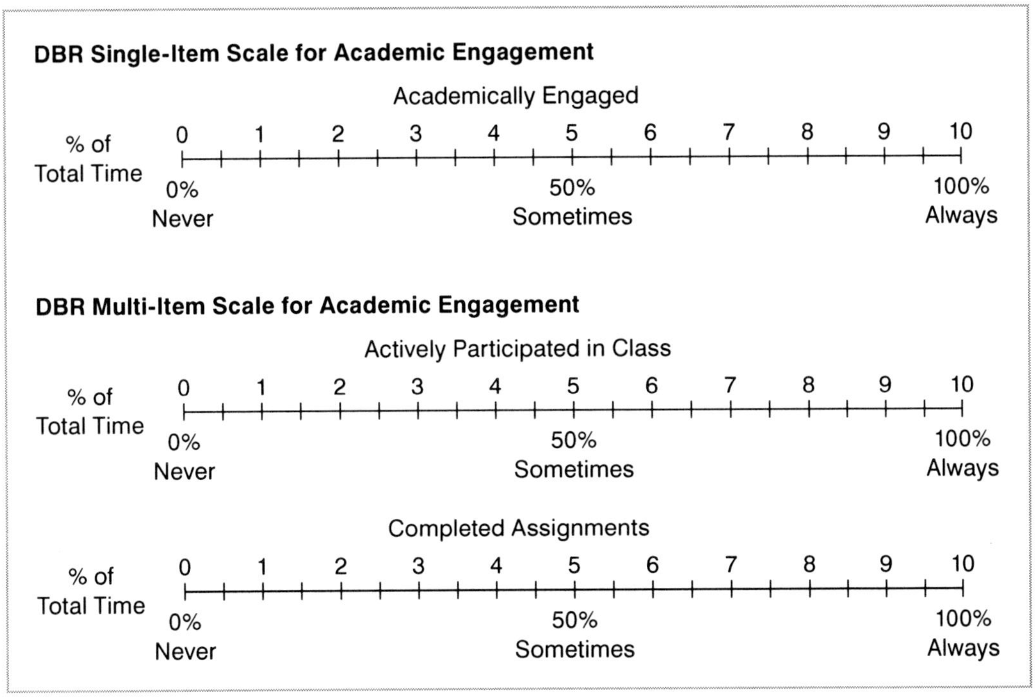

FIGURE 5.2. DBR single-item and multi-item scales.

Devon's disruptive behavior is impeding his ability to learn and that his classmates' frustration about the disruptions is also negatively impacting him socially. With these three questions answered, it is time to develop an operational definition of the target behavior.

Step 3: Develop an Operational Definition for Each Target Behavior

When progress monitoring, in order to obtain accurate and relevant data regarding student performance, a precise definition of the target behavior is needed because the same term can have different meanings to different people. Using the DBR-SIS Standard Form definition, we broadly define *disruptive behavior* as any student action that interrupts regular school or classroom activity (e.g., out of seat, fidgeting, playing with objects, acting aggressively, talking/yelling about things that are unrelated to classroom instruction). It is important to verify that the definition accurately captures the behavior(s) of concern. In Devon's case, the standard definition would work well if he engaged in several of the behaviors provided in the example. Conversely, if Devon's disruptive behavior was actually more aggressive in nature than the definition implies (e.g., throwing objects, threatening classmates), an alternative definition may need to be developed. Having identified and defined the target behavior(s), questions surrounding the logistics of data collection can next be answered.

Step 4: Determine Who Will Conduct the Ratings

When using DBR as a progress monitoring method, selecting an individual to perform the rating will most often be straightforward. The question to ask is, *Who is in the best position to provide the necessary information?* Often, DBRs are performed by the classroom teacher as he or she monitors student behavior during the time period of interest. However, further consideration is needed when selecting a rater (or raters) at the middle school level, given that students are taught by multiple teachers during the day. Because ratings may vary between raters, it is advisable that the rater remain consistent within and across an established observation period. For example, due to systematic differences in how each individual approaches the rating task, it could be problematic to have the classroom teacher complete a rating one day during math, and have a student teacher complete the rating the following day in the same class. However, if data were needed across multiple classes at the middle school level, one teacher could consistently complete the ratings in math class, whereas another could consistently complete the ratings in language arts. In this case, there would simply be two streams of data that can be graphed by period (i.e., content) and used for decision making.

Another option is for the student to use the DBR to self-monitor his or her own behavior. In this case, completion of the DBR functions as both an intervention (by increasing students' awareness of and accountability for their behavior) and as a progress monitoring tool (by collecting students' ratings of their own performance, which can be monitored over time). Particularly as students get older, self-monitoring may become a preferred method for collecting data on student performance given that doing so increases self-responsibility and also shifts the burden for data collection from the teacher to the student. Initially, student ratings can be compared to teacher ratings to determine whether self-reported levels of student behavior agree with teacher-reported levels of student behavior, and to calibrate ratings accordingly. For further information on using DBR as a self-monitoring intervention, the reader is referred to Chapter 10.

Step 5: Determine When, Where, and How Often Ratings Will Occur

Within a progress monitoring context, DBR data should be collected daily at a minimum, although the total length of the observation and rating period can vary widely. An essential consideration in this determination involves the tier of support that the student is currently receiving. Because data collection becomes more individualized and intensive at each tier, this information will help inform the intensity and level of specificity needed for decision-making. Next, a setting and time frame of interest needs to be specified (e.g., morning seatwork, math class), which can be informed by the problem statement. Referring to our previous problem statement, we specified that Devon's disruptive behavior occurred throughout the day. Therefore, in considering best options for progress monitoring Devon's behavior, a single rating could be completed at the end of each day. However, if more detailed information is needed, ratings could also be performed more frequently, such as twice per day or at the end of each instructional activity. These determinations require judgments based on the nature of the problem and the goals of the intervention, and must be considered on a case-by-case basis. Regardless of how the ratings are structured (e.g., once per day, twice per day), however, the observation period should remain consistent across days to facilitate decision making. For example, if ratings occur twice per day—once after lunch and once at the end of the day—that same schedule should remain consistent for all observations.

An important consideration related to the timing of the rating involves the recording of the rating. To help ensure reliable data collection, DBRs need to be recorded in close proximity (ideally, immediately) to the time period of interest. The longer the delay in recording a rating, the less reliable the rating may be. As a result, DBRs should not be completed retroactively, such as the period after or day after an observation period. As such, when articulating DBR logistics, it is important to ensure that there is adequate time built in following an observation period for a rater to record his or her rating.

Finally, it is important to consider how many times data will be collected before and then during the intervention. Ideally, enough data should be collected in each phase (preintervention and intervention) so that the level, trend, and variability of the behavior can be reliably determined (see Chapter 11 for a discussion of data summarization). As such, time should be allocated in each phase of the process to collect a sufficient stream of outcome data.

Step 6: Determine the Appropriate Scale and Develop the DBR Form

Once the procedures surrounding DBR data collection have been determined, the data collection forms must be developed. The ideal structure of the DBR scale depends on (1) the behavior of interest and (2) the developmental level of the student. As discussed previously, the flexibility of DBR allows for it to be structured using a variety of formats. Some behaviors, such as homework completion, may lend themselves to a simple checklist scale (i.e., yes/no), whereas other behaviors (e.g., academic engagement) may require a larger scale range (e.g., 0–100%). Within the context of progress monitoring, however, it is important to ensure that the scale is (1) capable of accurately reflecting behavior and (2) able to detect changes in behavior over time.

Let's consider a case in which a 3-point scale is developed to monitor a student's work completion. Two potential problems may arise in using the 3-point scale for progress monitoring purposes. First, the range of possible behaviors may not be adequately represented by the magnitude of the scale. If the 3 points on the scale corresponded to *no work completed*, *some work completed*, or *all work completed*, it would be impossible to differentiate between days when the student completed one out of 10 questions and days when the student completed eight out of 10 questions, as both would constitute completing "some work." This range variation would be an important distinction to make, however, particularly when setting goals for the student during intervention. Second, the number of scale gradients may be too few to adequately detect changes in behavior over time. If, for example, the 3 points on the scale instead corresponded to *completed 0–33% of work*, *completed 34–67% of work*, or *completed more than 67% of work*, any small improvements in work completion (e.g., from 40 to 60% work completion) would not be represented by the graphed data. In most cases, we recommend the use of a standard 11-point scale for progress monitoring in order to ensure that the scale reflects the range of possible behaviors and is sufficiently sensitive to detect changes in behavior. Returning to our prior example regarding work completion, an 11-point scale reflecting the percentage of work completed would better inform goal setting because it would more precisely estimate the actual extent of work completion and would have much greater sensitivity to detect changes in behavior. If, for example, only 30–40% of work was being completed on average during baseline, an initial goal may be to have 60% of work completed. This distinction could not be made using a scale with only three gradients.

In addition to the range of the scale, the behavioral dimension(s) of interest must be determined. As shown in Table 5.2, educators using DBR might be interested in collecting data relative to different dimensions of behavior, such as frequency, duration, or magnitude. The DBR-SIS Standard Form incorporates duration-based ratings such that the individual indicates the *percentage of time* that the target behavior was observed. However, DBR forms can also be structured to capture other dimensions of interest. In an initial investigation regarding the anchoring of DBR-SIS, Miller, Riley-Tillman, Chafouleas, and Schardt (in press) examined differences in ratings between a DBR-SIS that included percentage-of-time anchors (reflecting duration) and a DBR-SIS that did not include the anchors (instead, participants were instructed to rate the extent to which the target child exhibited the specified behavior during the observation session, with no explicit mention of duration). Ratings using the two scales were compared to systematic direct observation (SDO) scores, and rater error was examined relative to each of the scales. Results

TABLE 5.2. Potential Dimensions of Behavior to Consider in Building DBR

Dimension	Definition	Examples
Frequency	How often the behavior occurs	• Number of interruptions • Number of tantrums • Number of times hand was raised to participate
Duration	How long the behavior lasts	• Length of time the student was engaged • Length of tantrum • Length of time the student was disruptive
Magnitude	The intensity of the behavior	• Talking back quietly versus screaming • Looking out window versus head down on desk • Kicking furniture versus kicking another student

indicated that rater error did not substantially vary between the two versions of the scales, except in relation to academically engaged behavior. Thus, findings suggest that duration-based ratings are supported for academically engaged behavior and perhaps other state behaviors with a clear duration, though this has yet to be examined empirically. Further, either duration- or nonduration-based ratings may be acceptable for targets such as respectful and disruptive behavior. In Chapter 9, examples of DBR formats to measure other dimensions can be found.

After these determinations have been made, DBR forms can be developed for progress monitoring purposes. Predeveloped forms can also be obtained from the website *http://directbehaviorratings.org*. In addition, alternative DBR scales and forms can be developed to meet the needs of the assessment. One option that is freely available on the web (*interventioncentral.com*) is the Behavior Rating Scales Report Card Maker, which can be used to customize your own DBR. One caveat to creating your own forms is that there may be limited evidence to support the use of alternative instrumentation and procedures. As such, the advantages and disadvantages of creating alternative scales should be weighed carefully.

Step 7: Conduct Rater Training

Once the materials have been created, training in DBR procedures is needed to promote the collection of reliable and valid data. It is important that the rater understand what examples (and nonexamples) of the target behaviors include, as well as what might constitute a rating of 4 versus 5, for example. As discussed in Chapter 7, an online training module is available at *www.directbehaviorratings.org/training* to assist in training individuals in how to conduct ratings of the three core behavioral competencies of academic engagement, respectfulness, and nondisruptive behavior using the DBR-SIS Standard Form. The training module provides raters with feedback regarding the accuracy of ratings and provides additional opportunities for practice. If alternative scale formats are used, training procedures should be designed and implemented in order to ensure that raters have the skills and knowledge necessary to complete the DBRs accurately.

Step 8: Collect Baseline Data, Set Intervention Goals, and Begin Intervention

With the target behavior(s) selected and defined, student(s) selected, scales and forms developed, and teachers trained, DBR progress monitoring data collection can begin. An essential first step involves the collection of baseline data. That is, prior to implementing any changes, it is important to collect information about typical student performance that will serve as the standard against which to measure subsequent changes. Without baseline data, it is difficult (if not impossible!) to determine whether meaningful change has occurred. As a general guideline, a minimum of three to five baseline data points are typically recommended, and those data should be relatively stable before implementing intervention supports (Kratochwill et al., 2010). Data collection procedures (including the person who does the rating!) should stay consistent across baseline and intervention phases so that meaningful comparisons can be made. That is, if changes are made to the data collection procedures, it will be difficult to determine if changes are due to the effectiveness of the intervention itself or the variations in data collection procedures (e.g., collecting data over a longer period of time or in a different setting).

Once adequate baseline data are collected, the data-based decision-making process begins. At this stage, the important question to ask is, *How is the student functioning relative to a reasonable goal*? As part of this process, baseline data should be analyzed using the summarization strategies outlined in Chapter 11. Once the baseline performance is determined, a reasonable goal can be set for the intervention phase. Progress monitoring data can then continue to be collected to evaluate student progress in response to the intervention.

Step 9: Use Data to Inform Interventions, Strategies, and Supports

Progress monitoring data are only meaningful if they are used to inform the selection of student supports and facilitate decision making surrounding student performance. In order to facilitate decision making and problem solving, DBR data must therefore be regularly reviewed and aggregated. As reviewed in Chapter 11, there are numerous options for presenting and aggregating DBR data in meaningful ways. These data are then used to make several determinations as part of the data-based decision-making process:

1. Based on the data, was the program/strategy/intervention effective?
   a. Evaluate graphs of student performance in terms of level, trend, and variability.
   b. If not, why was it ineffective and what changes could be made to improve it?
      i. What do the data suggest?
         1. The target behavior has improved slightly.
            a. Does the plan need to be modified to increase effectiveness?
         2. The target behavior has not changed at all, or has become worse.
            a. Assuming the intervention has been implemented correctly, consider a different plan.
   c. If it is working, what steps should be taken?
      i. Increase goal for further improvements?
      ii. Implement in different settings?
      iii. Fade support if no new goals identified?

Summarizing and graphing the data will assist in these determinations. As shown in Figure 5.3, a visual display of the data and the intended goal can be used to answer the primary question, *Was the program/strategy/intervention effective*? Based on these data, Devon's disruptive behavior did improve, though we might consider modification to increase his goal so that continued improvements can be made. Conversely, if progress monitoring data suggest that an intervention is not working as intended, problem solving can address how to improve upon the current plan. In particular, if a student is not progressing as intended based on progress

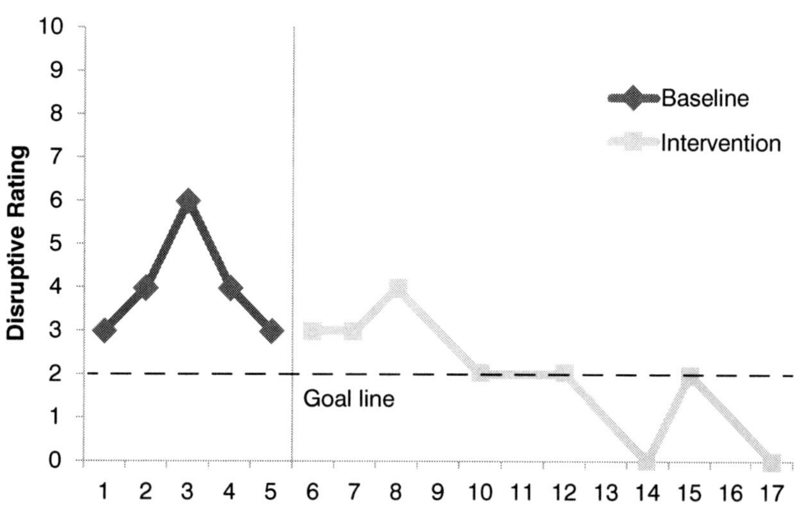

FIGURE 5.3. Data-based decision making using DBR.

monitoring data, decisions must be made about whether to (1) modify the plan or (2) discontinue the plan. As part of the problem-solving process, differing courses of action can be taken based on the data (see Table 5.3). If modifications are needed, numerous options exist: modifying goals, reteaching prerequisite skills, modifying antecedents and/or consequences, changing reinforcement options and/or schedule, modifying target behaviors, improving treatment fidelity, and more.

A very important and perhaps often overlooked component of data-based decision making related to progress monitoring involves having structures and systems in place for timely data review and interpretation. To the extent that school systems and personnel can incorporate this process into existing structures, data-based decision making will be facilitated and become more streamlined. To guide administrators and school personnel in this process, the National Association of State Directors of Special Educators (*www.nasdse.org*) developed blueprints for response-to-intervention implementation, which provide recommendations for how to build systems for data review. Specific actions are recommended, such as building infrastructure by forming a leadership team and developing an action plan, leading to implementation of a systematic support structure. Regular review of

TABLE 5.3. Data-Based Decision Making Using Progress Monitoring Data

Circumstances	Possible course(s) of action
Student is making adequate progress.	Continue progress monitoring to determine if progress is sustained.
Behavior is improving but at a slow rate.	Determine if the intervention is being implemented with fidelity. If so, pare back goals and determine if reinforcement options and schedule are sufficient.
Behavior improved and then plateaued.	Determine if the intervention is still being implemented with fidelity. If so, increase goals, if needed, and amplify reinforcement options.
Behavior did not improve.	Determine if the intervention is being implemented with fidelity. Determine if reteaching is needed to establish prerequisite skills. Evaluate reinforcement options and modify, if needed. If prerequisite skills are established and reinforcement options are sufficient, modify antecedent strategies and/or consequence strategies.
Behavior got worse.	Determine if the intervention is being implemented with fidelity. Allow sufficient time to rule out a short-term extinction burst. If the intervention is determined to be detrimental, discontinue it.

Note. Based on Chafouleas, Riley-Tillman, and Sugai (2007) and Wolery, Bailey, and Sugai (1988).

academic and behavioral data in tandem is recommended to best support student success. One of the advantages of DBR is the opportunity to collect a large amount of timely data. This advantage, however, is lost if the data are not reviewed and appropriate interventions decisions are not made.

Putting It All Together: Case Examples

Next, we illustrate the process of using of DBR as a progress monitoring tool to review the process outlined in sum. Specifically, we review DBR within two different contexts: using DBR to monitor student progress in response to targeted supports and using DBR to monitor response to a classwide intervention. It should be noted that procedures involved in individual progress monitoring at different levels of support intensity would be similar; however, DBR data collection procedures might need to intensify to increase the level of specificity provided by the data. This intensification might be accomplished by evaluating the student's behavior in multiple settings or on a more frequent basis.

Example 1: Individual Progress Monitoring

"Ms. Carter," a school psychologist at Washington Middle School, provides supplemental support to students with emotional and behavioral difficulties. "Mr. Williams," a sixth-grade teacher, recently approached her about a student in his math class, "Ron," who is frequently off task and is starting to fall behind as a result. Despite moving Ron's seat to the front of the classroom and providing frequent prompts and redirects, Mr. Williams continues to struggle with keeping Ron on task and engaged in classroom instruction. Together, Mr. Williams and Ms. Carter decide that Ron could likely benefit from targeted supports to help improve his on-task behavior and work completion. Ms. Carter suggests using DBR as both an intervention and progress monitoring tool for Ron.

In discussing Ron's behavior, Mr. Williams decides that Ron's behavior would best be monitored using two 11-point DBR-SIS to measure on-task behavior and work completion. In considering how to structure the ratings, Mr. Williams decides that ratings can be completed once per day at the end of math class. Ms. Carter works with Mr. Williams to prepare the forms and the scales. They define on-task behavior as Ron remained seated with his eyes focused on the teacher or work materials during math class. They define work completion as Ron actively worked on the assigned activity. Ms. Carter and Mr. Williams discuss examples of various ratings (e.g., What does a rating of 7 look like?) and the following day, Mr. Williams begins collecting baseline data on Ron's behavior. At the end of each class, he rates Ron on each scale, and finds that Ron is on task approximately 60% of the

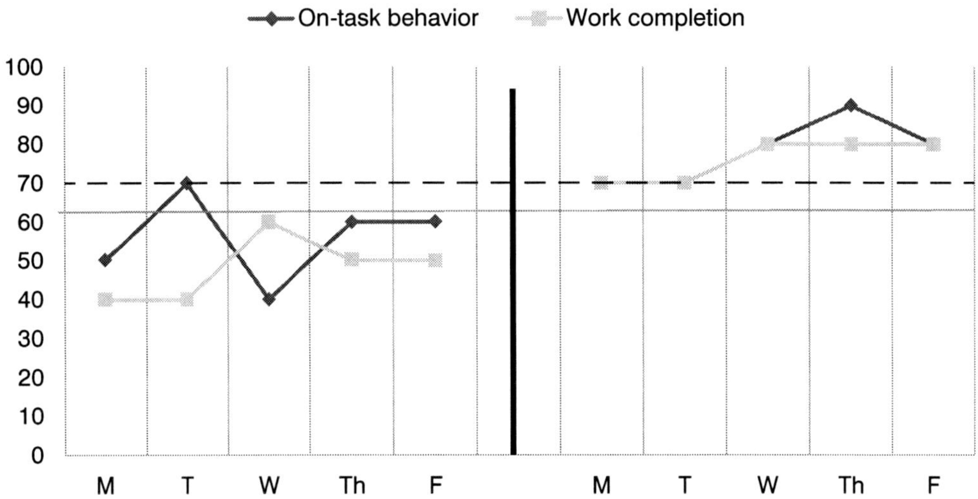

FIGURE 5.4. Baseline and intervention data for Ron.

time and his work completion averages 50%. Equipped with this information, Mr. Williams meets with Ron to talk about his observations and introduce the intervention phase. They discuss what Ron's behavior has looked like during baseline and set initial goals of 70% on task and 60% work completion. Each day, Mr. Williams completes the ratings and meets with Ron at the end of math to provide feedback on his behavior. Together, Mr. Williams and Ron graph the daily DBR ratings so that Ron can see his progress over time (see Figure 5.4). If Ron meets his goals at the end of each week, Mr. Williams allows him to choose a prize from the class prize box. Gradually, Mr. Williams sees that Ron is improving in his on-task behavior and work completion.

Example 2: Group Progress Monitoring

"Ms. James" is a third-grade teacher at Carter Elementary School. She has a particularly challenging group of students this year, whose frequent interruptions are causing her to stop instruction to address behavior more frequently than usual. Eager to get her class on the right track, Ms. James decides that she will start measuring student behavior in her class. She begins by considering the nature of the problem and decides to take note of the types of interruptions she is experiencing and the students involved. The following day, she pays careful attention to the interruptions and notices that many of the disruptions occur because (1) students aren't paying attention to instructions and (2) several students frequently call out or socialize with their peers during instruction. With this information, Ms. James develops a problem statement: Her third-grade class is not meeting behavioral expectations due to frequent interruptions during instruction. She decides that the standard DBR-SIS definitions for academic engagement and disruptive behavior would be well suited for progress monitoring, given the types of behavior she is seeing and the scope of the assessment.

To complete the ratings on her class, she decides to divide the school day in half, so that she can complete a rating before students go to lunch and again before the end of the day. This way, she can give her students specific feedback about their behavior twice per day. She decides to use the standard DBR-SIS forms with smiley faces, so the students can better understand which ratings are desirable. She completes the online training module and begins collecting baseline data for a

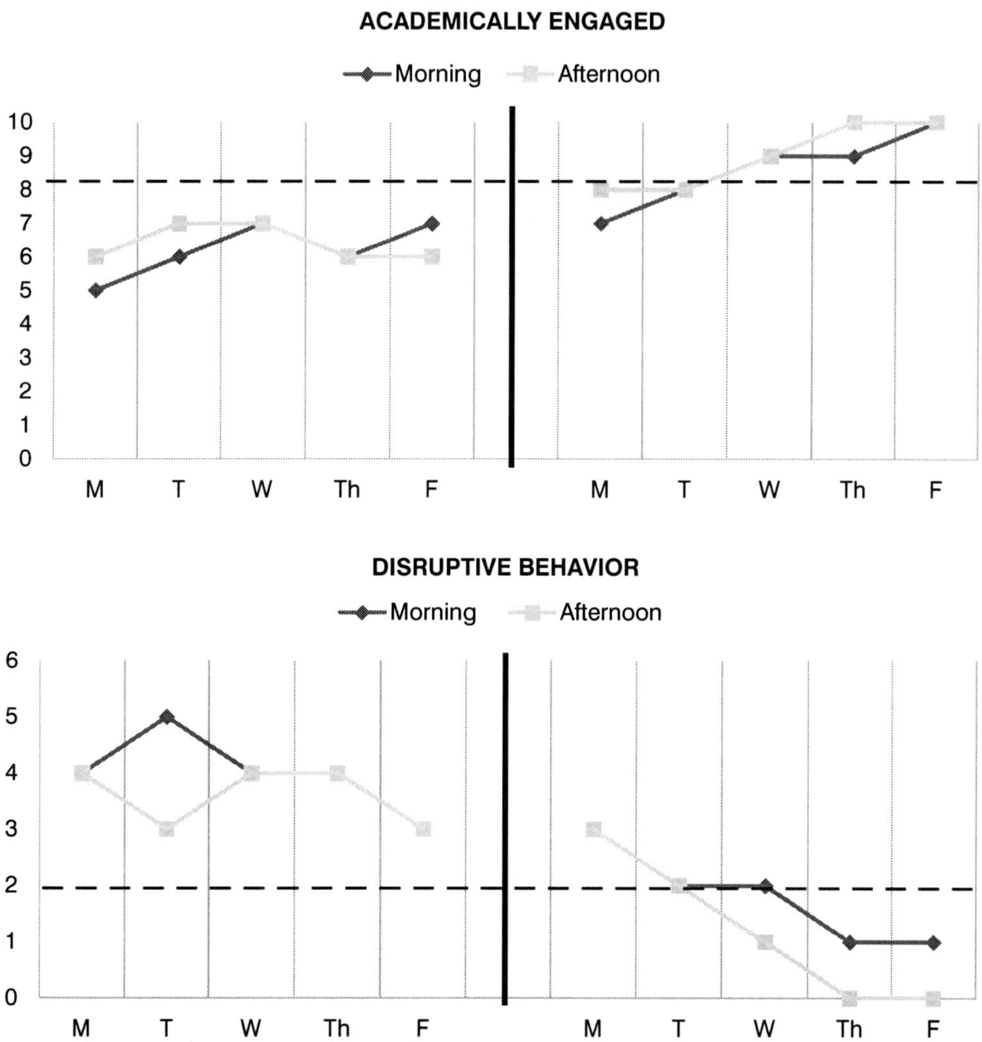

FIGURE 5.5. Classwide data for Ms. James's class.

week, unbeknownst to her students. She monitors levels of engagement and disruptive behavior, and after the observation period, immediately records her ratings. In reviewing the data at the end of the week, she sees that her class consistently received ratings of 6 and 7 on academic engagement and ratings of 3 and 4 on disruptive behavior across rating periods. As an initial goal, Ms. James decides that she would like to see levels of academic engagement at 8 or higher, and levels of disruptive behavior at 2 or lower. She shares this information with her class, and together, they develop a plan. They decide that the class can earn extra time at recess, contingent on meeting their specified daily goal. She reteaches behavioral expectations to her class and provides specific praise to students when she sees exemplary behavior. She posts her ratings on the whiteboard to share with the class and they discuss the ratings after each rating period. Within several days, she sees improvements in her students' behavior, as her ratings reflect that they are reaching their goal (see Figure 5.5).

Conclusions

This chapter outlined the process of progress monitoring student performance within MTSS. After reviewing existing options for progress monitoring, we hold that DBR provides an advantageous method to monitor student progress due to its efficiency, repeatability, flexibility, and defensibility. When incorporated within a problem-solving framework, DBR provides data that can be readily used to inform data-based decision making regarding student supports. DBR can be contextualized and customized to fit the needs of the assessment, and it has complementary applications as an intervention and communication tool. It will be critical over time for other methods of DBR to be studied more thoroughly as the overall class of assessment is ideally suited for this purpose.

CHAPTER 6

Use of DBR for Systematic Screening

Stephen P. Kilgus, Faith G. Miller, Austin H. Johnson, and Sandra M. Chafouleas

It has been estimated that although one in every five students are at risk for social–behavioral problems, approximately only 30% of these individuals receive the support they require to achieve social and academic success (U.S. Public Health Service, 2000). Recognition of this disparity between need and service provision has resulted in increased calls for school participation in the prevention of social–emotional and behavioral problems (Hoagwood & Erwin, 1997; National Research Council & Institute of Medicine, 2009; Severson et al., 2007; Walker & Shinn, 2002). Historically, schools have identified students struggling with social–emotional and behavioral problems via informal teacher referral. Unfortunately, research suggests that such processes may miss many at-risk students (Dowdy, Doane, Eklund, & Dever, 2013), particularly those struggling with internalizing behavior (e.g., anxiety, depression) or less severe externalizing behavior (Pearcy, Clopton, & Pope, 1993; Stranger & Lewis, 1993). In contrast, research has supported the use of *screening* in order to maximize the number of correct classifications of at-risk students (Levitt, Saka, Romanelli, & Hoagwood, 2007; Severson et al., 2007). Given the crucial role of screening in prevention, repeated calls have been made by scholars, professional organizations, and federal legislation for school adoption of screening practices (Individuals with Disabilities Education Improvement Act [IDEA], 2004; National Association of School Psychologists, 2002; National Research Council & Institute of Medicine, 2009; No Child Left Behind, 2002).

The purpose of this chapter is to review information from ongoing work regarding the use of DBR-SIS within screening applications. We first describe the process of screening and discuss its importance in supporting positive student development.

Next, we consider the desirable characteristics of school-based screening instruments and examine the research in support of the use of DBR-SIS in screening. Finally, we outline the steps involved in using DBR-SIS to conduct systematic screening and provide case studies to illustrate this process.

What Is Screening?

Screening is defined as the systematic evaluation of a prespecified group of individuals (e.g., school, district) through the use of efficient assessment methods and procedures. Although school-based screening began as a way to identify those students with diagnosable disorders, over time the scope of screening has widened to encompass those students demonstrating early signs or symptoms of more serious problems that do not yet warrant diagnosis of a disorder (i.e., behavioral and emotional risk; Kamphaus, 2012). Many different constructs can be used to define behavioral and emotional risk, including underperformed adaptive behaviors (e.g., engagement, respect), overperformed maladaptive behaviors (e.g., disruption), and the presence of both risk and protective factors (e.g., multiple school transitions, good problem-solving skills). The selection of an appropriate screening tool must therefore be made in consideration of the underlying construct of interest. For instance, if risk for externalizing disorders is of concern, then educators should utilize screening tools that assess those behavioral symptoms known to predict later development of the disorders, such as noncompliance, disruption, temper outbursts, and limited empathy (Bennett, Lipman, Racine, & Offord, 2003; Loeber, 1982; Loeber & Dishion, 1983; Miller & Eisenberg, 1988; Moffitt, 1993). If, on the other hand, a school wishes to identify those students who demonstrate behaviors that may impact their ability to learn and thrive in school without specific concern for diagnostic status, screening tools should focus on those constructs considered most relevant to school-based success (e.g., academic engagement, respectful behavior, social skills).

Although screening instruments can take several forms (e.g., teacher nomination, rating scales or checklists, systematic direct observations), all result in data that indicate the likelihood of the condition of interest. Some screeners are inherently dichotomous (i.e., yes/no), such as teacher nomination, in which a student is either nominated or not. Other measures, such as the Behavioral and Emotional Screening System (BESS; Kamphaus & Reynolds, 2007), are associated with norm-referenced cut scores. Students are considered to be at risk for behavioral disorders if their performance is more than one standard deviation away from the standardization sample mean (*T*-score > 60), and they are considered to show clinically significant levels of disordered behavior if they are more than two standard deviations away from the mean (*T*-score > 70). Still other measures, such as the Student Risk

Screening Scale (SRSS; Drummond, 1994), are associated with criterion-referenced cut scores. Students are considered to possess the condition of interest if their score falls above a prespecified level. For example, students receiving between 4 and 8 points on the SRSS are considered to demonstrate moderate risk, whereas students receiving 9 or more points are considered to demonstrate high risk.

In concert with considerations regarding various types of screening instruments, another important facet of screening involves the *scope.* That is, screening instruments can be used (1) universally, such that all students are screened; (2) in a targeted manner, such that only a select group is screened; or (3) with an indicated group to evaluate the presence of a specific disorder (Levitt et al., 2007). Within a prevention-focused framework, universal and targeted screening approaches are of particular interest. In these contexts, we use the term *systematic screening* to refer to either a universal or targeted approach. It should be noted that although a universal approach is optimal in "casting a wide net" to identify students at risk, disadvantages include time and resources required to screen all students. Thus, feasibility may necessitate a targeted approach to screening, whereby a smaller number of students are selected for evaluation. For example, students deemed to be performing below their peers in terms of functioning might be nominated for screening. In this example, half of a class might be screened as opposed to the whole class.

Why Is Screening Important?

Despite calls for implementation of screening for social–emotional and behavioral risk in schools, adoption remains limited (Cook, Volpe, & Livanis, 2010; Romer & McIntosh, 2005). Recent estimates suggest only one in eight schools have begun to screen for behavioral purposes (Bruhn, Woods-Groves, & Huddle, 2014). One factor contributing to limited adoption relates to the limited efficiency and usability of existing screening methods and procedures (Kilgus, Chafouleas, & Riley-Tillman, 2013; Severson et al., 2007). Until recently, many of the psychometrically defensible screening tools available to schools required a large amount of educator time, effort, and resources. Furthermore, although more efficient tools exist (e.g., SRSS), several of these tools are limited by their focus on the pathological medical model (Chafouleas, Kilgus, & Wallach, 2010). In this model, student behavioral problems are viewed as the result of dysfunction located within the student. This perspective stands in contrast to more modern models that relate student problems to the mismatch between student needs and environmental supports in the educational setting (Sheridan & Gutkin, 2000). When viewed only within a pathological framework, schools might conclude that (1) behavioral concerns are beyond their educational mandate and (2) it is therefore not the school's responsibility to screen for students who are at risk for social–emotional and behavioral problems.

Limited educator motivation to engage in social–emotional and behavioral screening may also be related to the relatively low priority given to social outcomes in school settings. Educator prioritization of academic outcomes is made obvious through the focus on various indicators of educational success, including grades, grade promotion, graduation, and performance on statewide achievement tests. Schools have an understandable interest in ensuring adequate student performance on these indicators, given the influence of these statistics on public perception, accountability standards, and funding. The lack of similar indicators with direct relevance to social success and ties to educator accountability may somewhat explain the reduced emphasis on the screening of social behavior. Schools are unlikely to be as concerned about detecting students who are at risk for behavioral problems in the absence of a "goal" or statewide standard toward which student progress should be monitored.

Given each of the aforementioned factors, multiple efforts can be undertaken to promote the adoption and sustained implementation of systematic screening for socially risky behavior. Educational staff, including school psychologists, should work with administrators and faculty to change how social–behavioral concerns are perceived. An attempt should be made to shift away from a pathological point of view to one founded within ecological theory, wherein the manipulation of high-priority environments (e.g., school) is emphasized. In addition, researchers might look to develop novel screening methods that possess many of the methodological and psychometric characteristics that have encouraged widespread adoption of curriculum-based measurement (CBM) within the academic domain. To date, such efforts have represented an attempt to establish a "CBM analogue," or a GOM for social behavior (Chafouleas, Riley-Tillman, & Christ, 2009; Gresham et al., 2010). Although many candidates have been suggested for social–behavioral GOM status, support for DBR-SIS may be particularly promising.

Systematic Screening within MTSS

Within an MTSS, the goal of systematic screening is to determine which students have not responded to universal supports within the general education setting, suggesting the need for either targeted or individualized intervention (depending upon the severity of the concerns). Because the goal is to identify the presence of risk (e.g., risk of maladaptive behavior, risk of experiencing school failure), all students identified for screening are evaluated on common criteria related to a condition of interest. Systematic screening is not necessarily concerned with determining the nature of the risk or the category of symptoms that has resulted in the condition (e.g., externalizing problems, attentional problems); rather, the goal is to identify only the presence of risk for negative outcomes (Keller-Margulis, Shapiro, &

Hintze, 2008). Once a decision is made regarding the presence of risk, educators must determine how each student will be assigned to intervention. As discussed by Shinn (2010), educators may opt to (1) assign all students to receive targeted supports (referred to as *titration*) and then monitor them for response to intervention, or (2) assign each student to a tiered support based on the severity of his or her need (referred to as *triage*).

Whether implemented via titration or triage, it is necessary that schools establish a systematic plan for moving from screening to intervention. As part of this plan, educators must choose the frequency with which they will engage in the systematic screening of students throughout the school year. Within the academic domain, it is common practice to screen students three times per year (fall, winter, and spring; Hosp et al., 2016). Repeated administrations serve two functions: (1) the identification of students who are newly at risk, and (2) the evaluation of the continued risk status of previously identified students. Although it has been suggested that behavioral screening should mirror this triannual process (Lane, Kalberg, Bruhn, Mahoney, & Driscoll, 2008), initial research by Miller, Welsh, Chafouleas, Riley-Tillman, and Fabiano (2015) suggests that recommended practices may vary, in part, by the screening instrument being used. In general, however, the use of at least two or three yearly administrations is recommended, given noted variability in student behavior and the need to detect changing risk status (Miller et al., 2015).

DBR-SIS as a Screening Tool

As discussed in Chapter 4, it is essential that systematic screening tools demonstrate three key features: contextual relevance, usability, and technical defensibility (Glover & Albers, 2007). We believe that DBR-SIS holds particular promise for use within school-based social–emotional and behavioral screening, given the growing evidence in support of these three features.

Contextually relevant screeners are aligned with school service delivery needs in that they can be administered at times and with the particular frequency necessary to support intervention-related decision making. They are also predictive of age and developmentally appropriate conditions (e.g., internalizing problems, risk factors) that are of interest to educational stakeholders. DBR-SIS has high contextual relevance, given that targets are representative of behaviors considered crucial to the development of social competence (Walker, Irvin, Noell, & Singer, 1992). Thus, DBR-SIS data may provide information regarding the appropriateness of school support efforts, as well as each student's potential for success within school and beyond (see Chapter 2 for more information regarding social behaviors of interest within the school setting). We consider DBR-SIS to be particularly well aligned for school-based behavioral screening.

Usable screeners are efficient in terms of time, effort, and resources, thus permitting their simultaneous use across multiple students. They are also supported by a schoolwide infrastructure, are acceptable to stakeholders, and yield student-related benefits that exceed the costs associated with data collection, interpretation, and use. Usability is perhaps the most obvious strength of DBR-SIS when included within a screening assessment. DBR-SIS are highly efficient, as they may be adopted and applied with minimal educator time, effort, and resources (Chafouleas, Riley-Tilman, & Christ, 2009; Christ et al., 2009).

Technically adequate screeners produce data with psychometric evidence supporting their interpretation and use as predictors of behavioral risk. Such evidence includes reliability, validity, and classification accuracy, as evaluated through conditional probability statistics (i.e., sensitivity, specificity, positive predictive power, and negative predictive power). Conditional probability statistics provide information regarding the extent to which risk is consistently identified (and not identified) between measures. These statistics are particularly helpful in identifying cut scores to use in identifying students as at risk. To date, a number of studies have examined the technical adequacy of DBR-SIS data for use in screening.

Reliability

Reliability refers to the consistency of scores and the extent to which scores are free from measurement error. Evidence for the reliability of DBR-SIS scores has been collected using several different methods. One method that has been used to estimate the reliability of DBR-SIS involves the calculation of an intraclass correlation coefficient (ICC) derived from classical test theory. Using this approach, DBR-SIS score variance is parceled into two components: (1) variance of student scores, nested within teacher; and (2) error variance. Ranging from 0 to 1, higher ICCs reflect higher reliability estimates. Because DBR-SIS scores are obtained over multiple observations, ICCs are calculated as a function of a specific number of observations. Across six to ten observations, ICCs have ranged from 0.90 to 0.97 across individual targets of academically engaged (AE), respectful (RS), and disruptive behavior (DB) (Johnson et al., 2014). These data support the reliability of scores obtained using DBR-SIS.

A second method used to evaluate reliability of DBR-SIS scores has been in studies employing generalizability theory, which permits a more detailed analysis of reliability. Evaluating multiple facets of variance simultaneously allows for examination of DBR-SIS score variance that is due to factors such as the student, the rating occasion, the rater, and combinations thereof. Findings from generalizability studies suggest that (1) a *minimum* of five observations is advised for low-stakes decisions; (2) the dependability of DBR-SIS scores increases as the number of observations increases; and (3) the rater should remain consistent due to the influence of the rater on the scores (e.g., Chafouleas, Briesch, et al., 2010; Christ, Riley-Tillman, Chafouleas, & Boice, 2010).

Validity

Evidence of the validity of DBR-SIS scores has been supported primarily by examining the relationship between DBR-SIS and existing validated screeners. For example, Miller et al. (2015) examined the relation between DBR-SIS and two screeners: the Social Skills Improvement System—Performance Screening Guide (SSIS-PSG) and the BESS. Strong correlations (>.50) were found between DBR-SIS and the SSIS-PSG and the BESS. Similarly, moderate to strong correlations have also been found between DBR-SIS and the Social Skills Rating System (SSRS; Gresham & Elliott, 1990) as well as the SRSS (Chafouleas, Kilgus, et al., 2013; Kilgus, Riley-Tillman, Chafouleas, Christ, & Welsh, 2014). These findings provide evidence of a strong relation between DBR-SIS and existing validated screeners. In addition to traditional correlational studies, studies examining classification accuracy also provide information regarding the validity of DBR-SIS scores.

Classification Accuracy

As previously described, classification accuracy can be evaluated using conditional probability statistics, which provide information regarding the extent to which risk is consistently identified between measures. Typically, a newly developed measure is evaluated against a well-established measure, and consistency of risk identification is determined across both measures. To this end, the true positive rate (sensitivity) and true negative rate (specificity) are often of interest, as are positive and negative predictive values. Additionally, conditional probability statistics are particularly helpful in identifying cut scores to use in identifying students as at risk.

In order to validate DBR-SIS for use in identifying students at risk, a series of classification accuracy studies have been completed in recent years. Initial studies examining classification accuracy examined screening procedures using two approaches to identify risk: (1) individual targets and (2) a combination of targets (e.g., Kilgus, Chafouleas, Riley-Tillman, & Welsh, 2012). That is, researchers were interested in examining how to best use the scales for screening purposes. For example, would risk status on a combination of the three targets best identify students in need of additional support, as opposed to considering each target in isolation? To this end, Kilgus et al. (2012) evaluated the value added by considering multiple DBR-SIS targets in a simultaneous fashion, called *multiple gating*. Through this multiple gating procedure, students were considered at risk overall when they were found to be at risk on more than one target (e.g., AE and DB). Examinations of this multiple-gating procedure have yielded mixed results, with this approach working well with some grade levels and poorly with others (Chafouleas, Kilgus, Jaffery, Riley-Tillman, Welsh, et al., 2013; Kilgus et al., 2014). Similarly, individual targets were found to function better for screening with certain grades than others. For example, Chafouleas, Kilgus, et al. (2013) found that, for screening of lower elementary students, the single target of DB functioned best, whereas at upper elementary a single target of AE functioned best. In light of these inconsistencies, Johnson et al. (2014) developed a new approach using combined scale summary scores to identify risk.

The most comprehensive study of screening using DBR-SIS ratings to date, conducted by Johnson et al. (2016), included a multisite sample of 1,863 students in grades 1, 2, 4, 5, 7, and 8. Because of inconsistencies supporting the use of a multiple-gating procedure, an alternative method was developed to determine overall risk: a combined summary score was created by taking the average (mean) rating for each target (AE, DB, RS) and summing them together (with DB reverse-scored). This approach was found to offer several advantages, including optimal classification accuracy indices across grades and a consistent approach to determining risk regardless of grade level. Further, DBR-SIS ratings also demonstrated high levels of reliability. Cut scores were developed for both individual targets and combined summary scores (see Tables 6.1–6.4). Although the summary scores are best used to identify risk overall, examining the individual targets can be informative regarding intervention efforts. The recommended rating procedures outlined in this chapter reflect the most current research-based practices for using DBR-SIS in targeted screening.

Although Johnson et al. (2014) identified preliminary normative ratings, we note that local norms can be used as well. One potential benefit of these norms over larger empirically derived cut scores may lie in their implications for decision making based on screening results. For instance, if a screener identifies 75% of students in a school as "at risk" when educational professionals are already aware of a significant need for behavior supports among most of their students, it may be beneficial to use locally derived norms for this population to identify students who are particularly atypical when compared to their peers. Although research on the development of behavioral local norms is limited, individuals interested in learning more about their development are referred to the literature regarding best practices in academic local norm development (e.g., Stewart & Silberglitt, 2008).

Finally, an additional, unique advantage of the use of DBR-SIS is that it can be used across assessment purposes. Although recent research has begun to support the use of DBR for screening purposes, initial research primarily supported the use of DBR-SIS in progress monitoring (see Chapter 5). The link between progress monitoring and screening offers numerous benefits for schools, including a

TABLE 6.1. Cut Scores and Conditional Probability Statistics for Single-Target Summary Score: Academic Engagement

Grade group *Time point*	Cut score[a]	Sensitivity	Specificity	PPV	NPV
Lower elementary					
Fall	8.2	.79 [.71, .87]	.72 [.68, .75]	.38 [.34, .42]	.94 [.92, .96]
Winter	8.4	.88 [.81, .94]	.70 [.66, .74]	.40 [.37, .44]	.96 [.94, .98]
Spring	8.5	.85 [.78, .92]	.74 [.70, .77]	.39 [.35, .43]	.96 [.94, .98]
Upper elementary					
Fall	8.4	.84 [.77, .90]	.73 [.69, .76]	.37 [.33, .41]	.96 [.94, .98]
Winter	8.4	.81 [.73, .89]	.80 [.77, .83]	.39 [.35, .44]	.96 [.95, .98]
Spring	8.7	.77 [.69, .85]	.74 [.70, .78]	.37 [.33, .41]	.94 [.92, .96]
Middle school					
Fall	8.6	.83 [.76, .90]	.73 [.69, .77]	.43 [.39, .48]	.95 [.93, .97]
Winter	8.8	.86 [.79, .92]	.74 [.70, .79]	.49 [.45, .54]	.95 [.93, .97]
Spring	8.8	.83 [.75, .90]	.71 [.66, .75]	.41 [.37, .46]	.94 [.92, .97]

Note. Conditional probability statistics are presented alongside a 95% confidence interval (in brackets).
[a]If a student's summary score for academically engaged behavior is equal to or less than this value, he or she is classified as at risk.

TABLE 6.2. Cut Scores and Conditional Probability Statistics for Single-Target Summary Score: Disruptive Behavior

Grade group *Time point*	Cut score[a]	Sensitivity	Specificity	PPV	NPV
Lower elementary					
Fall	1.2	.85 [.78, .91]	.71 [.68, .75]	.39 [.36, .43]	.96 [.94, .97]
Winter	1.3	.73 [.64, .81]	.74 [.70, .77]	.39 [.34, .43]	.92 [.90, .94]
Spring	1.0	.73 [.64, .81]	.70 [.65, .73]	.32 [.28, .36]	.93 [.91, .95]
Upper elementary					
Fall	0.7	.81 [.74, .88]	.71 [.68, .75]	.36 [.32, .39]	.95 [.94, .97]
Winter	0.7	.81 [.74, .89]	.72 [.69, .76]	.32 [.28, .36]	.96 [.94, .98]
Spring	0.6	.74 [.65, .82]	.74 [.71, .78]	.37 [.33, .41]	.93 [.91, .95]
Middle school					
Fall	0.6	.82 [.74, .88]	.71 [.67, .75]	.41 [.37, .45]	.94 [.92, .96]
Winter	0.4	.83 [.76, .90]	.71 [.66, .75]	.45 [.41, .50]	.93 [.91, .96]
Spring	0.5	.74 [.65, .82]	.70 [.66, .74]	.38 [.34, .42]	.92 [.89, .94]

Note. Conditional probability statistics are presented alongside a 95% confidence interval (in brackets).
[a]If a student's summary score for disruptive behavior is equal to or greater than this value, he or she is classified as at risk.

TABLE 6.3. Cut Scores and Conditional Probability Statistics for Single-Target Summary Score: Respectful Behavior

Grade group *Time point*	Cut score[a]	Sensitivity	Specificity	PPV	NPV
Lower elementary					
Fall	9.1	.71 [.62, .79]	.70 [.66, .74]	.34 [.30, .38]	.92 [.89, .94]
Winter	9.1	.72 [.63, .80]	.70 [.66, .74]	.36 [.32, .40]	.92 [.89, .94]
Spring	9.2	.73 [.64, .81]	.72 [.68, .76]	.34 [.30, .38]	.93 [.91, .95]
Upper elementary					
Fall	9.5	.77 [.69, .85]	.74 [.70, .78]	.36 [.32, .40]	.95 [.93, .96]
Winter	9.4	.76 [.67, .85]	.72 [.68, .75]	.30 [.26, .34]	.95 [.93, .97]
Spring	9.7	.72 [.64, .80]	.69 [.65, .73]	.32 [.28, .35]	.92 [.90, .95]
Middle school					
Fall	9.7	.79 [.71, .86]	.71 [.66, .75]	.40 [.36, .44]	.93 [.91, .95]
Winter	9.7	.72 [.63, .80]	.75 [.71, .79]	.45 [.40, .51]	.90 [.88, .93]
Spring	9.7	.74 [.65, .82]	.70 [.65, .74]	.38 [.34, .42]	.92 [.89, .94]

Note. Conditional probability statistics are presented alongside a 95% confidence interval (in brackets).
[a]If a student's summary score for respectful behavior is equal to or less than this value, he or she is classified as at risk.

TABLE 6.4. Cut Scores and Conditional Probability Statistics for Combined-Scale Summary Score (AE + RS + DB)

Grade group *Time point*	Cut score[a]	Sensitivity	Specificity	PPV	NPV
Lower elementary					
Fall	26.2	.86 [.79, .92]	.72 [.68, .76]	.40 [.36, .44]	.96 [.94, .98]
Winter	26.4	.81 [.74, .88]	.71 [.67, .74]	.39 [.35, .43]	.94 [.92, .96]
Spring	26.5	.82 [.74, .89]	.75 [.71, .78]	.39 [.35, .43]	.95 [.94, .97]
Upper elementary					
Fall	27.3	.87 [.81, .93]	.71 [.68, .75]	.37 [.34, .41]	.97 [.95, .98]
Winter	26.8	.84 [.76, .90]	.80 [.77, .84]	.40 [.36, .45]	.97 [.95, .98]
Spring	27.8	.79 [.71, .86]	.71 [.67, .75]	.35 [.32, .39]	.94 [.92, .96]
Middle school					
Fall	27.5	.83 [.76, .90]	.71 [.66, .75]	.41 [.37, .45]	.95 [.92, .97]
Winter	28.2	.90 [.83, .95]	.72 [.68, .77]	.49 [.45, .54]	.96 [.94, .98]
Spring	28.1	.83 [.75, .90]	.71 [.66, .75]	.41 [.37, .45]	.94 [.92, .97]

Note. Conditional probability statistics are presented alongside a 95% confidence interval (in brackets).
[a]If a student's combined summary score is equal to or less than this value, he or she is classified as at risk.

reduction in the resources and effort needed for implementation over time, and increased ease in understanding and interpreting behavioral data across different assessment purposes. For instance, DBR-SIS screening data could be used as a baseline of performance, and then teachers could continue to collect these data following the introduction of Tier 2 or 3 supports in order to assess student response to intervention. These newly collected progress monitoring data can then be compared to the initial DBR-SIS baseline data to determine student progress (see Chapter 11 for additional information regarding the visual analysis of DBR-SIS data).

Using DBR in Behavioral Screening

As noted above, research to date has yielded support for the use of DBR-SIS within screening applications. With this evidence in mind, how might schools use the tool for this purpose? Although DBR-SIS can be used in various ways to support screening decision making, to date, most research has focused on the standalone application of DBR-SIS at the universal level for systematic screening purposes. In this capacity, three core DBR-SIS individual targets would be administered to all students within a population of interest, such as a particular grade level. Resulting single-target summary scores and combined-scale summary scores would then be calculated and compared to cut scores in determining each student's risk status. We next outline the steps associated with DBR-SIS use within a systematic screening process (see Table 6.5), noting different options available to schools to customize a screening plan that meets the needs of each school context.

Step 1: Establish a Decision-Making Plan

First, it is necessary for the Problem-Solving Team (PST) to establish a decision-making plan that defines the way in which systematic screening data will be utilized. The plan should specify guidelines for identifying and responding to at-risk and not-at-risk students. Specifically, the scope of the screening (universal or targeted) will need to be identified in relation to needs and resources. Potential recommendations for responding to students who are not found to be at risk include continued provision of universal behavior supports and consideration within subsequent systematic screenings. Those students who are found to be at risk, on the other hand, could either be referred for additional assessment or directly placed in an intervention group. Referral for additional assessment might take place if the PST is interested in corroborating risk status and/or determining the extent of need. Alternatively, at-risk students could be assigned to intervention via either a triage or titration approach. At this time, titration is likely to be most appropriate for use

TABLE 6.5. DBR Blueprint for Systematic Screening

☐ 1. Establish a decision-making plan.

Determine the scope of the screening and if at-risk students will be referred for (a) additional assessment or (b) intervention (via a titration or triage approach).

☐ 2. Determine who will conduct ratings.

Raters will likely be head teachers of the classroom in which each student spends the majority of his or her instructional time.

☐ 3. Conduct rater training.

Raters should be directed to complete DBR-SIS training of the type available at directbehaviorratings.org.

☐ 4. Determine the order in which students will be rated.

Create groups of three to five students that will be rated at the same time using DBR-SIS. Grouping should be quasi-random to avoid rating too many "well-behaved" or "poorly behaved" students at one time.

☐ 5. Select DBR-SIS target behaviors.

Include all single targets and combination scales that are pertinent to relevant cut scores and school context. Determine the targets/scales that will determine the students who were at risk and should be considered for additional assessment or intervention (see Step 1).

☐ 6. Determine when and how often ratings will occur.

Identify the days (e.g., October 1–5) and times (e.g., 9:00 A.M.–12:00 P.M. and 12:30–3:30 P.M.) during which each group of students will be observed and rated. An attempt should be made to schedule 10 ratings for each student within each group.

☐ 7. Complete DBR-SIS ratings.

Teachers should complete DBR-SIS ratings as soon as possible following each rating period.

☐ 8. Calculate summary single-target scores and combined-scale scores (if applicable).

For single-target scores, compute the mean of scores within each DBR-SIS target (e.g., mean of all AE ratings). For combined-scale scores, compute the mean within each DBR-SIS target, remembering to reverse-score all DB scores. Sum the means of each target to derive the DBR-SIS combined-scale summary score. It is recommended that means comprised of less than six ratings not be used.

☐ 9. Compare resulting summary target/scale scores to their corresponding cut scores.

Ensure that identified cut scores are appropriate for the target/scale under consideration, as well as the grades and time of year within which DBR-SIS was administered. Use cut scores to generate a list of at-risk students to refer for additional assessment or intervention.

with DBR-SIS, given that triage requires cut scores associated with multiple levels of risk (e.g., moderate risk and high risk).

Step 2: Determine Who Will Conduct Ratings

Next, the PST should convene to identify one rater for each student who will be screened. These individuals will be responsible for rating all students enrolled in their respective setting. Rater selection is relatively straightforward at the elementary level, as the most appropriate rater is likely to be the head teacher of the classroom in which each student spends the majority of his or her instructional time. This process is slightly more complex at the middle or high school level because each student has several teachers across multiple classrooms. In this scenario, the PST, in collaboration with faculty and administration, should select a single class period in which screening will be conducted. For example, a high school could determine that each teacher will screen all of the students in his or her Period C classroom. Doing so ensures that each student is rated by at least one teacher.

One rater per student is likely to be sufficient for screening purposes, and the cut scores provided in this chapter are derived from ratings by a single head teacher. Previous research has found DBR-SIS ratings to be most reliable when completed by teachers who have the opportunity to observe and interact with all students without having to substantially divide their attention, such as during one-on-one supplemental instruction (Chafouleas, Briesch, Riley-Tillman, Christ, Black, et al., 2010). However, the ability to corroborate ratings across multiple raters may allow for more accurate and less biased screening decisions. Therefore, another option is for the PST to select an additional individual to rate each student. At the elementary level, appropriate additional raters would likely be co-head teachers, instructional support staff (e.g., classroom aide), or specialist teachers (e.g., art, music, physical education). At the middle and high school levels, an additional rater is easily identified through the selection of an extra class period within which a second round of ratings would be completed. However, consideration of how ratings will be combined or compared across raters should be established prior to implementation.

Step 3: Conduct Rater Training

Following their selection, raters should be trained to complete DBR-SIS ratings. This training process should be systematic and founded upon research indicative of the nature and extent of training necessary to yield psychometrically defensible DBR-SIS data (see Chapter 7). Recommendations from this research have informed the construction of an evidence-based online training module, available at *directbehaviorratings.org*. Once finished, trainees are e-mailed a certificate of successful training completion.

Step 4: Determine the Order in Which Students Will Be Rated

Once all raters have been trained to complete DBR-SIS ratings, it is time to establish a plan for the collection of these data. First, each student should be placed in one of several rating groups in the classroom. Rating groups include students who will be rated at the same time and should be comprised of three to five students. How many groups should be established within a classroom is dependent upon the number of enrolled students. For example, in a classroom of 20 students, it would be necessary to create four to seven groups. The purpose of grouping and conducting simultaneous student ratings is to shorten the total amount of time required to screen all students. If each rater evaluated only one student at a time, it would take several weeks to complete the screening process for an entire classroom. At the same time, however, rating accuracy would likely suffer if one teacher had to rate the behavior of all students in the classroom simultaneously. For these reasons, groups are limited to a small number of students so that the rater is capable of observing all students at the same time.

Groups should be rated one at a time. For instance, when collecting DBR-SIS data for Group 1, a rater should only be observing and rating the behavior of the three to five students in that group. Group 1 students would be observed and rated across consecutive days until sufficient data were collected (see Step 6 for recommendations regarding what should be considered "sufficient" data). At this time, the rater would no longer consider Group 1 students, and would begin to observe and evaluate the behavior of Group 2 students. It is recommended that groups be assigned in a quasi-random fashion to reduce the likelihood of rating too many students with similar behavioral profiles at once. It might appear intuitive to rate the behavior of all "well-behaved" students at once, given that the resulting rating process would be relatively straightforward. However, to do so would mean that it would eventually be necessary to simultaneously rate multiple "poorly behaving" students as well. Given that these students are likely to be the most difficult to rate with accuracy (Chafouleas, Kilgus, et al., 2012), it is preferred that each group includes a variety of students demonstrating differing levels of problem behavior.

Step 5: Select DBR-SIS Target Behaviors

With rating groups now established, it is necessary to determine the DBR-SIS targets on which each student will be screened. It is recommended that schools employ all three targets (i.e., DB, AE, and RS) in the interest of deriving a comprehensive depiction of each student's potential for behavioral risk (Johnson et al., 2014). Additionally, use of all three targets permits the calculation of a combined-scale summary score (as described in greater detail in Step 8), which has demonstrated many desirable classification accuracy statistics. At the very least, it is suggested that schools employ the DB and AE targets, as research has supported their particular relevance to screening decisions (Chafouleas, Kilgus, et al., 2013; Kilgus et al., 2014), and these targets have been shown to demonstrate more desirable classification accuracy statistics than the RS target when considered in isolation (Johnson et al., 2014).

Step 6: Determine When and How Often Ratings Will Occur

In continuing with the establishment of a DBR-SIS data collection plan, it is necessary next to schedule when and how many ratings will be completed for each student. Within an elementary school setting, it is recommended that ratings be completed twice a day for 5 consecutive days for each rating group. The first rating should correspond to the student behavior observed by the rater between arrival to school and departure for lunch (e.g., 8:30–11:30 A.M.). The second should represent behavior observed between the return from lunch and the end of the school day (e.g., 1:15–3:30 P.M.). In a middle or high school setting, it is recommended that the first rating correspond to the behavior displayed by the student during the first half of a class period (e.g., 12:15–12:40 P.M.), and the second rating to behavior displayed during the second half (e.g., 12:40–1:05 P.M.).

Data collection should continue for the first group until 6–10 data points have been collected for all students in the group. This recommendation is informed by the results of generalizability and dependability studies investigating the number of ratings needed to achieve an adequate level of dependability (Briesch et al., 2010; Chafouleas et al., 2010). Once the requisite number of data points has been collected for each group member, the rater should begin to observe and evaluate Group 2 students. This process should continue until all groups have been rated and a sufficient amount of data has been collected for all students in the classroom.

Step 7: Complete DBR-SIS Ratings

Once DBR-SIS targets have been chosen and the rating schedule has been established, raters can begin to rate Group 1 students. Raters should be reminded to complete each rating as soon as possible following each rating period. PST members should work with raters prior to screening to identify times during which it is most convenient to complete each rating. A logical time to record morning ratings is right before the rater's lunch period, whereas afternoon ratings may be completed at the end of the school day. As discussed in Chapter 4, raters should rate only the behavior that they observe (i.e., behavior observed outside of the target rating period should not be taken into consideration) and should skip any ratings wherein they feel that they did not have the opportunity to sufficiently observe the target student. Furthermore, any ratings that cannot be conducted immediately following the observation period should be skipped in order to avoid introducing unnecessary rating error.

Step 8: Calculate Single-Target Scores and Combined-Scale Summary Scores (If Applicable)

After 6–10 data points have been collected, schools must determine how DBR-SIS data will be interpreted relative to the aforementioned decision-making plan. One of two approaches could be taken: Consider either a *combined-scale summary score* or a *single-target summary score*. In the first approach, each student would be considered at risk only if he or she fell below cut scores on a DB + AE + RS summated combined scale. Although such an approach does not immediately identify the specific area of risk, ratings for DB, AE, and RS can be reviewed after determining overall risk in order to evaluate potential areas of specific difficulty. The combined approach may be preferred when a premium is placed on classification accuracy (given research support for the technical performance of these scales for screening purposes), as well as on the generation of multiple behavioral targets for progress monitoring and evaluation.

To derive combined-scale summary scores, it is necessary to pool mean scores across all individual targets of interest. Prior to doing so, all individual target summary scores should be rounded to the first decimal place (e.g., 3.44 = 3.4; 8.79 = 8.8). If DB is to be represented in the combined scale (as it is in the provided cut scores in Step 9), the rounded mean score for this particular target must be reverse-scored prior to summing the individual scores. This is accomplished by subtracting the rounded score from 10 (e.g., 10–7.9 = 2.1). Combined-scale summary scores are then derived by calculating the sum of all rounded mean target scores. If one was interested in the interpretation of the DB + AE + RS scale, then it would be necessary to add the rounded mean scores of AE, RS, and reverse-scored DB to calculate each student's combined score.

To derive single-target summary scores for each student, it is necessary to calculate the average (i.e., mean) rating for each of the target behaviors rated using DBR-SIS. The number of mean scores that should be calculated is dependent upon the number of DBR-SIS targets that were administered. If DB, AE, and RS were administered, then three mean scores should be calculated for each student. Mean scores are calculated by deriving the sum of all ratings within a target and dividing that sum by the number of data points collected within that target. Mean target scores should then be rounded to the first decimal place (e.g., 3.44 = 3.4; 8.79 = 8.8) to prepare for comparison to individual target cut scores. After mean scores are calculated, the score being used for overall behavioral risk determination (e.g., AE) would be compared to the cut score for that grade group and time point. This approach may be most appropriate when the purpose of screening is to identify general behavioral risk while attending to a specific area of concern (e.g., AE, DB), or when efficiency calls for rating fewer than three target behaviors.

Alternatively, a student may be considered at risk if he or she falls in the at-risk range for one or more individual targets. For instance, a student would be considered at risk overall if his or her score were at risk within DB alone; within both DB and AE; or across DB, AE, and RS. Educators are cautioned, however, that there is less support for the classification accuracy of this approach than there is for use of a combined-scale or single-target summary score, and that the conditional probability statistics associated with each cut score will change with the use of this multiple-gating approach.

Step 9: Compare Resulting Target/Scale Summary Scores to Their Corresponding Cut Scores

Once all single-target and combined-scale summary scores have been calculated, each score should be compared to its corresponding cut score in determining each student's risk status. To safeguard the appropriateness and accuracy of screening decisions, PSTs should ensure that each cut score is specific to the appropriate target/scale, grade, and time of year during which data were collected (see Tables 6.2–6.5). Comparing observed scores to cut scores should allow one to generate a list of at-risk students who are to be referred for either additional assessment or intervention in accordance with the previously specified decision-making plan (see Figure 6.1).

Alternative Procedures

Alterations to the aforementioned data collection procedures are also possible. For instance, it may be possible to rate more students at once (e.g., eight or nine), to collect more than 2 data points per day, or to collect a smaller number of DBR-SIS data points for each student. Modifications are easily made to the size of rating groups and the schedule of data collection (e.g., three daily ratings across the elementary school day). Alterations to the number of data points collected is also relatively straightforward and supported by the results of Chafouleas, Kilgus, et al. (2013), which indicated that 2–3 data points may be sufficient to yield reliabilities of equal to or greater than .90. However, researchers have not yet examined how different data collection procedures will influence DBR-SIS classification accuracy. Therefore, until such evidence is available, the most defensible approach to DBR-SIS screening will employ those procedures described above and outlined in Table 6.5.

Student Name	Combined Scale Summary Score	Cut Score	At Risk	Action Taken
			☐ Yes ☐ No	
			☐ Yes ☐ No	
			☐ Yes ☐ No	
			☐ Yes ☐ No	
			☐ Yes ☐ No	
			☐ Yes ☐ No	
			☐ Yes ☐ No	
			☐ Yes ☐ No	
			☐ Yes ☐ No	
			☐ Yes ☐ No	

Teacher: ______________________ Date: ______________ Time Point: Fall Winter Spring

FIGURE 6.1. Screening summary sheet.

Putting It All Together: Case Example

Now that we have outlined the steps involved in using DBR-SIS to screen for social–emotional and behavioral concerns, we illustrate the process using a case example. The following case study focuses on the use of combined-scale summary scores to conduct systematic screening at the elementary school level.

Systematic Screening Using Combined-Scale Summary Scores

The Behavior Support Team at North Elementary School (grades K–5) was interested in conducting systematic screening for behavioral risk and elected to use DBR-SIS. First- and second-grade students were selected to participate in the screening, given concerns regarding the prevalence of behavioral issues in these grades. An initial screening was conducted during the fall (October), with plans to screen again in the winter (January) and spring (April). After reviewing the literature and instructional materials available at *directbehaviorratings.org*, the Behavior Support Team decided that all students in grades 1 and 2 would be rated universally, using all three DBR-SIS targets in order to provide a comprehensive assessment of school-based competencies. They then decided that these data would be used to implement a titration approach to intervention, such that those students deemed to be at risk would be provided with targeted supports.

It was decided that each head teacher would rate the students in his or her classroom. For the majority of students, no additional ratings were collected; however, the team chose to have a second staff member conduct ratings for a small number of students for whom data collection problems were noted (e.g., rater bias, problems with data collection). Prior to asking teachers to collect screening data, the team provided each teacher with an electronic link to the online DBR-SIS training module. Once completed, teachers submitted their certificate of training completion to the team. The decision was made to periodically review the record of training completion to determine who was eligible to screen students using DBR-SIS, and who was in need of an annual booster training session to ensure the defensibility of ratings.

Once data collection began, the team provided each teacher with the appropriate DBR-SIS forms to rate four or five students during each rating period. The order in which all students were rated was randomized within each classroom to reduce bias that might result from nonrandom selection (e.g., simultaneous rating of all students thought to be typically disruptive). For instance, in "Mrs. Harris's" class of 20 students, the team randomly assigned each student to one of four groups using a random number generator (e.g., *randomizer.org*), resulting in four groups of five students. Group 1 was rated across each day of the first week of each screening month. Following this week and the collection of all necessary data points, the teacher began to collect ratings for Group 2 across each day of the second week of each screening month. This process continued in this fashion until each group had been rated.

Ratings were completed twice a day. The first rating corresponded to behavior displayed by the students during the morning portion of the school day, spanning from the morning routine activities to the end of the transition to lunch. Once all students had transitioned to lunch, each teacher took a moment to rate his or her students on the DBR-SIS targets of interest. The teacher only considered the behavior he or she had directly observed during the morning when rating each student's behavior. Ratings were completed as soon as possible following the morning observation period to ensure that impressions of student behavior were still clear in each teacher's mind. The second rating corresponded to behavior displayed during the afternoon, spanning from the return from lunch to students' departure to their waiting buses or cars. Once all students had left for the day, the teacher took another moment to rate each student's behavior.

Once all DBR-SIS ratings were completed, the team calculated combined-scale summary scores by computing the average score for each target behavior, then summing the rounded mean scores (with DB reverse-scored). A student's summary score was only computed and considered in screening decisions if at least 6 data points had been collected across the five possible data collection days. Resulting summary scores were then compared to their corresponding cut scores, which were specific to each grade level and time of year under consideration. For the fall, students in grades 1 and 2 were considered at risk if their combined-scale summary score was equal to or greater than 26.2. The PST then generated a list of at-risk students to be referred for targeted behavioral intervention.

Conclusions

The aforementioned recommendations for the use of DBR-SIS in screening are founded upon findings of multiple investigations (e.g., Chafouleas, Kilgus, et al., 2013; Kilgus et al., 2012, 2014; Johnson et al., 2016). As such, they may be reasonably described as evidence-based approaches to screening and defensible for use within school settings. Though encouraging, additional investigations are necessary to further define the parameters of DBR-SIS applications, and to broaden the support for interpretation and use of DBR-SIS targets as screeners of behavioral risk. Several specific areas of inquiry can be identified. First, there is need for continued examination of DBR-SIS criterion-related validity through examination of relationships with various criterion measures. To date, research has supported the concurrent and predictive relationship between DBR-SIS and multiple measures, including the SSRS, SSIS-PSG, SRSS, and BESS. Future examinations should expand these investigations to other assessments of interest—for example, through examination of additional criterion measures, such as the Strengths and Difficulties Questionnaire (Goodman, 1997), or the Student Internalizing and Externalizing Behavior Screeners (Cook et al., 2011). Further, longitudinal studies are needed to evaluate the predictive validity of DBR-SIS and to gain insights regarding how risk status changes over time.

Second, it may also be of interest to identify an optimal means by which to combine DBR-SIS targets to derive more accurate screening decisions. As outlined previously, DBR-SIS work to date has considered (1) single-target summary scores, which represent mean ratings for individual behavioral targets (e.g., AE); (2) combined-scale summary scores, representing sums of mean DBR-SIS target ratings (e.g., DB + AE + RS; Johnson et al., 2016); and (3) single-method multiple-gating procedures, wherein overall risk status is defined as risk in two or more DBR-SIS targets (Chafouleas, Kilgus, et al., 2013; Kilgus et al., 2012, 2014). Future investigations might also consider more advanced statistical means by which to utilize information contributed by multiple DBR-SIS targets. Such statistical procedures have been considered in the CBM literature and include logistic regression (e.g., Clemens, Shapiro, & Thoemmes, 2011), discriminant analysis (e.g., Hintze & Silberglitt, 2005), and classification tree analysis (e.g., Compton, Fuchs, Fuchs, & Bryant, 2006). Each analytical approach should also be subjected to a cost–benefit analysis. The optimal approach is the one that affords superior classification accuracy and is also feasible for application in schools by practitioners with minimal to moderate statistical training.

Third, the use of DBR-SIS in multiple-gating procedures should be explored, wherein DBR-SIS targets and scales are combined with an additional screener to potentially increase classification accuracy. Researchers may wish to examine DBR-SIS performance within this particular application, and evaluate whether this novel use of the tool is associated with either (1) differential classification accuracy or (2) a need for alternative DBR-SIS data collection procedures (e.g., different cut scores, greater minimum number of data points).

Finally, targeted screening applications for DBR-SIS may also warrant additional exploration, wherein students are screened prior to and/or during implementation of targeted or individualized interventions. Such assessment might afford data regarding the clinical significance of treatment effects (Jacobson, Follette, & Revenstorf, 1984), or the potential for intervention to move a student outside the range of risk and lessen the likelihood of eventually receiving a behavior disorder classification. This information would be highly useful in decision making regarding an ongoing intervention, including whether it should be continued, modified, or terminated.

CHAPTER 7

Considerations and Developments in DBR-SIS Assessment Training

Austin H. Johnson, Nicholas J. Crovello, and Sandra M. Chafouleas

Before embarking on a new activity, whether in our personal or professional lives, we often first take some time to learn how to do that activity. For those simpler tasks that involve lower stakes, such as programming the clock on a microwave, we might briefly read an instruction manual. For more moderately challenging tasks, like learning how to do a squat at the gym, we might supplement step-by-step instructions by watching videos online to observe how a squat is correctly performed. Finally, for complex tasks, such as changing the serpentine belt in a sedan, we might read a manual, watch some videos, and finally call a mechanically inclined friend to come over and give us feedback on how we are doing. Similarly, educational professionals are often charged with embarking upon new and novel activities with varying degrees of support and training. There are many components of DBR that may benefit from comprehensive training, including the communication of results and implementation of corresponding interventions. In this chapter, we focus specifically on training in assessment procedures, both generally and with respect to DBR. Given that single-item scales (DBR-SIS) have received the greatest attention within the DBR-specific training research, we will limit our discussion to training for DBR-SIS.

Why Provide Training?

Whether it is a microwave, a squat, or a serpentine belt, we seek out training because we want to do something correctly. However, *correctly* is defined differently for each of those individual tasks (although we might sometimes wish we could achieve the outcome of squats just by setting the clock on our microwave!). When we talk about conducting an assessment correctly, typically our focus is on the quality of the resultant data: that is, their reliability and validity. Both of these concepts, however, are multifaceted. *Reliability* is generally concerned with consistency in scores over certain dimensions of interest (Hintze, 2005), whether across raters (i.e., interrater reliability), across time (i.e., test–retest reliability), or across items (i.e., internal consistency). High reliability indicates that the data derived from a measure are consistent across some dimension considered meaningful for that measurement context. Similarly, *validity* consists of a number of distinct concepts such as face validity and construct validity, with an overarching concern being whether data derived from an instrument result in meaningful decision making (Messick, 1995).

Accuracy is related to, but distinct from, reliability and validity and may be defined as the relationship between (1) the instrument-derived score and (2) an acceptable comparison score (Guion, 1965). As demonstrated in Figure 7.1, although results from an assessment may be considered reliable if minimal differences exist across ratings from separate individuals, this does not necessarily mean that the ratings are accurate. Looking down the column reflecting high reliability/

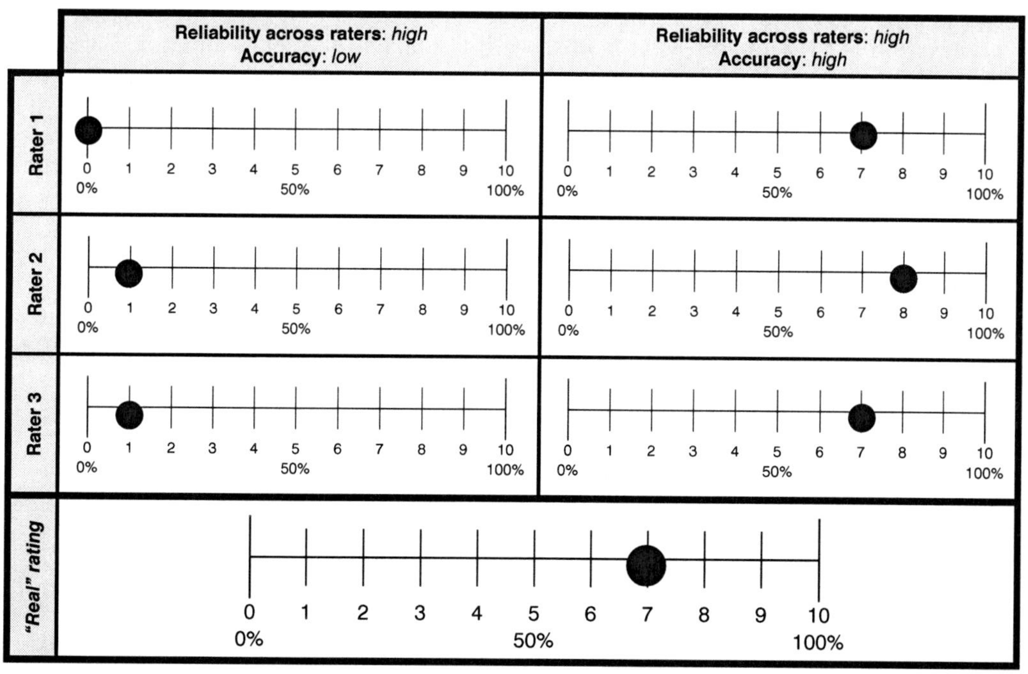

FIGURE 7.1. Examples of reliability and accuracy: Multiple raters measuring academic engagement at a single time point.

low accuracy, all raters rated academic engagement consistently (i.e., in the 0–1 range); however, they also rated the behavior much lower than the comparison score would indicate (i.e., academic engagement rating = 7). In contrast, looking down the column reflecting high reliability/high accuracy, ratings of academic engagement are not only consistent with one another (i.e., in the 7–8 range), but also with the "real" score. If scores from an assessment do not measure what they intend to measure (i.e., construct validity), then conclusions about accuracy are meaningless because comparisons between the derived score and the comparison score are not representative of the intended outcome. In other words, reliability may be present independent of accuracy, whereas validity is a prerequisite for meaningfully interpreting accuracy (Sulsky & Balzer, 1988).

In the case of DBR-SIS, rating accuracy is often of most interest due to the nature of the rating data. One important advantage of DBR-SIS is that it allows the rater to make a brief rating or ratings at the end of an observation period (i.e., a "retrospective" rating), rather than multiple ratings over an extended time period. However, because a defining feature of DBR-SIS involves retrospective ratings of student behavior, the data are inevitably influenced to some degree by the rater's subjective view of the behavior (Schlientz et al., 2009). Rater characteristics (e.g., ability level, prior observational experience) have been noted to be one of the three core factors associated with rating accuracy, alongside characteristics of the recording procedure (e.g., complexity of the coding system) and the conditions of the observation (e.g., who and what is observed; Cronbach, Gleser, Nanda, & Rajaratam, 1972). In some cases, individuals may be harsher or more lenient in their overall assessment of behavior, resulting in ratings that are consistently depressed or elevated. A rater may also have difficulty discriminating between different behaviors or individuals, leading to ratings that do not accurately reflect distinctions that may actually be present. In still other cases, individuals may enter a rating situation with preconceived notions of what a particular student acts like or can do, which may unduly influence ratings based on a specific time frame.

Rater characteristics are important to consider in any rating situation, but are particularly relevant to the use of DBR. This is because one of the critical features of DBR involves the ability of persons in the environment (i.e., participant observers) to serve as raters of student behavior, rather than requiring the use of an external observer. Although the use of participant observers (e.g., teachers, students) is certainly a strength in terms of feasibility, these raters are unlikely to have received prior training in behavioral assessment. Therefore, training may be particularly beneficial in order to promote the accuracy of DBR-SIS-derived behavior ratings. Before moving to discuss considerations with regard to DBR-SIS training in particular, we first review the broader literature on training across intervention and assessment contexts.

Use of Training Procedures to Promote Treatment Usage and Assessment Accuracy

Understanding the efficacy of training procedures has long been of interest in schools, given the central role that professional development plays in promoting new knowledge and skills. One of the more well-known models for staff development, first articulated by Joyce and Showers (1980), should look familiar to anyone who has conducted social skills training, in that training is conceptualized as occurring within five major categories: knowledge, modeling, practice, feedback, and coaching (Merrell & Gimpel, 1998; see Table 7.1). Both knowledge and modeling components are implemented by a trainer without the active participation of a trainee. Knowledge consists of the didactic presentation of the theory or rationale for implementing a new strategy or technology, whereas modeling involves actual demonstration of how the strategy or technology is used. Practice and feedback, on the other hand, require audience participation. After receiving initial instruction, trainees practice implementing the strategy on their own and receive feedback regarding their performance within the training setting. Finally, coaching involves the delivery of ongoing feedback in the actual implementation setting (e.g., classroom) as the strategy is enacted for real.

Joyce and Showers (1980) first reviewed over 200 articles relating to best practices in inservice training for teachers. Although their conclusions were complicated by the packaged nature of most training programs and the lack of component

TABLE 7.1. Core Components of Effective Training Procedures

Type	Component	Description
Indirect	Tell (knowledge)	Trainer introduces the strategy or technology and provides the underlying research or theoretical rationale.
	Show (modeling)	Trainer demonstrates how to implement the strategy or technology.
Direct	Do (practice)	Trainer gives trainees time to practice implementing the strategy or technology on their own within the practice setting.
	Feedback	Trainees are provided with feedback regarding their efforts from either the trainer or their colleagues within the practice setting.
	Generalize (coaching)	Trainees implement the newly learned strategy or technology in the actual classroom and receive in-vivo feedback from a trainer or colleague.

analysis across articles, the authors did suggest that evidence for modeling and feedback was the strongest across the reviewed studies. However, these authors noted that indirect methods (or "presentation of theory") also possessed some positive qualities despite difficulties in generalization. The authors concluded that for the majority of inservice teacher trainings, a combination of (1) presentation of theory, (2) modeling or demonstration, (3) practice, (4) feedback, and (5) coaching for application or generalization would likely be most effective. Bush (1984) later found that generalization of skills into actual classroom practice occurred only when training consisted of all five components.

More recently, the role of training has been explored as a way of promoting treatment integrity within the school-based literature. Sterling-Turner, Watson, Wildmon, Watkins, and Little (2001) conceptualized training components as belonging to either indirect or direct procedures. Indirect procedures are those that expose trainees to an intervention or assessment through didactic training or the review of written materials (e.g., lecture). In contrast, direct methods more actively involve trainees by incorporating opportunities for individuals to observe and practice training content (e.g., modeling and practice/feedback). Research has repeatedly shown the use of direct training procedures to result in higher levels of treatment integrity than indirect training (Sterling-Turner et al., 2001; Sterling-Turner, Watson, & Moore, 2002; Watson & Kramer, 1995).

Behavioral Assessment Training

Although the aforementioned studies contributed to our understanding of the role of training with school-based professionals, most dealt with promoting treatment usage. As outlined at the outset of this chapter, promoting rating accuracy is of central importance when considering the use of DBR. There are a handful of studies that have examined the role of training more specifically in promoting rating accuracy.

Spool (1978) was one of the first to review the research on observer training that had been conducted across various fields in the social sciences. Of the 27 studies reviewed, most training programs included a combination of didactic instruction and demonstration, opportunities for practice, and feedback. General conclusions from this literature review suggested that training programs were effective in increasing observer accuracy; however, given that few studies involved a comparison of different training procedures, more nuanced analyses of individual training components could not be conducted. Spool (1978) therefore wrote at the time that "one can only conclude that some training is better than none" (p. 879).

Madle, Neisworth, and Kurtz (1980) examined the effects of training upon 6-point Likert-type ratings of hyperactivity and attention span. Half of the participants were assigned to a brief familiarization condition, in which they received verbal instructions in terms of how to use the assessment and then practiced rating four tapes without feedback. The other half of participants received the same familiarization, but also watched a 20-minute training module and completed exercises in a study guide before they viewed the practice tapes. Results suggested that the more comprehensive training reduced bias in Likert-type ratings of hyperactivity and attention. This examination of the effect of training upon rating quality is particularly noteworthy, given that the ratings were similar in format and scope to what we now refer to as *DBR-SIS*.

Additional research has expanded upon the indirect methods employed by Madle and colleagues (1980) to look at the benefit of direct methods such as practice and feedback, plus frame-of-reference training. Frame-of-reference training utilizes modeling procedures in which participants observe a stimulus and then discuss which aspects of that stimulus are most critical for consideration during assessment. For instance, in a study by McIntyre, Smith, and Hassett (1984), participants were asked to rate the quality of a lecture using a 12-item rating scale, and expert consensus procedures (i.e., having experts conduct ratings individually and then discuss until a single comparison score is agreed upon; Borman, 1977) were utilized to derive a comparison score for determining rating accuracy. Results suggested that trainings involving frame of reference resulted in more accurate ratings than no training or trainings that emphasized common errors made when rating (e.g., halo, leniency, central tendency) and how to avoid them. Additionally, Angkaw, Tran, and Haaga (2006) compared the effectiveness of varying intensities of frame-of-reference training on ratings of anxiety, social skills, and alcohol-related coping skills using an 11-point Likert-type scale. Whereas the moderate training group rated five cases independently during training, the intensive training group

Using Frame-of-Reference Training

In order to provide raters with detailed models of DBR-SIS training procedures, frame-of-reference training is integrated into the DBR-SIS online training module. For example, prior to watching the module's first demonstration clip, raters are instructed to attend to the behavior displayed by a student, "Bob," in relation to the construct of *respect*. As the video plays, a teacher walks around a group of eight desks, instructing the class on the components of a story. We watch as Bob rolls his eyes and makes a "talking" motion with his hand, and at the end of the clip, we are asked how we would rate the degree of respectful behavior exhibited by Bob. Descriptive anchors are provided under each rating to help facilitate interpretation of the scale, and the narrator describes the steps he took to arrive at a final rating of 6 on the respect continuum for Bob's behavior, citing specific examples of behaviors he observed throughout the clip.

compared and discussed their ratings of 10 cases. The authors found that moderate and intensive levels of frame-of-reference training produced comparable estimates of behavior, with limited differences between rater scores.

Taken together, some research suggests that both direct and indirect methods may serve important roles in rater training; however, the resources required to fully deliver both methods may preclude their intensive utilization. Although some treatment integrity research suggests that direct methods may be associated with more positive outcomes (e.g., Sterling-Turner et al., 2001), these methods also require the provision of more sophisticated information in the form of modeling, practice, and feedback.

Online Training

One potential method for delivering individualized and responsive direct training is through the use of web-based modules. Computerized modules are not only capable of depicting various types of information (e.g., text, images, video, sound), but can also utilize decision rules to determine the amount and type of feedback to provide participants. This format may also help ameliorate issues of dosage or exposure (Chafouleas, Kilgus, Riley-Tillman, Jaffery, & Harrison, 2012) by permitting the mass dissemination of information with a significantly reduced resource cost on the part of the trainer.

Given that much of the research on rater training was conducted prior to the widespread adoption of the Internet, it is unsurprising that limited research exists on online rater training. However, within the broader educational research literature, some research has suggested that web-based teacher training may result in outcomes that are comparable to face-to-face training (Russell, Carey, Kleiman, & Venable, 2009). As pointed out by these researchers, however, issues with participants' technical competency and comfort may need to be considered prior to implementation. Additionally, depending on the method of delivery, online trainings may also reduce the opportunity for participants to socialize and collaborate with peers (Brown & Green, 2003). That said, potential benefits of web-based training may include convenience for individual participants and increased availability to larger numbers of individuals (Chafouleas et al., 2015). In addition, web-based training offers potential benefits to the developers of trainings, given the low per-user cost of delivering a web-based module when compared to an in-person training.

Simultaneously, the resource requirements for participants to efficiently benefit from web-based training must be considered. These include computer and Internet access, the ability of participants to save their progress in the event of a program crashing or Internet outage, and the software/hardware requirements expected by the training module. In our own work, we have precorrected for potential problems associated with technology access in schools by having our web development partners develop an offline version of the DBR-SIS module in case access issues occurred. We loaded this offline module onto small, relatively inexpensive "netbook" laptops, which were then provided to teachers. This method allowed us to (1) avoid complications with school-based computer labs during DBR-SIS trainings, as well as (2) provide access to the module for individuals who could not, or did not want to, use their own technology to access the module.

The DBR-SIS Online Training Module

The product of several years of research and development, the DBR-SIS online training module is one method of training educational professionals to use DBR-SIS to rate academically engaged, disruptive, and respectful behavior. As described later in this chapter, preliminary research indicates that the DBR-SIS online training module may improve rating accuracy depending on the type of rating made and comparison score utilized. The module is designed for individuals with varying degrees of previous training in behavioral assessment and observation, including general and special education teachers; school-based mental health professionals (e.g., school psychologists, counselors, social workers); paraprofessionals; and educational and psychological researchers.

The online training module, which is estimated to typically take between 25 and 40 minutes to complete, is located at *www.directbehaviorratings.org/training*. After a brief description of, and instructions on using, the module, users are asked to enter in some brief information about themselves. Users are also encouraged to print out a copy of the DBR-SIS Standard Form, which specifies procedures and operational definitions for rating each behavior.

Upon beginning the module, some initial indirect training is provided on the basics of DBR using a prerecorded slideshow with voice-over narration. The overview begins with a discussion of DBR-SIS: what it is, how it works, and the various ways in which DBR-SIS can be used for the assessment of student behavior. The three behaviors included on the DBR-SIS Standard Form are explained using operational definitions, examples, and nonexamples. Next, both quantitative and qualitative anchors are provided for the rating scale, which are included on the DBR-SIS Standard Form. Quantitative anchors take the form of both (1) the values on the scale from 0 to 10, and (2) estimated percentages of time that a student was engaged in a target behavior. Qualitative anchors are provided in a stepwise fashion. That is, the extremes and midpoint (i.e., 0, 5, 10) of the scale are first labeled as *Never*, *Sometimes*, and *Always* in order to facilitate considerations around scale usage. In order to provide additional opportunities for anchoring of the other points on the DBR-SIS scale, qualitative anchors are then also provided for each group of 2 scale points (although these additional anchors do not appear on the Standard Form). For instance, 3 and 4 are labeled as *a little less than half of the time*, whereas

8 and 9 are labeled as *very frequently*. Finally, additional considerations regarding DBR-SIS usage are provided (e.g., completing the form, making sure ratings of behaviors are independent). After completion of this section, participants move on to the second section of the module.

In the second section of the training module, participants are provided with five opportunities for modeling and frame-of-reference training. In each opportunity, a 1-minute video clip is shown that depicts elementary-age students in a typical classroom setting. Before each clip, participants are (1) instructed to observe a particular target student; (2) shown both a pseudonym for, and an image of, the target student; and (3) told which behavior or behaviors to attend to during the clip for subsequent rating. After viewing the clip, participants view a DBR-SIS scale and are asked to consider how they would rate the student's behavior in the previous clip (see Figure 7.2). After a brief pause, a target rating that was derived from expert-consensus procedures is shown as the correct score for that clip. The relevant operational definition and examples are shown again, along with a voice-over narrative description of how the experts arrived at that specific rating. For example, in the second demonstration clip for disruptive behavior, the narrator explains that "Tyler was frequently disruptive. At first, Tyler was sitting properly in

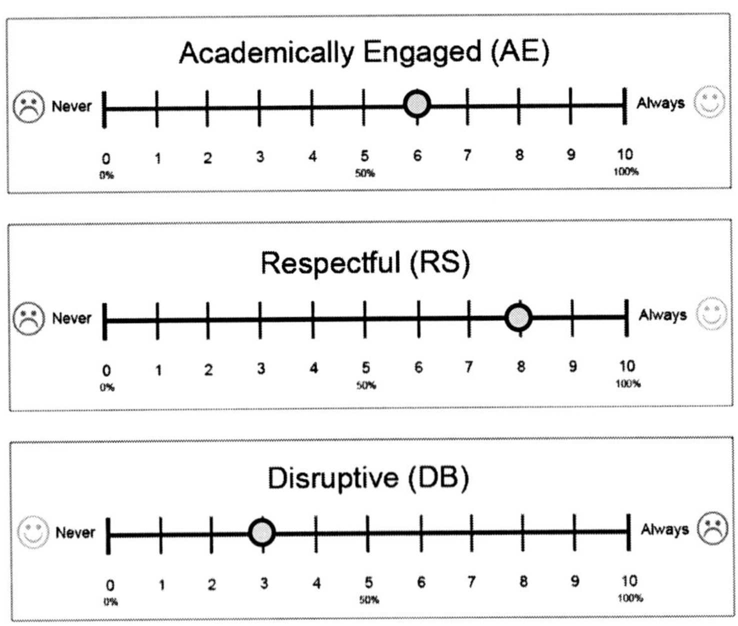

FIGURE 7.2. DBR-SIS Online Training Module Rating Form. The training module can be found at *www.directbehaviorratings.org/training*. Reprinted with permission from Sandra M. Chafouleas.

his seat, passively listening but not disruptive. Soon, he began rummaging through his desk and took out paper to make a paper airplane. This behavior constitutes 'playing with objects,' which he continued to do for the remainder of the clip. In summary, Tyler was observed performing actions that interrupt regular classroom activity 'very frequently' throughout most of the clip. This translates to a rating of 9" (see Figure 7.3). After participating in four such examples of rating individual student behavior, all three target behaviors are rated simultaneously in a fifth and final example.

After this modeling and frame-of-reference training, participants engage in practice and feedback in the final section of the training module. At a minimum, practice and feedback consist of participant ratings of all three target behaviors on the Standard Form. For low- (i.e., 0–2) and high-level (i.e., 8–10) behaviors, ratings are considered accurate if they are within 1 point of the correct rating; however, ratings of medium-level (i.e., 3–7) behaviors are considered accurate if they are within

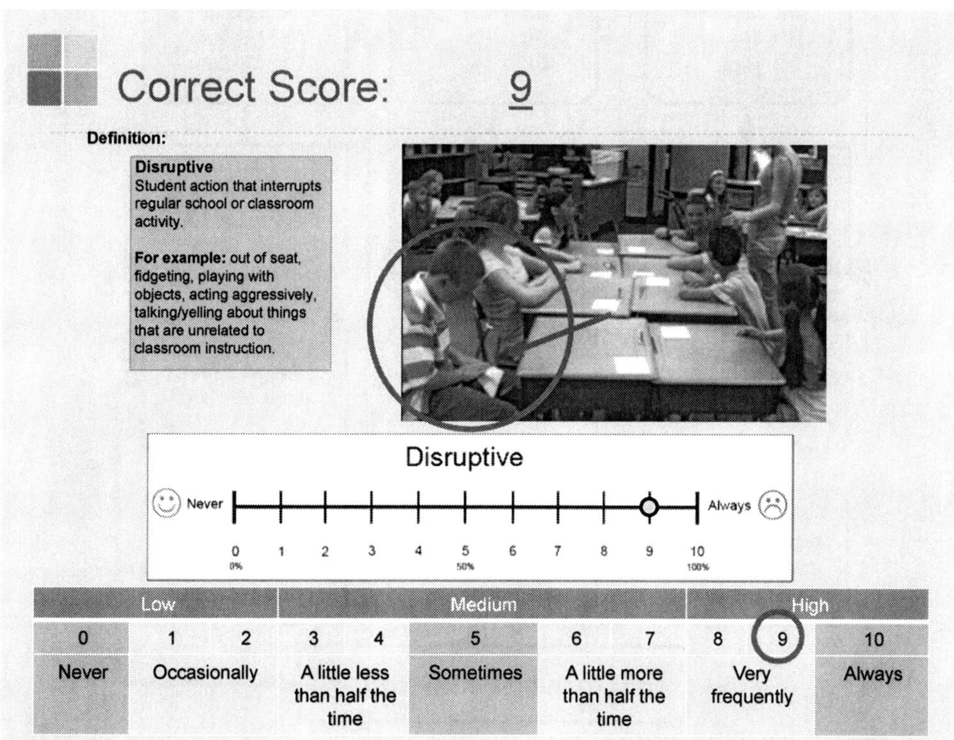

FIGURE 7.3. Provision of expert consensus rating in DBR-SIS Online Training Module. The training module is available at *www.directbehaviorratings.org/training*. Reprinted with permission from Sandra M. Chafouleas.

2 points of the correct rating. The determination of appropriate accuracy criteria was made based upon prior DBR-SIS training research (Chafouleas, Jaffery, et al., 2013; Chafouleas, Kilgus, et al., 2012). Participants who are not accurate in each of their initial ratings view and rate at most two additional practice clips per behavior, with additional practice individualized based upon a participant's responses as demonstrated in Figure 7.4. Upon finishing the module, a certificate in PDF format is emailed to the participant as a record of module completion.

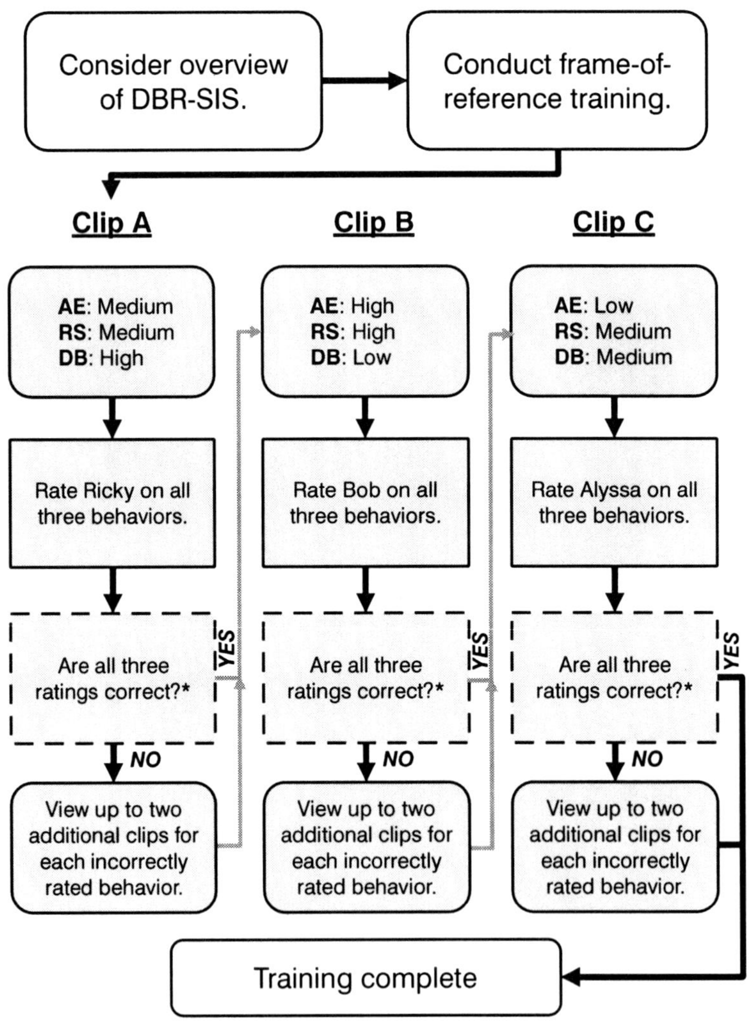

FIGURE 7.4. DBR-SIS Online Training Module component flowchart. *Ratings must be within 1 point of low (0–2) and high (8–10) comparison scores to be considered correct. Ratings must be within 2 points of medium (3–7) comparison scores to be considered correct. Levels of behavior shown here for Clips A, B, and C are for demonstration purposes only. Adapted from Chafouleas, Riley-Tillman, Jaffery, Miller, and Harrison (2014).

Research in DBR-SIS Training to Improve Rater Accuracy

The ability to produce accurate, reliable, and valid data is a critical feature of any assessment tool. As previously discussed, the literature suggests that rater training that includes components of modeling, practice, and feedback can improve rater accuracy. Particularly because DBR-SIS requires raters to estimate the degree to which a student engaged in a behavior (e.g., academically engaged, respectful, disruptive) during a specified observation period, each rating is influenced by a rater's subjective perception (Schlientz et al., 2009). As such, strategies to increase objectivity and accuracy are particularly important to implement when using DBR, given that ratings are typically used to inform educational decision making. In turn, systematic evaluations of individual rater training have been conducted to gauge the influence of training on the accuracy of DBR-SIS data (see Table 7.2).

In a study designed to examine the concurrent validity between DBR and direct observation data, Chafouleas et al. (2005) assigned teachers to one of two training conditions. In the control condition, each teacher received a one-on-one

TABLE 7.2. Brief Summary of Findings from DBR-SIS Training Research

Study	Participants	Key finding
Chafouleas et al. (2005)	Teachers	No significant differences in rating accuracy based on practice and feedback when rating written vignettes.
Schlientz et al. (2009)	Undergraduates	Training that included practice and feedback improved the accuracy of DBR-SIS ratings more than a brief familiarization.
LeBel, Kilgus, et al. (2010)	Teachers	Only a moderate level of training is needed to prepare teachers to accurately assess student behavior using DBR-SIS.
Chafouleas et al. (2012)	Undergraduates	A standard training package resulted in improvements in rater accuracy; a more extensive package may not always result in additional improvements.
Harrison et al. (2014)	Undergraduates	Behaviors occurring at low or high rates are rated more accurately than behaviors occurring at medium rates. Additional rater training did not always result in improvements in accuracy above and beyond brief familiarization.
Chafouleas et al. (2015)	Undergraduates	Findings support the use of a web-based model for improving rater accuracy.

explanation of what DBR was, how it should be completed, and how the target behaviors were defined. Participants in the training condition were also asked to read two or more vignettes, provide their ratings, and then these ratings were compared with predetermined consensus scores. No significant differences were identified in rating accuracy between the two conditions, suggesting that the rating practice based on written vignettes did not have a significant influence.

In the first study to explicitly investigate the effect of training on rater accuracy using DBR-SIS, Schlientz et al. (2009) divided undergraduate participants into two groups that were equated for time (both lasting approximately 30 minutes). Participants in the DBR training condition listened to a PowerPoint presentation that explained the target behaviors, and then they received opportunities for practice and feedback while viewing videotaped segments. Although participants in the comparison condition received a brief familiarization to the DBR forms, they did not receive opportunities for practice and feedback. Results suggested that participants who received the DBR training produced more accurate ratings than those in the brief familiarization condition. Additionally, the authors noted that there was less variability in the ratings completed by the participants that received direct training. Schlientz et al. (2009) argued that practice and feedback may have allowed raters to set anchors, which, in turn, improved the accuracy of the ratings. Given that this was a preliminary investigation involving undergraduate participants, however, additional research was needed to examine the effect of training on the accuracy of intended users (i.e., teachers).

LeBel et al. (2010) randomly assigned 53 middle and high school teachers to one of three training conditions. In the no-training condition, participants received general instructions to complete the DBR after watching three video clips; however, no additional information was provided. The indirect training condition consisted of watching an instructional DVD and then practicing rating the video clips with standardized feedback provided. Procedures in the direct training condition were identical to those in the indirect condition; however, participants also had the opportunity to discuss their ratings and receive individualized feedback. Interestingly, results suggested that training only significantly influenced accuracy when rating academic engagement (LeBel et al., 2010). That is, there were few differences between trained and untrained teachers' ratings of disruptive behavior.

These initial studies yielded important but inconsistent information in regard to training recommendations for DBR. Taken together, preliminary investigations suggest that practice and feedback using videotaped (rather than written) examples may be important elements in promoting rating accuracy (Chafouleas et al., 2005; Schlientz et al., 2009); however, the provision of standardized feedback may be sufficient to prepare teachers to assess student behavior (LeBel et al., 2010). It is important to note, however, that these studies differed both in terms of the training components included and the target behaviors assessed (Chafouleas, Kilgus, et al., 2012). Thus, it may be necessary to systematically evaluate differences in rating accuracy that result when different training package variations are used.

Chafouleas, Kilgus, et al. (2012) sought to directly compare the effects of frame-of-reference and rater error training on the accuracy of DBR ratings. As discussed previously, *frame-of-reference training* refers to an examination of the targets and a brief discussion of aspects of the behavior that are relevant to evaluation, whereas *rater error training* refers to the provision of information related to common forms of rater error. In addition, the authors examined the effect of *exposure*, or the dosage of overall training received. Results indicated that training did result in improved accuracy, but the most comprehensive package (including frame-of-reference training, rater error training, and longer exposure) did not always result in greater accuracy than a standard training procedure including modeling, practice, and feedback. That is, more comprehensive training resulted in greater accuracy when rating medium and high rates of disruptive behavior, but showed no improvement over a standard when rating low rates of academic engagement and disruptive behavior. Thus, results of this study further supported findings using direct training with undergraduates (Schlientz et al., 2009) and indirect training with teachers (LeBel et al., 2010), in that a feasible level of training resulted in relevant improvements in accuracy.

Given initial findings that the effects of training were moderated by the rate of behavior (i.e., high, medium, or low), this issue was further explored by Harrison, Riley-Tillman, and Chafouleas (2014) using undergraduate participants. Accuracy was found to vary substantially depending on the rate at which academic engagement, compliance, and disruption occurred. A greater degree of accuracy was found when target behaviors were demonstrated at either low (< 33% of the time) or high (> 67% of the time) rates, whereas accuracy was significantly lower for those behaviors occurring at medium rates. Furthermore, this investigation supported earlier findings (e.g., LeBel et al., 2010), in that rater training involving practice and feedback did not enhance the accuracy of ratings of compliance (respectful) and academic engagement above and beyond brief familiarization training. Results did indicate, however, that participants receiving direct training rated disruptive behavior more accurately (Schlientz et al., 2009; Chafouleas, Kilgus, et al., 2012). Based on the accumulated research, a web-based training module for using DBR that includes brief familiarization, modeling with frame-of-reference training, and multiple opportunities to practice and receive immediate feedback was developed (Chafouleas et al., 2015). Generally, preliminary findings support the utility of the web-based module for improving accuracy, although statistically significant improvements in accuracy were found only for high rates of academic engagement as well as high and medium rates of respectful behavior. These findings support earlier work (Chafouleas, Kilgus, et al., 2012) suggesting that the accuracy of ratings depends on the target behavior and the rate at which it is displayed.

Throughout this line of inquiry, a few themes have emerged. First, it appears that a moderate, feasible level of training is sufficient to improve the accuracy of DBR ratings (Schlientz et al., 2009; LeBel et al., 2010, Chafouleas, Kilgus et al., 2012; Harrison et al., 2014; Chafouleas et al., 2015). In other words, lengthening the time or amount of training does not necessarily improve accuracy under universal conditions. Second, the evidence suggests that medium rates of behavior are more difficult to rate accurately (Harrison et al., 2014). More comprehensive training, specifically the inclusion of frame-of-reference training and increasing exposure, resulted in some improvements for difficult-to-rate target behaviors, such as medium rates of disruptive (Chafouleas, Kilgus, et al., 2012) and respectful (Chafouleas et al., 2015) behavior; however, similar results were not found for other target behaviors occurring at various rates. As such, it is necessary to weigh feasibility and efficient use of resources versus the type of training package that could produce the most accurate ratings in most settings. This sentiment frames support for the use of the web-based training module, although further investigation is needed to more fully explore its effect on the accuracy of teacher-produced DBR ratings.

Conclusions

Accuracy, or the degree to which ratings reflect actual levels of behavior, is a key component of the quality of data derived from DBR-SIS. Numerous training components have been hypothesized to increase rater accuracy, including the provision of information about the rating procedure (i.e., indirect methods) and opportunities for modeling, practice, and feedback (i.e., direct methods). The blueprint provided in Table 7.3 outlines steps that should be taken in order to select and prepare raters to use DBR regardless of the format of training employed. However, training delivered over the Internet may provide a particularly unique and efficient way to train individuals on how to use behavioral assessment methods. This chapter described an online training module for assessment with DBR-SIS that combines indirect and direct training methods and utilizes video, audio, and decision-making rules to provide targeted feedback and practice to trainees.

The research reviewed in this chapter focused mainly on teacher raters, with results suggesting that the use of indirect and direct components, particularly frame-of-reference training, may increase the accuracy of DBR-SIS-derived ratings of behavior. However, there is limited knowledge about the design and effectiveness of DBR-SIS training for other raters, including students themselves. Furthermore, although this chapter focused on the use of training to increase DBR-SIS rating accuracy within an assessment context, the role of training in promoting implementation of DBR interventions has received less emphasis. In one preliminary study,

TABLE 7.3. Blueprint for Selecting and Preparing Raters to Use DBR

- ☐ 1. Determine appropriate rater.

  The most appropriate rater is often the head teacher of the target classroom; however, ratings may also be conducted by support staff or the student herself.

- ☐ 2. Familiarize rater with requirements for DBR use.

  Raters should receive instruction regarding what the target behaviors are (e.g., definition, examples, non-examples) and how the scale should be used.

- ☐ 3. Model rating procedures and provide opportunities for practice and feedback.

  Raters should first receive a demonstration of how to carry out the assessment procedures. Once the procedures are clarified, raters should practice conducting ratings on their own and receive feedback regarding their accuracy within the training setting.

- ☐ 4. Determine if additional training is needed.

  If rating accuracy during initial training is found to be low, additional instruction and practice may be necessary.

- ☐ 5. Begin using DBR.

  Once rating accuracy is found to be sufficient in the training setting, raters may begin implementing DBR in the target setting. Ongoing accuracy checks may be employed to guard against rater drift.

teachers reported a greater likelihood of adoption if training in a DRC intervention was provided by a respected colleague than by a mental health professional in the school building (Holdaway & Owens, 2015); however, research investigating the relationship between training and actual implementation is needed. Implementation science is a large and varied field, and the literature may benefit from additional research regarding training to improve fidelity of implementation across all key aspects of DBR-SIS.

PART III

DBR Applications

Intervention

CHAPTER 8

Use of DBR in Targeted Intervention

Leanne S. Hawken, Kaitlin Bundock, Gregory A. Fabiano, and Amy M. Briesch

Contemporary service delivery systems involve provision of a continuum of academic and behavior supports designed to meet the needs of all students (National Center on Response to Intervention, 2010). At the universal level, all students (ideally) receive high-quality core instruction. In the realm of behavior, this may include the explicit teaching of schoolwide expectations, implementation of evidence-based classroom management strategies, and use of social–emotional learning curricula across all classrooms. Although it is expected that this level of behavior support will prevent many problems from developing or worsening, students who do not respond to universal prevention may benefit from targeted interventions. Interventions at this level are targeted toward approximately 10–15% of the student population who are at risk for developing severe problem behavior due to their (1) poor peer social skills, (2) low academic achievement, (3) poor organizational or time management skills, and/or (4) less than optimal home environments (Crone et al., 2010; Hawken, Adolphson, MacLeod, & Schumann, 2009; Lewis & Sugai, 1999). These students typically require additional teaching, practice, and feedback in order to be successful (Fairbanks, Sugai, Guardino, & Lathrup, 2007; Kincaid, 2007; Lee, Sugai, & Horner, 1999). In contrast, students who are engaging in extremely disruptive, violent, or aggressive behavior need more support than targeted interventions can provide and thus would likely benefit from intensive, individualized interventions (Hawken et al., 2009; see Chapter 9 for more information on individualizing interventions).

There are several key features that distinguish targeted interventions (Crone et al., 2010; OSEP, n.d.). First, in order to be efficient, targeted interventions need to be implemented similarly across students. This consistency allows teachers to build fluency and practice in implementing the intervention. Having interventions that follow a standardized protocol and/or are scripted (e.g., by providing teachers with step-by-step instructions on how to implement the intervention) increases the likelihood that the interventions will be implemented with fidelity. Second, to prevent problem behavior, students should be able to access targeted interventions quickly, usually in less than a week. Once a student is identified through universal screening or teacher referral, it should not be necessary to conduct additional lengthy assessments prior to giving students access to the intervention. Third, targeted interventions should supplement, rather than substitute for, universal supports. Within a schoolwide positive behavior supports (SWPBS) model, for example, targeted interventions can be seen as a way to provide students with additional practice with and feedback on the schoolwide expectations that have been taught universally. Fourth, targeted interventions should be flexible to allow for modification based on functional assessment data if the intervention is not working. For example, some students engage in problem behavior to gain peer attention, and a targeted intervention should be modifiable to support this function. Alternatively, for those students who are engaging in a problem behavior to escape or avoid a demand, there must be a cache of interventions available to address this function as well. Finally, data must be collected and analyzed on a frequent basis to measure student response to the intervention. For example, response to intervention may be measured by tracking the percentage of points students earn on a daily progress report (DPR), the number of office discipline referrals (ODRs) earned, or the amount of work completed.

There are many different types of targeted behavioral interventions (e.g., social skills instruction, problem-solving training); however, this chapter focuses specifically on two interventions that involve the regular provision of behavioral feedback to students using DBR-like tools: check-in/check-out (CICO) and the daily report card (DRC). The underlying premise of DBR-like tools is that a teacher rates a student's behavior at least once a day, and this information is shared with both the student and his or her family (Chafouleas et al., 2002). It is important to note that for both the CICO intervention and the DRC intervention, the DBR is only one component; each intervention incorporates several other features key to implementation. The remainder of this chapter describes the critical features and implementation guidelines of CICO and DRC. Whereas CICO is a schoolwide intervention designed to maximize feasibility and efficiency through use of the same materials across multiple students, the DRC may be individualized, more or less, depending on the level of student need.

Check-In/Check-Out

What Is CICO?

CICO is a targeted intervention that is structured around a daily check-in and check-out system (CICO is also referred to in the literature as the *behavior education program* [BEP]). Schools that implement CICO should have a well-established Tier 1 positive behavior support system that includes (1) defining and teaching behavioral expectations to all students in all settings; (2) providing reinforcement for following expectations; (3) establishing a hierarchy of consequences for students who do not follow expectations; and (4) maintaining a team in the school who examines data for decision making. CICO builds on schoolwide expectations by providing students with more frequent feedback on classroom social behavior as well as more frequent reinforcement for demonstrating appropriate behavior.

Students begin the school day by checking in with the CICO coordinator. During check-in, the CICO coordinator ensures that students have school supplies (e.g., paper, pencil, notebook) and provides each student with a DPR. The DPR lists the behavioral expectations (which are aligned with the schoolwide expectations) for the student and provides space for the student's teacher(s) to rate how well these expectations were met throughout the day. The purpose of morning check-in is to provide a positive contact between the student and an adult, allow an opportunity for the coordinator to prompt the student to work on specific goals for the day (e.g., "Remember that yesterday you had a hard time sitting in your seat, so what are you going to do today to work on that?"), and to prevent problem behavior by ensuring students have the necessary materials for the school day to be successful in class.

Students then take the DPR with them throughout the school day. At predetermined points (e.g., transition periods at the elementary level, end of each period at the secondary level), students meet with their teacher for a brief feedback session. Each teacher feedback session is seen as a quick teaching opportunity, in which behavioral expectations can be reviewed and reinforced. If students are following expectations, they are given feedback about how they met the expectations (e.g., behaviors they engaged in that demonstrated "being respectful"), receive praise, and earn higher scores on their DPRs. If students are not following expectations, they are given corrective feedback by the teacher, an opportunity to explain how to improve their behavior, and an opportunity to practice following the expectation during the next marking period.

At the end of the day, students then return to meet with their CICO coordinator to review their overall performance for that day (i.e., check-out). At check-out, the CICO coordinator calculates each student's points earned for the day, provides praise and encouragement, and gives the student a small reward such as a sticker or small snack based on his or her performance. A copy of the DPR is given to the student to take home for parent signature. Members of the Behavior Support Team then meet weekly or every 2 weeks to evaluate student progress and determine if the program needs to be modified, or if students are ready to transition from CICO to a self-monitoring program (Crone et al., 2010; see Chapter 10 for more information on self-management interventions).

Students who benefit from CICO typically engage in mild acting-out behavior (e.g., talking out, talking back, off task) in the classroom throughout the day. If students only demonstrate problem behavior during one or two periods of the day or during unstructured times (e.g., recess), other targeted interventions should be considered to best support these students. In addition, students who benefit from CICO are those who are just beginning to engage in problem behavior at school and whose behavior is not severe or extreme, such as hitting a peer or starting fires. Those students with more pronounced behavioral needs should be considered for individualized intervention (see Chapter 9).

CICO is designed to be an efficient way to intervene simultaneously with multiple students who have not responded to universal behavior supports. As such, the materials and procedures should be developed with group applicability in mind. In this section, we highlight the considerations that must be made in implementing CICO with a targeted group of at-risk students (see Table 8.1 for the CICO intervention blueprint).

Step 1: Determine with Whom CICO Will Be Used

Schools use many different methods to identify students who may be appropriate for CICO. First, for schools that have a well-defined ODR system, the number of ODRs received can be used to trigger the need for CICO. Sugai, Sprague, Horner, and Walker (2000) have recommended guidelines for using ODRs to make data-based decisions regarding necessary levels of support including: (1) students who receive zero to one ODR per year are likely adequately supported by universal interventions; (2) students receiving two to five ODRs potentially require targeted interventions; and (3) students who receive six or more ODRs may require targeted interventions. These recommendations are only guidelines, however, and schools should adapt them to fit the context of their school population.

Second, many schools rely on teacher referral as a method for identifying students who would be appropriate for CICO (Crone et al., 2010). In these cases, a teacher would refer the student to a team in the school that is responsible for providing behavior support. Teacher referral can be an important supplement to ODR data, as often the students who are just starting to act out may have problem behavior in the classroom that is not severe enough to warrant an ODR.

TABLE 8.1. Steps in Implementing the CICO Intervention

☐ 1. Determine with whom CICO will be used.

Different methods can be used to identify students for participation in CICO, including review of ODR data, teacher referral, and/or universal screening.

☐ 2. Determine who will serve as the CICO coordinator.

An effective CICO coordinator is someone who can commit to implementing the intervention 10–15 hours per week, the students enjoy meeting with, and is experienced in interacting with multiple students and tasks at one time.

☐ 3. Determine when ratings will occur.

Depending on the nature of the students' schedules, rating may occur during transitions (e.g., end of morning meeting), at the end of a class period (e.g., at the end of math class), or based upon a longer block of time (e.g., 9:00 A.M. to morning recess).

☐ 4. Create the daily progress report.

The DPR lists the behavioral expectations for the student, the scale on which expectations will be rated (e.g., 0–2 Likert scale), and the times of day when ratings will occur.

☐ 5. Conduct training.

Training for the CICO coordinator, teachers, and students' parents should focus on the procedural elements of the intervention, including how to talk to each student about obtained ratings. (Note: Student training should not occur until after baseline data have been collected.)

☐ 6. Collect baseline data.

Teachers should complete the DPR in the absence of intervention in order to obtain an estimate of current behavior.

☐ 7. Establish daily point goals and identify reinforcers.

The criterion for reinforcement (i.e., percentage of points needed) can be set for all students or individualized in relation to baseline data. It is important to determine which potential rewards (e.g., verbal, social, edible, material, or activity-based) the student finds most reinforcing.

☐ 8. Train the student, implement the intervention, and monitor progress.

Implementation of CICO begins after training the student in intervention procedures. DPR data should be entered into a database daily, with progress reviewed at least once every 2 weeks. Once students have consistently met their goals, they may enter a self-monitoring phase.

Third, some schools utilize more formal screening instruments to identify students for the CICO intervention. The Systematic Screening for Behavior Disorders (SSBD; Walker & Severson, 1992) is one such screening measure used during the elementary grades to identify students likely to be engaging in externalizing (i.e., aggression, acting-out, noncompliance) or internalizing (i.e., depression, anxiety, withdrawal) behaviors (Walker, Cheney, Stage, & Blum, 2005). The SSBD utilizes a three-stage process to identify potentially at-risk students. The first stage involves teacher nomination of students with behavioral characteristics predictive of school failure. Students identified in the first stage are then further screened using a series of rating scale items to determine behavioral severity and the form of the problem behavior. In the final stage, students are systematically observed in the classroom and on the playground to determine their performance in classroom and social situations. Those students identified through systematic screening (e.g., passing through multiple assessment gates) may then be prioritized for participation in CICO.

Step 2: Determine Who Will Serve as the CICO Coordinator

One of the key determinants of a successful CICO intervention is consistency. As such, it is important to select a CICO coordinator whose schedule allows him or her to check in and out with the students each day. The school principal, for example, would not be the ideal CICO coordinator because his or her ability to meet with students may be determined by the number of unexpected problems or crises that arise in a given day. More than one person can check students in and out, but it is critical that the person is reliable, works in the school every day, and understands factors that influence problem behavior. Due to the flexibility needed and the time commitment involved (i.e., 10–15 hours a week implementing the intervention), this role is often filled by a paraprofessional. However, the coordinator can be anyone from the administrative assistant in the front office to the school librarian. Regardless of role, the person who checks the students in and out should be positive and someone the students like, can bond with, and look forward to seeing on a daily basis. If students find meeting with the coordinator to be aversive, the intervention will likely be unsuccessful. Furthermore, the CICO coordinator needs to be experienced at interacting with multiple students and tasks at a time, given that multiple students will typically check in and out before and after school.

Step 3: Determine When Ratings Will Occur

Although a critical component of CICO is the provision of behavioral feedback at multiple points throughout the day, rating frequency must be determined locally in consideration of the students' schedules. In elementary school, the marking periods are typically related to natural breaks in the school day. For example, ratings may be conducted during transitions based upon a particular activity or instructional block (e.g., end of morning meeting, end of literacy instruction) or may be based upon a longer period of time (e.g., from 9:00 A.M. to morning recess). In middle and high school settings, on the other hand, students typically receive feedback from each teacher after each period of the day.

Step 4: Create the DPR

The DPR is a specific type of DBR that is used to rate how well students met behavioral expectations. Typically, each row of the DPR corresponds with an assessment target (e.g., be respectful, be responsible) and each column represents a different rating occasion (e.g., math, language arts). Although individualized expectations may be developed for a particular student, schools are encouraged to put their schoolwide expectations on the DPR, as these are the expectations that all faculty and staff have agreed upon and taught. In addition, using the schoolwide expectations allows for increased efficiency because the same materials can be used with all students. Typically, ratings are conducted using a 3-point scale, wherein a score of 1 indicates that the student did not meet expectations, a score of 2 indicates that the student partially met expectations, and a score of 3 indicates that the student fully met expectations. It is also important that the DPR includes space for (1) the teacher to initial that ratings were conducted, (2) the parent to sign that the DPR was received, and (3) the CICO coordinator to total the number of points earned each day. A sample DPR that could be used in a middle school setting is presented in Figure 8.1.

Step 5: Conduct Training

Once the materials have been developed, training is needed for the CICO coordinator, teachers, and students' parents. The procedural elements of the intervention (e.g., how and when the DPR will be completed, how reinforcement will be earned) should be reviewed with all parties involved. The training for the CICO coordinator should include the rationale behind CICO, how to check students in and out, how to provide positive comments and corrective feedback to students, how to train students to participate in the intervention, how to select and distribute reinforcers, and how to communicate effectively with teachers and parents.

Training should be provided to all school personnel—not just those with students participating in CICO—to ensure that all teachers are aware of how students are identified for the intervention and what their role is if one of their students participates in the intervention in the future. Staff training should focus on how students are identified for CICO support, as well as how to provide feedback to

A-Day B-Day

Name: ______________________________ Date: ______________

Teachers: Please indicate YES (2), So-So (1), or No (0) regarding the student's achievement for the following goals:

Goals	Period 1	Period 2	Period 3	Period 4	Period 5
Be respectful	2 1 0	2 1 0	2 1 0	2 1 0	2 1 0
Be responsible	2 1 0	2 1 0	2 1 0	2 1 0	2 1 0
Keep hands and feet to self	2 1 0	2 1 0	2 1 0	2 1 0	2 1 0
Follow directions	2 1 0	2 1 0	2 1 0	2 1 0	2 1 0
Be there—be ready	2 1 0	2 1 0	2 1 0	2 1 0	2 1 0
TOTAL POINTS					
TEACHER INITIALS					

CICO Daily Goal /50 CICO Daily Score /50

In training _____ CICO Member _______ ______________________________
Student signature

FIGURE 8.1. Sample of daily progress report.

students. It is important, for example, for feedback to be brief and specific. Students should know why they received the score that they did and should understand what they need to do differently if a low score was received. Additionally, staff training should emphasize that teachers need to provide positive comments on the DPR and to avoid writing negative comments. One of the main goals of CICO is to provide positive contact with adults. As such, it is important that teachers use the card to provide positive feedback, rather than writing comments to vent their frustration. For example, a positive comment that provides corrective feedback could be, "Nice job keeping your hands and feet to yourself today! Tomorrow, let's work harder on being respectful to your peers by saying only kind words," instead of, "James was horrible today! He would not stop saying rude things to his classmates!" Parent training should focus on how to review the DPR with their child, including providing positive verbal feedback for achieved goals. For more detailed information regarding training procedures, please see Crone et al. (2010).

Step 6: Collect Baseline Data

In order to judge whether CICO was effective, it is first necessary to collect baseline data. Teachers should be instructed to complete the DPR as they would during intervention; however, data at this stage are not shared with students, and students do not check in or out with the CICO coordinator. The number of data points needed depends on the nature of the behavior. If the baseline data are highly stable (i.e., the student earns a similar number of points on the DPR each day), three data points may be sufficient to provide a clear picture of baseline functioning. If data are highly variable, however, baseline data collection should continue until it is possible to make a confident prediction as to what behavior would look like if no changes were made to the status quo.

Step 7: Establish Daily Point Goals and Identify Reinforcers

The next step is to determine the criterion for receiving reinforcement. A daily point goal specifies the number, or percentage, of points that a student must receive on his or her DPR to earn a predetermined reward. Although one goal may be established for all students participating in CICO in order to maximize feasibility (e.g., 80–85% of total points), it is important that the goal be challenging yet attainable. That is, if goals are set too high and exceed the student's level of capability, frustration may quickly set in, leading to disengagement in the program. Baseline data may therefore be used to determine an individual level of performance that would be challenging yet attainable.

At this stage, the team should also identify appropriate reinforcers. Students may receive verbal praise for meeting expectations throughout the day as well as for meeting their goal at the end of the day (e.g., "Awesome job today of meeting the East Street expectations! You received perfect ratings for following directions and keeping your hands and feet to yourself!"). Other possibilities, however, include social (e.g., spending time with a friend or adult), edible (e.g., snack), material (e.g., pencil, sticker), or activity (e.g., computer time) reinforcers. Regardless of the type of reinforcement used, it is important to ensure that the student finds the reward to be adequately reinforcing. For example, although many students in the early elementary grades enjoy receiving stickers, not all students will find stickers motivating. Reinforcement surveys can be used at the outset of intervention to identify those tangibles or activities that a student enjoys, or students can be allowed to choose from several available options on a daily basis.

Step 8: Train the Student, Implement the Intervention, and Monitor Progress

The final step before beginning the intervention involves training the student in the intervention procedures as well as how to appropriately accept feedback. The CICO coordinator is typically responsible for training the student. To prevent the student from feeling like CICO is a punishment, this person should explain what CICO is and why it might help the student. Student training should also involve role plays of examples and nonexamples of how to receive feedback during check-out. Throughout the CICO intervention, the CICO coordinator should enter the DPR data into a database daily for summarization and monitoring (see Figure 8.2). The team should meet at least once every 2 weeks to review individual student data and determine whether progress has been made (see Chapter 11 for more information

Coordinator: ______________________________

Week of: ______________________________

Student	Daily percentage of points earned					Weekly average
	Monday	Tuesday	Wednesday	Thursday	Friday	

FIGURE 8.2. CICO weekly summary sheet.

on data-based decision making). Once students are consistently meeting their goals, they can be entered into a self-monitoring phase, in which each student rates his or her own behavior and compares these ratings to those the teacher makes (see Crone et al., 2010, for more information on fading CICO).

Research on CICO

A recent review found that CICO, and interventions closely related to CICO, are the most commonly researched targeted interventions within the context of SWPBS (Bruhn, Lane, & Hirsch, 2014). Furthermore, CICO has been found to effectively decrease observed problem behavior, to reduce ODRs, to improve academic engagement or work completion, and to improve students' percentage of DPR points in the majority of studies (Hawken et al., 2014). Most of the studies on CICO have been conducted in elementary and middle school settings (Hawken et al., 2014); however, evidence is now being collected to support the use of CICO with high school students. Of the studies included in their review, Hawken et al. (2014) evaluated two studies conducted at the high school level, eight at the middle school level, and 10 at the elementary school level. The results of their review suggest that CICO is slightly more effective at the elementary than the secondary level, but these results should be interpreted cautiously, due to high levels of variability in the data. Across 10 studies conducted at the secondary level, approximately 50% of the 32 participants were responsive to the intervention. An additional 13% of participants were somewhat responsive to the intervention (Hawken et al., 2014).

The Daily Report Card

What Is the DRC?

DRCs have long been used effectively to treat children with challenging behaviors, monitor outcomes, and open a daily line of communication between teachers and each child's parent(s) (DuPaul & Eckert, 1997; Kelley, 1990; O'Leary & Pelham, 1978; Pelham et al., 2005; Pelham, Wheeler, & Chronis, 1998; Vannest et al., 2010; Volpe & Fabiano, 2013). It is a procedure aligned with a long tradition of using contingency management with children who display disruptive behavior in general education (e.g., Hops & Walker, 1988) and special education settings (Reid, Maag, Vasa, & Wright, 1994; Schnoes, Reid, Wagner, & Marder, 2006; Vannest et al., 2010). A DRC is first created for each participating student, targeting the individualized problem behaviors believed to be of greatest concern. Periodically throughout the day, the classroom teacher rates the student's behavior using the DRC and shares this information with the student. Teachers provide specific, positive feedback when performance goals are met and help the student problem-solve what changes could be made when performance falls short of the goal. At the end of the day, the card is sent home with the student so that the parent can review the child's daily performance. Home-based reinforcement is used in order to motivate students to achieve their daily goals.

The DRC is similar to CICO in that it involves (1) daily recording of behavior using a DBR-multi-item scale (DBR-MIS), (2) provision of behavioral feedback to the student, (3) reinforcement based on goal attainment, and (4) daily home–school communication about the targeted behaviors. One key difference, however, is that the DRC has an idiographic focus. This means that rather than rating all students on the same behavioral expectations, DRC goals are individually developed relevant to the targeted case. In addition, parents serve a key role in implementation of the DRC, as a student's performance during the school day is reinforced at home. In this way, parents are generally able to provide rewards that are more motivating than those typically available in the school context, and the child becomes accountable at home for behaviors exhibited during the school day. There are many individualized considerations that must be made in the development of the DRC. Next, we outline the steps involved in developing and subsequently using the DRC as both an intervention and progress monitoring tool (see Table 8.2 for the DRC blueprint).

Step 1: Identify and Define Target Behaviors

The first step in creating a DRC involves the identification of appropriate target behaviors. Our goal at this stage is to identify those behaviors that result in the greatest level of impairment to the student's functioning on a daily basis. Depending on the age and developmental level of the students, somewhere between three and eight target behaviors may be included on the card (Center for Children & Families, n.d.). Although DRCs can be used to assess a wide range of observable problem behaviors, one line of research has focused on specifically linking DRC items to IEP goals (e.g., Fabiano et al., 2010). In this way, the selection of targets was made more student-driven (i.e., based on identified idiographic needs) rather than educator-driven (i.e., selecting behaviors based on teacher perceptions). Regardless of how the target behaviors are selected, however, it is essential that each be operationally defined in observable, measurable terms to ensure that the individual responsible for conducting the ratings can reliably assess each target behavior. It is also important to use terminology that is developmentally appropriate, given that ratings will be shared with the student as part of the intervention. For example, a teacher may feel that noncompliance is an important target behavior for a 6-year-old student; however, labeling this behavior as "arguing" or "listening to directions" would put the behavior in terms that the student would be more likely to understand.

TABLE 8.2. Steps in Implementing the DRC Intervention

☐ 1. Identify and define target behaviors.

Identify between three and eight target behaviors that result in the greatest impairment to the student's functioning on a daily basis. Operationally define the behaviors and ensure that language is developmentally appropriate for the student.

☐ 2. Determine when ratings will occur and who will conduct them.

Because ratings also serve as behavioral feedback to the student, ensure that they occur throughout the day. Weigh both behavioral needs of the student and feasibility for the teacher in determining optimal frequency.

☐ 3. Determine the appropriate dimension of behavior.

Ratings may simply indicate whether a behavior occurred or not (i.e., yes/no) or may focus on a specific dimension of behavior (e.g., frequency, latency, duration).

☐ 4. Create DRC items.

Each DRC item should specify the criteria for success. Dichotomous items can be used to judge (a) if a behavior occurred at all or (b) if an established goal was met. Creation of a DRC goal should be informed by an estimate of the current level of behavior.

☐ 5. Conduct training.

Both teacher and parent training should focus on understanding the target behavior, recording procedures, and intervention procedures. An additional goal of parent training should be the establishment of a home-based reward system. Student training is also necessary to ensure understanding of intervention purpose and procedures. (Note: parent and student training should not occur until after baseline data have been collected.)

☐ 6. Collect baseline data, set intervention goals, and begin intervention.

Teachers should complete the DRC in the absence of intervention in order to obtain an estimate of current behavior. Subsequent to student and parent training, these DRC ratings become a source of behavioral feedback with rewards provided for obtained goals.

Step 2: Determine When Ratings Will Occur and Who Will Conduct Them

The second step is to identify the appropriate time periods during which ratings will occur. Given that DRC ratings will be shared with students as a means of providing behavioral feedback, it is important that the ratings occur throughout the day rather than providing one summative rating before the student leaves to go home. How often these ratings should occur, however, is a question that should be answered with the behavioral needs of the individual student in mind. Whereas providing feedback every couple of hours may be sufficient for some students, those students with more intensive behavioral needs might require feedback at the end of each instructional block (e.g., reading, math). In considering when ratings should occur there is also an important balance that must be struck between providing the student with a sufficient amount of feedback and ensuring that ratings are not being conducted too frequently that the feasibility for the classroom teacher is diminished. As a result, the number of ratings conducted each day will inevitably vary depending on both the student and teacher involved. Figure 8.3 presents an example of a DRC that could be used to rate the same five target behaviors across multiple activity blocks throughout the day.

Step 3: Determine the Appropriate Dimension of Behavior

Once we have determined which behaviors will be included on the DRC, it is necessary to determine how they will be assessed. The most basic type of assessment involves simply delineating between whether a behavior occurred or did not occur (e.g., arrived at class on time, turned in homework). In such a case, the assessment can be recorded directly on the DRC. In contrast, if the target behavior is one that can be counted (e.g., calls out, out of seat), it is necessary to determine which dimension of behavior is of most interest and to record data on an appropriate recording sheet. If frequency is of concern (e.g., how often the student calls out or raises hand), a simple tally system might be used to record the number of behavioral occurrences. Latency might also be recorded if the concern is with how long it takes a student to initiate a behavior (e.g., begin working after instructions are given). Although duration is often more challenging for a classroom teacher to measure (because it requires the use of a stopwatch or other timing device), possible assessment targets could include the amount of time a student takes to transition from lunch to the classroom or the amount of time that the student works quietly during independent seatwork. Finally, there may be some situations in which measuring teacher behavior is of most interest, such as recording the number of teacher prompts needed before the student begins working.

Child's Name: ______________________ Date: ____________

Target Behavior(s)	Morning Meeting	Reading Circle	Math	Journal Time	Learning Centers
	Activity/Period				
1. Interrupted group less than five times.	Y / N	Y / N	Y / N	Y / N	Y / N
2. Followed directions with three or fewer reminders.	Y / N	Y / N	Y / N	Y / N	Y / N
3. Sat in assigned area with two or fewer reminders.	Y / N	Y / N	Y / N	Y / N	Y / N
4. Complied with 70% or more of teacher's requests.	Y / N	Y / N	Y / N	Y / N	Y / N
5. Had two or fewer instances of whining.	Y / N	Y / N	Y / N	Y / N	Y / N
6.	Y / N	Y / N	Y / N	Y / N	Y / N
7.	Y / N	Y / N	Y / N	Y / N	Y / N
8.	Y / N	Y / N	Y / N	Y / N	Y / N
Total number of Y					
Total number of N					

Comments:

FIGURE 8.3. Sample of daily report card (consistent goals across rating periods).

Step 4: Create DRC Items

Once the target behaviors and corresponding dimensions have been determined, it is time to create the DRC items, which will specify the criteria for judging success. Typically, DRC items have been written to evaluate behavior via a dichotomous (i.e., yes/no, smiley face/frowning face) scale. However, the dichotomous scale can be used in two ways: (1) to judge "all-or-nothing" behaviors (i.e., either the behavior occurs or it does not), or (2) to judge whether an established goal was met. For those behaviors that involve a simple yes/no judgment (i.e., either the student performs the behavior or not), setting the goal is quite straightforward. For example, the goal for a student who comes to class without a pencil and notebook would simply be that the student "comes to class with the appropriate materials," with the materials needed operationalized ahead of time. Similarly, the goal for a student who routinely comes to class late might be that the student "arrives at class on time."

In many other cases, however, assessment of the target behavior may be more complex than making a simple yes/no determination. For example, with a behavior such as the use of inappropriate language, simply asking the question of whether the student used inappropriate language during class or not may provide an oversimplification of the target. A classroom teacher would likely be more interested in assessing factors such as how often the student used inappropriate language (i.e., frequency), how long the inappropriate language was used for (i.e., duration), or what specific words were used or whether they were directed toward someone (i.e., severity). When assessments involve some type of numerical measurement, we want to first set a goal for what improved performance would look like. The creation of a DRC goal should be informed by an estimate of the current (i.e., baseline) level of behavior. In some cases, it may be possible to make a best guess about the current level of behavior, whereas in other cases it may be necessary to collect a few days' worth of baseline data. Returning to the target behavior of calling out, for example, we would first want to know how often the student is currently calling out in order to develop an appropriate goal for intervention. The classroom teacher might therefore be asked to record any occurrences of calling out for a week and then a realistic goal could be established in relation to these baseline data. The resultant DRC item (e.g., "Calls out fewer than five times during an instructional block") could then be evaluated using a yes/no scale.

As noted previously, a DRC can be implemented across different activities (e.g., independent reading, centers) or different periods (e.g., math, language arts) within the same day. It is therefore important to carefully consider how the behavioral expectations may vary across different settings. In some cases, the selected DRC goals may be broadly applicable, such that the same goals can be used across multiple rating periods (e.g., followed directions with three or fewer reminders; see Figure 8.3). In other situations, however, it may be necessary to allow goals to vary

Child's Name: ______________________ Date: ______________

Target Behavior(s)	Morning Meeting	Reading Circle	Math	Journal Time	End of Day
	Activity/Period				
1. Followed directions with three or fewer reminders.	Y / N	Y / N	Y / N	Y / N	
2. Started work with two or fewer reminders.			Y / N	Y / N	
3. Turned in assignments appropriately.			Y / N	Y / N	
4. Raised hand to speak with two or fewer reminders.	Y / N	Y / N			
5. Contributed to discussion appropriately.	Y / N	Y / N			
6. Writes homework in assignment book.					Y / N
7. Cleans up desk before going home.					Y / N
Total number of Y					
Total number of N					

Comments:

FIGURE 8.4. Sample of daily report card (goals vary across rating periods).

across rating periods. As an example, the behavior *turned in assignments appropriately* would be applicable to math or writing, but would not make sense for morning meeting. Therefore, the DRC may need to be amended such that it is clear which goals should be rated at which times (see Figure 8.4).

In a recent study involving students between the ages of 6 and 12 who had been diagnosed with ADHD, the most common DRC targets included "Returns completed homework," "Stays on task with fewer than *X* reminders," "Follows directions with *X* or fewer reminders," "Respectful to teacher/accepts feedback appropriately," and "Completes assignments in specified amount of time" (Fabiano et al., 2010). A comprehensive list of sample target behaviors can be found under the Resources section of the Center for Children and Families website at *http://ccf.fiu.edu.*

Step 5: Conduct Training

It is necessary to train both teachers and parents in the use of the DRC, given that each party will be involved in a slightly different way. When meeting with a classroom teacher, there are several logistical considerations that should be covered. First, it is necessary to ensure that the teacher has a clear understanding of the target behaviors by reviewing the operational definitions and discussing both examples and nonexamples of each behavior. Second, the method for recording behavior should be determined and any necessary materials identified. If the behavior involves a one-time assessment, it can be recorded directly on the DRC. If the behavior involves more than a simple dichotomous judgment, however, it may be necessary to use a secondary data collection sheet in order to record data and then use these data to inform the overall DRC rating. Third, it is important to review the intervention procedures. A schedule should be established that specifies when the ratings will be conducted and when they will be shared with the student. It may also be useful to talk about how teacher–student meetings will be structured (e.g., *How long will meetings last? How will feedback be delivered?*), as well as what system will be used for sending DRC ratings home.

Although procedural elements (e.g., what target behaviors will be evaluated and when) should also be discussed with parents, the focal point of the parent meeting should be on establishing a home-based reward system. It is important to work with the parents to establish a menu of potential rewards that are both motivating to the student and feasible for the parents to provide. The schedule and criteria for delivering rewards should also be reviewed with parents at this stage to ensure that rewards are being provided daily, but are only contingent upon goal attainment. Finally, the positive nature of the DRC intervention should be emphasized. Parents should understand that the goal of the DRC is to reward students for achieving goals and not to punish them if their performance falls short. Parents should be encouraged to provide positive feedback for goal attainment and to acknowledge failure to meet a goal using a neutral, matter-of-fact tone. Ideally the parent training meeting should occur after baseline data have been collected in order to prevent a potential reactivity effect, in which the parents change the way they interact with their child as a function of knowing about the upcoming intervention. It may be necessary, however, to meet with the parents prior to baseline data collection to ensure that they are on board with the intervention. In such a case the purpose of collecting baseline data should be described (i.e., in order to get a sense of the behavior in the absence of intervention) so that parents understand the importance of waiting until the intervention period begins to make any changes to "business as usual" at home.

Step 6: Collect Baseline Data, Set Intervention Goals, and Begin Intervention

Once the teacher has a clear understanding of how the DRC will be used, it is time to begin baseline data collection. Similar to CICO, one of the strengths of the DRC is that the intervention generates data on a daily basis that can be used within a progress monitoring context. During baseline, the teacher therefore completes the DRC according to the predetermined schedule; however, ratings are not shared with the student or the student's parents. It is important to check in during the first week of baseline data collection to ensure that (1) the behavior is sufficiently problematic to warrant intervention and that (2) the established DRC goals continue to be appropriate (i.e., that they were not set too high or low).

Once a predictable pattern of behavior has been identified during baseline, the DRC should be introduced to the student. This meeting should focus on ensuring that the student has a clear understanding of what the target behaviors are and what the intervention will look like. This process begins similarly to the teacher meeting by reviewing the definitions of the target behaviors. Depending on the developmental level of the student, however, it may be necessary to use role plays in addition to a verbal discussion in order to ensure that both examples and nonexamples of the target behaviors are clear (Volpe & Fabiano, 2013). Once the student understands which behaviors will be evaluated, the criteria for earning rewards should be discussed. It should be clear to the student what he or she needs to do in order to receive a reward and what the possible reward options are. Time can be spent at this stage discussing those rewards that had been identified and approved by the student's parents and determining which the student finds most motivating. Finally, it is important to review the procedural routine that will be used to implement the DRC, including when the student will receive rating feedback, how the student will share ratings with his or her parent(s), and where the DRC will be stored to ensure that it does not get lost on the way to and from home.

Each time that the classroom teacher meets with the student to discuss the DRC ratings, the student should be praised for meeting any goals; in contrast, missed goals should be discussed matter-of-factly (Volpe & Fabiano, 2013). At the end of the day, the number of yeses and nos should be calculated and recorded on a progress monitoring log or chart before the DRC is sent home with the student. These data are then used to make decisions regarding intervention effectiveness and to determine whether changes should be made to the plan. For instance, DRC goals met across a period of time (e.g., marking period or school year) can be used to determine whether changes in intervention are warranted. This was illustrated in a study by Nahum-Shani and colleagues (2012), which used the percentage of DRC goals met as one of the main criteria on which to make clinical judgments about the effectiveness of current treatment. In this study, the need for additional treatment was identified if children had a monthly DRC average of less than 75% and current impairment as rated by parents and teachers.

Research on the DRC

Although much of the research on DRC in recent years has focused heavily on students with ADHD (Evans & Youngstrom, 2006; Fabiano et al., 2010; Pelham & Fabiano, 2008), this type of intervention has been used successfully with a range of students over the past several decades. For example, one of the first published reports of using the DRC can be traced back to work in the 1960s when middle school students in a residential program attended a special summer classroom (Bailey et al., 1970). Children were given specific feedback on behavioral goals established for the classroom, and the specific feedback was linked to rewards in the home. Following this intervention, the children improved their behavior in class to consistently acceptable levels. More recent examples involve the use of DRC to improve the behavioral functioning of K–5 students in general education classrooms (Chafouleas, Sanetti, Kilgus, et al., 2002) and to reduce disruptive behavior in preschool students (LeBel et al., 2013).

In addition to being an effective intervention, the DRC has also been shown to be an efficient and effective procedure for monitoring outcomes in important areas of children's psychosocial functioning (Cheney, Flower, & Templeton, 2008; Fabiano et al., 2009; Pelham et al., 2005; Vannest et al., 2010). One study illustrated that the DRC may be a viable vehicle for monitoring progress on IEP goals and objectives (Fabiano et al., 2010). Further, the DRC has been shown to be sensitive to changes in treatment status for youth with ADHD. Multiple studies illustrate that the DRC is a sensitive indicator of changes in pharmacological (e.g., Pelham et al., 2001) and behavioral interventions (Pelham et al., 2005) for ADHD. Thus, changes in the percentage of goals met under differing environmental (e.g., establishment of special education goals) or intervention-related contexts can be analyzed to determine the relative effectiveness of modifications to an intervention.

As the DRC continues to be used in practice, future directions include determining how to best integrate the progress monitoring information generated into school (e.g., instructional support team discussions) and clinical (e.g., pediatrician discussions with parents on the efficacy of medication for ADHD) settings.

Putting It All Together: Case Examples

Now that we have reviewed the steps involved in designing the CICO and DRC interventions, we illustrate the use of each within two different contexts. In the first case example, CICO is used to target minor misbehavior of a student in third grade. The second case example describes the use of a DRC to improve a seventh-grade student's on-time arrival to class, the frequency with which she brings required materials to class, and her initiation of independent work.

CICO Example: Elementary School

"Daniel," an 8-year-old boy in third grade at Sunset Elementary School, frequently engages in problem behavior and consistently shows poor academic performance. He often gets out of his seat during lessons, group work, and independent reading, and disrupts class by talking, making noises, and poking other students.

Daniel's teacher, "Ms. Andrews," is concerned with his academic performance and frustrated by his constant class disruptions. Ms. Andrews spoke with "Carlos," the school counselor, who mentioned that along with some academic support in reading and math, Daniel might be a good candidate for the school's targeted intervention, CICO. When the Behavior Support Team members developed CICO to fit the culture of their school, they renamed the intervention the *Shark Program* to match the shark mascot of their school. After meeting with Daniel's parents and teachers to explain the intervention and obtain permission, Carlos explained the intervention to Daniel. The team went over three main objectives, all of which aligned with the schoolwide behavioral expectations. Daniel would focus on the "SHARK Code": Safe, Honest and Accountable, Respectful and Kind. More specifically, Daniel would focus on walking (not running) in the building; keeping hands, feet, and objects to himself; following directions; using kind words and actions; taking care of himself and his belongings; and being in the right place and ready (see Figure 8.5).

Carlos met with Daniel on a Monday morning to train him on behavioral expectations, the CICO procedures, and how to respond to feedback. After this meeting, Carlos gave Daniel a DPR and prompted him to have a good day in class. Daniel checked in with Ms. Andrews at four designated times: before morning

Shark Code

Sunset Elementary School

Checked in	YES NO
Checked out	YES NO
Parent signature	YES NO

Goal: 50% 55% 60% 65% 70% 75% 80%

Student: ______________ **Date:** ______________ **M Tu W Th F** **Goal:** ______________

Expectations	Arrival to Recess				Recess to Lunch				Lunch to Recess				Recess to Dismissal				Total
	Tough Time	So-So	Good	Awesome	Tough Time	So-So	Good	Awesome	Tough Time	So-So	Good	Awesome	Tough Time	So-So	Good	Awesome	
Safe	1	2	3	4	1	2	3	4	1	2	3	4	1	2	3	4	
Honest & Accountable	1	2	3	4	1	2	3	4	1	2	3	4	1	2	3	4	
Respectful & Kind	1	2	3	4	1	2	3	4	1	2	3	4	1	2	3	4	
Keep Practicing	☐				☐				☐				☐				

Successes:

4 = AWESOME: Met expectations with positive behavior; worked independently without any corrections/reminders.

3 = GOOD: Met expectations with only one reminder/correction.

2 = SO-SO: Needed two to three reminders/corrections.

1 = TOUGH TIME: Needed four or more reminders/corrections.

Note: Parent comments can be included on the back of this form.

Parent/Guardian Signature: ______________

FIGURE 8.5. Daniel's daily progress report at Sunset Elementary School.

recess, before lunch, before afternoon recess, and at the end of the day. During each check-in, Ms. Andrews rated Daniel's behavior on a scale of 1–4, and provided verbal praise. At the end of the day, Daniel checked out with Carlos, who totaled the points earned for the day, discussed common behavior problems Daniel had exhibited, and provided reinforcement for meeting expectations throughout the day. For every day Daniel met his goal of earning at least 80% of the daily points possible, he was given one Star Ticket, which he could cash in for prizes at the school store. Daniel also had the opportunity to earn small, tangible rewards such as stickers, pencils, and erasers. Daniel took the DPR home to be signed by his parents, and was prompted to check in with Carlos the next morning before school.

After participating in the program for 2 weeks, Daniel was still frequently coming to class unprepared and using verbal and physical aggression to resolve conflicts. The CICO team determined that Daniel was not making as much progress as they would like, and arranged to have a meeting to discuss possible changes they could make to CICO with Daniel. At the meeting, the team asked Daniel how he felt about CICO, and what changes could be made that would help him be successful. Daniel had a good understanding of the behavioral expectations and the CICO procedure. He mentioned, however, that he wasn't motivated to earn points toward school store items and felt that having more time with his friends would be motivating. The CICO team decided that an appropriate adjustment to make to CICO would be changing the reinforcement to spending time with his friends and peers. The team replaced the opportunity to receive school store prizes with the opportunity to earn a special lunch with a friend of his choice.

Three weeks after making changes in the reinforcements of CICO, Daniel was coming to class prepared and interacting with his peers more appropriately. When the CICO team met with him to evaluate his progress, Daniel said he was motivated by the opportunity to earn extra time with friends and by the increasingly positive interactions he was having with the CICO coordinator and his teacher. Daniel will continue to be involved in CICO for at least 6 weeks, at which point the CICO team will discuss the option of fading off the intervention with Daniel.

DRC Example: Middle School

Let's consider the case of "Julia," a middle school student, who came to the attention of the school's Problem-Solving Team (PST) through a referral from her language arts teacher, "Ms. Martin." Ms. Martin is concerned that Julia often shows up late for class without the necessary materials (e.g., writing utensils, notebook, homework) and that she often has difficulty initiating independent work. Under the consultation of the PST, Ms. Martin decides to create a 5-item DRC that includes the following dichotomously scored items: (1) arrives at class on time, (2) brings completed homework to class, (3) brings necessary materials to class, (4) starts work with two or fewer reminders, and (5) writes homework in assignment book. After collecting a week's worth of baseline data, Ms. Martin finds that Julia is earning approximately 50% of the possible yes ratings. The teacher then discusses the intervention with Julia's parents, who agree to provide Julia with home-based incentives (e.g., extra TV time, choice of after-dinner snack, use of computer for social networking) if she earns 80% of the possible yes ratings for the week.

After 1 month of implementing the intervention, Ms. Martin returns to the PST to discuss how Julia has been doing. In reviewing the data, they find that Julia has earned 90% or more of the possible yes ratings for the past 2 weeks. Ms. Martin has been very pleased with Julia's performance in class and suggests that this intervention may benefit Julia in her other classes. During the next seventh-grade team meeting, Ms. Martin introduces the idea to her colleagues, who are receptive to trying it out. A more comprehensive DRC is created for Julia, with a column for each of her six classes (see Figure 8.6). Although the five initial target behaviors are used across Julia's core academic classes (language arts, science, history, Spanish, math), only two of the items are deemed appropriate for chorus (i.e., arrives at class on time, brings necessary materials to class). The school team, in cooperation with Julia's parents, decides to keep the current goal of 80%, but the goal will now be calculated based on 150 possible ratings for the week instead of 25. In this way, all participants hope that Julia's improved classroom preparation behaviors will generalize across the school day.

Conclusions

The goal of this chapter was to introduce readers to two different ways of using DBR as part of a targeted behavior intervention. CICO and DRC may look similar at a surface level, given that daily ratings are used to provide behavioral feedback to students and to reward them based on goal attainment. At the same time, however, we hope that this chapter has shed light on a few key distinctions across these two tools as well. The specific elements of each intervention are important to consider when determining which one to use when, in relationship to each particular school setting and the students in need of support.

One key difference between CICO and the DRC involves the management of the intervention. Whereas the individual teacher would retain primary responsibility for DRC implementation, CICO is a schoolwide intervention designed to minimize the burden on individual teachers through the use of a central coordinator. CICO therefore requires a coordinator who is charged with responsibility not only for evaluating student performance, but also for recording and monitoring performance over time. Additionally, although the DRC may be used in one class or block of time during the day (thereby potentially requiring the participation of only one

Child's Name: ______________________ Date: ______________

Target Behavior(s)	Period Language Arts	Science	Chorus	History	Spanish	Math
1. Arrives at class on time.	Y / N	Y / N	Y / N	Y / N	Y / N	Y / N
2. Brings completed homework to class.	Y / N	Y / N		Y / N	Y / N	Y / N
3. Brings necessary materials to class.	Y / N	Y / N	Y / N	Y / N	Y / N	Y / N
4. Starts work with 2 or fewer reminders.	Y / N	Y / N		Y / N	Y / N	Y / N
5. Writes homework in assignment book.	Y / N	Y / N		Y / N	Y / N	Y / N
Total number of Y						
Total number of N						

Comments:

FIGURE 8.6. Sample of daily report card for use across middle school periods.

teacher), CICO is a schoolwide intervention that is implemented across a student's schedule in all classes and blocks of time throughout the day.

A second key difference involves the number and nature of adult–student interactions. Although students meet with their teacher to review DRC ratings at the end of a period, the DRC does not incorporate the checking in or out components found in CICO. These components of CICO are essential elements of the intervention because they provide opportunities to precorrect and address behavioral challenges, as well as to facilitate positive interactions with an adult at the school prior to and after engaging with teachers. An additional difference involves the role of parents in intervention implementation. Although parents participate in CICO by reviewing and signing the student's DPR each night, they are not responsible for critical intervention components. In contrast, the use of home-based reinforcement for points earned during the school day with the DRC makes parent participation critical.

Finally, whereas CICO emphasizes the use of similar materials and procedures across student participants in order to maximize feasibility, the DRC maintains an idiographic focus wherein all goals are specific to the individual. Because implementation of DRC does not require the implementation of SWPBS at the universal level, the DRC can be used with students in need of additional supports regardless of the type of universal behavior supports in place. In schools with SWPBS in place, however, practitioners may choose to use CICO, in the interest of efficiency and feasibility, for students in need of additional supports. In these cases, practitioners could implement the DRC with students who are nonresponsive to CICO to match their needs for more intensive and individualized interventions while still maintaining the feasibility of targeted supports.

CHAPTER 9

Use of DBR in Individualized Intervention

Rose Iovannone and Amy M. Briesch

In Chapter 8, DBR was discussed as part of a targeted intervention involving behavioral feedback and reinforcement in order to meet the needs of a targeted group of students that was believed to be at risk for negative behavioral outcomes. Given that a notable percentage of students (i.e., 10–15% of the school population) may participate in targeted interventions, it is important that the interventions look similar across different students to ensure the feasibility of implementation. However, when students have severe behavioral needs (i.e., exhibit behaviors that are extreme or dangerous) that exceed the reach of targeted interventions or simply do not respond to this level of support, it is necessary to provide tertiary, or intensive, levels of support. Interventions at the tertiary level are characterized by their focus on the individual needs of students, taking into consideration each student's unique characteristics and the specific circumstances related to the problem behaviors (e.g., intensity of behaviors, surrounding environmental events); thus, tertiary interventions require more resources in order to implement. There are many ways to individualize interventions, such as (1) broadening assessment information gathered to better understand the behavior and its relation to the environment, (2) increasing the specificity and number of hypotheses developed based on the assessment information, (3) implementing multicomponent interventions aimed to prevent and reduce problem behavior and increase replacement behaviors, (4) providing more opportunities to monitor response to interventions, and (5) individualizing the data collection tools. Most important at the intensive level, however, is that the design of strategies is based on functionally relevant data to meet the individual needs of students.

The initial starting point when designing individualized, intensive behavior supports is to conduct a functional behavioral assessment (FBA). Although the process looks different depending on the individual case, the primary goal of an FBA is to examine the relationship between a specific problem behavior and its environmental context in order to identify a predictive pattern of when and why the behavior occurs (Scott, Alter, Rosenberg, & Borgmeier, 2010). A hypothesis about the function of a problem behavior, or why the behavior is occurring, is informed by identifying both behavioral antecedents (i.e., events immediately preceding the targeted behavior) and consequences (i.e., events that immediately follow the targeted behavior). *Antecedents* are defined as events that trigger occurrences of the problem behavior, whereas *consequences* serve to maintain, or reinforce, the behavior.

Effective intervention at the intensive level should include two core features. First, the behavior intervention plan (BIP) developed should reflect the FBA data and knowledge of the student's context. The BIP should therefore include strategies that (1) address the environmental antecedents so that behavior problems are prevented by rendering them irrelevant (Carr, Langdon, & Yarbrough, 1999); (2) teach the student an appropriate replacement behavior that makes the problem behavior inefficient (Kahng, Iwata, & Lewin, 2002; Pelios, Morren, Tesch, & Axelrod, 1999); and (3) deliver reinforcement following performance of the replacement behavior so that the problem behavior becomes ineffective (O'Neill et al., 1997). A wealth of research has confirmed that the FBA process of developing behavioral interventions is effective in reducing problem behaviors and increasing appropriate replacement skills for students with and without disabilities (e.g., Blair, Umbreit, & Bos, 1999; Burke, Hagan-Burke, & Sugai, 2003; Duda, Dunlap, Fox, Lentini, & Clarke, 2004; Dunlap & Carr, 2007; Lane, Weisenbach, Phillips, & Wehby, 2007).

The second core feature of effective individualized interventions is that the student's response to the intervention must be consistently monitored and analyzed so that adjustments can be made quickly to the intervention strategies through a dynamic, iterative process designed to meet the student behavioral goals established by the school team. The progress monitoring data should have utility and timeliness and be ongoing to enhance the likelihood that the BIP will be effective (Epstein et al., 2005).

At the intensive level, evidence-based intervention is no longer a set of research-validated procedures but is rather determined based on each individual's response to the intervention. Although individualization helps to ensure that each student receives the most appropriate type and level of behavior support, it also brings with it additional complexity, given that assessment targets and related intervention plans look very different from one student to the next. Whereas targeted interventions such as CICO (see Chapter 8) can employ the same intervention and assessment materials across multiple students (e.g., evaluating behavior in relation to the same schoolwide expectations using the DPR), customizable tools are needed to address unique needs. Data collection therefore becomes especially crucial at the intensive level. The focus of this chapter is on an intervention and assessment model that uses functionally derived data to design intervention strategies and an individualized DBR tool to monitor the response of those students with the most intensive behavioral needs. In addition to describing the critical features of this tool and how it may be used to support intensive intervention implementation, we provide a brief review of research conducted to date.

Prevent–Teach–Reinforce and the Individualized Behavior Rating Scale Tool

Prevent–Teach–Reinforce (PTR; Iovannone, Greenbaum, Wang, Kincaid, & Dunlap, 2009) is an individualized behavior intervention model that is based upon the principles of applied behavior analysis (Carr et al., 2002; Skinner, 1953) and aligned with the values of positive behavior support (Koegel, Koegel, & Dunlap, 1996; Sugai & Horner, 2002). The PTR model uses a multistep process that includes (1) teaming; (2) goal setting (i.e., identifying the problem); (3) PTR assessment (i.e., analyzing the problem); (4) PTR intervention (i.e., developing and implementing the intervention); and (5) evaluation (i.e., evaluation and monitoring). The PTR model is team driven and results in a BIP "package" that includes, at a minimum, three categories of intervention strategies. Each plan has at least one *Prevent* strategy that modifies the antecedents predicting the problem behavior, one *Teach* strategy that provides instruction in a new skill to replace the problem behavior, and one *Reinforce* strategy that arranges contingent consequences so that the new skill is more likely to be repeated and the problem behavior is less likely to occur (Dunlap, Iovannone, Kincaid, et al., 2010; Dunlap, Iovannone, Wilson, Strain, & Kincaid, 2010). Teachers and team members use a menu to select evidence-based interventions from each of the three categories (i.e., Prevent, Teach, Reinforce). Once the interventions are selected, the team ensures that the strategies link to the hypothesis and develops the precise steps that describe exactly how each intervention will be implemented in the teacher's classroom or other relevant context. Once it is developed, teachers are coached on the plan so that it is implemented with fidelity.

The PTR model was subjected to a randomized controlled trial involving more than 200 student-centered school-based teams and was shown to be significantly more effective than typical behavior interventions (i.e., services as usual) in improving student behavior skills, social skills, and academically engaged time (Iovannone et al., 2009). Further, most teachers implemented the behavior interventions at 80% or higher fidelity (mean fidelity score = .83). Teachers found the PTR process to be highly acceptable and effective as indicated by social validity ratings, with an overall mean of 4.16 on a 5-point Likert scale (Iovannone et al., 2009).

What Is the IBRST?

Essential to the success of the PTR model is the use of assessment data to determine strategy effectiveness. The Individualized Behavior Rating Scale Tool (IBRST) was therefore developed to be an efficient and nonintrusive way for teachers and other educators to determine the impact of the intervention on the student's targeted behaviors in a standardized fashion. Each team first selects the specific behaviors targeted for intervention (i.e., at a minimum, one problem behavior and one appropriate replacement behavior) and defines them so that they clearly describe how the student performs the problem behavior and how he or she *should* perform the replacement behavior. Respondents then utilize a 5-point Likert scale to record their perceptions of the student's performance daily across baseline and intervention periods. The 5 points on the Likert scale represent levels or dimensions of behavior occurrence and are individually defined for the student, based on the current estimated rate of the behavior occurrence and the desired goals.

Although the IBRST is uniquely defined for each individual student, the meaning of the ratings is standardized. That is, for problem behaviors a 5 always represents an estimate of a *very bad day* for the behavior, a *4* always represents a *typical bad day,* a *3* represents *a so-so day* (neither bad nor good), a *2* represents a *good day,* and a *1* represents a *great day.* For appropriate replacement behaviors, the scale is reversed (i.e., *5* representing a *great day, 1* representing a *very bad day*). The rating of *3* therefore retains the same meaning on the scales targeting both problem and appropriate behavior. The goal for the student can be set at the *1* or the *2* rating for the problem behavior or a *4* or *5* rating for an appropriate behavior. To record data, a teacher simply circles the rating that best matches his or her perception of the behavior occurrence during the time period specified. Phases of intervention trials can be labeled on the IBRST by drawing vertical dashed lines whenever a strategy is introduced, withdrawn, or modified. Figure 9.1 shows an example of a completed IBRST targeting hitting and engagement with baseline and two phases of intervention.

At the heart of all progress monitoring tools is the ability to evaluate the effectiveness of interventions on changes in student behavior. The IBRST data recordings allow the teacher/team to answer the following questions:

1. Are the data showing that the targeted behaviors are occurring at a rate indicating a need for intervention (i.e., baseline)?
2. Are the intervention strategies being implemented effective in reducing the student's problem behavior and increasing the student's appropriate replacement behaviors (i.e., postintervention)?
3. Are the goals of intervention being met?
4. Are modifications to the intervention plan needed, and if made, are they resulting in the desired student outcomes?

Student: *Tracy* School: *Maple*

Rater: *Joe*

Problematic Behavior	Date	02/01/15	02/02/15	02/03/15	02/04/15	02/05/15	02/08/15	02/09/15	02/10/15	02/15/15	02/12/15	02/15/15	02/16/15	02/17/15	02/18/15		
		Baseline			Interention 1					Intervention 2							
Hitting	>10 times	5	5	5	5	5	5	5	5	5	5	5	5	5	5	5	5
	8–10 times	4	4	4	4	4	4	4	4	4	4	4	4	4	4	4	4
	5–7 times	3	3	3	3	3	3	3	3	3	3	3	3	3	3	3	3
	2–4 times	2	2	2	2	2	2	2	2	2	2	2	2	2	2	2	2
	1 or less	1	1	1	1	1	1	1	1	1	1	1	1	1	1	1	1
Engagement	>60%	5	5	5	5	5	5	5	5	5	5	5	5	5	5	5	5
	45–60%	4	4	4	4	4	4	4	4	4	4	4	4	4	4	4	4
	30–44%	3	3	3	3	3	3	3	3	3	3	3	3	3	3	3	3
	20–29%	2	2	2	2	2	2	2	2	2	2	2	2	2	2	2	2
	<20%	1	1	1	1	1	1	1	1	1	1	1	1	1	1	1	1

KEY: *Hitting definition:* Touching peers or adults with an open hand, fist, foot, or object. Record estimate of number of hitting events each day: *5* = very bad day; *4* = typical bad day; *3* = so-so day; *2* = good day; *1* = very good day. *Engagement definition:* Record estimate of percentage of time engaged during independent work time—eyes on work materials or teacher, pencil moving or hand raised to ask question: *1* = very bad day; *2* = typical bad day; *3* = so-so day; *4* = good day; *5* = very good day.

FIGURE 9.1. Sample IBRST completed for a student with one problem behavior and one appropriate behavior with three phases: Baseline, Intervention 1, and Intervention 2.

Given the individualized nature of the IBRST, many considerations must be made in the development of this tool. In this section, we outline the steps involved in developing and subsequently using the IBRST to monitor student response to intervention (see Table 9.1 for the IBRST blueprint).

Step 1: Identify and Define Target Behaviors

The first step in using the IBRST is to identify, define, and come to consensus on a minimum of one problem and one appropriate replacement behavior to be targeted for intervention. It is important that the target behaviors be operationally defined so that they are observable and measurable. This will enable consistent communication about the behavior among team members and will increase the accuracy and reliability of rating the student's behaviors. The team can designate a general descriptive name to label the behavior (e.g., cussing, aggression); however, the clear

TABLE 9.1. Steps in Creating the IBRST

- ☐ 1. Identify and define target behaviors.

  Select a minimum of one problem and one appropriate replacement behavior to be targeted for intervention. Ensure that both are operationally defined in the KEY section of the IBRST.

- ☐ 2. Determine when ratings will occur and who will conduct them.

  Ratings can be conducted throughout the day or within particular time periods/ routines. If more than one teacher will provide ratings, consider whether separate forms should be used or if all ratings will occur on the same form.

- ☐ 3. Determine the appropriate dimension of behavior.

  Several different dimensions of behavior may be of interest, including frequency, duration, latency, and intensity. Determine whether one or more dimensions will be assessed.

- ☐ 4. Determine scale points and develop the *IBRST*.

  For problematic behaviors, begin by estimating a typical "bad day" and "very bad day" and set these estimates at 4 and 5, respectively. Next, estimate a "great day" and set this estimate at 1. Finally, set ratings at 2 ("good day") and 3 ("so-so day") by subtracting the top number of rating 1 from the bottom number of rating 4 and splitting the resulting range between the two scale points. The same procedures are followed with the scale flipped (5 = "great day") for appropriate behaviors.

- ☐ 5. Train raters to use the IBRST.

  Use discussion, practice, and feedback to familiarize raters with use of the IBRST. Changes can be made to the scale at this stage prior to beginning data collection.

- ☐ 6. Collect baseline data, set intervention goals, and begin intervention.

  The IBRST can be used to record and graph baseline data in the absence of intervention. Once an intervention is implemented, a dashed vertical line is drawn and ratings continue to be plotted throughout the intervention phase.

definition of the behavior(s) should be written in the KEY section at the bottom of the IBRST. Figure 9.1 provides an example of defining behaviors in the KEY section.

Although there is no limit to the number of behaviors that can be tracked using the IBRST, the team should come to consensus on the problem behaviors that, if addressed, would result in widespread improvement in the quality of the student's, peers', and adults' lives. Let's consider the example of a second-grade student named "Winnie." In discussing Winnie's case, the school-based team may initially identify three problem behaviors: verbal callouts, low rates of academic engagement, and destruction of property. After defining the behaviors and determining that each is unique, the team might then discuss which behavior is of the highest priority. Although property destruction is a high-impact behavior, Winnie's teacher reports that, on average, Winnie has engaged in this behavior only once or twice a month. Because the behavior is occurring so infrequently, the team agrees that addressing it would not make a significant improvement on daily quality of life. On the other hand, the teacher reports that Winnie calls out frequently and is unengaged with the classroom instruction throughout most of the school day. These problem behaviors have created major disruptions in both Winnie's ability to progress through the curriculum and her teacher's ability to provide instruction to the larger class. The team therefore agrees that verbal callouts and low rates of academic engagement would be more appropriate targets for daily data tracking and intervention development at this point in time, whereas property destruction might be targeted once these primary problem behaviors have been addressed.

Step 2: Determine When Ratings Will Occur and Who Will Conduct Them

After identifying and defining the behaviors targeted for intervention, the team then determines the period of time in the day that the behaviors will be tracked. The team can decide to rate the behavior occurrences throughout the whole day, during problematic routines, over specific time periods (e.g., morning, afternoon), or by subjects/activities. If multiple teachers will be using the IBRST, the team can provide each teacher with an individualized copy of it or designate each row or column for a different teacher. Figure 9.2 shows an example of Winnie's IBRST scale rating academic engagement during different time periods of the day as well as during different situations (e.g., group time vs. independent work time). Rather than each column representing a different date, each represents a scheduled activity. Using this specific IBRST, the designated recorder would circle the rating indicating his or her perception of the student's academic engagement during each activity and setting.

Step 3: Determine the Appropriate Dimension of Behavior

After determining the time period for rating behavior, the next step is to identify the particular dimension of behavior (e.g., frequency, duration, intensity) that is most appropriate and feasible to assess using the 5-point scale. To do this, the team must answer a series of questions for each problem and appropriate behavior that will be included on the IBRST. First, team members must determine which method they believe would be best for estimating the occurrence of the problem behavior.

Student: *Winnie* School: *Orange*

Behavior	Date:	Morning Routine	System 44	Computer Time	Reading Instruction	Specials	Math	Computer Time	Dismissal
Academic Engagement (*whole-group instruction*)	65%+	5	5	5	5	5	5	5	5
	51–65%	4	4	4	4	4	4	4	4
	34–50%	3	3	3	3	3	3	3	3
	16–33%	2	2	2	2	2	2	2	2
	0–15%	1	1	1	1	1	1	1	1
Academic Engagement (*independent work time*)	65%+	5	5	5	5	5	5	5	5
	51–65%	4	4	4	4	4	4	4	4
	34–50%	3	3	3	3	3	3	3	3
	16–33%	2	2	2	2	2	2	2	2
	0–15%	1	1	1	1	1	1	1	1

KEY: *Academic engagement (whole-group instruction)*: Remains in designated area, head facing toward person speaking, lets others speak by remaining quiet, responds with related topic comments to direct questions, raises hand and waits to be called on when offering comments. *Rate your perception of the percentage of time Winnie was engaged during whole-group instruction in relevant activities. Academic engagement (independent work time)*: Remains in designated area, appropriately interacts with materials, lets others speak by remaining quiet, responds with related topic comments to direct questions, raises hand and waits to be called on when offering comments. *Rate your perception of the percentage of time Winnie was engaged during independent work time in relevant activities.*

FIGURE 9.2. Sample IBRST showing multiple times and situations for recording academically engaged time.

Is it easier to estimate the number of times the behavior occurs during the specified time period for rating (i.e., frequency)? The length of time the behavior event lasts during the time period (i.e., duration)? The amount of time that passes before a student initiates a behavior (i.e., latency)? The overall proportion of a time period in which the behavior occurred (i.e., percentage of time)? The degree to which the behavior interfered with classroom instruction (i.e., intensity)? Measuring intensity is often best suited to behaviors that are defined as an escalating chain, whereas estimating percentage of time may be more appropriate for those behaviors for which students do not have the same number of opportunities to perform each day (e.g., initiate social interactions, remain academically engaged during independent work times). In some cases, a team may decide that measuring teacher behavior (e.g., number of teacher prompts needed to elicit desired behavior from the student or to redirect from a problem behavior) is of most interest. For example, a teacher may estimate that on a *typical bad day* of independent work time, a range of 10–15 prompts may be delivered to the student to redirect him or her back to the assignment. A *very bad day* would be more than 15 prompts. A *great day* would be delivering two or less prompts.

The IBRST can also be set up to measure multiple dimensions of the same behavior if this is of interest. For example, during a team discussion concerning "Joe's" tantrum behaviors, it was decided that both the duration and the intensity of tantrums were important to monitor on a daily basis. Although Joe's tantrum behaviors typically occurred only once a day, they varied in their duration as well as the extent the tantrum reached in the escalating chain. Figure 9.3 shows an example of the type of IBRST that might be created for Joe. Note that the first row allows raters to record the length of a tantrum event in minutes, whereas the second row allows for recording the intensity of the same event. If tantrums occur more than once a day, this scale could be further adapted by using the columns to record each event rather than a daily rating.

Student: *Joe* School: *Manor*

	Problematic Behavior	**Date**	**9/1/15**	**9/1/15**	**9/2/15**	**9/3/15**	**9/3/15**	**9/3/15**					
Tantrum Duration	>10 min.		5	5	5	5	5	5	5	5	5	5	5
	8–10 min.		4	4	4	4	4	4	4	4	4	4	4
	5–7 min.		3	3	3	3	3	3	3	3	3	3	3
	2–4 min.		2	2	2	2	2	2	2	2	2	2	2
	<2 min.		1	1	1	1	1	1	1	1	1	1	1
Tantrum Intensity	Runs & screams		5	5	5	5	5	5	5	5	5	5	5
	Throws objects		4	4	4	4	4	4	4	4	4	4	4
	Screams		3	3	3	3	3	3	3	3	3	3	3
	Stomps feet		2	2	2	2	2	2	2	2	2	2	2
	Whines		1	1	1	1	1	1	1	1	1	1	1

KEY: *Tantrum definition:* Chain of behaviors that includes whining, stomping feet, screaming and throwing objects, running around the classroom while screaming. *Directions: Duration—Rate your perception of the length of time Joe's tantrum behavior lasts during an event. 5* = very bad day (>10 minutes); *4* = typical bad day (8–10 minutes); *3* = so-so day (5–7 minutes); *2* = good day (2–4 minutes); *1* = very good day (<2 minutes). *Intensity—Rate your perception of the highest level of intensity Joe displayed during the tantrum even. 5* = very bad day (running around and screaming); *4* = typical bad day (throwing objects); *3* = so-so day (screams); *2* = good day (stomps feet); *1* = great day (whines).

FIGURE 9.3. Sample IBRST showing two different measurement categories for one behavior during baseline.

Step 4: Determine Scale Points and Develop the IBRST

After establishing the time period for tracking the problem behavior and the measurement type to be used, the team is asked a systematic set of questions for the purpose of setting the scale points for each target behavior. Starting with the first problem behavior, the team is asked to estimate a typical bad day of behavior occurrence. Often, using a time range is useful to assist the team in estimating the behavior. For example, a team can be asked to think back over the last 2 or 3 weeks or since a recent holiday or major event. The estimate provided is set at rating *4, typical bad day.* The estimation does not need to be an exact number but can be a range (e.g., 4–6 times, 3–5 minutes, 20–40% of the time).

After the rating *4* is set, the team is asked to think back again over the same time frame to estimate the behavior occurrence on a *very bad* day (rating *5*). This is typically accomplished by merely setting 5 at one more than the top range of the rating for *4*. That is, if the team states that a typical bad day (i.e., *4*) for Joe's screaming is 7–8 episodes, a *5* would then be 9 or more episodes. Next, the rating *1* is set by asking the team for an estimate of behavior occurrence on a *great* day. The team can also be asked if this would be considered the reasonable goal for determining whether the intervention is effective. Finally, to set up ratings *2 (good day)* and *3 (so-so day)*, the top number of rating *1* is subtracted from the bottom number of rating *4*, giving a range of estimation that can be split between the two ratings. For example, Joe's team set rating *1* as 0–2 screaming episodes. To set the ratings for 2 and *3*, the team subtracts the *2* (top of the estimate for rating *1*) from the estimate for rating *4* (7, which is the low estimate of the range), giving the team 3–6 screaming episodes to split between the ratings of 2 and 3. Joe's team decided that a 2 *(good day)* would be 3–4 screaming episodes, whereas a *3 (so-so day)* would be 5–6 screaming episodes. This sequence of questions is repeated for any additional problem behaviors. For appropriate behaviors, the scale, as described earlier, is flipped. Therefore, the team estimate of the *typical bad day* for appropriate behavior occurrence would be set at rating *2*, and the *great day* would be set at rating *5*. Figure 9.4 shows an example of an IBRST in which two problem behaviors and two appropriate behaviors were targeted. Note that the IBRST is flexible enough to allow the team to use different measurement methods to track each behavior, yet have only one tool for collecting the information.

Step 5: Train Raters to Use the IBRST

Once the IBRST is set up, the next step is training teachers or raters to use it. This is usually accomplished at the end of the meeting in which the IBRST is being developed by asking the teacher to think back to the previous day and, for each target behavior, circle the rating that best represents his or her perception of what

Behavior	Date										
Screaming	>8 times	5	5	5	5	5	5	5	5	5	5
	7–8 times	4	4	4	4	4	4	4	4	4	4
	5–6 times	3	3	3	3	3	3	3	3	3	3
	3–4 times	2	2	2	2	2	2	2	2	2	2
	0–2 times	1	1	1	1	1	1	1	1	1	1
Hitting	>7 times	5	5	5	5	5	5	5	5	5	5
	5–6 times	4	4	4	4	4	4	4	4	4	4
	3–4 times	3	3	3	3	3	3	3	3	3	3
	1–2 times	2	2	2	2	2	2	2	2	2	2
	0 times	1	1	1	1	1	1	1	1	1	1
Expressing Frustration	Frequent (40%+)	5	5	5	5	5	5	5	5	5	5
	(31–40%)	4	4	4	4	4	4	4	4	4	4
	Occasional (21–30%)	3	3	3	3	3	3	3	3	3	3
	(11–20%)	2	2	2	2	2	2	2	2	2	2
	Rare (0–10%)	1	1	1	1	1	1	1	1	1	1
Transition to Nonpreferred	Whimper or squeal	5	5	5	5	5	5	5	5	5	5
	Louder than indoor voice	4	4	4	4	4	4	4	4	4	4
	Outdoor play voice scream	3	3	3	3	3	3	3	3	3	3
	Louder than outdoor play	2	2	2	2	2	2	2	2	2	2
	Ear penetrating scream	1	1	1	1	1	1	1	1	1	1

KEY: Screaming: *Definition*—loud, high-pitched sound heard outside the classroom. *Directions:* Rate your perception of the number of screaming events the student has during a whole day. **Hitting:** *Definition*—touching peers or adults with an open hand, fist, foot, or object while screaming. *Directions:* Rate your perception of the number of hitting events the student has during a whole day. **Express frustration:** *Definition*—Use communication (voice output device, signs, pictures) to request a break or attention. *Directions:* Rate your perception of the percentage of times the student expressed frustration appropriately within the opportunities available each day. **Transition to nonpreferred tasks:** *Definition*—moving from previous task to a nonpreferred task within one minute of request using a quiet voice and body. *Directions:* Rate your perception of the highest level of intensity the student displayed in transitioning to nonpreferred tasks.

FIGURE 9.4. Sample IBRST with two problem and two appropriate behaviors.

the student's performance looked like during the specified time periods. After the teacher rates the previous day's behavior, we would then ask how he or she reached the decision on the rating. The provided explanation will demonstrate whether the teacher understands the use of the IBRST and may also identify some potential problems with the scale's initial setup. If a teacher seems to struggle with arriving at a rating, the IBRST can be modified to address any issues. For example, the teacher may decide that frequency would be a better method for rating the behavior than intensity, or may decide that the definition of a target behavior needs to incorporate additional examples. Both of these issues can be addressed by editing the IBRST to change the measurement method or to further refine the definition of the behavior, etc.

Step 6: Collect Baseline Data, Set Intervention Goals, and Begin Intervention

After the team confirms that the behavior can be rated with the existing IBRST, it is time to begin baseline data collection. A good rule of thumb is to check in with the teacher within 1 week of initiating use of the IBRST, for two reasons. First, the baseline period will allow the team to determine whether the behaviors targeted for intervention are occurring at a rate that truly suggests the need for intervention. Second, the team needs to ensure that the estimates used to set up the IBRST are accurate. Teachers often become more cognizant of behavior occurrence once they begin using the IBRST, so if the original scale points appear to be over- or underestimates after baseline data have been collected for a few days, they can be adjusted. During baseline data collection, the IBRST ratings can be displayed as a graph showing the trend of the data points by drawing a line connecting each rating in each column. If preferred, the team can also easily transfer the ratings into a spreadsheet software program such as Excel, which will make more visually pleasing graphs.

Collection of IBRST baseline data continues through intervention development. Once an intervention is implemented, the team draws a vertical dashed line after the last date of baseline, and ratings of behavior continue to be collected and plotted throughout the intervention phase. It is recommended that the team meet within 3 weeks after starting the intervention to review the first phase of postintervention IBRST ratings and determine if the targeted behaviors are improving, remaining the same, or getting worse. It is important when reviewing postintervention data that measurement of intervention implementation fidelity is also available to assist in making the most accurate and appropriate decisions related to the intervention. If data indicate that the targeted behavior is not improving, but the interventions have not been implemented with fidelity, the team must first address the reasons for low fidelity prior to changing the intervention.

Using the IBRST in Data-Based Decision Making

Although data-based decision making is used throughout all levels of behavior support, it is conducted more frequently and continuously at the tertiary level. This approach allows a team to be proactive in making any necessary plan adjustments that will prevent problem behavior from intensifying. It is recommended that the team establish an ongoing monitoring schedule to continuously review data and make next-step decisions (Goh & Bambara, 2012). Initially, the team may want to meet more frequently (e.g., once a week) so that the plan can be quickly refined in response to fidelity and/or student outcome data. After the plan is showing effectiveness, a systematic schedule of monitoring and decision making can be established. For example, the team may establish that data will be reviewed every 3 weeks. Though strategies for data summarization and analysis are discussed in detail in Chapter 11, here we provide several case study examples to illustrate the use of the IBRST to make data-based decisions regarding intervention effectiveness. Specifically, we consider how to make modifications if an intervention plan has not been shown to be effective as well as how to promote skill maintenance when data do suggest positive change.

No Change Postintervention

Although we hope that the intervention will be successful, postintervention data may not always demonstrate positive behavior changes. Instead, the data may indicate a lack of improvement toward behavioral goals for the student. "Tracy's" first intervention phase in Figure 9.1 shows an example of a stable or "no movement" data pattern. By comparing the baseline data points to the first postintervention data points, it is clear that the targeted behaviors are not improving. In this situation, the team will want to first determine if the intervention has been implemented with fidelity prior to determining whether the plan needs to be modified. In the absence of fidelity data, it is impossible to know whether lack of student progress is due to an ineffective intervention or insufficient implementation. If implementation has been inconsistent or the implementer has struggled with particular intervention components, strategies for boosting fidelity should be considered. One potential problem may involve implementer knowledge and comfort with the intervention. It is possible that specific strategies are not well understood and that additional training is needed. Performance feedback may also be helpful in identifying implementer-specific struggles and in problem-solving how to improve rates of implementation. The team may discover that the behavior plan was not written explicitly so that it would describe the precise behaviors the teacher would perform in order to implement the behavior plan with fidelity. In this situation, the team may decide to provide more detail and clarity so that the behavior plan is task-analyzed into the specific steps the teacher or any school staff could perform.

If, however, fidelity measures indicate that the intervention is being implemented, the plan will need to be reviewed for modifications. Several issues should be considered when reviewing the plan. First, confirmation that the hypothesis derived from the FBA is correct should be explored. This can be done through a problem-solving meeting, or if more data are needed about the behavior, additional FBA data may be gathered. For example, the original hypothesized function of the problem behavior for Tracy (Figure 9.1) was attention. When Tracy performed her replacement behavior of academic engagement, she was reinforced with positive attention. A review of the data indicated that the intervention was not effective even though the teacher was implementing it with high fidelity. The team then reviewed the FBA information and came to a consensus that the primary function of Tracy's problem behavior was to escape/delay a nonpreferred activity rather than to get attention. As a result, the intervention was changed to accommodate the new hypothesis by reinforcing Tracy with allowable escape contingent upon performance of engaged behavior. As shown in Figure 9.1, a second phase line indicates the new intervention plan. The data recorded following implementation of the new strategies showed a steady improvement in Tracy's behaviors.

If the team determines that the hypothesis is accurate, members may next want to consider modifying the current interventions to enhance their effectiveness. In some cases, the delivery of the interventions may need to be increased or intensified, such as by providing more frequent reinforcement following replacement behaviors, adding additional prompts to remind the student when and how to use the replacement behavior, or providing additional visual cues that could serve as salient prompts. In some cases, the reinforcement being provided contingent upon performance of the replacement behavior may need to be strengthened so that the student is motivated to use the new behavior. To illustrate, consider "Roger," whose problem behavior is calling out (Figure 9.5) and the replacement behavior is engagement. Roger's IBRST shows that the first intervention phase, indicated by the first dashed vertical line, showed no change in behavior. The team members reviewed the hypothesis and found the function of escape for his calling-out behaviors to be accurate. They then reviewed the plan and determined that the reinforcement intervention, which was designed to provide Roger with a 5-minute escape at the end of the day contingent upon meeting his academic engagement goal, was too lengthy of a delay for Roger to experience the desired escape. That is, Roger's problem behavior, which occurred, on average, six to eight times a day, allowed him to escape more efficiently and effectively than did the replacement behavior, which only earned him escape once a day. The team decided to modify the plan by having Roger obtain 5 minutes escape time at the end of each nonpreferred academic activity, contingent upon meeting his engagement goal, rather than have him wait for one escape at the end of the day. After implementing the modified plan for 1 week, the IBRST data showed an improved trend in both the problem and replacement

Student: *Roger* School: *Main Street*

Problematic Behavior	Date	02/01/15	02/02/15	02/03/15	02/04/15	02/05/15	02/08/15	02/09/15	02/10/15	02/15/15	02/12/15	02/15/15	02/16/15	02/17/15	02/18/15		
					Escape one time a day					Escape multiple times a day							
Calling Out	>8 times	5	5	5	5	5	5	5	5	5	5	5	5	5	5	5	5
	6–7 times	4	4	4	4	4	4	4	4	4	4	4	4	4	4	4	4
	4–5 times	3	3	3	3	3	3	3	3	3	3	3	3	3	3	3	3
	2–3 times	2	2	2	2	2	2	2	2	2	2	2	2	2	2	2	2
	<2 times	1	1	1	1	1	1	1	1	1	1	1	1	1	1	1	1
Engagement	90%+	5	5	5	5	5	5	5	5	5	5	5	5	5	5	5	5
	75–89%	4	4	4	4	4	4	4	4	4	4	4	4	4	4	4	4
	50–74%	3	3	3	3	3	3	3	3	3	3	3	3	3	3	3	3
	25–49%	2	2	2	2	2	2	2	2	2	2	2	2	2	2	2	2
	<25%	1	1	1	1	1	1	1	1	1	1	1	1	1	1	1	1

KEY: *Calling out definition*: Shouting out comments unrelated to the task or topic in a louder than inside voice without raising hand. *Directions:* Rate your perception of the number of times Roger called out over the day. *Engagement definition:* Interacts appropriately with materials in a way that gets the task completed; raises hand to ask for help, ask a question, or volunteer a response; eyes and body directed toward the materials or speaker. *Directions:* Rate your perception of the percent of independent work time that Roger remained engaged.

FIGURE 9.5. Sample IBRST showing behavior intervention plan modification.

behavior. The team can now make decisions on whether to maintain the current dosage of the reinforcement or to begin fading.

Another consideration for the team is to determine whether the behavior may be so complex that more FBA data need to be collected. The additional information may provide a clearer understanding of the problem behavior, specifically if the behaviors occur in multiple contexts and have multiple purposes. Particularly for students who have significant communication deficits (e.g., students on the autism spectrum who may be nonverbal) and who exhibit behaviors that are intense and durable, an additional assessment procedure, called *functional analysis*, can be conducted to confirm the various functions of the multiple behaviors. A functional analysis is a systematic procedure that manipulates antecedents and consequences through a series of experimental conditions and examines the effect each condition has on the problem behavior occurrence (Cooper, Heron, & Heward, 2007). By confirming the hypothesis, a more effective intervention plan could be developed.

For example, "Joy" (Figure 9.6) is a student with an autism spectrum disorder who has exhibited self-injurious behaviors (SIB) for several years. The first

Name: *Joy* School: *Smith*

Behavior	Date	10/1	10/2	10/3	10/4	10/5	10/8	10/9	10/10	10/11	10/12	10/15	10/16	10/17	10/18	10/19
							Intervention 1—attention				Intervention 2—modify plan to increase attention			Intervention 3—add break		
Self-Injurious	>20/day	5	5	5	5	5	5	5	5	5	5	5	5	5	5	5
	16–20	4	4	4	4	4	4	4	4	4	4	4	4	4	4	4
	11–15	3	3	3	3	3	3	3	3	3	3	3	3	3	3	3
	6–10	2	2	2	2	2	2	2	2	2	2	2	2	2	2	2
	0–5/day	1	1	1	1	1	1	1	1	1	1	1	1	1	1	1
Ask for Attention	>50%	5	5	5	5	5	5	5	5	5	5	5	5	5	5	5
	40–49%	4	4	4	4	4	4	4	4	4	4	4	4	4	4	4
	30–39%	3	3	3	3	3	3	3	3	3	3	3	3	3	3	3
	20–29%	2	2	2	2	2	2	2	2	2	2	2	2	2	2	2
	<20%	1	1	1	1	1	1	1	1	1	1	1	1	1	1	1
Ask for a Break	>50%	5	5	5	5	5	5	5	5	5	5	5	5	5	5	5
	40–49%	4	4	4	4	4	4	4	4	4	4	4	4	4	4	4
	30–39%	3	3	3	3	3	3	3	3	3	3	3	3	3	3	3
	20–29%	2	2	2	2	2	2	2	2	2	2	2	2	2	2	2
	<20%	1	1	1	1	1	1	1	1	1	1	1	1	1	1	1

FIGURE 9.6. Sample IBRST showing three phases of intervention modification/change.

hypothesis surmised that the primary function of the SIB was to get attention. However, as indicated by the data following the first phase, the intervention plan that taught Joy to perform a replacement behavior to obtain immediate attention was not effective at reducing the SIB and increasing use of the replacement behavior. The team modified the intervention by increasing the opportunities for Joy to use her replacement behavior, thus giving Joy attention more consistently and efficiently. The data indicated that although her behavior showed some improvement, it was not yet at the desirable level during specific academic activities. The team was concerned about potential injuries if the SIB continued and decided to request a district behavior analyst to conduct a functional analysis. After the functional analysis, it was confirmed that during some contexts, such as nonpreferred academic work, Joy engaged in the behavior for the purpose of escaping the work rather than for attention. During other activities in which demands were low or Joy tolerated them, the behavior was primarily exhibited for adult attention. The team developed a BIP in which an escape replacement behavior would be taught and reinforced during the nonpreferred academic activities, and the original attention replacement behavior would continue to be implemented during the situations in which attention was the primary function. The data after the third phase line in Figure 9.6 shows a decreased trend in the SIB behavior and an increased trend in using the replacement behavior. Note that the team added an additional row to the IBRST that indicated that an additional replacement behavior (i.e., ask for a break) was being added to the plan.

Positive Postintervention Outcomes

Our hope in implementing any intervention plan is that the selected strategies result in positive behavior change. However, just because behavioral improvements have been made does not necessarily mean that it is time to terminate the intervention plan and discontinue progress monitoring. Figure 9.7 shows an example of an

Name: *Randy* School: *Washington*

		Baseline Data					Postintervention Data									
Behavior	**Date**	**10/1**	**10/2**	**10/3**	**10/4**	**10/5**	**10/8**	**10/9**	**10/10**	**10/11**	**10/12**	**10/15**	**10/16**	**10/17**	**10/18**	**10/19**
Screaming	>20/day	5	5	5	5	5	5	5	5	5	5	5	5	5	5	5
	16–20	4	4	4	4	4	4	4	4	4	4	4	4	4	4	4
	11–15	3	3	3	3	3	3	3	3	3	3	3	3	3	3	3
	6–10	2	2	2	2	2	2	2	2	2	2	2	2	2	2	2
	0–5/day	1	1	1	1	1	1	1	1	1	1	1	1	1	1	1
Academic Engagement	50%+	5	5	5	5	5	5	5	5	5	5	5	5	5	5	5
	40–49%	4	4	4	4	4	4	4	4	4	4	4	4	4	4	4
	30–39%	3	3	3	3	3	3	3	3	3	3	3	3	3	3	3
	20–29%	2	2	2	2	2	2	2	2	2	2	2	2	2	2	2
	<20%	1	1	1	1	1	1	1	1	1	1	1	1	1	1	1

KEY: Screaming: *Definition*—short, high-pitched, loud noises lasting about 1 second. *Directions:* Rate your perception of the number of screaming events the student has during a whole day. **Academic engagement:** *Definition*—eyes directed toward task materials, appropriate physical interactions with task-related materials, raising hand to ask for help. *Directions*: Rate your perception of the percentage of time Randy was engaged during independent work time.

FIGURE 9.7. Sample IBRST showing positive postintervention outcomes.

IBRST developed for "Randy," who had a targeted problem behavior of screaming and a targeted appropriate behavior of academic engaged time. IBRST ratings were developed to be collected during his morning independent work time in reading/language arts. Baseline data were collected for 5 days, and intervention began on day 6, as indicated by the dashed vertical phase line between the dates of 10/5 (last day of baseline) and 10/8 (first day of intervention implementation). The baseline data points confirm that the problem and appropriate behaviors were appropriate for intervention because both screaming and academic engagement were consistently rated as *typical bad days* or *very bad days*. More specifically, Randy's IBRST baseline data indicated that he was engaging in approximately 16 or more screaming incidents and that he remained on task for less than 30% of the reading/language arts routine. Postintervention data points show a decrease in his screaming episodes and an increase in his academic engagement. After 2 weeks of intervention implementation, the teacher reported that Randy was screaming five times or less per independent routine and his academic engagement had increased to 50% or more. By comparing the IBRST baseline data points to intervention data points, this example clearly demonstrates a pattern of movement toward the desired goals for Randy's performance of the targeted behaviors.

Although the data suggest a reason to celebrate, the work does not end here. Rather, the team's next step is to brainstorm strategies for ensuring that the student moves from acquisition level to mastery and finally to maintenance, just as would occur if academic goals and skills were being addressed. Depending upon the breadth and depth of the interventions, the team may consider several avenues, including extension, shaping, fading, and self-management.

EXTENSION. One way to move the student from acquisition to mastery and finally to skill maintenance is to extend the scope of the intervention plan. If the plan is being implemented in only one routine or setting, the team may want to extend the plan so that generalization, and eventually mastery, of the desired new skills is attained. Extending the plan may involve implementing the intervention in additional routines/settings or teaching a new interventionist to implement the strategies (e.g., another teacher, paraprofessional, parent). In order to extend the scope of the intervention plan, the team should determine the goals of extension, develop appropriate IBRST anchor points, discuss modifications necessary to the current intervention plan, and train individuals to implement the modified strategies, if applicable. Finally, just as in the original intervention setting, it is important to develop a monitoring plan to support implementation and to continue to review data routinely to determine whether the intervention retains effectiveness.

SHAPING BY MODIFYING ANCHOR POINTS OR GOALS. If the intervention plan is already being implemented throughout the day or in multiple settings, the team may choose to change the IBRST anchor points in an attempt to shape the student's target behavior. Such a modification would be most appropriate if the initial goal was set at a lower level than was ultimately desired by the team.

As one example, an IBRST that was designed to track "Maria's" tantrum behaviors is presented in Figure 9.8. Due to the chronic nature and longevity of Maria's tantrum behaviors prior to intervention, the team decided that a reasonable initial goal would be to decrease the tantrums to 1–3 minutes in duration. Because the FBA hypothesis was that Maria engaged in tantrum behaviors when presented with nonpreferred independent work tasks (e.g., worksheets) in order to escape the task, the intervention plan had the teacher, after requesting that Maria do a nonpreferred task and hearing her emit a short squeal (which was a typical precursor behavior to a full tantrum), prompt Maria to use her replacement behavior of asking for a break. Two weeks of postintervention data showed that Maria's tantrums had decreased to 1–3 minutes with a concurrent increase in using her replacement behavior. The team therefore decided to change the tantrum goal to zero minutes (i.e., anchor 1 on the IBRST = no tantrums) and make the respective changes to the other anchors. The team agreed that the BIP strategies would be continued with a minor modification of when to prompt Maria to use her replacement behavior. Rather than waiting for the precursor of the squeal, the teacher would teach Maria to communicate a need for a break immediately after hearing a request to do a nonpreferred task (i.e., prior to Maria emitting a short squeal). As seen in Figure 9.8, a new IBRST row was added to the original form showing the revised rating anchors. In addition, a vertical line was drawn on the IBRST immediately prior to the first date of implementing the modified plan with the new anchor points, thus allowing for accurate comparison and evaluation of the changes in Maria's behaviors using the new criteria. Finally, the teacher wrote a comment in the original row used for rating tantrum behaviors, indicating that the measurement points had changed.

FADING. If the postintervention data indicate that the student is performing at the expected level, the team may want to consider fading procedures, such as fading the delivery of reinforcement. However, prior to fading the reinforcement, the team should review the data to confirm that the student is consistently using the new behavior or skill intended to replace the problem behavior and that the problem behavior occurrence has been extinguished or decreased to an acceptable level. If the data establish that both of these factors are occurring, a plan for fading the reinforcement can be developed. As one option, the team may choose to fade reinforcement by decreasing the frequency of delivery or thinning the rate of reinforcement. For example, a fading procedure may begin by changing the delivery of reinforcement from 100% (after each occurrence of the replacement behavior) to every other time the student exhibits the desired behavior. This may continue for several days, and if IBRST data indicate that behavior remains at desirable levels,

Behavior	Date	4/1/15	4/2/15	4/3/15	4/4/15	4/5/15	4/8/15	4/9/15	4/10/15	4/11/15	4/13/15	4/16/15	4/17/15	4/18/15	4/19/15	4/20/15
Tantrums	>12 min	5	5	5	5	5	5	5	5	5	5	5	5	5	5	5
	10–12 min	4	4	4	4	4	4	4	4	4	4	4	4	4	4	4
	7–9 min	3	3	3	3	3	3	3	3	3	3	3	3	3	3	3
	4–6 min	2	2	2	2	2	2	2	2	2	2	2	2	2	2	2
	1–3 min	1	1	1	1	1	1	1	1	1	1	1	1	1	1	1
Ask for a Break	85%+	5	5	5	5	5	5	5	5	5	5	5	5	5	5	5
	60–85%	4	4	4	4	4	4	4	4	4	4	4	4	4	4	4
	40–59%	3	3	3	3	3	3	3	3	3	3	3	3	3	3	3
	20–39%	2	2	2	2	2	2	2	2	2	2	2	2	2	2	2
	<20%	1	1	1	1	1	1	1	1	1	1	1	1	1	1	1

Behavior	Date	*4/23/15	4/24/15	4/25/15	4/26/15	4/27/15	4/30/15	5/1/15	5/2/15	5/3/15	5/4/15
Tantrums	>12 min	5	5	5	5	5	5	5	5	5	5
	10–12 min	4	4	4	4	4	4	4	4	4	4
	7–9 min	3	3	3	3	3	3	3	3	3	3
	4–6 min	2	2	2	2	2	2	2	2	2	2
	1–3 min	1	1	1	1	1	1	1	1	1	1
		Anchor rating points changed; see row below									
*Tantrums	>9 min	5	5	5	5	5	5	5	5	5	5
	7–9 min	4	4	4	4	4	4	4	4	4	4
	4–6 min	3	3	3	3	3	3	3	3	3	3
	1–3 min	2	2	2	2	2	2	2	2	2	2
	*0 min	1	1	1	1	1	1	1	1	1	1
Ask for a Break	85%+	5	5	5	5	5	5	5	5	5	5
	60–85%	4	4	4	4	4	4	4	4	4	4
	40–59%	3	3	3	3	3	3	3	3	3	3
	20–39%	2	2	2	2	2	2	2	2	2	2
	<20%	1	1	1	1	1	1	1	1	1	1

FIGURE 9.8. Sample IBRST showing change in rating criteria for tantrums.

additional fading can occur by reinforcing after every third or fourth display of behavior, and so on. Another method for fading reinforcement is by using delayed gratification. Delayed gratification involves teaching the student to wait a specified period of time, complete a certain amount of work, and/or exhibit a specific number of desired behaviors before receiving the reinforcer. If the team decides to begin fading reinforcement, the same method of drawing a dashed vertical line immediately prior to the column representing the date the fading strategy is implemented should be done so that the team can review the new, incoming data to ensure that the positive trend is continuing.

Fading could also involve reducing steps or strategies contained in the BIP. As problem behaviors decrease and replacement behaviors increase, some parts of the BIP may no longer be necessary to maintain behavior change. For example, in Figure 9.9 "Lilly" initially had a multicomponent behavior plan that included providing choices to her as an antecedent intervention to prevent problem behavior occurrences, teaching a replacement behavior of engaging in a task that would result in incremental escape earned contingent upon meeting an engagement goal, and reinforcing the entire class with an additional 10 minutes of free time if Lilly met her engagement goal 3 out of 5 days. Lilly's team reviewed the data after 2 weeks and found an improved trend in her behaviors. Lilly's teacher stated that the choice-making intervention did not seem to be that important to Lilly. The team decided to modify Lilly's plan by fading out the choice intervention and agreed to review data again in 5 days to ensure that Lilly's behavior continued to maintain its improved status. Depending upon the data review, the team would either reinstate the choice intervention (if data showed behaviors going back to baseline performance) or continue to fade out the choice intervention. Figure 9.9 shows that Lilly's behavior continued to maintain its desired performance after discontinuing the choice intervention; thus, the team decided that the choice intervention was no longer necessary.

SELF-MANAGEMENT. When the data show steady behavioral progress toward the desired goals, the team may consider having the student use the IBRST as part of a self-management system. Self-management involves shifting responsibility to the student for monitoring, evaluating, and reinforcing his or her own performance of specific behaviors. Such a system allows the student more ownership of the intervention strategies, fosters greater independence, and allows the student to take responsibility for his or her behaviors, resulting in greater intrinsic control. If the team decides to use the IBRST as part of a self-management system, the members will consider how to determine the goals of the intervention with the student and then train the student in rating his or her behavior occurrence during designated time periods. Initially, the team will want to have an adult continue to rate the student with a duplicate rating form and schedule time to compare ratings

Behavior	Date	4/1/15	4/2/15	4/3/15	4/4/15	4/5/15	4/8/15	4/9/15	4/10/15	4/11/15	4/13/15	4/16/15	4/17/15	4/18/15	4/19/15	4/20/15
Cursing	>15 times	5	5	5	5	5	5	5	5	5	5	5	5	5	5	5
	12–15 times	4	4	4	4	4	4	4	4	4	4	4	4	4	4	4
	8–11 times	3	3	3	3	3	3	3	3	3	3	3	3	3	3	3
	4–7 times	2	2	2	2	2	2	2	2	2	2	2	2	2	2	2
	0–3 times	1	1	1	1	1	1	1	1	1	1	1	1	1	1	1
Engagement	85%+	5	5	5	5	5	5	5	5	5	5	5	5	5	5	5
	60–85%	4	4	4	4	4	4	4	4	4	4	4	4	4	4	4
	40–59%	3	3	3	3	3	3	3	3	3	3	3	3	3	3	3
	20–39%	2	2	2	2	2	2	2	2	2	2	2	2	2	2	2
	<20%	1	1	1	1	1	1	1	1	1	1	1	1	1	1	1

Intervention 1: Multicomponent plan—choices; replacement behavior; reinforce replacement behavior

Behavior	Date	*4/23/15	4/24/15	4/25/15	4/26/15	4/27/15	4/30/15	5/1/15	5/2/15	5/3/15	5/4/15
Cursing	>15 times	5	5	5	5	5	5	5	5	5	5
	12–15 times	4	4	4	4	4	4	4	4	4	4
	8–11 times	3	3	3	3	3	3	3	3	3	3
	4–7 times	2	2	2	2	2	2	2	2	2	2
	0–3 times	1	1	1	1	1	1	1	1	1	1
Engagement	85%+	5	5	5	5	5	5	5	5	5	5
	60–85%	4	4	4	4	4	4	4	4	4	4
	40–59%	3	3	3	3	3	3	3	3	3	3
	20–39%	2	2	2	2	2	2	2	2	2	2
	<20%	1	1	1	1	1	1	1	1	1	1

Intervention 2: Modified plan—removal of choices; retain replacement behavior; reinforce replacement behavior

FIGURE 9.9. Sample IBRST showing change in intervention (fading of one component of a comprehensive behavior plan).

with the student and discuss discrepancies. Once the student self-rates accurately (i.e., matches the adult's ratings), the adult can implement a gradual fading of rating the student. For more information on self-management strategies, see Chapter 10.

Research on the IBRST

To date, the IBRST has been subjected to one preliminary study exploring interrater agreement (Iovannone, Greenbaum, Wang, Kincaid, & Dunlap, 2014a). Two independent observers, one a school-based practitioner who worked directly with the student (e.g., teacher, paraeducator), the other a data collector from the university research team, used the IBRST to rate their perceptions of targeted behavior occurrences during specific observation times. Repeated data measurements (N = 354) were collected across 19 students in grades K–8 in order to assess agreement between raters. Resulting linear- and quadric-weighted kappa coefficients indicated adequate agreement between raters on both problem and appropriate behaviors with overall quadric-weighted kappa coefficients of .77 for baseline behavior ratings and .72 for postintervention behavior ratings. Furthermore, among the disagreements, the majority only varied by 1 point on the 5-point rating scale, indicating that both observers generally agreed that the behavior was characteristic of a *good day* (e.g., problem behavior was rated at a *1* or a *2*; appropriate behavior at a *5* or a *4*) or of a *bad day* (e.g., problem behavior was rated at a *5* or a *4*; appropriate behavior at a *1* or a *2*). The agreement remained stable from baseline to postintervention as well as across type of measurement dimension (e.g., frequency, duration, percentage, intensity). Behaviors that were more salient (i.e., with clear beginning and ending), however, such as hitting, screaming, or cussing, had higher levels of agreement than did behaviors that were less salient, such as academic engagement, compliance, and communicating needs (e.g., quadric-weighted kappa coefficients of .83 vs. .65). It does need to be noted that interrater agreement estimates were at adequate levels for both salient and less salient behaviors. The difference between the two types of behaviors, though, may suggest that the IBRST is more suitable for use with behaviors that are discrete (i.e., have a distinct beginning and ending) and countable than with behaviors that are continuous in duration and are not easily counted. It could also suggest that more training is needed to use a tool such as the IBRST when less salient behaviors are identified for intervention and tracking purposes. Additional research is needed to further examine these potential questions.

Conclusions

The goal of this chapter was to illustrate how DBR can be used as part of a comprehensive individualized behavior intervention. The IBRST was designed to be used with the PTR FBA/BIP process (Iovannone et al., 2009) and utilizes a 5-point Likert scale to assess both problem and replacement behaviors. One of the most important characteristics of this tool is its inherent flexibility to target a wide range of potential behaviors of interest, assuming that they are both observable and measurable. This feature means that teams are able to assess and intervene with an individualized set of behaviors that are most relevant to a particular student and context. Given that individualization is one of the key features of intensive intervention (National Center on Intensive Intervention, 2013), the IBRST holds particular promise for use with students with more pressing behavioral needs.

Although the IBRST aligns with many other forms of DBR that have been described throughout this book, it is important to keep in mind that intervention design and implementation require a different level of expertise at the intensive level. That is, it is essential to have members of the team who possesses expertise in behavioral principles and measurement in order to guide both the setup and use of the plan and the measure. The guidelines presented in the IBRST blueprint (Table 9.1) may seem fairly simple; however, each step requires a greater level of decision making than necessarily meets the eye. The first step of identifying and defining target behaviors, for example, can be one of the most challenging. In fact, Bergan and Tombari (1976) found that problem identification was the key variable in predicting whether or not an intervention plan was implemented. If the team selects the wrong behavior from the outset or does not spend sufficient time defining and prioritizing behavioral targets, the chances of meaningful behavioral change occurring are inevitably reduced. As one example, a target behavior may be selected that occurs too late in a behavioral chain (i.e., sequence in which minor behaviors lead to more extreme behaviors). A student who is frustrated by an assigned task may begin by muttering under his or her breath; however, these quiet comments may turn into loud profanity and eventually property destruction. In order for efforts to be most effective, it is important to intervene early in the chain with precursor behaviors (i.e., muttering behavior) rather than targeting problem behavior that is full-blown (i.e., property destruction). It is therefore essential that team members who participate in intensive, individualized intervention not only understand the procedures involved in creating and using DBR, but also possess advanced knowledge related to the problem-solving process and behavioral principles as well.

CHAPTER 10

Use of DBR in Self-Management Interventions

Amy M. Briesch and Sandra M. Chafouleas

As discussed earlier in this book, DBR has a long history in the context of teacher-directed intervention. This means that even though ratings are typically shared with the student, the teacher maintains primary responsibility for assessing and recording behavior. Teacher-directed DBR interventions have been shown to be successful at improving a range of student behaviors, from math work completion (Blechman, Schrader, & Taylor, 1981) to the rest-time behavior of kindergarteners (Lahey et al., 1977). However, limitations of teacher-directed interventions are worth noting. First, from a logistical point of view, teachers may not be able to find the time to implement and monitor interventions over time due to competing classroom demands. Although DBR is intended to be far less intrusive and time-consuming than many intervention alternatives, implementation integrity may suffer if teachers do not feel that they have the time or support to implement the intervention (Gresham, 1989). Second, and perhaps even more important from a philosophical point of view, is that teacher-directed intervention may limit the opportunity for skill building. Skill building, such as learning to self-manage behavior, is a critical component of reducing inappropriate behavior (e.g., disruption, aggression) and increasing academic engagement (Epstein et al., 2008). Teacher-directed interventions can keep the locus of control away from the student, thereby diminishing personal responsibility for one's own behavior. Furthermore, when the student's behavior is externally regulated, the likelihood of behavioral generalization is limited (Gross & Wojnilower, 1984). That is, positive behavior change may be evidenced in the presence of the teacher; however, once the student is not under the teacher's watchful eye, the behavior may revert to previous levels.

In contrast, in a self-managed intervention approach, students are charged with the responsibility for their own behavior. As a result, the person whose behavior is being changed and the person doing the changing are one and the same (Copeland, 1982). One of the central advantages of this type of approach is that students tend to become more knowledgeable about their own behavior (McCurdy & Shapiro, 1992), in effect, building skill in self-management. The effectiveness of self-management interventions in helping to empower students by increasing independence and self-reliance has been noted both in the literature (Cole & Bambara, 1992) and by school-based professionals (Briesch, Briesch, & Mahoney, 2014). Students are taught skills that they can take with them beyond the classroom setting, such as how to set personal goals and regulate their own behavior. As a result, self-management strategies have been shown to be at least as effective (e.g., Bolstad & Johnson, 1972), if not more so (e.g., Autry & Langenbach, 1985), at decreasing off-task and disruptive behaviors than teacher-managed interventions. Taken together, the theory behind self-management is that when those skills are within the student's repertoire, supports provided by others are diminished and there is increased likelihood that skills may generalize to new contexts. In this chapter, we expand on this rationale, providing clarification to the terminology surrounding the construct of self-management, and then review options and considerations in design and implementation of self-management techniques.

What Is Self-Management?

What exactly do we mean when we say *self-management*? This question may seem like a simple one; however, posing this question can be like asking one to define intelligence—you are likely to get a different response depending on whom you ask. The number and configuration of specific components has been found to vary substantially from one self-management intervention to the next, with one review of the literature identifying a total of 16 different intervention configurations across 30 studies (Briesch & Chafouleas, 2009). Although self-management interventions may vary in terms of configuration (as we highlight in this chapter), the two core components are inarguably self-observation and self-recording. Together, use of these components has been referred to as *self-monitoring* (Cole & Bambara, 2000). *Self-observation* refers to the process of personal self-reflection, in which the individual's awareness of a target behavior is heightened. As adults, we tend to engage in self-observation on a daily basis without even thinking about it. Take, for example, the speed regulation that inevitably results from passing a police car on the highway, or the act of counting calories in order to maintain one's weight. In either situation, we are engaging in a self-reflective process that ultimately leads to behavioral change.

Within the context of a classroom, students can similarly be taught to assess those behaviors that are critical to, or impeding, school success. For example, a student who struggles with calling out and making disruptive noises during class might be taught to assess his or her overall level of disruption (e.g., *How disruptive was I being on a 1–4 scale?*) periodically throughout the day. In some cases, self-observation may occur at the same time as the problem behavior (e.g., "Sam" realizes that he was making noises when he asks himself the question and then stops this behavior), thereby serving as a prompt to change one's behavior. However, it is not always necessary for self-observation to occur at the same time as the problem behavior in order to be effective. In some cases, self-observations made prior to, or following, a target behavior may also effect behavior change, albeit through different mechanisms (Kanfer, 1970). Taking the example of verbal disruption once again, if Sam is asked to reflect on his behavior before he has actually started making noises or calling out, this self-reflection may preempt the behavior from ever occurring. Alternatively, if Sam is asked to reflect on his behavior after he has already been disruptive, the negative feedback that he receives through self-reflection may be punishing enough to prevent the behavior from recurring. The process of documenting these self-observations is called *self-recording*.

Although self-monitoring forms the foundation of any self-management intervention, it is possible to incorporate several additional components. In our work, we have found the definitions of possible components as proposed by Fantuzzo, Rohrbeck, and Azar (1987) to be useful in understanding the options. These authors suggested that beyond basic self-monitoring procedures (i.e., observing and recording a predetermined, operationally defined behavior), self-management interventions may also involve (1) use of rating prompts, (2) setting goals for student performance and comparing actual performance to these goals, (3) use of primary (e.g., rewards) and/or secondary (e.g., points, tokens) reinforcers, and (4) monitoring performance over time. Each of these components is discussed in greater depth in this chapter to illustrate the different ways in which self-management interventions can be designed and implemented.

Using Self-Management Interventions to Promote Appropriate Student Behavior

As is the case for any DBR-related intervention, flexibility is one of the central advantages for using self-management techniques. In this section, we both outline the general steps involved in using a self-management intervention and highlight the different ways in which particular components may be implemented (see Table 10.1). Although a wide variety of options exists in selecting specific components to incorporate into a self-management plan, it is important to know that few studies

TABLE 10.1. Steps in Designing and Implementing a Self-Management Intervention

☐ 1. Determine with whom the self-management intervention will be used.

Self-management has been shown to be effective for a wide range of students across ages and ability levels.

☐ 2. Identify and define target behavior(s).

The goal may be to increase a positive behavior (e.g., peer interactions) or decrease a negative behavior (e.g., calling out). One or several related behaviors may be chosen.

☐ 3. Determine what method of self-recording will be used and create a DBR-SM card.

Event-based behaviors may best be measured using frequency counts, whereas time-based behaviors may be more easily monitored using a time-sampling or global evaluation technique.

☐ 4. Determine whether self-monitoring prompts will be used.

Although verbal teacher prompts are the most common in the literature, other options include nonverbal cues (e.g., hand signals) or student-centered methods (e.g., timers, pagers).

☐ 5. Determine whether self-evaluation will occur with or without rewards.

In goal-based self-evaluation, students compare performance to a prespecified goal (e.g., 50% on-task behavior). In accuracy-based evaluation, students earn points for matching self-ratings with those of their teacher.

☐ 6. Determine whether self-charting will be used.

Performance may be graphed across days in order to monitor one's progress toward an established goal.

☐ 7. Collect baseline data.

The DBR-SM card can be used by the teacher to collect baseline data and establish appropriate goals.

☐ 8. Conduct training and begin intervention.

Training the student in implementation should focus on two goals: (a) understanding the target behavior and (b) understanding the intervention procedures.

have directly compared the relative efficacy of self-management components. Additional research is therefore warranted in order to determine the independent contribution of particular components and to establish guidelines for applied use.

Step 1: Determine with Whom the Self-Management Intervention Will Be Used

The first step in implementing any intervention is to determine with whom its use is appropriate. Self-management interventions have been used with students across age (e.g., elementary through high school) and ability levels. Although most studies have involved upper-elementary or middle school students (Briesch & Chafouleas, 2009), promising examples involving preschool students can also be found in the literature, wherein self-management has been used to improve classroom transitioning (e.g., Connell, Carta, & Baer, 1993; Connell, Carta, Lutz, et al., 1993), on-task behavior (DeHaas-Warner, 1991, 1992), independent work skills (Sainato, Strain, Lefebvre, & Rapp, 1990), and social interactions (Sainato, Goldstein, & Strain, 1992; Shearer, Kohler, Buchan, & McCullough, 1996). Self-management has also been used successfully with students who have learning disabilities (e.g., Dalton et al., 1999; Maag, Rutherford, & DiGangi, 1992), behavioral disorders (e.g., Levendoski & Cartledge, 2000; McDougall & Brady, 1995), autism spectrum disorders (e.g., Sainato et al., 1990; Strain, Kohler, Storey, & Danko, 1994), as well as with students without exceptionalities (e.g., Rock, 2005). In addition, a review of 16 studies employing self-management interventions with students with ADHD found significant improvements in on-task and appropriate behavior for interventions containing self-monitoring (average effect size [ES] = 2.15), self-monitoring plus reinforcement (average ES = 1.39), and self-evaluation (average ES = 1.96) (Reid, Trout, & Schartz, 2005) components. The positive results established thus far across different populations and contexts support the use of self-management as an intervention option for teaching and reinforcing appropriate behavior with a wide range of students.

Step 2: Identify and Define Target Behavior(s)

Once the target student has been identified, the next step is to select and operationally define an appropriate target behavior. In selecting a behavior to target within a self-management intervention, the "rules" are similar to those of any DBR intervention. That is, the goal is either to increase a positive behavior (e.g., peer interactions during free play) or to decrease a negative behavior (e.g., peer interactions during independent reading). In addition, regardless of the valence of the behavior, it is crucial that it be operationally defined in order to ensure that all parties (e.g., student, teacher) have a clear, shared understanding of the behavior being evaluated. In the research literature, among the behaviors most frequently targeted using self-monitoring have been on-task and disruptive behaviors. We discuss both of these behaviors and additional examples next.

On-Task Behavior

Self-management interventions have been most commonly used to increase on-task behavior, with the overwhelming majority (93%) of studies included in a review of the self-management literature (Briesch & Chafouleas, 2009) targeting this particular outcome. Most typically, students are asked to record whether or not they were paying attention when a recording prompt is given. Such an approach has proven effective with students in both self-contained (e.g., Amato-Zech, Hoff, & Doepke, 2006) and general education classrooms (e.g., Dalton et al., 1999), in addition to alternative school placements (e.g., Wood, Murdock, Cronin, Dawson, & Kirby, 1998) and residential treatment programs (e.g., Axelrod, Zhe, Haugen, & Klein, 2009).

Disruptive Behavior

Self-management interventions have also been commonly used to reduce disruptive classroom behavior such as calling out, being out of one's seat, and making inappropriate noises. In a study by Barry and Messer (2003), for example, elementary school students diagnosed with ADHD were asked to answer the questions "Did I play or fight with my classmates in the classroom?" and "Did I talk loudly or make noise in class?" during a general education classroom period. Self-management interventions have also been found to be successful in reducing the disruptive behavior of students either at risk for (Hoff & DuPaul, 1998), or diagnosed with (Dunlap et al., 1995), behavioral disorders.

Targeting Multiple Behaviors

Although students have most commonly been taught to assess a single classroom behavior, in some cases multiple behaviors have been rated simultaneously. In a study by Guerasko-Moore et al. (2007), for example, male students diagnosed with ADHD were taught to complete a classroom preparation checklist consisting of four targets: (1) *seated when bell rang*, (2) *eye contact with teacher when instruction began*, (3) *pen or pencil on desk*, and (4) *relevant instructional materials open when lesson began*. Peterson, Young, Salzberg, West, and Hill (2006) taught students to rate six target behaviors related to classroom social skills (i.e., *on-task*, *off-task*, *following instructions*, *accepting no for an answer*, *accepting teacher feedback*, *appropriately getting teacher attention*) using a 4-point scale (i.e., *honor*, *satisfactory*, *needs improvement*, *unsatisfactory*). Finally, Chafouleas, Sanetti, Jaffery, et al. (2012) worked with middle school teachers to design and implement a classwide intervention involving individual monitoring of engagement, homework completion, and class preparedness. Examples of forms and intervention training materials for these three target behaviors can be freely accessed at *www.directbehaviorratings.org*.

Internalizing Behaviors

Far less is known about the efficacy of self-management interventions in the treatment of internalizing disorders (e.g., anxiety, depression). In the literature on internalizing behaviors, self-monitoring has been applied as an assessment method through which self-ratings are used as a source of outcome data rather than as the intervention agent. For example, individuals struggling with anxiety may be asked to record their responses to anxiety-provoking situations (e.g., increases in heart rate, dysfluent speech; Donohue, Van Hasselt, & Hersen, 1994). Recommendations have been made with regard to use of self-management as an intervention strategy, such as asking depressed students to monitor positive life events (e.g., Reynolds & Stark, 1987). Empirical evidence is not currently available, however, to support the use of self-management as an intervention for internalizing behaviors.

Other Target Behaviors

Although self-management has most commonly been used to address the problem behaviors discussed above, other unique applications have been noted in the literature. Some researchers have used self-management strategies to teach and promote social interactions between children with autism spectrum disorder (ASD) and their typically developing peers (e.g., Sainato et al., 1992; Strain et al., 1994). Across these studies, strategy training alone did not lead to increases in strategy usage; however, the introduction of self-recording (i.e., having the child mark *yes* or *no*, depending on whether a particular strategy was used successfully) resulted in significant increases in strategy usage. Stahmer and Schreibman (1992) also used self-management with children with ASD in order to teach appropriate play behaviors (e.g., driving toy car instead of sucking on or throwing toy car). In this case, the child self-monitored by marking a box at the end of a predetermined interval to indicate whether he or she had played appropriately.

Step 3: Determine What Method of Self-Recording Will Be Used and Create a DBR-SM Card

As was stated above, the process of documenting self-observations is called *self-recording*. The next step in setting up a self-management intervention is to determine what method of self-recording best matches the behavior of interest. That is, it is necessary to first determine whether the target behavior is event-based (i.e., discrete) or time-based (i.e., continuous), and then to select a recording system that is consistent with the type of behavior (Chafouleas, Riley-Tillman, & Sugai, 2007). Table 10.2 provides a brief review of characteristics and examples of each recording system.

Event-Based Behaviors

If the behavior of interest has a clear beginning and end (e.g., inappropriate comments, contributing to classroom discussion), use of a frequency count may be most appropriate. An example of a simple form for the self-recording of count data is presented in Figure 10.1. An overall frequency count can be monitored across days if the time period is consistent (e.g., 45-minute math period), or, more typically, a rate of behavior (e.g., three hand raises per hour) can be calculated to provide a standardized estimate across time. Although frequency counts are fairly easy to learn to self-monitor, one potential limitation is that it can become highly intrusive if the behavior occurs at a high frequency. Therefore, another option may be to record the permanent products of a target behavior. The most common application of this within school-based settings has been the self-recording of work completion. A student, for example, may be asked to record the number of math problems completed by the end of class or the number of pages read in a story. Self-monitoring of

TABLE 10.2. Examples of Event and Time-based Behaviors

What kind of behavior is it?	Event-based (i.e., discrete)	Time-based (i.e., continuous)
How do you know?	The behavior . . . • Is relatively short in duration. • Has a clear beginning and end. • Is easy to count or record duration.	The behavior . . . • Varies in duration. • Has a less defined beginning and end. • Occurs too quickly or frequently to count meaningfully and accurately.
What are some examples?	• Calling out • Punching a neighbor • Asking a question • Breaking a pencil • Hand raising • Social initiations • Positive verbal statements	• Active or passive attention to task • Disruption • Throwing a tantrum or crying • Roaming around the classroom • Social interaction • Playing with objects

Name: ______________________________

Date: ______________________________

Activity: ______________________________

Place an *X* in the box every time that you raise your hand to answer a question.				

FIGURE 10.1. A simple format for event recording, in this case, each occurrence of hand raising.

performance is discussed more specifically later in this chapter. Finally, a checklist format might be used to assess whether the student completed certain tasks. In a study by Guerasko-Moore, DuPaul, and White (2006), students with ADHD used a checklist to document the presence or absence of classroom preparation behaviors such as having their materials ready.

Time-Based Behaviors

Alternatively, some behaviors have a more meaningful duration and therefore are not easily counted. Such behaviors may be measured using either time-sampling techniques or a global evaluation. Time-sampling techniques require the student to record his or her behavior at regular intervals throughout the target period (e.g., every minute, every 5 minutes). One option within a time-sampling approach is for students to base their ratings on what their behavior looked like at the time of the prompt (akin to traditional time-sampling methods). For example, an inattentive student may be instructed to periodically stop and ask him- or herself "Was I paying attention right now?" and then mark the answer in a chart containing yes and no boxes. A second option is for students to more generally assess their behavior since the time of the last prompt. For example, the same inattentive student may be instructed to ask him- or herself "Was I paying attention over the past 5 minutes?" and then mark the answer accordingly. An example of a dichotomous (i.e., yes/no) DBR form that utilizes time sampling is presented in Figure 10.2. The number of intervals in which a target behavior was observed can then be divided by the total number of recording intervals to provide a percentage estimate of how often the behavior occurred.

One question that arises when using a time-sampling approach is how frequently ratings should be conducted. As opposed to a teacher-completed DBR, less is currently known about the ideal frequency with which behaviors should be self-rated. In the majority of studies, self-monitoring intervals have been set at fairly short latencies, with students self-observing and recording as frequently as every 1–5 minutes. It is likely that frequency may be flexibly determined based on the particular situation however. For example, it may be unreasonable to use very short latencies (e.g., 30 seconds) when engaged in a reading comprehension activity, whereas it is likely impractical to use a longer latency (e.g., 2 hours) when frequent prompts are needed.

The other option for self-recording time-based behaviors involves having the student conduct a more global evaluation (e.g., rating behavior once at the end of class), such as is typically done by adult DBR users. Ardoin and Martens (2004), for example, trained students to rate the amount of time that they spent looking around, playing with objects, engaging in peer interactions, and being out of seat, using a 4-point scale (i.e., *none of the time, just a little of the time, some of the time, all of the time*) at the end of each period. Furthermore, middle school students in a study by Chafouleas, Sanetti, Jaffery, and Fallon (2012) used an 11-point DBR-SIS to rate degree of engagement along with class preparedness and homework completion at the end of the targeted instructional period. In Figure 10.3, an example of two different formats for DBR is provided to illustrate how a scale can be flexibly modified for younger and older student populations. First, the use of pictures may help to make the rating scale more interpretable. Whereas older students are better able to discriminate between values on a Likert-type scale (e.g., 1 = *not following classroom rules*, 5 = *perfectly following classroom rules*), use of a smiley-face scale may facilitate more accurate rating with younger students. Pictures have also been used to increase the saliency of target behaviors and to facilitate evaluation. In Figure 10.4, one example of a form for monitoring outdoor play behavior is provided.

Although either time-sampling or traditional DBR ratings can be used when assessing time-based behaviors, remember that a key feature of using DBR involves recording a rating in close proximity to the actual occurrence of the behavior; thus, retrospective recordings (e.g., "What did you eat for breakfast last Monday?") are not included. Future research is needed in order to determine the optimal timing of self-monitoring, as well as how recommendations may vary depending on the behavior of interest.

Name: ______________________________

Date: ______________________________

Activity: ______________________________

Directions: Each time you are asked to self-record, consider your current behavior and then make a mark in the appropriate box.

STUDY RECORD		
	Record + if you were studying	Record – if you were not studying
1		
2		
3		
4		
5		
6		
7		
8		
9		
10		
Total +'s = ___/ 10 = ___% of intervals studying		

FIGURE 10.2. A sample of a DBR format for time-based recording, in this case, related to studying behavior.

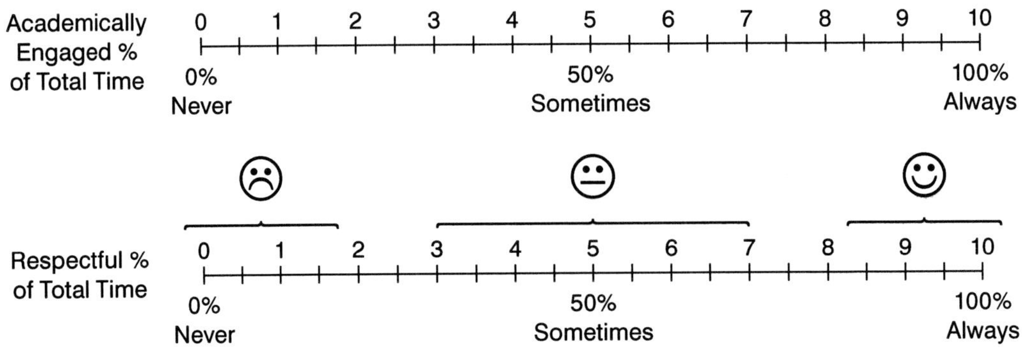

FIGURE 10.3. Examples of DBR scales modified for a younger and an older student population. Note that although the scale is consistent across both examples (0–10), the qualitative descriptors are adapted. The original formats are available at *www.directbehaviorratings.org*. Reprinted with permission from Sandra M. Chafouleas, T. Chris Riley-Tillman, Theodore J. Christ, and George Sugai.

Step 4: Determine Whether Self-Monitoring Prompts Will Be Used

Once a target behavior has been defined and the method of self-monitoring has been selected, one question that arises is how the student will know when it is time to engage in self-monitoring. Throughout the research literature, use of various monitoring prompts has been noted, and similar diversity in prompting approaches has been reported in practice as well. Verbal prompts have been commonly noted in the literature (e.g., Barry & Messer, 2003), and a recent survey of school psychologists (Briesch et al., 2014) found these to be the most popular cues. Other prompts commonly provided by teachers included nonverbal cues such as hand signals or a tap on the shoulder. Prompts need not, however, be the responsibility of the adult. In some cases, a student's self-monitoring schedule may be determined by having the student look at the clock, using a timer or pager, or it may correspond with natural transitions that occur in the classroom (e.g., end of classroom lesson).

Step 5: Determine Whether Self-Evaluation Will Occur with or without Rewards

The next consideration that must be made is whether or not to engage the student in the process of self-evaluation. Across several studies, self-monitoring has been used effectively in isolation (e.g., Levendoski & Cartledge, 2000; Prater, Hogan,

Name: ______________________________

Date: ______________________________

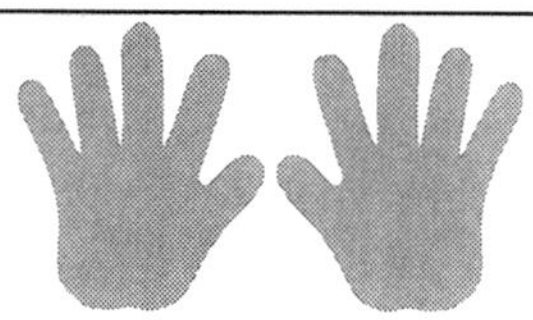	Keep hands to self	☺	😐	☹
	Play with equipment nicely	☺	😐	☹
	Use kind words	☺	😐	☹

FIGURE 10.4. A sample of a DBR form targeting outdoor play activities for preschool students.

& Miller, 1992), suggesting that the simple act of increasing self-awareness may be enough to cause meaningful behavioral change. An additional option, however, involves the use of self-evaluation. Two options for evaluation can be used in isolation or combination: (1) comparing performance to a goal to assess absolute performance, or (2) comparing performance to an external standard to determine accuracy of rating. An example of comparing performance to a goal might include 80% correct on math computation worksheets, whereas comparison of performance to an external standard might involve comparing ratings with those completed by a teacher. Each is further described below.

Use of Goal-Based Evaluation

In the first option, a goal for student behavior can be prespecified and student performance compared to the established standard. For example, given low levels of attention noted prior to intervention (e.g., 50% on-task behavior), the teacher could work with a student to set a reasonable goal for attention during the intervention phase (e.g., 70% on-task behavior). Each day, the teacher and student would meet at the end of class and compare the student's ratings to the predetermined standard to see whether he or she has met this goal.

Most typically, adults establish performance goals with minimal input solicited from students. This is likely because one of the major concerns voiced surrounding student determination of performance goals is that children may select goals that are not reasonably challenging (i.e., standard set too low). Consider, for example, the response you are likely to get if you ask a fifth grader how much homework he or she thinks would be reasonable to assign! One suggestion would therefore be that adults provide explicit guidance and instructions regarding goal setting (e.g., setting performance goal above previous baseline performance) to ensure that the standard chosen is reasonably stringent.

Use of Accuracy-Based Evaluation

There is no requirement that the accuracy of student ratings be examined when comparing performance to a goal, and some studies have demonstrated that significant behavioral change can occur in the absence of rating accuracy (e.g., Broden, Hall, & Mitts, 1971; Lipinski & Nelson, 1974). However, the accuracy issue has generally raised some concern and controversy because although self-observation and self-recording largely occur in tandem, it is possible that a student might observe him- or herself engaging in inappropriate behaviors but choose not to record the behavior as inappropriate in order to present a more favorable impression. This is akin to a response bias known as "faking good" or social desirability. For example, when asked to rate the amount of sugary foods consumed over the course of a day, it is easy to see how a person enrolled a weight management course might under-record sugar consumption despite self-observation.

In order to address this potential problem, the second option for self-evaluation involves assessing the accuracy of student ratings by comparing them to ratings conducted by an external observer. For example, both the student and teacher would conduct ratings simultaneously during class and then meet at the end of class to compare their assessments. Typically, bonus points are awarded if the student's ratings exactly match the teacher's, and points are lost if major rating discrepancies are noted. However, one of the concerns with including an accuracy-based evaluation component is that an external observer (e.g., teacher, aide) is needed. At a logistical level, this may be a concern because of the adult resources required.

Use of Reinforcement

Evaluation is frequently linked to use of reinforcement (e.g., tokens, rewards). For example, students receive a "prize" for meeting an established goal or for achieving a particular level of rating accuracy. Some studies have demonstrated that incremental effects may be achieved when rewards are added to self-monitoring alone (e.g., Gansle & McMahon, 1997; Maag et al., 1992); however, a recent meta-analysis found stronger effect sizes for those self-management studies that did *not* incorporate reinforcement (Briesch & Briesch, 2015). Although many studies have included reports on students in the process of selecting rewards (e.g., Dalton et al., 1999; Hertz & McLaughlin, 1990), students have not typically been charged with the responsibility of determining when and how to administer their own rewards. This fact is likely due to concerns that students may recruit rewards even if they were not earned. For example, imagine what might happen when a puppy is left to independently administer his bag of training treats! Given that limited research (e.g., Bolstad & Johnson, 1972; Felixbrod & O'Leary, 1973) has found self-administered and externally administered rewards to be equally effective, however, suggests that the management choice for reinforcement components may be left to the discretion of the individual implementer, and might best be based on considerations related to individual situations, such as the student, type of reinforcer, etc. For example, in the case of one of us (S. M. C.) in particular, it would generally not be a wise decision to rely on appropriate independent delivery of Girl Scout cookies (particularly the Thin Mint variety)!

Step 6: Determine Whether Self-Charting Will Be Used

Perhaps the least frequently utilized component in the literature has been self-charting, which involves the regular graphing of performance across days and monitoring one's progress toward an established goal. Research has shown that providing students with graphical feedback may serve to improve behavior (e.g., Fuchs & Fuchs, 1987). Although a handful of studies have incorporated charting into the larger intervention package (e.g., Moore, Prebble, Robertson, Waetford, & Anderson, 2001; Shimabukuro, Prater, Jenkins, & Edelen-Smith, 1999), the independent contribution of self-graphing to self-monitoring procedures has generally been neglected. Figure 10.5 contains a blank graph to illustrate the simple steps involved in making a graph by hand.

Step 7: Collect Baseline Data

As with all interventions, it is important to collect baseline data to ensure that the behavior warrants intervention and to establish appropriate goals. During the baseline phase, the teacher can utilize DBR to complete the same rating of the student's target behavior. Once baseline behavior stabilizes (see discussion in Chapter 11), the self-management intervention can then be introduced to the student.

Student Self-Chart

Name: ______________________________

Date: ______________________________

Activity: ______________________________

y-axis label: ______________

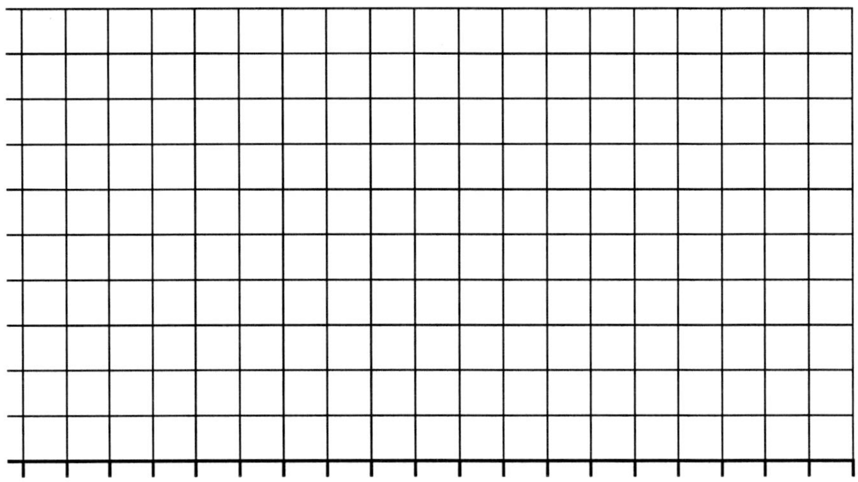

x-axis label: ______________________________

Directions:

1. Label the *x*-axis to represent the time period (e.g., sessions or days).
2. Label the *y*-axis to represent what is being measured (e.g., hand raising).
3. Write in the units (i.e., numbers) along the *y*- and *x*-axes. Numbers should be equal intervals (e.g., 1, 1.5, 2, 2.5 or 1, 2, 3, 4).
4. Enter the data points on the graph by marking a dot at the corresponding number on the *y*-axis for each session or day (e.g., if the total number of times you raised your hand on day 1 was five, you would mark a circle that lines up with day 1 on the *x*-axis and the label 5 on the *y*-axis).

FIGURE 10.5. A blank graph for teaching students self-graphing.

Step 8: Conduct Training and Begin Intervention

The last step to implementing a self-management intervention is training the student in the implementation procedures. Although the content of training sessions will inevitably vary depending on the age of the student and the level of the problem behavior, most sessions will focus on two common goals: the student's understanding of (1) the target behavior and (2) the intervention procedures. Training can occur either in or outside the actual classroom setting. If training occurs outside of the classroom setting, however, it may be necessary to implement practice sessions in the classroom before the actual intervention begins to make sure the student and any involved adults fully understand the procedures. For example, in our work, we have found it important to review and practice procedures around how recording will occur (when completed and reviewed, where materials will be kept). Each of the training goals is further described next.

Understanding the Target Behavior

The first goal is focused on ensuring that the student has a detailed understanding of the behavior or behaviors that he or she will be asked to monitor. As noted previously, it is necessary to first define the target behavior in observable and measurable terms, such that the student and adult have a shared understanding of what the behavior looks like. Both examples and nonexamples of the target behavior should be presented as well to maximize definitional clarity. The rationale behind training participants to understand the targets becomes crystal clear if we consider a situation in which a child has claimed to his parent, "Yes, I've cleaned up my room." Whereas the child might believe that a clean room is defined by no clothes on the floor, a parent might disagree that simply shoving all the clothes into the closet does not constitute a clean room, given that the clothes were not neatly put away. In addition to didactic instruction, the adult may choose to model the examples and nonexamples for the student. This modeling component can be especially important for targets involving social behavior, such as use of appropriate language. Modeling language indicating respectful (e.g., "Could I please borrow your yellow marker for a few minutes?") versus disrespectful (e.g., "I need that marker—give it to me!") behavior can be a key element to effective training. To check for understanding, students can then be given different practice scenarios (e.g., reading vignettes, participating in role plays) and asked to indicate whether the target behavior occurred.

Understanding the Intervention Procedures

The second goal of training should be to ensure that students understand how to carry out the actual intervention procedures. During this phase, the adult reviews the recording sheet with the student, explains any applicable prompts, and has the student practice recording his or her behavior using the form. Although recording practice may occur solely in the training context, in many cases (e.g., Dalton, Martella, & Marchand-Martella, 1999; Edwards, Salant, Howard, Brougher, & McLaughlin, 1995), a trial recording period has been incorporated into the classroom as well. Before the intervention officially begins, the student may be asked to implement the procedures in the actual classroom setting, with more frequent accuracy checks built in to ensure that he or she is rating correctly. During this period, it is helpful to incorporate adults who will responsible for assisting the student as well to ensure that all are knowledgeable about, and comfortable with, the procedures.

One of the concerns that practitioners may have relates to a student's ability to provide useful and reliable behavioral data. Problems with self-report data in children have been noted (LaGreca, 1990), including the potential for children to provide information that is socially desirable rather than accurate. Research has shown, however, that even students at the elementary level can be trained to conduct accurate self-evaluations (e.g., Ardoin & Martens, 2004). In fact, interobserver agreement levels of 80% and above have been noted repeatedly in the literature (e.g., Carr & Punzo, 1993; Wood et al., 1998). Even studies conducted with preschool students have demonstrated moderate to high correlations (range = 0.61–1.00) between self-ratings and data from external observers (DeHaas-Warner, 1992; Sainato et al., 1990), suggesting that even very young children can be taught to make accurate assessments.

Putting It All Together: Case Examples

Now that we have reviewed the steps involved in designing a self-management intervention, we illustrate its use in two different contexts. In the first case example, self-management is used to target attending behavior in a kindergarten student. The second case example describes the use of a self-managed DBR to improve the homework completion, class preparation, and independent organization of a middle school student.

Example 1: Kindergarten

"Ms. Smith" has approached "Ms. Lee," the school psychologist, to discuss some concerns regarding one of her kindergarten students, "Josie." According to Ms. Smith, Josie engages in high levels of off-task behavior during independent seatwork. In particular, Ms. Smith is concerned that Josie does not seem to be following along when she gives directions and does not see tasks to completion without getting distracted and requiring several prompts. Josie's off-task behavior manifests in a variety of ways, including looking out of the window, doodling, and talking to neighbors. After talking together, Ms. Smith and Ms. Lee decide that self-management would be an appropriate intervention strategy for Josie to increase her overall on-task behavior in the classroom.

First, Ms. Smith and Ms. Lee decide that the target behavior in this case will be "paying attention," which they define as "the student being oriented toward the teacher and/or actively engaged in instructional activities." Next, they determine that the intervention will consist of the following components: self-monitoring, goal-based self-evaluation, verbal reinforcement, and charting. Ms. Smith will verbally prompt Josie to self-record how well she was paying attention periodically throughout the day and then meet with her at the end of the day to review her ratings and compare them to a preset goal. They determine that an appropriate goal would be to earn 5 out of 6 possible points for each day. Because Ms. Smith feels that self-charting would be too difficult a task for a kindergarten student, she decides to collect and graph the data each day and then provide verbal reinforcement to Josie after reviewing the graph.

Ms. Smith feels that the best time and place for the self-recording would be during the periods devoted to independent work involving literacy. Due to the fact that on-task behavior has a meaningful duration, Ms. Lee decides that a momentary time-sampling technique would be the best approach to utilize. About every 5 minutes during the 30-minute period, Ms. Smith will prompt Josie to record whether or not she was paying attention, using the sample DBR form in Figure 10.6.

To ensure that Josie knows what *paying attention* means and is able to appropriately self-monitor and record her behavior, Ms. Smith conducts a brief training. First, Ms. Smith verbally discusses the problem behavior and provides Josie with examples, nonexamples, and pictorial representations of what paying attention looks like. Second, Ms. Smith explicitly shows Josie how to complete the DBR form, providing multiple chances to practice recording her own behavior and receive feedback regarding her rating accuracy.

Over the next 2 weeks, Josie completes the self-monitoring form using the described procedures. At the end of each day, Ms. Smith computes Josie's overall DBR score (out of a possible 6 points) and adds this data point to her cumulative

Was I paying attention during classroom activities?						
1	2	3	4	5	6	TOTAL ☺
☺ YES ☹ NO	☺ YES ☹ NO	☺ YES ☹ NO	☺ YES ☹ NO	☺ YES ☹ NO	☺ YES ☹ NO	

FIGURE 10.6. DBR form for Josie.

graph. When Ms. Lee and Ms. Smith meet to review the data, Ms. Smith indicates that the intervention was effective and that Josie's attention during independent literacy tasks has improved. Although preintervention data had not been collected, trends in the DBR data also supported Ms. Smith's perception. Josie's DBR data are provided in Figure 10.7.

Example 2: Middle School

"Sam" is a sixth-grade student who was recently referred by his classroom teachers due to trouble with organization. Sam's teachers note that he is often unprepared for class and seems to forget materials as well as his assignments. Sam's teachers contacted "Mr. Green," the school psychologist, to discuss the problem and develop an intervention plan. Through discussions with Sam and his parents, Mr. Green revealed that Sam has typically had difficulty with organization, but that the difficulties became more problematic when he entered middle school and was required to change classes and track multiple assignments throughout the day. Together, they decide that a self-management intervention may help Sam bolster needed organizational skills.

Mr. Green works with Sam, his teachers, and parents to identify the behaviors that they want to target. They decide on three: homework, class preparation, and independent organization. After speaking with Sam's teachers, Mr. Green finds that Sam seems to have the most difficulty at the beginning of the day and after changing classes for English and social studies. Mr. Green suggests that it might be best if Sam self-records his behaviors once at the end of his morning math and science block, and then again following his English and social studies block in the afternoon. Using this information, Mr. Green creates the DBR form in Figure 10.8.

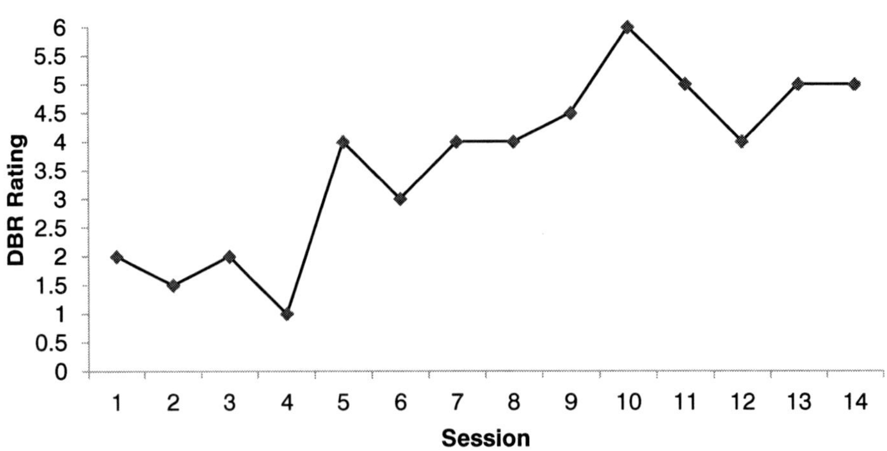

FIGURE 10.7. DBR data for Josie.

Daily Self-Monitoring Form	
Student's Name: *Sam*	Date: *April 3rd*
Class: Circle one Math/Science or English/Social Sciences	
How well did I do with homework completion? Examples: Completed today's homework assignments, remembered to bring assignment with me to school, handed in assignment on time when requested.	0 1 2 3 4 5 6 7 8 9 10 Not at all Somewhat Very well
How well was I prepared for class? Examples: Had all necessary materials for class (pens, pencils, etc.), had materials ready to go when needed, wrote down important information, packed all materials at end of class.	0 1 2 3 4 5 6 7 8 9 10 Not at all Somewhat Very well
How well did I independently organize? Examples: Remembered homework, wrote down important information, remembered materials without being reminded, and followed and understood directions without needing multiple prompts.	0 1 2 3 4 5 6 7 8 9 10 Not at all Somewhat Very well
	Average Rating
	# Bonus Points
	Total for class

FIGURE 10.8. DBR form for Sam.

The team decides that it would be most appropriate for Sam to have a self-evaluation procedure that was goal-based but also where he could earn extra points for accuracy. Sam's primary teachers, "Mr. Franklin" (math and science) and "Ms. Draper" (English and social studies), agree to briefly meet with Sam after class every day to review the DBR form. They agree that an appropriate goal for Sam would be to receive a score of at least 7 on his DBR form total for the day (average of the two class totals), and that he will receive 1 extra point on his form if his self-recording is accurate (as compared to the teacher ratings). Mr. Green and Sam talk together to determine an appropriate reinforcer for reaching the preselected goal and decide upon extra computer time. In addition, they agree that if Sam meets his goal for at least 4 of the 5 days, he will receive an additional reinforcer for meeting his goal across the week. Because Sam is in the sixth grade, the team feels that he is

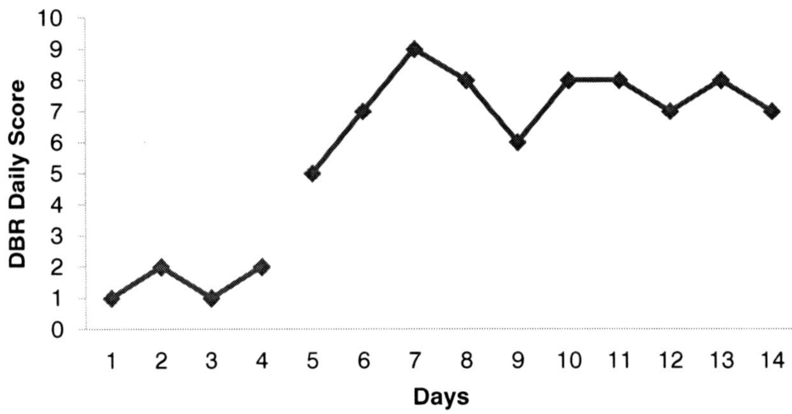

FIGURE 10.9. DBR data for Sam.

old enough to self-chart his DBR data at the end of each school day. Ms. Draper will then meet with Sam to review his chart and provide the reinforcement, if appropriate.

Mr. Green reviews the DBR form with Sam, supplies him with a blank graphing chart, and provides instructions regarding how to calculate his total score for the day and plot his data. Once Sam has demonstrated his understanding of the procedures, he begins self-monitoring as described. At the end of 2 weeks, Mr. Green checks in with both of Sam's teachers to review overall progress. Both teachers report that the intervention has been successful, in that Sam was much more organized. Sam likewise reports that he is doing better and is happy to continue with the self-management program. Review of Sam's DBR data further supports the comments from both Sam and his teachers (see Figure 10.9).

Conclusions

The goal of this chapter was to provide an overview of the ways in which self-management interventions have been used in research and what considerations must be pondered before incorporating self-managed DBR in practice. As this chapter illustrates, a singular term has been used to describe a wide range of intervention configurations that vary with regard to the number of components, the level of student involvement, and the format of the DBR. Although additional work is still needed to identify components and to explore the effects with additional populations (e.g., young students) and on additional behaviors (e.g., internalizing), the demonstrations of effectiveness and flexibility with which the intervention can be adapted offer a highly valuable option for supporting students.

PART IV

DBR Communication

Linking Assessment and Intervention

CHAPTER 11

Summarizing DBR Data for Interpretation and Decision Making

Austin H. Johnson, T. Chris Riley-Tillman, and Sandra M. Chafouleas

The purpose of data collection in schools is to inform decision making, whether it is a teacher giving a test to determine student comprehension of academic material or a school psychologist collecting DBR data with a seventh grade teacher to determine if a student is responding to an intervention to improve academic engagement. Data without context are just numbers, and graphs without critical examination are just pictures. If data are to help support students in schools, we must move beyond simply collecting and storing the information to summarizing and interpreting it to inform decision making.

As has been discussed earlier in this book, two of the critical components of an effective multi-tiered system of support are the use of (1) screening data to identify those students who require intervention and (2) progress monitoring data to understand each student's response to intervention. Each component entails unique considerations and data analyses. Behavioral screening typically involves a one-time decision: Students are administered a measure, the resultant data are summarized, and these data are used to identify students in need of supports. In order to assess a student's response to intervention, however, we need to understand what his or her behavior looked like before and after an intervention was implemented. As a result, the steps of summarizing, presenting, and interpreting cannot occur just once during a case if the data are to inform current and ongoing practices. Rather, the school team will need to set a goal for meaningful change and collect and evaluate data repeatedly to determine if that change is occurring in response to intervention.

The importance of making data summarization procedures efficient and flexible is relevant to both screening (given the large amounts of data typically collected) and progress monitoring (given the repeated nature of data collection). As a result, preparing data ahead of time in a way that makes them easy to use, access, and manipulate can save a lot of effort later on when preparing presentations, graphs, and reports. This chapter reviews three key steps in preparing DBR data for interpretation and decision making. First, DBR data must be *organized* to establish a central location for collected information. Second, DBR data must be *summarized* in a way that facilitates meaningful interpretation by school professionals and stakeholders, such as parents and sometimes the students themselves. Third, DBR data patterns must be *interpreted*—or translated from numbers, bars, and lines—into actionable information (see Table 11.1 for an outline of these steps).

Organization

The first step to making a data system easy to use and manipulate is organization: the task of gathering together and preparing data for presentation. After collecting multiple sessions', periods', or days' worth of data, practitioners are often left with a stack of data collection forms and the intimidating task of putting them all together in a way that makes sense. Generally, the first step in any data organization process is determining *where* to put the data.

Step 1: Select a Data Management System

Although data entry is rarely an enjoyable task, moving information from paper form into an electronic storage system can serve to simplify the subsequent activities necessary to interpret the data. Thankfully, the wide availability of digital spreadsheet tools (as outlined in Table 11.2) allows for complex data sets to be quickly and easily entered and summarized. Paid options include Microsoft Excel, part of the Microsoft Office Suite, and Apple Numbers, which belongs to the iWork package for Mac operating systems. A number of free options for data organization exist as well. For a solution with no download necessary, Google Drive provides fairly comprehensive spreadsheet software with cloud storage. In addition, Apache's OpenOffice suite includes Calc, a free-to-use downloadable data management tool comparable to Microsoft Excel. A simple web search of either of these application names will direct you to each company's website for more information.

Before choosing and implementing any data management system, digital or otherwise, it is crucial to review the ethical and legal obligations to which educational professionals are subject in relation to student data. It is incumbent upon educational professionals who collect and store student data to ensure that they

TABLE 11.1. Steps in Preparing DBR Data for Interpretation and Decision Making

- ☐ 1. Select a data management system.

  Both paid (e.g., Microsoft Excel, Apple Numbers) and free (e.g., Google Docs, Calc) options are available for storing and organizing data. The use of digital records, however, involves unique considerations related to data security, confidentiality, and disclosure.

- ☐ 2. Enter the data.

  A minimum of three columns of data is needed when entering formative data (i.e., date/session, phase, DBR score); however, additional aspects of the observation may be entered in subsequent columns (e.g., activity type, number of students present).

- ☐ 3. Generate summary statistics.

  The typical level of behavior can be represented by the mean, median, or mode value. Bar graphs can be used to visually compare summary statistics (e.g., across target behaviors, across periods of time).

- ☐ 4. Create bar graphs.

  Bar graphs can be used to visually depict the typical DBR score obtained across categorical groups (e.g., boys vs. girls, baseline vs. intervention, academic engagement vs. respectful behavior).

- ☐ 5. Create line graphs.

  Line graphs can be used to visually depict changes in DBR scores over time for a target student or group.

- ☐ 6. Conduct a visual analysis.

  Examine changes in level, trend, and variability within and across phases. Assess the immediacy of effects from baseline to intervention.

- ☐ 7. Use quantitative metrics to supplement visual analysis.

  The magnitude of an effect can be determined by calculating quantitative metrics such as percentage of nonoverlapping data, improvement rate difference, or standardized mean difference.

- ☐ 8. Determine next steps.

  Once data have been analyzed, one must determine whether the intervention was effective, ineffective, or inconclusive. Follow-up strategies are then selected based on this determination.

TABLE 11.2. Descriptions of Popular Spreadsheet Software

Name	Description	Cost	Where to find
Microsoft Excel 2013	Part of the Microsoft Office software suite. Widely used, with many tutorials available online. Available for Windows and Mac.	$109.99	*http://office.microsoft.com/en-us/excel*
Apple Numbers	Part of the iWork software suite. More visually driven and less spreadsheet-driven than Excel. Available only for Mac.	$19.99	*www.apple.com/iwork/numbers*
Google Drive	Hosted in the "cloud," or exclusively online. Use regular Internet browser to enter and manipulate data. Available on most Internet-enabled computers and devices.	Free	*http://drive.google.com*
OpenOffice Calc	Part of the OpenOffice software suite. Similar features to those found in Excel. Can open and edit Excel files. Available for Windows, Mac, and other operating systems.	Free	*www.openoffice.org/product/calc.html*

are stored in a manner that both protects student confidentiality and does not contain information about the student that is unnecessary for service provision (Jacob, Decker, & Hartshorne, 2010). In addition to reviewing relevant professional codes of conduct regarding student records, educational professionals should also attend to provisions laid out in both the Family Educational Rights and Privacy Act (FERPA; 1974) and the Individuals with Disabilities Education Act (IDEA; 2004).

Given their unique attributes, digital records require some additional upkeep provisions that must be considered. These include issues of *security* and *disclosure.* In terms of security, unlike a lockable filing cabinet, securing files on computers can be a tricky and at times unwieldy task. The Excel, Calc, and Numbers programs all feature password protection for files; a web search of "password protect [program name] file" should yield results that describe the steps involved for each program. Furthermore, free and robust encryption tools such as TrueCrypt are available for download; these tools allow users to secure data stored digitally. Many computers that contain sensitive or identifiable data can be loaded with systemwide encryption; district IT departments should be able to provide additional information about the use of these options.

Stripping data and records of all identifiable information is one excellent way to protect against breaches of confidentiality, and should be considered whenever data are stored or transmitted digitally. For example, names in a digitally stored spreadsheet could be replaced by an ID number, with a separate "key" connecting that ID number to the student's name stored locally in a locked filing cabinet. With data stored in this manner, the digitally stored data may not be able to be linked to the student's real name unless the key is also accessed—which should be unlikely if it is securely stored in a separate location.

It is crucial to note that these are just recommendations. Practitioners should consult with their school, district, or state education agencies; IT departments; and other appropriate authorities to understand the restrictions regarding student records that are relevant to their circumstances.

Step 2: Enter the Data

After selecting a data entry tool and reviewing relevant policies and recommended procedures surrounding the use of electronic data entry systems, it's time to figure out how best to actually enter the data. When entering screening data, each row should reflect the data for a different student. Because screening using DBR data entails collecting ratings across multiple days, each day of data collection should be represented in its own column. These data points can then be used to generate a column of mean scores reflecting the student's average DBR score over the data collection period. Assuming that multiple students are included in the screening, then each row will represent a different student. In this case, you can look down a column (e.g., DBR-AE) and consider students in comparison to their peers. You can also include columns to highlight risk status based on the result. If data are collected across multiple behaviors, the same set of columns can be copied to separate spreadsheets, each representing a relevant target (e.g., academic engagement, disruptive behavior). See Figure 11.1 for an example of this method of summarizing screening data.

When entering formative data for summarization, it is necessary to have at least three columns: one that represents time (e.g., day, session), one that represents the intervention condition (e.g., baseline, intervention), and one for the obtained DBR score. Each row therefore represents a unique observation (e.g., all of the data from 4/5/15, 4/6/15, and 4/7/15 on separate rows). The first column might be labeled *Day* if a single observation was conducted daily; however, *Session* would be a more meaningful label if data collection periods were consistent across activities but inconsistent across time (e.g., collected during a social skills group that meets only on Mondays and Thursdays). The second column, *Phase*, allows the user to quickly match each data point to its relevant phase (e.g., baseline, intervention), and subsequently include phase change lines or other information as necessary.

Student	Grade	Observation on 10/20/2015	Observation on 10/29/2015	Observation on 11/6/2015	Average	Cut Score	Next Steps
Hank R.	3	10	7	8	8.33	8	—
Elise P.	3	7	8	10	8.33	8	—
Tavon M.	3	4	0	10	4.67	8	Refer to Child Study Team
Michael S.	3	5	3	10	6	8	Refer to Child Study Team
Jayden W.	3	6	4	10	6.67	8	Refer to Child Study Team
Talia B.	3	7	9	9	8.33	8	—
Maria R.	6	8	1	10	6.33	9	Refer to Child Study Team
Jessica Y.	6	5	3	10	6	9	Refer to Child Study Team
Juan H.	6	10	8	10	9.33	9	—
David M.	6	9	0	9	6	9	Refer to Child Study Team

FIGURE 11.1. Table depicting screening data for academic engagement.

Although the phases of interest are typically baseline and intervention, any changes to a given intervention can also be indicated in the Phase column. For instance, if a student's DRC goal was raised from 80 to 90%, recording when this change was made in the Phase column of the spreadsheet will allow users to match any potential effects with this intervention modification. A final column is needed for the actual DBR score. This third column could be labeled *DBR Score* if a single score (e.g., academic engagement) is of interest; however, if multiple DBR scores will be entered, one column should be created for each individual score.

Although only three columns are necessary to graph progress monitoring data, it is often preferable to enter all recorded aspects of the observation (e.g., instructional activity, whether teacher's aide was present) that may be useful to avoid the need to find and retrieve paper forms at a later date and time. Some potential variables appear in Table 11.3, which provides details regarding (1) the type of data, (2) the purpose of those data, and (3) how those data might be recorded on a spreadsheet. After determining what information will be entered on the spreadsheet, the columns can be labeled with each aspect of the observation that should be recorded, and details for each observation can be entered row by row. An example of a spreadsheet for a standard DBR-SIS form with three behaviors is shown in Figure 11.2. Now, with a complete spreadsheet prepared, the data are ready for summarization.

TABLE 11.3. Potential Variables for Data Entry

Type	Purpose	Recording suggestions
Date	When were ratings made?	"Date" format with MM/DD/YY
Day of week	Trends across days	M, T, W, Th, F
Changes to routine	Note influence on ratings, help explain outliers	Narrative description or coded categories (e.g., 1 = sent to office, 2 = fire drill)
Unable to observe	Explain absent ratings, don't get confused by blank cells	Y/N, 1/0, *X*/blank
Number of students present	Note influence on ratings	Integer (e.g., 23)
Activity type	Note influence on ratings	Narrative description or coded categories (e.g., 1 = math, 2 = reading)
Instruction type	Note influence on ratings	Narrative description or coded categories (e.g., 1 = small group, 2 = independent seatwork)
DBR rating	Used as outcome variable	Integer (e.g., 7) or percentage (e.g., 70%)

Date	Day	Session	Phase	Unable	Changes	AE	DB	RS	Start	End
4/15/15	M	1	Baseline			6	3	8	8:30 A.M.	10:30 A.M.
4/16/15	T	2	Baseline		Fire drill	7	2	10	8:30 A.M.	9:40 A.M.
4/17/15	W	3	Baseline			4	0	10	8:30 A.M.	10:30 A.M.
4/18/15	Th	4	Baseline	Y	Field trip					
4/19/15	F	5	Baseline			6	4	10	8:30 A.M.	10:30 A.M.
4/22/15	M	6	Intervention			7	2	9	8:30 A.M.	10:30 A.M.
4/23/15	T	7	Intervention			8	1	10	8:30 A.M.	10:30 A.M.
4/24/15	W	8	Intervention			5	3	10	8:30 A.M.	10:30 A.M.
4/25/15	Th	9	Intervention		Dad in class	10	0	10	8:30 A.M.	10:30 A.M.
4/26/15	F	10	Intervention			9	0	9	8:30 A.M.	10:30 A.M.

FIGURE 11.2. Spreadsheet depicting data collected on three behaviors using standard DBR-SIS form.

Summarization

Once DBR data have been organized, the next overarching step is to summarize those data so as to provide stakeholders with a picture of student performance. Although numerical values (i.e., summary statistics) can be used to provide a quick snapshot, the use of graphs in communicating results has been shown to be associated with improved outcomes over simply describing results verbally (Fuchs & Fuchs, 1986).

Step 3: Generate Summary Statistics

In order to get a quick and rough estimate of what a given set of data might look like, the calculation of summary statistics may be useful. Summary statistics involve collapsing a set of data into one value to provide a general description and most typically come in the form of means, medians, or modes.

Summary statistics have relevance within both screening and progress monitoring contexts. As discussed in Chapter 6, summary scores for screening are calculated after 6–10 data points have been collected. Summary scores are based on either the mean of all ratings conducted within a given DBR-SIS target (i.e., *single-target summary scores*) or the sum of all mean scores across targets (i.e., *combined-scale summary scores*). When analyzing progress monitoring data, the mean, median, or mode can be calculated using all data points in a given phase (i.e. baseline, intervention) to summarize student performance.

Data can also be summarized over a particular dimension or characteristic, depending on the questions to be answered. Possible dimensions other than phase include subject/content areas (e.g., data collapsed across math periods), activity types (e.g., across small-group activities), and potential setting events (e.g., across days when the student did not report eating breakfast). For instance, a practitioner may wish to understand the average level of disruptive behavior that was observed during small-group instruction versus that observed during individual seatwork. In this case, a mean could be calculated for those ratings that are specified as "small-group instruction" on the spreadsheet, and those that are specific as "individual seatwork."

Step 4: Create Bar Graphs

One popular method for visually presenting a small number of summary statistics is use of the bar graph. Whereas time is represented on the x-axis in a line graph, the x-axis in a bar graph represents a categorical variable (i.e., one that has two or more distinct, unordered categories); therefore bar graphs are most appropriate when the goal is to compare different groups. If looking at DBR screening data, for example, different bars can be used to depict the average DBR score obtained across grade levels or across boys and girls (see Figure 11.3). In the context of progress monitoring, a bar graph might be used to represent the average DBR-SIS ratings a target student obtained during a given phase for (1) academic engagement, (2) disruptive behavior, and (3) respectful behavior. Alternatively, bar graphs with two different-colored bars can be used to compare an individual student's ratings to the average ratings of all students in a group or class.

Although summary statistics provide a snapshot of behavior and may jumpstart discussions about the data, it's crucial to remember that summary statistics reduce a rich and varied formative data stream to a single value. An average rating for engagement during baseline may provide a general idea of a student's functioning for that phase, but without seeing each data point individually, consumers of these data will have little idea what was actually occurring across time. This lack of specificity is of particular concern in the context of progress monitoring. Given these limitations, the use of techniques that capitalize on the entire data set and allow the consumer to discern individual data points and their relationship to the student, the context, and the intervention are almost certainly more valuable when making progress monitoring decisions.

Step 5: Create Line Graphs

Line graphs are most appropriate for depicting changes over time within the same individual or group. Because they allow for the presentation of large amounts of

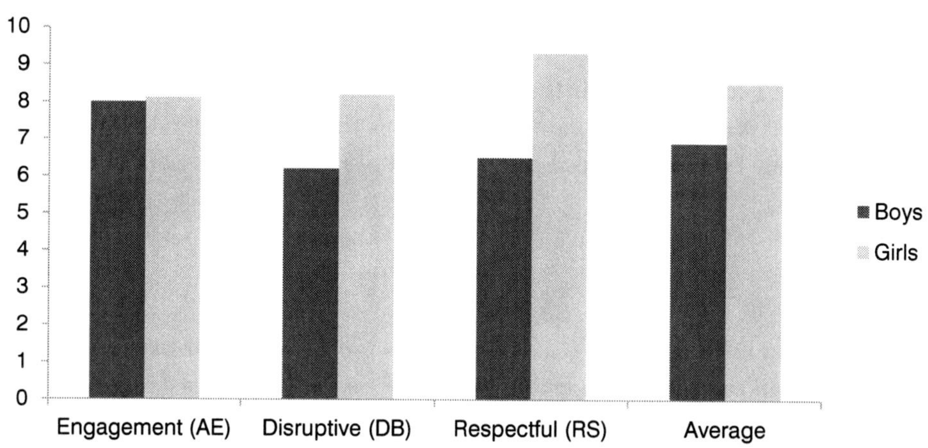

FIGURE 11.3. Bar graph depicting average DBR scores obtained for sixth-grade boys and girls.

quantitative information in a simple visual manner, line graphs may be the most effective way to present formative DBR data. Although most people are likely familiar with how to construct a simple line graph, the specific conventions of formative data presentation bear some review. A number of unique symbols and specific recommendations are pertinent to preparing DBR data for presentation and interpretation, as these allow for the clear presentation of large, rich data sets. The key components of a line graph depicting formative data include the *x*-axis, the *y*-axis, data points, data paths, and phase change lines. In order to facilitate quick and easy interpretation of line graphs for formative progress monitoring, it is recommended that sites adopt and adhere to a consistent set of graphing rules, as described next.

The X-Axis

For formative data, the *x*-axis represents time and should increase from the earliest data point collected on the left side of the axis to the most recent data point collected on the right side of the axis. Determining how to represent time along the *x*-axis, however, is not always a straightforward decision. For instance, if data are collected at unevenly spaced intervals of time (e.g., Monday morning, Thursday morning and afternoon, and Friday morning and afternoon), should each hash mark along the *x*-axis correspond with a half-day period, with missing data points from Monday afternoon to Wednesday afternoon? These decisions should be anchored in the question that is being investigated with the collected data. If the data collection periods correspond with rating respectful behavior toward peers during art class for a student, and art class only occurs on Mondays and Thursdays, it may not be useful to indicate that data were collected with long gaps of time between sessions. If the question is restricted to behavior within each session of art class, consumers and interpreters of the data may be better served by using "Session" as the unit of time along the *x*-axis. Although the spacing between each data point may not be equal in time, it is equal in the number of sessions the student attended. If a session is missed, it may be useful to indicate that with the absence of a data point for the relevant session.

The Y-Axis

When graphing DBR data, the *y*-axis represents the specific DBR score and therefore should span the range of possible values for that scale. For instance, if a DBR-SIS with a range of possible values from 0 to 100% is used to rate academically engaged behavior, then it may be preferable to depict each of the 11 possible scores (0%, 10% . . . 100%) as a discrete mark along the *y*-axis. Thus, even if ratings of only 80 or 90% have been collected, the full range of possible values is displayed to demonstrate that the student could have been rated at any of these alternative values.

Data Points

For those cases in which multiple dependent variables have been collected, each dependent variable should be represented using a distinct symbol and/or color to easily differentiate between them. For instance, if "Ms. Tonazzi" were using a DBR form with three target behaviors (academic engagement, respectful behavior, and disruptive behavior) to rate "Wei" during her math block every day, she would have data for three dependent variables to present. She could either (1) create three separate line graphs, each one demonstrating the data for a single behavior, or (2) create one line graph showing the data for all three behaviors. If she opted to represent all three dependent variables on one line graph, she might use blue circles for academic engagement, green triangles for respectful behavior, and red squares for disruptive behavior to help consumers read the graph accurately.

Data Paths

A *data path* is a straight line that connects meaningfully similar (i.e., adjacent in time and similar in type) data points that should be interpreted together rather than viewed as isolated points scattered through space. For instance, if all of the DBR data collected before intervention implementation are plotted and then connected by an unbroken data path, the consumer can take this to mean that these data may be interpreted together as a whole. On the other hand, broken data paths indicate either unexpectedly missing data or changes in the intervention, assessment method, or other relevant variable. For instance, if a data sheet for the third day of baseline data collection was unexpectedly misplaced, the path between the first two data points and all subsequent data points in baseline would be broken in order to indicate the absence of data for the third day.

In a similar manner to the treatment of data points, data paths for distinct outcome variables can be given different patterns and/or colors to differentiate between them. Options for patterns include solid, dashed, dotted, or starred lines, or any other combination of symbols that is small enough to be arranged in a line between data points.

Phase Change Lines

Often, graphed data are used to determine if a change (or lack of change) in a dependent variable can be attributed to the introduction or removal of an intervention.

In order to clearly demonstrate the point at which an intervention is introduced or removed, a vertical phase change line is drawn upwards from the *x*-axis at the point where the change occurred. This line is traditionally a solid line spanning the height of the *y*-axis, and signals that the two phases separated by this line can be compared to see if any change in behavior occurred. Use of a dashed phase change line typically indicates that an intervention was changed in some way that could affect behavior after the change.

As an example, let's consider the case of "Ray," who is struggling with academic engagement during Mrs. Graham's math period. In consultation with the school psychologist, Mrs. Graham decides that a possible way to increase Ray's academic engagement would be to allow Ray to earn points toward a homework pass if he is rated as engaged for at least 70% of the class period. After 1 week of consistently meeting his goal and thereby earning his reward, Mrs. Graham and the school psychologist decide to increase the goal to 80% academic engagement. When graphing these data, Mrs. Graham would use a solid phase change line to indicate the point at which the reward system was first introduced and then a dashed line to indicate the point at which Ray's goal was increased from 70% to 80%. In the case of an intervention wherein multiple changes may occur over the course of that intervention (e.g., progressive goal changes), it is helpful to indicate the contingencies in place during each phase of the intervention by entering a small amount of descriptive text above each portion of the phase.

If a target intervention involves changes in the goal, one popular alternative to the use of dashed vertical change lines is horizontal goal lines. For example, if a student's goal for respectful behavior was increased from 60 to 70%, a separate dashed horizontal line for each goal may be placed parallel to the relevant sessions along the *x*-axis. For those days on which the 70% goal was in place, a dashed horizontal line at 70% on the *y*-axis allows for quick identification of where a goal is in relation to a specific student's data point, and for a quick assessment of discrepancies or alignment between the student's score and his or her goal (see Figure 11.4).

Interpretation

After *organizing* and then *summarizing* DBR data, practitioners and consumers of data are finally faced with the task of *interpretation*. As was discussed at the beginning of this chapter, data without subsequent interpretation and action are just numbers on a spreadsheet or dots and dashes on a graph. With analysis and response, however, data become a tool for making meaningful and demonstrable differences in the lives of parents, teachers, and students.

At its core, the implementation of single-case design with a student involves (1) collecting an initial set of data, (2) making a prediction about the future performance

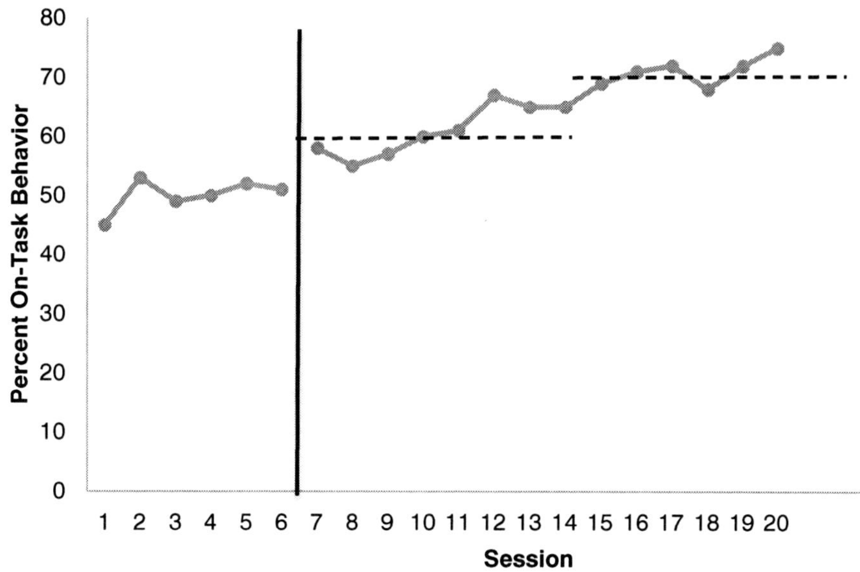

FIGURE 11.4. Use of horizontal goal lines to assess student progress.

of those data, and (3) testing whether the implementation of an intervention is associated with change in the behavior from their predicted performance. The more opportunities to demonstrate the effects that a given design provides, the more confidence practitioners and stakeholders can have in their conclusions regarding the relationship between the intervention and any behavior change that may or may not have occurred. Single-case design methodology generally recommends that *three* demonstrations of effects are necessary in order to be confident that an intervention is functionally related to changes in a target behavior.

Although more sophisticated designs are needed in order to determine whether a functional relationship exists between the introduction of an independent variable and changes in a dependent variable (e.g., reversal design, multiple baseline design; see Riley-Tillman & Burns, 2009), the most common design used within school-based decision making is the AB design. An *AB design* refers to a situation in which formative data are collected prior to the implementation of an intervention (i.e., the A phase, or baseline) to understand current functioning and then again after an intervention was implemented (the B phase). Although such a design cannot be used to infer a functional relationship, the data can be used to make tentative conclusions about student progress after the implementation of an intervention. Although we cannot say whether the intervention is responsible for the change, we can say whether change is occurring and how we may wish to proceed accordingly. Decisions regarding progress can be made using visual analysis, and possibly be supplemented by quantitative analysis, as is discussed in the following sections.

Step 6: Conduct Visual Analysis

The most common method for analyzing school-based formative assessment data likely involves the use of a visual analysis. Such an analysis involves the use of established decision rules to determine if and how aspects of the behavior stream change upon implementation or removal of a given intervention. Specifically, data are inspected both within and between phases with regard to three general characteristics: level, trend, and variability. First, the *level* of a set of data points refers to the value along the y-axis around which most of the data points congregate. Referring back to the summarization section, level could be summarized for a set of data as the mean, median, or mode for those data. Therefore, when examining changes in level, we are interested in knowing whether the typical level of behavior changed from baseline to intervention. Depending on the type of data, the level may have particular importance. For example, with DBR data, a level under 8 for academic engagement may be considered the at-risk range (see Chapter 6 for specific information on determining risk). As such, the level alone can be an important manner in which to consider graphed data.

Second, the *trend* of a set of data points refers to whether those data points appear to be systematically increasing, decreasing, or remaining stable over time. The line that best fits the trajectory of a given data set is called the *trend line*, and *slope* refers to how steep or flat a trend line appears. Slopes can be positive, negative, or zero. If the level of the outcome variable increases over time, the slope is positive; if the level of the outcome variable decreases over time, the slope is negative. Large changes in shorter amounts of time in the outcome variable correspond to larger or steeper slopes. However, if each additional session results in no change in the outcome variable, the trend line would be horizontal with a slope of zero. When examining changes in trend, we are generally interested in knowing whether the slope of the data has changed from baseline to intervention in the expected direction. For example, if data reflecting disruptive behavior were either consistent (i.e., no slope) or increasing (i.e., positive slope) within the baseline period, we would want to see a decrease in these data (i.e., negative slope) subsequent to the intervention.

Third, the *variability* of a set of data points refers to the "bounce" in the data. The amount of variability in the data has a considerable influence on one's ability to predict future data points. If little to no variability is present in the baseline data, then a prediction past the observed data may be made with some confidence. If a lot of variability is present, then predictions of future behavior are much harder to confidently make. For this reason, many research studies opt to wait to implement interventions until baseline variability has decreased to some prespecified amount. It is important to recognize, however, that behavioral variability may represent a meaningful and significant component for treatment (i.e., with the goal of stabilizing behavior over time). When examining changes in variability, we are typically interested in knowing whether variability decreased subsequent to intervention implementation.

In addition, immediacy can be considered when examining changes between phases. *Immediacy* refers to how quickly an effect is seen after an intervention is introduced. The longer the period of time between the implementation of an intervention and the demonstration of an effect, the less confident we can be that the intervention was responsible for the observed change (as opposed to other unmeasured variables). One helpful way to determine the immediacy of effect is to apply comparisons of level, trend, and variability to the last three data points of the baseline and the first three data points of the intervention (Kratochwill et al., 2010). In this way, the remainder of the data is temporarily trimmed away to allow the immediacy of the effect postintervention to be more easily interpreted.

Note that when considering level, trend, variability, and immediacy, it is important to consider the context. For example, if DBR data were used to monitor a social skills training intervention, one might not expect that there would be an immediate intervention effect. As such, immediacy would be devalued when looking at those data. Trend, however, may be more important, given that growth over time is expected when measuring a behavioral learning outcome. In contrast, a reward-based intervention with little delay to reinforcement may be expected to show an immediate effect, making immediacy a more salient feature to attend to. Basing the plan for analysis on the case will also be important with the quantitative metrics reviewed next.

Step 7: Use Quantitative Metrics to Supplement Line Graphs

Although line graphs can facilitate the simple communication of results to others, it may sometimes be easier to speak in hard numbers. A number of simple statistical formulae have been developed to summarize specific aspects of change within single-subject data. These are sometimes referred to as *single-subject effect sizes*; however, some of these bear only a slight resemblance to the effect sizes used in group-design research and the assumptions and qualities associated with them. For this reason, it may be more appropriate to refer to this class of statistical techniques as *quantitative metrics*. Although many different metrics are available (for more information, see Parker, Vannest, & Davis, 2011; Maggin, O'Keeffe, & Johnson, 2011), two quantitative metrics are described next as simple options in evaluating change in single-subject data.

Percentage of Nonoverlapping Data

The percentage of nonoverlapping data (PND) metric captures the percentage of data points in an intervention phase that do not overlap in the intended direction of the treatment effect with data points in baseline (Scruggs & Mastropieri, 2013).

In other words, if an intervention is intended to increase academically engaged behavior as measured using DBR, PND will represent the percentage of intervention data points that were higher than the highest DBR score in baseline. Thus, a PND score of 100% indicates that all data in the intervention were "better than" those in baseline. Guidelines for interpretation of PND magnitude have suggested that a PND greater than 90% reflects a *very effective* intervention, a PND between 70 and 90% reflects an *effective* intervention, a PND between 50 and 70% reflects a *questionable* intervention, and a PND below 50% reflects an *ineffective* intervention (Scruggs & Mastropieri, 1998). Given that all data points during the intervention phase are compared to the most extreme data point in baseline, one important limitation of PND is that the presence of an outlier (i.e., an extreme value) in the baseline phase has the potential to seriously alter the resulting PND value. Using the previous example, if data during baseline generally corresponded to DBR ratings of 0 or 1 but one baseline session demonstrated a DBR rating of 9, the PND value would likely be 0% even if there was a potentially meaningful overall change in DBR ratings (e.g., all intervention data points were 6's and 7's).

Improvement Rate Difference

Adopted from the health care literature, the improvement rate difference (IRD) metric represents the difference between the ratio of "improved" data points in treatment and the baseline data points (Parker, Vannest, & Brown, 2009). "Improvement" in the case of IRD is defined as a data point that demonstrates a more desirable value in one phase when compared to its counterpart phase; therefore, an improved data point in an intervention phase is one that exceeds all data points in baseline in the intended direction of effect. An improved data point in baseline is one that meets or exceeds any data point in the intervention phase.

IRD has the added advantage of allowing readily calculable confidence intervals, which depict the relative precision of a given estimate. Parker et al. (2009) also demonstrated that IRD correlates highly ($r > .80$) with other parametric and nonparametric quantitative metrics. For interpretation purposes, it has been suggested that *large* effects may be associated with an IRD value at or greater than 70 or 75%, *moderate* effects with those between 50 and 70%, and *small to questionable* effects at or below 50% (Parker et al., 2009).

Using Quantitative Metrics in Practice

The debate over how, when, and why to use quantitative metrics in single-subject research is lively and ongoing. As mentioned earlier, these values are probably most valuable in practice when they are used to supplement line graphs and quickly communicate information about an intervention's effectiveness to others. For instance, if a consultant was utilizing an alternating treatments design to test the relative effectiveness of two interventions for disruptive behavior, he or she may wish to both visually and numerically present information at an IEP team meeting regarding how each intervention performed in comparison to baseline. The consultant could calculate quantitative metrics, presented in a table alongside the graph, and discuss both (1) the implications of a visual analysis of these graphs, and (2) how each intervention compared to the other and to baseline in quantitative terms. In this way, quantitative metrics provide a "snapshot" of student data that may supplement information presented for high-stakes meetings and other decision-making contexts. Given that progress monitoring is chiefly driven by formative visual interpretation, however, quantitative metrics may most appropriately be considered as secondary sources of information when used for this purpose. Additionally, when used, simple but accurate descriptions of the metrics, such as PND or IRD, may help stakeholders interpret these values and make a determination of the best course of action for an individual student.

Step 8: Determine Next Steps

Once the data have been analyzed using the aforementioned visual and quantitative strategies, one of two conclusions may be drawn: student progress was or was not made after the intervention was implemented (see Figure 11.5). If the team determines that satisfactory progress has been made, several options may be considered. If the teacher finds the intervention to be feasible, implementation may continue without any substantial changes. If difficulties with implementation have been noted, modifications may be made to the intervention to enhance feasibility. If it is no longer perceived to be necessary, the intervention may also be withdrawn entirely (Erchul & Martens, 2010).

If either no change has been observed or behavior appears to be worsening, it is necessary to brainstorm possible reasons for a lack of response. One of the first points that should be determined is whether the intervention was implemented in the way in which it was intended (i.e., implementation integrity). An intervention may be carried out less frequently than prescribed, or particular components of the intervention may be skipped altogether. Observational checks or integrity checklists can then be used to determine where the problems with implementation lie. It is also possible, however, that an evidence-based intervention may not be the right match for a particular student. If an intervention is implemented with fidelity but not found to be effective, the team may consider such factors as whether the intervention is developmentally appropriate for the individual student, whether there is a mismatch with the hypothesized function of behavior, and whether the student requires more intensive supports (e.g., more frequent, in a more individualized setting).

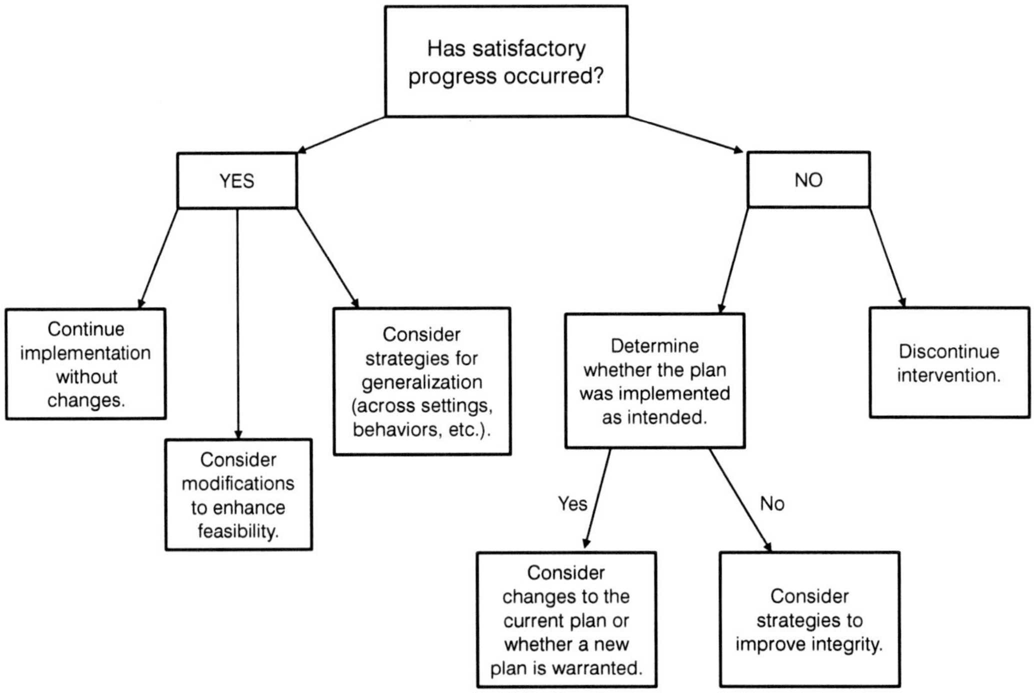

FIGURE 11.5. Decision-making tree for determining next steps based on progress monitoring data.

Putting It All Together: Case Example

Now that we have outlined the steps involved in organizing, summarizing, and interpreting DBR data, let's consider the case of "Saffron," a fourth-grade student in "Ms. Abboud's" class. Saffron has been exhibiting disruptive behavior, especially during her math block, for the first month and a half of school, and nothing that Ms. Abboud has tried (e.g., seating Saffron closer to her desk, time-outs, submitting minor discipline referrals) has, in Ms. Abboud's opinion, ameliorated the problem. After speaking with "Mrs. Perry," the school psychologist, Ms. Abboud begins collecting data regarding Saffron's current levels of disruptive behavior using a standard DBR scale ranging from 0 to 100%. Mrs. Perry asks Ms. Abboud to observe Saffron's disruptive behavior during each day's math block for the next week and to estimate the percentage of time Saffron was engaged in disruptive behavior during that block. They agree to meet briefly during Ms. Abboud's planning period the following Monday to discuss the results and plan the intervention.

On the school psychologist's recommendation, Ms. Abboud decides to record her data in a password-protected Microsoft Excel spreadsheet, saved on the school's secure server. She creates the spreadsheet with three columns of data: date, phase, and DBR score for disruptive behavior. This system will provide convenient access and data entry features, and password protection and a secure server will help protect the data.

After 5 days of collecting data, Ms. Abboud and Mrs. Perry meet to summarize the findings. They first look to determine the level of disruptive behavior for the baseline phase. For Saffron's baseline data (i.e., 30%, 40%, 50%, 50%, 60%), the mean would be 46%, the median would be 50%, and the mode would be 50%. These summary statistics converge around 50%; therefore, Mrs. Perry concludes that the *level* of Saffron's data at baseline lies around 50% and draws a line at this point (see Figure 11.6). Next, they examine the trend of the data. With the exception of Session 4, Saffron's data appear to be increasing at a rate of about 10% per session. After drawing a trend line (see Figure 11.7) for Saffron's baseline data, it is clear that little variability is present. Each data point is relatively close to, or on, the trend line (see Figure 11.8). In summary, we could say that the data for Saffron's disruptive behavior during baseline (1) hover around a level of 50%, (2) exhibit a positive trend that suggests an increase of about 10% per session, and (3) demonstrate little variability. With a summary of Saffron's behavior during baseline, Ms. Abboud and Mrs. Perry now have a point of reference against which to judge any behavior change after the intervention is implemented.

After supplementing her DBR data with teacher and parent interviews, direct observations, and some brief antecedent–behavior–consequence (ABC) charts, Mrs. Perry forms a hypothesis that Saffron is engaging in disruptive behavior to obtain teacher attention. The team decides to utilize a daily report card (DRC) as an intervention to provide specific teacher feedback to Saffron three times during her math block. Furthermore, Ms. Abboud will provide noncontingent attention to Saffron by checking in with her briefly as she moves, scans, and interacts during small-group math activities. Saffron will be rewarded with computer time by her parents for a positive DRC. With a behavior plan established, Ms. Abboud agrees to begin implementation the next day.

Ms. Abboud continues to use her spreadsheet to collect and graph data regarding Saffron's disruptive behavior, using DBR for the next 5 days, and both educators meet the following week to monitor the progress of the intervention plan. Ms. Abboud has now collected two full phases of data: one for the baseline phase and one for the intervention phase. Using the conventions of (1) *level*, (2) *trend*, and (3) *variability*, as well as (4) the *immediacy* of change between phases, these data can be compared to one another, and the student's response to the intervention can be inferred. At the same time, however, Mrs. Perry and Ms. Abboud will want to brainstorm if anything else may have occurred that could be responsible for any observed changes in behavior. That is, if these data are to be presented at a team meeting, the practitioners may wish to check in with Saffron's parents to ask if any changes occurred between data collection periods that may have influenced her behavior. In this way, data-based decision making is no different than solving a mystery; hypotheses are made and tested, and all other possible causes are investigated before drawing a tentative conclusion about what was responsible for an event's occurrence.

After confirming that no major changes have occurred between baseline and intervention periods that have influenced Saffron's classroom behavior, Mrs. Perry and Ms. Abboud sit down to analyze the DBR results and determine if behavior change occurred. First, the level of each phase is examined and compared. As discussed earlier, the level in the baseline phase appeared to hover around 50% across the three summary statistics. In the intervention phase (i.e., 40%, 55%, 50%, 35%, 50%), the mean is 46%, whereas both the median and the mode are 50%. After selecting the average to represent the level for this particular phase, both level lines are superimposed over the data paths, as depicted in Figure 11.6. Upon visual analysis, it is apparent that the level did not substantially change between baseline and intervention. In quantitative terms, Mrs. Perry might state that the average level of the behavior only decreased from 50 to 46%, or 4%—a minimal difference.

Second, trend lines are plotted across both baseline and intervention phases (see Figure 11.7). As noted previously, Saffron's disruptive behavior was increasing at a rate of about 10% per session during baseline. Given the low variability within this phase, Mrs. Perry may have predicted that Saffron's behavior would continue along the predicted trend line in the absence of any intervention. After the intervention was implemented, Saffron's disruptive behavior initially decreased, then increased and fluctuated. Visual analysis suggests that the slope of the intervention trend line is less steep. Although disruptive behavior was observed to increase during the intervention, this increase occurred at a slower rate.

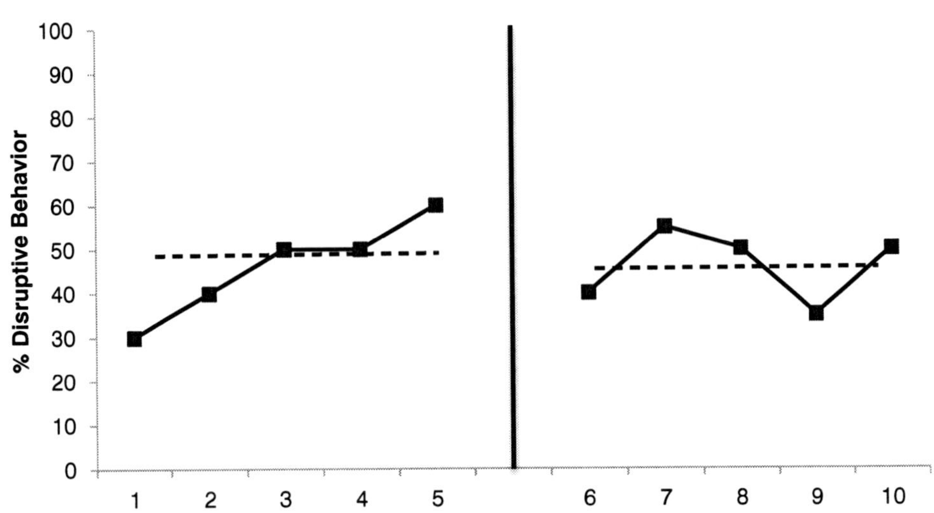

FIGURE 11.6. Changes in level from baseline to intervention for Saffron.

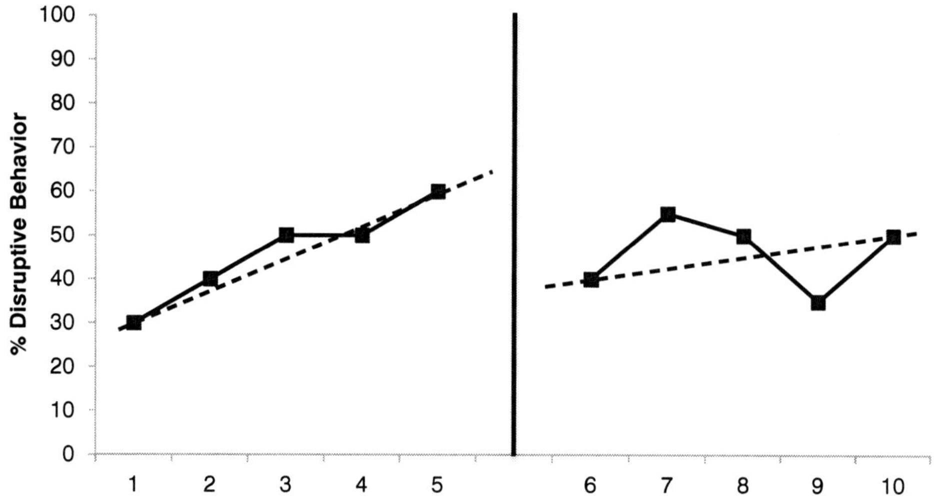

FIGURE 11.7. Changes in trend from baseline to intervention for Saffron.

Third, the degree of variability is compared between baseline and intervention phases, as depicted in Figure 11.8. Whereas there was relatively little variability during baseline, the intervention data points strayed further from the trend line. In many cases, it is anticipated that an intervention will reduce behavioral variability; therefore, finding that variability actually increased is not a desirable outcome. Mrs. Perry and Ms. Abboud conclude that there was no effect of the intervention on the level, there was a small effect on the trend, and there was a negative effect on the variability.

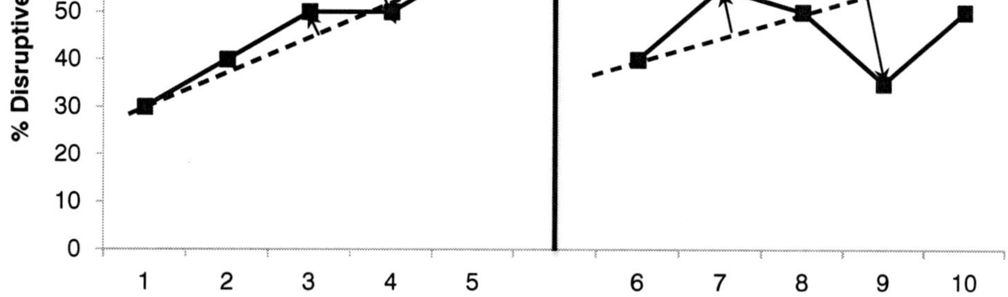

FIGURE 11.8. Changes in variability from baseline to intervention for Saffron.

Given that the DRC intervention was expected to reduce Saffron's disruptive behavior to a consistently low level, Mrs. Perry and Ms. Abboud need to brainstorm possible reasons for a lack of response. These could include:

1. The hypothesis regarding the function of the behavior was incorrect. For instance, perhaps Saffron's behavior is maintained by escaping math tasks, rather than by obtaining teacher attention.
2. Significant life events (e.g., trauma, divorce, special event) outside of school may be influencing Saffron's behavior. Ms. Abboud may want to contact Saffron's parents for more information.
3. The intervention was not implemented with fidelity. Ms. Abboud may be implementing only part of the behavior plan, or may not be implementing it correctly. For example, did Saffron receive DRC feedback from Ms. Abboud three times during math as outlined? Was noncontingent reinforcement also delivered throughout the intervention block? Were there some days that Saffron did not have her DRC checked and rewarded at home? Use of treatment fidelity measures might (a) assist Ms. Abboud in self-monitoring her own implementation of the behavior plan and (b) provide data concerning what portions of the intervention are not being implemented as planned.
4. The reward for meeting the goal on the DRC is not powerful enough, or not function-based. In other words, Saffron's behavior is not reinforced by the DRC reward and an additional reinforcer preference assessment of some type may be appropriate.
5. The intervention itself may not be effective for this particular student and her behavior. Saffron may require more explicit contingencies, perhaps in the form of a token economy or group contingency.

At the end of their progress monitoring meeting, Mrs. Perry and Ms. Abboud may conclude that no significant change has occurred for Saffron. Ms. Abboud consults with Saffron's father about outside factors that may have impacted Saffron's behavior and learns that Saffron's cousins had been visiting from out of town. As a result, the family had been inconsistent in rewarding Saffron's DRC results. The father assures Ms. Abboud that they will be more diligent from now on. The team also decides to provide an additional reward at school to increase the strength of the intervention. Mrs. Perry conducts a reinforcer preference assessment with Saffron to determine other potential reinforcers. Saffron communicates that she would like to earn time in the gym playing basketball to prepare her for team tryouts. Mrs. Perry and Ms. Abboud agree to continue implementing the DRC intervention with modifications for the next week and monitor Saffron's disruptive behavior to determine if it is effective. The two will meet each week to discuss Saffron's progress and consider whether a new plan is warranted.

Conclusions

This chapter has reviewed three key steps in preparing to communicate and utilize DBR data: organization, summarization, and interpretation. First, organization turns multiple discrete ratings into an easily manipulable data set. Next, summarization translates the overall data set into an easily digestible picture of behavior (e.g., summary statistic, graph). Finally, interpretation uses specific criteria (e.g., analysis of level, trend, and variability) to assess whether change has occurred from baseline to intervention. Together, these three steps facilitate data-based decision making that is efficient, simple, and communicable.

Moving forward, we challenge the field to consider organization, summarization, and interpretation for each of the assessment approaches utilized. Although much scrutiny is given to the psychometric properties of an assessment, the presented data are what are used to make educational decisions that impact a student's future. All of the data in the world can be collected, but in the absence of a plan for organization, summarization, and interpretation, it is unlikely that the practice will have any benefit for students in need. Over time, it will be critical for both researchers and applied professionals to embrace methods of evidence-based analysis just as they do evidence-based intervention and assessment.

CHAPTER 12

Use of Technology to Facilitate Assessment and Intervention

Stephen P. Kilgus, T. Chris Riley-Tillman, and Amy M. Briesch

Throughout this book, the case has been made that behavioral data are needed across multiple assessment purposes (e.g., screening, progress monitoring) to drive decision making within multi-tiered frameworks for service delivery (e.g., response to intervention [RTI], positive behavior interventions and supports [PBIS]). Because behavioral screening data have been shown to predict key academic and behavioral outcomes, such as grade-point average, out-of-school suspensions, ODRs, unexcused absences, and course failure (Lane, Bruhn, Eisner, & Kalberg, 2010; Lane, Kalberg, Parks, & Carter, 2008; Renshaw et al., 2009), these data can be used to proactively identify those students in need of more intensive behavior supports. Furthermore, although prior research and practice may be used to select instructional and intervention supports, progress monitoring data are needed to evaluate whether a particular approach works under a particular set of circumstances and for a particular individual (Stoner & Green, 1992). Data collection and use therefore become a critical part of intervention. As a result, procedures and materials that enable efficient and feasible data-based decision making within the demands of an educator's schedule are greatly needed to facilitate timely and effective intervention.

The Need for Electronic Data Systems

An effective multi-tiered model of support involves data collection and use to evaluate and inform services that are provided at the system, group, and individual levels. One of the key challenges is that a substantial amount of data is involved in such an endeavor! Let's say, for example, that a school of 500 students is interested in collecting DBR ratings for the purpose of behavioral screening. Even if the school were only interested in conducting targeted screening of the 20% of students found to be at risk for behavior problems, they would still have to collect 1,000 DBR data points (500 students × 20% × 10 data points per student = 1,000 data points!). The amount of data collected within the context of progress monitoring can also quickly become overwhelming. For example, if a teacher collected behavioral progress monitoring data for five students twice a day—a likely scenario for group-level supports within PBIS or RTI—50 data points would be generated in a single week. Such a data collection schedule would amount to 2,000 data points across the academic year. And if even two teachers per grade (K–8) used a similar progress monitoring schedule, this would result in 36,000 data points annually! You can quickly see how the management of these data might become unwieldy!

Given the rather daunting volume of potential data, it is critical for schools to consider how data will be handled. Any data system, whether it is electronic or paper-and-pencil based, must specify procedures and processes for four important data-related functions. First, the data must be *collected* and stored. If this is done via paper-and-pencil, the process will logically require two steps: (1) collecting the data at the time of the assessment via a data collection form, and (2) moving the data to a summary tracking sheet that includes multiple observations (see Figure 12.1 for an example of such a tracking sheet). If this is done electronically, however, data can be directly entered into the computer system (e.g., laptop, mobile device). Second, after recording, the teacher must *summarize* the data via graphs and simple computations (e.g., calculation of mean or standard deviation) to support eventual data interpretation. Again, these functions may be performed by hand or by the computer. Third, the teacher must *interpret* the collected data in order to draw conclusions regarding the effectiveness of the intervention. As discussed in Chapter 11, there are several different approaches to analysis and interpretation that may be considered. These include the use of visual analysis and/or the calculation of quantitative measures of effect size (e.g., PND). Finally, information must be *shared* with relevant stakeholders. Data may be distributed to a problem-solving team, a student's parents, and any other interested individuals. Again, this information could be distributed manually, sent electronically, or made available via an online system.

These four functions of data collection, summarization, interpretation, and communication are necessary to support effective data use. If traditional paper-and-pencil systems are employed, two central challenges may arise. The first challenge is that each step in this process can be rather time-consuming, requiring advanced and ongoing coordination. Simply put, it would be difficult to use any data that are collected in a formative fashion to guide service delivery without a data system to support efficient and effective data collection, summarization, interpretation, and communication. The rather extensive effort and time associated

Student: ______________________________

Grade: ______________________________

Rater: ______________________________

				Ratings	
Date	**Start Time**	**End Time**	**Activity**	**Disruptive Behavior**	**Academic Engagement**
12/5	8:30	11:45	Entire A.M.	5	6
12/5	12:30	3:15	Entire P.M.	4	7
12/6	8:30	11:45	Entire A.M.	3	9
12/6	12:30	3:15	Entire P.M.	6	5
12/7	8:30	11:45	Entire A.M.	2	8
12/7	12:30	3:15	Entire P.M.	1	8
12/8	8:30	11:45	Entire A.M.	2	10
12/8	12:30	3:15	Entire P.M.	0	10

FIGURE 12.1. Sample of summary tracking sheet for paper-and-pencil ratings.

with paper-and-pencil data collection and use might preclude the true purposes of such assessment, which include efficient and timely data-based decision making and inductive hypothesis testing. Although research has demonstrated the ability of screening and progress monitoring to enhance the effectiveness of service delivery (Eklund & Dowdy, 2014; Fuchs & Fuchs, 1986, 2006), we must recognize that potential effectiveness is inherently linked to the feasibility of associated data systems. That is, the collection of screening and progress monitoring data is unlikely to yield benefits if it is not supported by efficient and usable data systems.

Beyond questions of feasibility and utility, another reasonable concern pertains to whether teachers possess the training required to collect, summarize, interpret, and communicate data for the purpose of screening or progress monitoring. These concerns are founded in previous research, including findings pertaining to teacher capacity to develop and analyze graphs. Specifically, research has indicated a lack of adequate teacher training in graphical preparation and interpretation (Begeny & Martens, 2006), as well as the underutilization of graphing procedures in elementary and secondary classrooms (Moxley, 2007). These findings are unfortunate, given that the benefits of a graphical presentation of data have been clearly demonstrated (Fuchs & Fuchs, 1986; Kennedy, 2005; Smith, Best, Stubbs, & Archibald, 2002). If teachers lack graphing and graphical interpretation skills fundamental to the use of formative data, it is likely that assessment outcomes will not be consistently and/or accurately analyzed without the assistance of an electronic system for data-related functions (e.g., summarization, analysis). This would, in turn, reduce the likelihood of data being used effectively.

Current Applications of Technology to Support Data Use

In the interest of supporting the timely collection, interpretation, and use of assessment data, it is likely necessary that schools move beyond basic paper-and-pencil systems toward the use of electronic data systems. Computer software has long been used in applied school settings to score and interpret diagnostic measures such as the Woodcock–Johnson IV Tests of Cognitive Abilities (Schrank, Mather, & McGrew, 2015) and the Behavior Assessment System for Children, Third Edition (BASC-3; Reynolds & Kamphaus, 2015). The advantages afforded by software programs are numerous; however, three particular features are particularly important to note. First, use of such programs results in reduced time and effort because of the automated scoring and summarization features. Practitioners are free to spend their time interpreting the data and using them to inform instruction- or intervention-related decisions. Second, software use may reduce the likelihood of human error. The manual hand-scoring process, including correct score summation and comparison of results to appropriate normative tables (when necessary), is inherently susceptible to missteps that reduce the validity of score-based inferences and the defensibility of resulting decisions. Removing the need for hand scoring therefore enhances scoring reliability. Third, such systems reduce the need for specialized training or knowledge. Although test administrators must be able to appropriately interpret results, it is less important that they are able to construct sophisticated graphs or connect findings to specific curricula or intervention manuals when using computer software.

Despite these advantages, the scoring software and related electronic data systems described above were designed to drive summative assessments and decisions (e.g., diagnosis, classification). That is, such data are typically collected and used at one point in time to describe student performance during that period. Alternative electronic systems have recently emerged, however, designed specifically for the purpose of decision making within a multi-tiered model of supports. Importantly, these data systems can be used to identify students at risk for not reaching academic benchmarks or for poor behavioral outcomes. These at-risk students can then be monitored more frequently, and electronic data systems used to judge whether each student is progressing toward his or her individual goals for performance in response to the intervention. Two of the more widely known examples in the academic domain include AIMSweb (n.d.) and the Dynamic Indicators of Basic Early Literacy Skills (DIBELS) Data System (Good & Kaminski, n.d.), both of which can be used to collect, analyze, interpret, and report CBM data.

Although electronic systems have helped to improve the efficiency and effectiveness of data use in academic domains, they offer particular advantages for the use of behavioral data. One challenge when dealing with behavioral assessment data is that a wide range of target behaviors is possible. In the context of academic assessment, variables of interest represent a small and well-defined set of skills considered pertinent to all students at each particular grade/developmental level. In behavioral assessment, however, there is a tradition of idiosyncratic selection and definition of behaviors that are considered pertinent to each particular student case. Furthermore, it is common practice within formative behavioral assessment to select the instrumentation and measurement procedures that are most pertinent to an individual case and the behaviors to be evaluated. For instance, one educator might elect to continuously monitor the frequency of a particular behavior (e.g., callouts) during an observation period, whereas others might choose to evaluate the duration of a behavior (e.g., tantrums) or the percentage of intervals during which a behavior was displayed (e.g., disruptive behavior). In addition, it may be meaningful for the frequency and duration of observation periods to vary across students. In the case of one student, it may only be necessary to collect behavioral data twice a week for 30 minutes (e.g., Monday and Wednesday 9–9:30 A.M. and 12–12:30 P.M.), whereas another behavior might need to be monitored more frequently (e.g., twice a day 5 days a week for 2 hours). This level of flexibility in behavioral data collection stands in stark contrast to academic assessment, which typically employs standardized instrumentation and measurement (e.g., words read correctly per minute) and is of a standard duration (e.g., 1-minute CBM probe) with few options for frequency (e.g., once or twice a month, once a week). Although creating unique forms and keeping up with the analysis of outcome data across different cases can easily become overwhelming if using a paper-and-pencil approach, computerized systems have the potential to streamline this process.

A second potential challenge stems from the complex nature of behavior. Specifically, a core assumption of behaviorism pertains to the inherent variability of behavior as a function of the environment in which an individual resides (Cooper et al., 2007). Whereas academic skills (e.g., early literacy indicators) typically develop along a stable trajectory in a linear fashion, an individual student's behavior may change from moment to moment based upon within- or between-contextual differences. One issue that arises as a function of this variability is the need for greater amounts of data in order to facilitate valid interpretations. When data are consistent across time, it is possible to estimate a particular level or trend given relatively few data points. Alternatively, greater variability means that many more data points must be collected to support accurate estimation (Briesch, Volpe, & Ferguson, 2013). In a progress monitoring context, this means that educators must be prepared to collect, store, summarize, and interpret larger amounts of data within any given phase of service delivery (i.e., baseline, intervention) to support valid decision making regarding student functioning. Once again, the processes of data collection and management will be greatly simplified through the use of electronic, rather than paper-and-pencil, systems.

At this point, it should be clear that technology is needed to enhance schoolwide problem-solving models. Based upon the information provided above regarding the idiosyncrasies of behavior and behavioral assessment, we believe that such technology should possess multiple features to maximize its utility. These features are described next and outlined in Table 12.1.

TABLE 12.1. Steps in Assessing the Desirable Features of Electronic Assessment Systems

☐ 1. Ensure that measures produce data that are psychometrically adequate.

In addition to traditional reliability and validity indicators, consider sensitivity and specificity data when evaluating screening measures and whether progress monitoring measures are sensitive to change.

☐ 2. Assess whether the system is acceptable in terms of time, user effort, and resources.

Electronic systems should be easy to use and readily accessible to educators.

☐ 3. Determine whether there is sufficient capacity to store and enter data.

Systems should permit the storage and reporting of behavioral data across various dimensions (e.g., frequency, duration, percentage of time). Space should also be provided to collect and manage contextual data (e.g., time, location, instructional activity).

☐ 4. Determine whether the analysis and reporting of data are simple and clear.

Systems should permit the creation of line graphs and data summary reports. Decision rules should be integrated into systems in order to determine if a student is progressing and whether intervention should be modified.

☐ 5. Assess whether adequate training is provided.

Training should provide users with an overview of system features; allow users to practice using various features with feedback; and support users in developing the skills required to collect, enter, summarize, interpret, and report data.

☐ 6. Determine whether integration with other data sources is possible.

Integration within a larger electronic system that includes attendance, academic, and medical data may assist in decision making.

Step 1: Ensure That Measures Produce Data That Are Psychometrically Adequate

First and foremost, as is true within any assessment context, the data collection tools utilized in an electronic system must be psychometrically defensible. That is, although a system may be attractive and user-friendly, it must also provide data that are reliable and valid in order to support defensible decision making. As discussed in Chapter 4, critical indicators of reliability and validity vary depending on the purpose of assessment. For example, specificity and sensitivity are important when examining behavioral screening measures, whereas sensitivity to change is a critical indicator in the context of progress monitoring. In order to maximize their use within problem-solving systems, computerized systems must therefore incorporate measures that are psychometrically adequate for screening and/or progress monitoring, depending upon the measure's intended purpose.

Step 2: Assess Whether the System Is Acceptable in Terms of Time, User Effort, and Resources

Collection, summarization, interpretation, and communication of data must be acceptable in terms of time, user effort, and resources. Computerized systems have the potential to save users time over paper-and-pencil methods; however, software that is overly complicated to learn or use will greatly diminish this potential. Users of early word processors remember when it was easier for a good typist to use traditional methods rather than inefficient, albeit technologically sophisticated, tools in their infancy! As such, electronic data systems must be housed within a seamless user experience that places little between the accumulation of data and their use to improve student outcomes. Furthermore, in the interest of supporting efficient and effective decision making, data systems should be accessible to educators at any time and from any computer. Accessibility is considered high for systems that can be accessed via a web browser and somewhat lower for application-based systems requiring software installation prior to use.

Step 3: Determine Whether There Is Sufficient Capacity to Store and Enter Data

Beyond efficiency and rapid access, technological systems must possess the capacity to store a great deal of robust data. Given the wide range of target behaviors that educators may wish to track in school settings, it is important that systems are flexible enough to permit the storage and reporting of behavioral data across various dimensions (e.g., frequency, duration, percentage of time). Space should also be provided to collect and manage *contextual data*, indicative of the time (e.g., Monday

10–11:15 A.M.), location (e.g., Mrs. Martinez's classroom), and instructional activity (e.g., large-group math instruction) in which student behavior was exhibited. Such information is critical to allow for the appropriate interpretation of how behavior presents over time and in response to intervention.

Step 4: Determine Whether the Analysis and Reporting of Data Are Simple and Clear

Although our initial case for the use of technology was pragmatic, an even more exciting advantage is the enhancement of an educator's interpretive and problem-solving abilities. At its core, *problem solving* is defined by educator use of data to inform decisions; this stands in contrast to more subjective decisions that are founded upon educator intuition and beliefs regarding what is likely to be best for a student. *Any* data system should make the analysis and reporting of data simple and clear in the interest of promoting decision making within a problem-solving framework. Such analytic and reporting features should be in accordance with educational best practices, as they automate features related to single-case design and the visual analysis of formative data. In accordance with the principles of single-case design, data systems should permit the creation of (1) line graphs that depict student response both in the absence (i.e., baseline) and presence of intervention, and (2) data reports that summarize the graphed data via descriptions of student behavior both within and between phases. Graphs and reports should then be capable of informing ongoing decisions regarding which students are in need of additional supports and whether students who have received supports have responded as intended. Finally, decision rules (e.g., if a student is progressing and whether intervention should be modified) should be integrated into systems, thus supporting expedient decisions regarding changes to student supports. Such decision rules should also be incorporated into the aforementioned behavioral/contextual data structure, thus allowing for determination of specific settings and contexts within which a student is not progressing (e.g., time of day, location, instructional activity).

Step 5: Assess Whether Adequate Training Is Provided

Depending on the background of the individual, potential users may require different levels of training to ensure both initial adoption and sustained use of the system and its corresponding tools. Users should be provided with an overview of system features and should be given the opportunity to practice using various features with feedback. The training should support new users in acquiring and becoming fluent with the skills required to collect, enter, summarize, interpret, and report data. Continuing users should also be supported in maintaining fluency with existing features, as well as acquiring the skills needed to utilize features newly added to the system over time. In order to ensure that the system is used appropriately, it may be optimal to have a requirement that users complete training prior to actual use.

Step 6: Determine Whether Integration with Other Data Sources Is Possible

Although a behavioral assessment data system can be used in isolation, integration within a larger electronic system that includes general school (attendance), academic (e.g., grades, schoolwide achievement scores), and medical (e.g., medication) data may be particularly attractive to schools that are already managing large quantities of data. For these schools, system interoperability is a prerequisite for adoption and use. As such, it is important that behavioral data be considered seamlessly in line with other forms of data in making student-related decisions. This integration facilitates decision making, while also decreasing the need for training across multiple electronic systems.

Available Systems to Support Schoolwide Behavioral Assessment

Unlike electronic systems for the collection, summarization, analysis, and reporting of academic data that have existed for some time (e.g., AIMSweb, DIBELS), systems designed specifically for behavioral assessment are fairly new on the scene. In this section, we provide information regarding both existing (School-Wide Information System [SWIS], AIMSweb Behavior) and emerging (DBR Connect) systems, in light of the desirable features previously described.

School-Wide Information System

As within other multi-tiered models of support, the importance of data-based decision making is emphasized in a schoolwide positive behavior supports (SWPBS) model. In this model, decisions regarding which students require what level of behavior support are made by analyzing ODR data that are collected as a part of typical school routines. SWIS is a web-based system that was designed specifically to collect, summarize, interpret, and report ODR data. In addition to managing schoolwide ODR data, SWIS can be used to facilitate the collection, summarization, and use of targeted and intensive behavioral data as well. At the targeted level, check-in/check-out SWIS (CICO-SWIS) provides space for school staff to enter daily progress report (DPR) data for students participating in a CICO intervention (see Chapter 8 for more information on CICO and the behavior education plan, or BEP). Data can then be analyzed within or across classroom periods in order to assess student progress in relation to established goals. At the intensive level, the Individual Student Information System (ISIS-SWIS) can be used to monitor both plan implementation and behavioral outcome data for students receiving individualized, intensive supports. In addition to monitoring student progress and judging plan effectiveness, space is provided for teams to upload any documentation related to the student's individualized behavior support plan (PBIS Apps, 2014c).

Defensibility

Defensible data are those that are accurate, reliable, and valid. In order to promote accuracy, SWIS incorporates safeguards to protect against errors in data entry. Specifically, the Data Integrity system allows users to generate a summary of potential errors, including missing values and values that are outside of the expected range (e.g., dates that have not occurred yet). Use of this feature means that less time is spent double checking entered data, which often may be quickly entered into an electronic system.

With regard to the psychometric adequacy of SWIS assessment measures, at this point research has focused exclusively on the evaluation of ODR data. Validity evidence in support of the use of ODR data is promising, with several studies identifying moderate to strong correlations between ODR data and established behavior rating scales (Irvin, Tobin, Sprague, Sugai, & Vincent, 2004; McIntosh, Campbell, Carter, & Zumbo, 2009; Pas, Bradshaw, & Mitchell, 2011). With regard to screening in particular, however, research has demonstrated that the use of ODRs may underrepresent problem behavior (McIntosh, Horner, Chard, Boland, & Good, 2006; Walker et al., 2005). Studies have also indicated that use of ODRs may lead to high false-negative rates and thus missed intervention opportunities (Miller et al., 2015; Nelson, Benner, Reid, Epstein, & Currin, 2002). Given these concerns, researchers have recommended that ODR data be used in tandem with other assessment measures when conducting screening (McIntosh, Frank, et al., 2010). When considering the use of ODR data in a progress monitoring context, data that reflect sensitivity to change are of particular importance. Although data have supported the sensitivity of ODR data to detecting intervention effects at the schoolwide level (e.g., Nelson, Colvin, & Smith, 1996), these data are also needed at the level of the individual student. Further research therefore appears warranted to establish the psychometric research base in support of measures used in SWIS.

Efficiency

SWIS was designed to make data collection and analysis quick and easy. Time-saving features include the use of drop-down menus to simplify data entry and the ability to copy information from one referral to the next if multiple students are involved in the same incident. In a study of actual SWIS users, Irvin et al. (2006) found that most schools reported needing between 10 and 60 minutes per week for schoolwide ODR data entry. Users also reported that low effort was needed to generate reports and that the reports were useful across a variety of decision-making purposes (e.g., early identification, progress monitoring; Irvin et al., 2006). Furthermore, SWIS is a web-based system, which allows for accessibility via any computer through a web browser.

Capacity to Enter and Store Data

SWIS is designed to handle the information that is typically collected in a standardized fashion at the universal or secondary level (e.g., ODR, DPR) as well as the individualized data gathered at the tertiary level. Within the general system, relevant information from ODRs includes (1) the student's name, (2) the student's grade, (3) the staff member making the referral, (4) the date and time of incident, (5) where the incident occurred, (6) problem behavior observed, (7) additional students involved in the incident (if applicable), (8) action taken, and (9) perceived motivation behind the behavior (PBIS Apps, 2014c). In addition, individual schools can add up to 10 custom fields to meet local data collection needs. In CICO-SWIS, drop-down menus can be used to select the target student and to enter points earned on the DPR across different rating periods (PBIS Apps, 2014a). Finally, CICO-ISIS allows users to enter data from one or more unique assessment measures tailored for students at the tertiary level. Space is available to enter (1) the name of the measure; (2) the metric utilized (e.g., frequency count, percent of attempts, Likert scale); (3) the data collection schedule (e.g., daily, weekly); and (4) the student performance goal (PBIS Apps, 2014b).

Data Feedback and Reporting

In SWIS, it is possible to analyze data and create reports at the level of the individual student, classroom, grade, school, or district; however, different types of reports are available to the individual user depending on his or her level. For example, a classroom teacher may only be able to access ODR or ISIS-SWIS data for the students in his or her classroom, whereas the building principal could view data from across the school. Through the SWIS Dashboard, School Summary Reports can be generated to answer the "big five" questions of who (i.e., referrals by student), what (i.e., referrals by problem behavior), when (i.e., referrals by time or day of the week), where (i.e., referrals by location), and how many (i.e., average number of referrals per day/per month) (PBIS Apps, 2014c). Schoolwide reports are also available through CICO-SWIS and ISIS-SWIS. The Student Dashboard, on the other hand, is used to generate reports at the individual (i.e., student) level. With regard to ODR data, it is possible to answer the questions of what, when, where, and how many ODRs were received; however, users can also generate a report to examine the number of referrals by possible motivation, which may be used to help inform intervention planning. In CICO-SWIS, reports can be generated to examine points earned by a student both within and across rating periods. Student-level reports in CICO-ISIS permit the monitoring of data over time as well as the comparison of data across measures (PBIS Apps, 2014b). Across all levels, data from both individuals and groups can be represented in narrative form or using tables or graphs.

Training

Although users can log on to SWIS from any location using a password-protected account, the system is only available to schools through a local facilitator. The SWIS facilitator first conducts a readiness assessment to identify whether schools meet the requirements needed to obtain a SWIS license. In order to ensure the ability to use SWIS appropriately, schools must demonstrate that they not only have established procedures for discipline and appropriate discipline referral forms, but also that sufficient resources are dedicated to the use of SWIS, including administrative support, personnel, and physical resources (Todd & Horner, 2007). Similar checklists are also used to assess readiness for CICO- and ISIS-SWIS. The facilitator then trains key personnel in data entry and summarization, and works with the school team to ensure appropriate use of data in decision making before completing the licensing process (Irvin et al., 2006). Schools then purchase a subscription to the system, through which they receive access to the online database. Subscription fees are determined in relation to the number of participating schools. Information regarding these costs can be found on the PBIS Apps website (*www.pbisapps.org/Applications/Pages/Getting-Started-With.aspx*).

Integration

As was previously mentioned, SWIS was designed to accommodate multiple forms of behavioral data, including ODRs, DPRs, and individualized behavioral outcome measures. Schools can also use SWIS-ISIS to store any documents related to students receiving intensive/individualized supports, such as IEPs, behavior support plans, intervention checklists, observational forms, grades, and reports (e.g., psychoeducational, medical). Additionally, different options are available for integrating SWIS data within larger student information systems. For example, class rosters can be imported into SWIS or ODR data can be exported to existing electronic systems (see *www.pbisapps.org/Applications/Pages/Data-Integration.aspx* for more information).

AIMSweb Behavior

AIMSweb Behavior is a behavioral assessment and intervention module within the larger web-based AIMSweb system, designed for use within a multi-tiered model of support. At the universal level, AIMSweb Behavior includes two screening assessments that can be used to identify students in need of additional behavior supports: the Social Skills Improvement System—Performance Screening Guide (SSIS-PSG; Elliott & Gresham, 2008) and the Behavioral and Emotional Screening System (BESS; Kamphaus & Reynolds, 2007). The SSIS-PSG is a brief screener that can be used to quickly identify those students who may be at risk specifically for problems with prosocial behavior or motivation to learn. Teachers are asked to rate each student in their classroom on a scale from 1 to 5 with regard to these two constructs. Scores of 2 and 3 are considered to suggest moderate concern, whereas a score of 1 indicates a high level of concern. In contrast, the BESS is a more traditional multi-item rating scale that can be used to identify students at risk for a broader range of emotional and behavioral problems. One approximately 30-item form is completed for each student (in either English or Spanish), and forms are available for both teachers and students. Both tools can be used individually or in combination with one another and can be administered up to three times per year (Pearson, 2010).

At the targeted and intensive levels, the system offers tools for both intervention and progress monitoring. The Action Plan component of the system includes intervention strategies for use at the whole-class, group, and individual levels that were adapted from the BASC-2 Intervention Guide (Vannest, Reynolds, & Kamphaus, 2008) and the SSIS Intervention Guide (Elliott & Gresham, 2008), as well as step-by-step directions for how to implement these strategies. Depending on the level of support needed, individualized plans can be created, or more general plans can be developed to reflect schoolwide expectations. When screening data are available, intervention recommendations will be matched to the results of the assessment; however, users can also simply review the complete list of interventions (Pearson, 2010). The Action Plan component also allows users to create customizable assessment forms. Although any target behavior can be entered, AIMSweb Behavior also provides a list of recommended behaviors based either on screening results (i.e., those behaviors that received the highest ratings) or on a list of the most common problem behaviors. Depending on the target behavior selected, users can choose to use a Rating Scale form (i.e., dichotomous yes/no scale, 3-point Likert scale), a Frequency form (i.e., the number of times the target behavior occurred), or an Interval form (i.e., the percentage of time the target behavior occurred) (Pearson, 2010). The Progress Monitor component allows users to track student behavior over time and create progress reports. Reports can be generated to include mean or median scores within an intervention period, or to provide a line graph of student progress in relation to a preestablished goal.

Defensibility

Evidence in support of both the reliability and validity of the SSIS-PSG and BESS are provided in the AIMSweb Behavior Administration and Technical Manual (Pearson, 2010). The internal consistency of the BESS was found to be high across both teacher and student forms. Both test–retest reliability and interrater reliability were found to be within the desirable range for both the PSG and BESS (Pearson, 2010). Concurrent validity was demonstrated between the BESS and established measures of emotional and behavioral problems (e.g., BASC-2, Achenbach System of Empirically Based Assessment [ASEBA]), as well as between the SSIS-PSG and the full SSIS Rating Scales (i.e., SSIS-PSG Prosocial Behavior—SSIS Social Skills, and SSIS-PSG Motivation to Learn—SSIS Academic Competence). Finally, preliminary evidence of predictive validity was established when using the BESS Teacher and Student Forms to predict composite scores on the full BASC-2 measures. The proportion of true positives was found to range from .47 (Teacher Form, Internalizing Problems Composite) and .77 (Teacher Form, School Problems Composite), with classification accuracy found to be highest when teachers rated externalizing problems and students self-reported internalizing problems (Pearson, 2010). Additional research regarding the diagnostic accuracy of both the BESS and SSIS-PSG appears warranted.

In contrast, evidence is relatively absent regarding AIMSweb progress monitoring measures. The technical manual reports no psychometric evidence for any of the progress monitoring options. Previous independent research has examined tools similar to those afforded by AIMSweb Behavior (e.g., Volpe & Briesch, 2012), yet evidence regarding AIMSweb-specific methods is lacking. Although the Action Plan system permits the flexibility in design many educators desire, it is unclear at this time whether the various progress monitoring forms one might create via AIMSweb possess the sensitivity to change required of a formative measure.

Efficiency

One of the time-saving features of AIMSweb Behavior is the ability to prepopulate forms with student names and other demographic information. Such information can be exported from other systems (e.g., SWIS) and imported to the AIMSweb system. Screening and progress monitoring forms are relatively efficient, requiring only a few minutes to rate a student's behavior. For instance, it is estimated that the BESS can be completed in 3–5 minutes per student, whereas the SSIS-PSG requires only 20 minutes for an entire classroom. AIMSweb Behavior's automated suggestion system allows for the efficient selection of target behaviors and interventions, while also permitting educator choice and flexibility. User menus and dropdowns are intuitive and navigable.

Capacity to Enter and Store Data

A notable strength of the AIMSweb Behavior system is its integration with other AIMSweb modules. As a result, educators can concurrently evaluate behavioral data with the results of various academic assessments (e.g., CBMs of reading and mathematics), allowing for comparison of performance across domains in the process of reaching robust conclusions about student needs and possible supports. Though AIMSweb does not permit the storing of additional data (e.g., attendance, ODRs) or documents (e.g., behavior support plans, IEPs), the system's capacity to store and evaluate psychometrically defensible academic assessment data is a characteristic largely unique to the AIMSweb platform.

In addition, although one of the previously defined strengths of an online database is the ability to enter data directly into the system, AIMSweb Behavior also allows users to download and print hard copies of forms. Such flexibility allows schools to collect data in a manner that best suits their needs, while still providing electronic storage of information.

Data Feedback and Reporting

Similar to SWIS, AIMSweb reports can be generated at the level of the individual student, classroom, school, or district. Educators can generate reports for universal screening and progress monitoring purposes. As noted above, it is possible to generate reports that include both behavioral and academic data. The AIMSweb system makes it easy for teachers to identify those students in need of further assessment or intervention; screening results are color-coded in green (i.e., meets expectations), yellow (i.e., may be in need of individualized supports), or red (i.e., consult with behavior specialist) categories.

Training

A number of training options are available for new users of AIMSweb. In-person trainings that cover a range of content, from system management to data-based decision making, are available with certified trainers. Those users looking for greater flexibility may also opt for the online training, which can be completed at an individual pace during a 2-month period (see *www.aimsweb.com/training* for more information).

Integration

AIMSweb Behavior can be accessed as a standalone web-based system through a web browser. Although it is currently not possible to integrate AIMSweb with other data systems, options do exist for importing student demographic data from a school's student information system into AIMSweb.

DBR Connect

DBR Connect was designed to store, analyze, and provide reports of behavioral outcome data collected using DBR, in particular. This web-based system is intended to provide (1) enhanced utility of a problem-solving system though easy-to-use data entry on a variety of traditional and emergent platforms, (2) efficient and secure storage, (3) a wide range of easy-to-understand and customized analysis and reporting options, and (4) guided intervention-related decision making. The baseline prototype of DBR Connect (i.e., a preliminary software model that includes key features of the desired product) was developed through collaboration with faculty and graduate students at the University of Missouri, University of Connecticut, and East Carolina University in order to experiment with ideas and concepts related to the system. The current web portal has six core features: (1) easy-to-use data entry of student behavior ratings; (2) DBR data storage and organization, (3) analysis and customizable reporting of outcomes (e.g., individual and group charts); (4) a data initialization process that allows for preloading of school, classroom, and individual student information (e.g., names, IDs, demographics); (5) a user profile with capability to set preferences, such as organizing ratings by individual students and groups of students and customizing the behaviors being rated; and (6) a rudimentary help system. Currently, the capabilities and functions of the core features have been evaluated in the field with a limited number of teachers and administrators to gather basic information in regard to usability.

DBR Connect came online in December of 2015 and is available in a number of web platforms, including all versions of Google Chrome and Mozilla Firefox, Safari 6.0 and newer versions, and Internet Explorer 8 and newer versions. It is also responsive to browser-based screen size changes. The primary approach for tablet/smartphone data collection is to link directly into the web portal. In addition, specific applications ("apps") will be developed for a variety of platforms (iPhone and Android) based on customer feedback and usage of the desktop version. The use of smartphone/tablets represents a significant advancement in web-based data-based decision-making systems, and should help to make the entire process more feasible in actual classroom environments.

Defensibility

As noted above, DBR Connect is founded upon DBR methodology. As such, the system's defensibility is inherently linked to the DBR psychometric literature base (see Chapters 5 and 6 for evidence in support of progress monitoring and screening applications). Data collected and stored through DBR Connect are therefore thought to evidence reliability, validity, sensitivity to change, and classification accuracy.

Efficiency

DBR Connect allows for efficient loading of relevant data (e.g., schools, teachers, students) via Microsoft Excel spreadsheets. That is, rather than manually entering student- and teacher-related data into the system, as many educational systems require, instead educators can upload information in a format typically used in school settings. This feature is primarily intended to expedite the school adoption process, removing barriers between the decision to implement DBR Connect and its actual use.

An initial round of beta testing was conducted in 2010–2011 with educational professionals, including general education teachers, special education teachers, and student support service providers (e.g., school psychologists). Results suggested that individuals who utilized DBR Connect in an educational setting generally found it to be (1) easy to learn; (2) easy to use, both individually and when compared to other student data systems; (3) non-time-intensive; and (4) useful in making decisions often asked of educational professionals in data-based decision-making contexts.

Capacity to Enter and Store Data

DBR Connect has a web-based interface that facilitates data entry through a two-stage process. In the first stage, the parameters of data collection are defined. These parameters include (1) the student(s) targeted for rating, (2) the rating period (i.e., time, setting, and instructional activity, (3) the behavior(s) to be rated, and (4) type of rating (i.e., screening or progress monitoring). DBR Connect users can select any and all students and rating periods of interest. They can also choose from a prepopulated list of operationally defined behaviors, or opt to define their own behaviors in accordance with the particularities of each case. Users also have the option of grouping students in their classroom who possess common rating parameters. In other words, students within a group can be rated across the same behaviors (e.g., academic engagement, disruptive behavior) and within the same context (e.g., Tuesday and Thursday from 10–10:45 A.M. during social studies instruction).

In the second stage, the previously described parameters are used to create DBR ratings. These screens are to be accessed by educators after each rating period of interest and used to input ratings of student behavior. Rating screens include graphical sliders, which educators can move to record their specific rating for each student across all previously selected behaviors. Once submitted, all ratings are stored in a cloud-based server. All DBR Connect data are stored in accordance with Family Educational Rights and Privacy Act (FERPA; 1974) regulations.

Furthermore, the prototype version of DBR Connect provides secure storage of data via a number of enhancements, including *https* (i.e., secure web pages), secure log-on, secure database storage (via encryption), and automatic log-out (following 15 minutes of inactivity).

Data Feedback and Reporting

DBR Connect includes a basic analysis and reporting function in which users first select either the student or the group (if group, users have the option of selecting the student[s] within the group), and type of report (i.e., individual screening, group screening, or individual progress monitoring). The Individual Student Screening Report includes (1) the parameters of the selected rating period (e.g., time, setting, instructional activity); (2) the operational definitions of each rated behavior; (3) graphs of student behavior formatted in accordance with single-case design best practices; and (4) a summary of behavior, including ranges, means, and confidence intervals. The Group Screening Report provides identical information at the group level, while also yielding individual student data regarding means, ranges, and risk scores. The Individual Progress Monitoring Report provides similar information as the screening reports, but additionally provides all noted intervention changes (baseline, Intervention 1, Intervention 2, etc.) and their corresponding date ranges. Once a report is executed, results are displayed in a bar graph (see Figure 12.2) or a line graph (see Figure 12.3) and also summarized in a narrative fashion to promote educator interpretation.

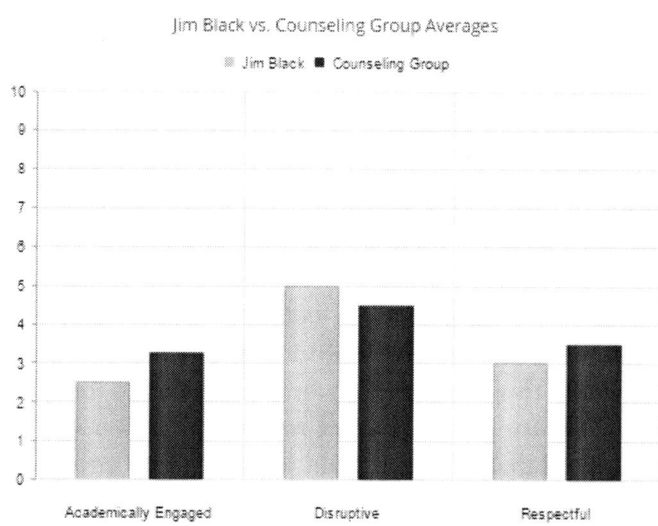

FIGURE 12.2. DBR Connect bar graph, displaying DBR-SIS ratings for both target and student groups.

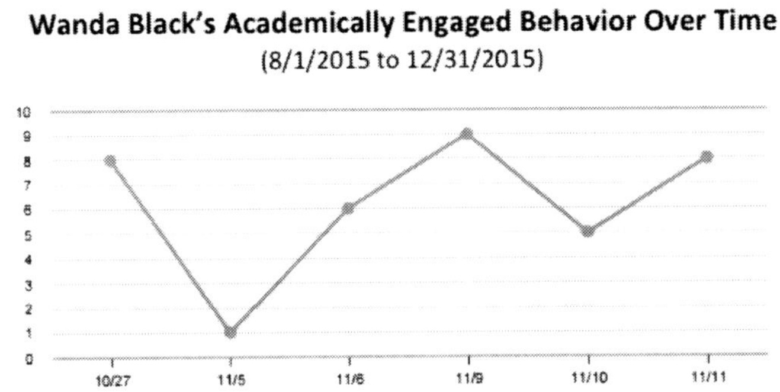

FIGURE 12.3. DBR Connect line graph of mean ratings for academically engaged behavior across days.

DBR Connect allows for stored data to be analyzed in a variety of ways in accordance with effective graphing and reporting strategies intended to enhance teacher responsiveness. Several options for predicted analysis exist at each level. At the individual level, data must be converted to an advanced single-case design, with line graphs based on experimental designs used in the intervention process. At the school level, it is important that data can be analyzed to observe any changes in social behavior across groups (e.g., classroom or school). In addition, at the district level, it is useful to have the ability to track a student's behavior across schools, comparing behavior over time as a student progresses from elementary to middle to high school. DBR Connect has advanced reporting options that allow users to present outcome data in a number of fashions.

Training

The current version of DBR Connect includes video-based online training modules intended to provide users with an overview of the DBR Connect system. The modules are based on previous research indicating the extent and nature of training necessary to promote accurate ratings of student behavior (Chafouleas, Kilgus, et al., 2012; LeBel et al., 2010; Schlientz et al., 2009). The online training modules have been developed through rounds of beta testing with faculty, graduate students, and educational professionals. As discussed in Chapter 7, the current training procedure includes three modules: (1) an introduction to the uses of DBR, (2) a demonstration of DBR use, and (3) practice rating student behavior (via video) with feedback. It is required that each user train to an accuracy criterion before engaging in the rating of students. Overall, training takes approximately 20–40 minutes to complete. Additional modules are currently in development and will focus on supporting educators to use data, graphs, and reports as part of evidence-based practice within a problem-solving framework.

Integration

DBR Connect currently operates as a standalone web-based system. Moving forward, it is of interest to expand DBR Connect functionality via the development of application programming interfaces (APIs). API development will allow for the integration of DBR Connect functionality within alternative software solutions. It will thus be possible to access DBR Connect features through a variety of data systems that choose to implement the DBR Connect APIs. Pending DBR Connect API integration, schools could therefore use DBR Connect without the need for dedicating resources to the adoption of a new data system or training school teachers/staff relative to system use. In our experience consulting with schools, the desire for such functionality is frequently noted by educators who are hesitant to adopt yet another data solution for their school. Should software developers choose to adopt APIs, educators will be able to access DBR Connect in the manner that best suits their needs.

Summary of Available Data Systems

Educators currently have access to a wide range of behavioral assessment data systems. A review of the current options indicates that systems vary widely in terms of functionality. SWIS allows for the collection and storage of ODRs across all students, DPR points for those participating in CICO, and individualized assessment data for students with unique behavior intervention plans. AIMSweb Behavior incorporates a variety of universal screeners (i.e., BESS and SSIS-PSG) and progress monitoring tools (e.g., teacher ratings, frequency- and interval-based direct observation), maximizing teacher flexibility in their approach to behavioral assessment. AIMSweb data also drive decisions regarding student supports through the systems' integration with multiple social skill and behavior intervention guides. Furthermore, AIMSweb Behavior integrates with academic data sources, allowing for more robust decisions regarding student performance. DBR Connect, the newest of the options, serves as a depository for all things DBR. An educator can use the system to collect, store, interpret, and communicate DBR information collected with regard to an individual or group of students. Detailed graphs and reports can be generated in accordance with best practice for single-case research and visual analysis, thus supporting evidence-based analysis of student data.

The noted systems collectively offer a variety of strengths. Each is considered user-friendly and capable of informing educator decisions regarding students, including their need for, and responsiveness to, intervention. SWIS and AIMSweb also permit the integration of behavioral data with other forms of information (e.g., behavior support plans, IEPs, academic assessment data), allowing the systems to serve as somewhat of a "hub" for data storage and interpretation. Despite these strengths, the reviewed systems are also associated with certain limitations. For instance, although research supports the use of DBR for progress monitoring purposes, research is limited regarding formative assessment options available via SWIS or AIMSweb. In addition, ODRs have been found to possess limited utility in universal screening, with the BESS, SSIS-PSG, and DBR possessing far greater support. Finally, although DBR Connect provides users with unique features (e.g., integration through existing data systems, rating notifications), continued development is necessary to ensure DBR Connect's stability (e.g., under the stress of simultaneous usage across hundreds and thousands of users). Additional research through expert focus groups and lab and field trials is needed both to examine DBR Connect's utility and to garner the feedback necessary for continued development and system expansion.

Conclusions

Universal screening and progress monitoring serve as the foundation of service delivery within multi-tiered systems of support, such as SWPBS interventions and supports. Research suggests that these two forms of assessment stand to promote the timeliness and effectiveness of behavioral service delivery. Yet, many educators lack the training to summarize and interpret these data in a manner that supports student outcomes. Furthermore, although paper-and-pencil approaches to assessment are common, they pose many difficulties given the complexities inherent in handling the large volume of data generated within multi-tiered frameworks. The current chapter offered a review of multiple behavioral assessment electronic data systems that serve to automate the collection, summarization, interpretation, and communication of behavioral data. Though these systems vary in terms of their structure, procedures, and content, each is intended to promote educators' use of data to inform student intervention. It is hoped that by using these systems, educators will enhance their capacity to serve students and promote positive academic and social outcomes.

CHAPTER 13

Using DBR in a Comprehensive Problem-Solving Model

Amy M. Briesch, Sandra M. Chafouleas, and T. Chris Riley-Tillman

This book has provided you with understanding of the ways in which DBR can be used to assess, intervene with, and communicate about student behavior. Although many benefits of DBR have been discussed across the different chapters, it would be presumptuous to think that DBR could be used to solve all child difficulties, given that it offers only one method of behavioral assessment and a single option for intervention programming. Thus, in this final chapter, we aim to demonstrate how DBR can be used in combination with other data sources and intervention strategies to create a comprehensive process for assessing and intervening with student behavior at multiple levels.

Comprehensive School-Based Problem Solving

As has been discussed throughout this book, changes in public policy at the federal, state, and local levels have enhanced accountability requirements in schools, thereby emphasizing the importance of data-based decision making. As a result, the traditional "wait to fail" model of service delivery, in which students only receive additional academic or behavior supports once their struggles are of considerable magnitude, is increasingly being rejected in favor of a problem-solving approach with a preventive focus. Data-based problem solving is a systematic process in which data are used to identify problems (*problem identification*), determine why they are occurring (*problem analysis*), implement interventions designed to improve student functioning (*plan implementation*), and monitor student progress over time to determine intervention effectiveness (*plan evaluation*). Within these four broad stages, however, there are several more specific problem-solving steps that must be carried out; these are outlined in Table 13.1 and discussed in detail next.

Problem Identification

The first stage that initiates the problem-solving process is the identification of a problem. Although this may seem fairly straightforward, it is important to note that problems can be identified through several different means (e.g., methods, persons, reasons). For many years, the predominant model of problem identification was through teacher referral. That is, once a problem reached a level at which the classroom teacher felt he or she could no longer handle it on his or her own, a referral was made to either special education or a school-based problem-solving team. Unfortunately, there are several limitations to this traditional referral process. For one, the process is reactive rather than proactive, in that problems must reach a significant-enough level that they are no longer tolerated in the classroom (Lane, Oakes, & Menzies, 2010). As a result, students who are struggling but whose behavior does not exceed this referral threshold are unlikely to be identified for supports. Teacher referral is also highly contextual, in that the chances of a student being referred depend on not only the student's behavior but also on teacher knowledge, attitudes, and behavior (Lane, Oakes, et al., 2010). Although a student may exhibit the same behavior across different settings, teachers may respond to it differently depending on factors such as how familiar each teacher is with the symptoms of a disorder or how high each teacher's tolerance level is for deviant behavior.

Step 1: Determine the Goal of Screening and Select the Appropriate Method

As discussed in Chapter 6, a more proactive approach to problem identification involves the use of screening procedures. Screening involves the systematic and efficient evaluation of a group of students in order to proactively identify potential risk. Before specific assessment tools can be selected, however, it is necessary to clarify what the school team sees as the purpose for conducting an assessment in the first place (Kazdin, 2005). Numerous theoretical assessment models for behavior exist; however, we believe that most school-based models can be classified according to one of three frameworks: (1) psychopathology, (2) risk and resilience, or (3) school-based success (see Table 13.2). A psychopathology-based framework is likely the most familiar, as it has traditionally been used in school settings. Within this framework, the goals of behavioral assessment are seen as the identification of symptoms or indicators related to a particular diagnosis (e.g., emotional and

TABLE 13.1. Steps in Conducting Comprehensive Problem Solving

☐ 1. Determine the goal of screening and select the appropriate method.

Screening may be used to (a) identify symptoms or indicators related to a particular diagnosis, (b) evaluate risk and protective factors, or (c) assess those behaviors that directly affect a student's ability to learn and thrive in school. Assessment tools should be selected to align with the intended goal of screening.

☐ 2. Define the problem and determine whether it exists at the individual or group level.

Problems are defined in terms of the discrepancy between current and expected performance. Screening data can be used to determine whether a problem exists for an individual student (thus warranting targeted intervention) or a group of peers (thus warranting a universal or small-group intervention).

☐ 3. Establish a baseline estimate of behavior.

Feasible methods for measuring behavior using participant observers (e.g., teachers, classroom aides) may include use of direct assessment procedures such as frequency counts, scatterplots, or DBR.

☐ 4. As needed, conduct additional assessments to determine why the problem may be occurring.

Additional assessments should be conducted to measure student skills and develop an understanding of those variables that may be maintaining problem behavior. Indirect assessments (e.g., semistructured interviews, rating scales) may be most appropriate during initial problem-solving stages, whereas more direct assessments (e.g., observation recording forms) should be used as the stakes of decision making increase.

☐ 5. Use assessment data to inform intervention selection.

Use of interventions involving DBR (e.g., check-in/check-out, daily report card, self-management) may be appropriate for addressing a number of school-based concerns at either the individual or group level.

☐ 6. Implement the intervention and monitor integrity.

Implementation integrity can be monitored using self-report (e.g., checklists, DBR-like ratings), direct observation, permanent products, or a combination of methods.

☐ 7. Monitor progress in response to intervention.

Progress should continue to be monitored with the same method used during baseline data collection. The frequency of monitoring should vary in relation to the intensity of student need.

☐ 8. Determine plan effectiveness.

If data indicate a positive effect, consider if it would be appropriate to continue to make modifications to enhance feasibility or to promote generalization. If data do not indicate effectiveness, assess implementation integrity and consider modification of the intervention.

TABLE 13.2. Theoretical Models of School-Based Behavioral Screening

Model	Goals of assessment	Examples of relevant constructs	Examples of measures
Psychopathology	Identify symptoms or indicators related to a particular diagnosis.	• Externalizing behaviors (e.g., aggression, defiance, hyperactivity) • Internalizing behaviors (e.g., withdrawal, anxiety, depression)	• Behavioral and Emotional Screening System (Kamphaus & Reynolds, 2008) • Child Behavior Checklist (Achenbach & Rescorla, 2001) • Student Risk Screening Scale (Drummond, 1994)
Risk/resilience	Assess individual and environmental factors that may predict, or protect against, negative outcomes.	• Risk factors (e.g., prenatal substance exposure, low socioeconomic status, exposure to violence) • Protective factors (e.g., gets along with other children, empathy, problem-solving skills)	• Communities That Care Youth Survey (Arthur, Hawkins, Pollard, Catalano, & Baglioni, 2002) • Devereux Student Strengths Assessment (LeBuffe, Shapiro, & Naglieri, 2009) • Social–Emotional Assets and Resilience Scale (Merrell, 2011)
School-based adjustment	Assess those behavioral constructs thought to relate to a student's ability to learn and thrive in school.	• Teacher adjustment (e.g., follows rules, disrupts instruction, listens politely) • Peer adjustment (e.g., gets along with peers, fights with peers)	• Direct Behavior Rating—SIS Standard Form (Chafouleas, Riley-Tillman, et al., 2009) • Social Skills Improvement System (Elliott & Gresham, 2008)

behavioral disorder), identifying students likely to meet diagnostic criteria, and initiating efforts to reduce symptoms. In contrast, the second option involves dual evaluation of risk and protective factors to identify both individual (e.g., aggressive behavior, problem-solving skills) and environmental (e.g., peer support, parental employment) factors that may predict, or protect against, negative outcomes (Severson et al., 2007). Some research has suggested that risk and protective factors may be more predictive of behavioral outcomes than even psychiatric symptom severity (Vance et al., 2002). Many risk factors may be difficult to change or are outside of the control of the school; however, many protective factors can be considered appropriate targets for intervention (e.g., problem-solving skills, social connections).

Finally, a school-based adjustment framework focuses on identifying behavior constructs thought to be relevant to students' ability to learn and thrive in school, without specific concern for diagnostic status. The goal of behavioral assessment is therefore seen as informing intervention directed at improving school functioning (e.g., Walker et al., 1992).

Once the general purpose of screening has been clarified, the more specific procedures can be determined. One aspect of establishing screening procedures is determining the scope of assessment efforts. Universal screening involves the assessment of all students in a given population (e.g., school, district). Given that assessment is conducted with large numbers of students, it is critically important that the procedures be efficient in order to maximize feasibility. The longer that an assessment measure takes to complete for one student, the lower the likelihood of the teacher completing it for 20–30 students. It is also important to consider the practicality of the assessment task from a logistical standpoint. For example, although a tool such as DBR is brief enough to be applied across large numbers of students, it may be difficult for a classroom teacher to simultaneously attend to the behavior of all students at one time. In those situations in which the feasibility of applying a particular tool universally is questionable, a multiple-gated screening procedure should be considered.

A multiple-gated framework capitalizes on the strengths and minimizes the weaknesses of any individual assessment method. Efficiency in screening is achieved through using a quick and simple identification procedure to initially screen all students, and then adding other more intensive methods and procedures at subsequent stages or "gates." Because the more intensive procedures are applied to only a reduced number of students that pass through each successive gate (Severson et al., 2007), a multiple-gated option offers a potentially more cost-effective approach to universal screening. An initial gate that provides all students the chance to be considered for risk status is desirable, yet potentially comes at a cost, given the resources that are necessary. For this reason, teachers are typically asked in the initial gate to simply nominate students using a common standard of reference. For example, each teacher might be given the operational definitions of academic engagement, disruptive behavior, and respectful behavior from the DBR-SIS Standard Form and asked to list up to three students in each class for whom the target behavior is most problematic (see Figure 13.1). Once a smaller subset of students is identified, one proposed second gate is to have teachers complete an established comprehensive rating scale for these students to confirm the problem. Additional gates (e.g., direct observation) may also be employed until a high-risk group is identified.

Depending on the purpose that screening is intended to serve in your particular setting, different assessment tools may be prioritized within universal or multiple-gated screening. If the goal of screening is to identify those students who have demonstrated, or are at risk for demonstrating, symptoms of psychopathology,

Instructions: The three behaviors listed below have been shown to be critically important in determining student success in the classroom. For each behavior, please read the definition and then list up to three students for whom you believe the behavior is of greatest concern. Each list should be mutually exclusive, meaning that you should not include the same student on multiple lists. If you feel that one student struggles in multiple domains, please list his/her name under the behavior that you believe to be the biggest problem.

Academically engaged is defined as actively or passively participating in the classroom activity. For example: writing, raising hand, answering a question, talking about a lesson, listening to the teacher, reading silently, or looking at instructional materials.

Student #1:

Student #2:

Student #3:

Respectful is defined as compliant and polite behavior in response to adult direction and/or interactions with peers and adults. For example: follows teacher's direction, pro-social interaction with peers, positive response to adult request, verbal or physical disruption without a negative tone/connotation.

Student #1:

Student #2:

Student #3:

Disruptive is defined as taking action that interrupts regular school or classroom activity. For example: out of seat, fidgeting, playing with objects, acting aggressively, talking/yelling about things that are unrelated to classroom instruction.

Student #1:

Student #2:

Student #3:

FIGURE 13.1. Sample of first-gate screening protocol for multiple-gating procedure.

there are several available rating scales that were designed for such identification purposes. As one example, the SRSS (Drummond, 1994) is a seven-item scale that can be accessed for free online and used to identify those students at risk for antisocial behavior. If the goal of screening is to identify risk and protective factors, however, a different set of measures would be needed. A wide range of risk factors may be assessed, ranging from low socioeconomic status to exposure to violence, using measures such as the Communities That Care Youth Survey (e.g., Arthur et al., 2002). A number of rating scales are also available that were designed to specifically measure social–emotional competencies (e.g., self-regulation, interpersonal functioning), including the Social–Emotional Assets and Resilience Scales (SEARS; Merrell, 2011). Finally, in those cases in which the goal is to identify those factors that most interfere with school-based success regardless of diagnostic status, tools such as the DBR-SIS Standard Form (Chafouleas, Riley-Tillman, Christ, & Sugai, 2009) or the SSIS (Gresham & Elliott, 2008) may be of most interest. Although the individual measure selected will depend on which behaviors are most important and relevant at the local level (see Chapter 2 for a discussion of target behavior selection), it is important that the measure be well aligned with the construct(s) of most interest.

One important point to keep in mind when selecting screening tools is the flexibility of DBR to assess a wide range of behaviors. As discussed in Chapter 1, as long as the behavior is observable and measurable, there is the potential to assess it using a DBR approach. The suggestion has been made, for example, that individual items can be selected from a longer rating scale in order to create tailored scales for the purposes of both screening and progress monitoring (Volpe et al., 2009, 2010). One option may therefore involve creating either single- or multi-item DBR scales to target the construct(s) of most interest. For example, DBR scales could be created to assess symptoms of underlying psychopathology (e.g., inability to sustain attention, loses temper) or even resilience factors (e.g., cooperation skills, problem-solving skills), as long as the target behaviors can be readily observed. One advantage of using DBR in screening is that these data can later be used to serve a second purpose in estimating performance under baseline conditions. It is important to note at the same time, however, that much of what we know regarding the psychometric properties of DBR is limited to the three core behavioral competencies/barriers (i.e., academically engaged, disruptive, respectful). Therefore, additional work is needed to evaluate the defensibility of emerging scales.

Step 2: Define the Problem and Determine Whether It Exists at the Individual or Group Level

Problem identification does not end, however, once concerns come to the attention of a teacher or a team. Given that behavioral concerns are often context dependent, the problem should be framed in terms of the discrepancy between current and expected performance (Tilly, Niebling, & Rahn-Blakeslee, 2009). Framing the problem in this way illustrates its magnitude, which, in turn, will help to determine the level of resources needed. Whereas expected performance in academic domains is often determined by objective standards or benchmarks (e.g., students should be able to read 40 correct words per minute by the end of first grade), expected performance in behavioral domains is often determined by the referring party. That is, the classroom teacher is asked to define what an acceptable level of behavior may be. As an example, let's imagine that the target behavior for "Joan" is calling out (e.g., providing answers without raising her hand, making unsolicited comments during instruction) and that Joan's teacher estimates that she calls out five times during a typical instructional block (e.g., literacy, math). If Joan's teacher believes in the value of a silent classroom, in which students always raise their hands before speaking, calling out five times an hour would be considered a significant problem warranting intervention. If, on the other hand, Joan's teacher values hand raising but considers the occasional blurt-out to be developmentally appropriate, calling out five times an hour might be viewed as less of a problem and addressed less urgently.

When discrepancy data suggest that a problem does exist for an individual student, the next question that we want to ask is whether it is an individual- or group-level problem. That is, we want to know not only whether the performance gap exists for the target student but also whether it exists for other students as well. Evidence of a performance gap only for the target student suggests the need for targeted intervention. However, a performance gap for both the target student and her peers suggests the need for group-level intervention (Batsche, Castillo, Dixon, & Forde, 2008).

Step 3: Establish a Baseline Estimate of Behavior

Once a problem has been identified and defined, baseline data are needed to better understand the current level of functioning. In some cases, baseline data may already be available and sufficient to estimate current performance. For example, if screening was conducted by either collecting DBR data or analyzing ODRs, these extant data could serve the purpose of estimating baseline levels of behavior. If, however, extant data are not sufficient or available, it would be necessary to collect new information.

Baseline data can be collected via several different means. If one were interested in obtaining a highly accurate estimate of performance, an external observer (e.g., school psychologist, social worker) might be employed to precisely measure the number of times that a behavior occurs or determine its duration. Alternatively, those individuals already in the classroom setting (e.g., teachers, classroom aides) can make direct recordings, such as through frequency counts or scatterplots. Other forms of DBR may also be helpful at this stage. For example, the use of performance-based behavioral recordings has been advocated when the behavior of interest is not easily measured using frequency, duration, or interval recording (Steege, Davin, & Hathaway, 2001). Steege and colleagues (2001) developed a 5-point Likert rating scale to record the stereotypic behavior of three individuals with ASD in a group home setting. In this case, each point of the Likert scale was designed to correspond with the estimated number of minutes during which the behavior was observed (e.g., *1* = 1 second to 2 minutes, 59 seconds; *2* = 3 minutes to 5 minutes, 59 seconds). Furthermore, participating teachers in a study by Wilkinson (2005) rated disruptive, off-task behavior using a 9-point Likert-type scale for which ratings of 1–3 represented "Poor" behavior, ratings of 4–6 represented "Needs Improvement," and ratings of 7–9 represented "Good" behavior.

Should the data suggest that the problem exists not only for an individual student but for his or her peers as well, baseline monitoring should occur at the group level. Although conducting observations or keeping a frequency count for multiple students in a classroom would quickly become unwieldy, preliminary research has suggested that DBR can be used to monitor classwide performance when implementing a group-level intervention. In a study by Riley-Tillman, Methe, et al. (2009), for example, the classroom teacher completed a DBR-SIS measuring the academic engagement of the class as a whole at the end of each silent reading period. Similar trends were observed across data collected using direct observation and DBR, leading to similar decisions regarding intervention effectiveness regardless of the data source utilized.

Problem Analysis

Step 4: As Needed, Conduct Additional Assessments to Determine Why the Problem May Be Occurring

Once a problem has been identified, the aim in this second stage of problem analysis is to derive hypotheses as to why the problem may be occurring in order to inform development of an intervention plan. Assessments must therefore be conducted in order to measure student skills and to develop an understanding of those variables that may be maintaining problem behavior. At this stage it is important to consider whether the problem represents a skill deficit, in that the student "can't do" a desired behavior, or a performance deficit, in that the student "won't do" it. For example, in the case of a student who has a meltdown (e.g., crying, banging head on desk) when work is too difficult, the desired replacement behavior might be for the student to ask for help from the teacher. The question that must be asked is whether the student does not know how to appropriately ask for help (thus requiring explicit instruction) or whether he or she simply is not doing so consistently (perhaps requiring additional practice or reinforcement).

Focus should also be placed on those environmental variables that can be measured and changed by the classroom teacher, as these are what will ultimately inform intervention efforts (Tilly et al., 2009). It has been argued that by focusing on skill deficits and environmental variables, psychology can truly be given away by empowering the classroom teacher to be able to effect needed change (Gutkin, 2009). Instructional (e.g., pace of instruction, opportunities to respond) or setting (e.g., seating arrangement, physical layout of room) variables, for example, are within a classroom teacher's control to change. In contrast, if the problem is viewed as existing entirely within the student (e.g., "He is hyperactive," "She is conduct-disordered"), changing the behavior appears to be a much more difficult task. Multiple data collection methods should be used at this stage, including review, interview, observation, testing, and self-report (RIOTS; Batsche et al., 2008).

Although DBR has most typically been used to rate a particular dimension of behavior rather than the context in which it is situated, initial work has begun to examine the utility of DBR in collecting such environmental data. Kilgus, Taylor, Kazmerski, and von der Embse (2015) developed four novel DBR-SIS targets corresponding to common consequences of students' problem behavior, including adult attention, peer attention, escape/avoidance, and access to items/activities (see Table 13.3 to review operational definitions for each consequence). Ratings of a particular consequence are interpreted similarly to conditional probabilities (Eckert, Martens,

TABLE 13.3. DBR Function-Based Targets and Operational Definitions

Behavior	Definition
Adult attention	Positive, negative, or neutral adult reaction that can be either verbal or nonverbal. Examples: reprimand, redirection to work, praise, discussion, high-fives, shushing.
Peer attention	Positive, negative, or neutral peer reaction that can be either verbal or nonverbal. Examples: talking, laughing, arguing, high-fives, hitting, kicking, yelling.
Escape/avoidance	Removal or avoidance of task, activity, or performance expectations. Examples: removal of academic materials, allowed to delay task completion, permission to leave room, elimination of task demands.
Access to items or activities	Acquisition of items or activities. Examples: toys, food, prizes, games, preferred tasks, sleep, technology, homework pass.

& DiGennaro, 2005), representing the percentage of target problem behaviors that were followed by that consequence. Like other forms of DBR, multiple data points should be collected over time prior to comparison. Ratings can then be aggregated within each target and compared, with the highest ratings corresponding to the likely function of the student's behavior.

In addition, other indirect and/or direct tools may be used to gather relevant information, depending on the rigor of assessment required at this stage (readers are directed to Steege & Watson, 2009 for a comprehensive discussion of assessment tools for assessing behavioral function). A number of semistructured interviews (e.g., Functional Assessment Checklist: Teachers and Staff; March et al., 2000) and rating scales (e.g., Motivational Assessment Scale; Durand & Crimmins, 1992) can be used to identify those conditions that may trigger problem behavior (e.g., room arrangement, type of instruction), intraindividual factors that may be associated with problem behavior (e.g., skill level, health factors), and those variables that typically follow problem behavior (e.g., adult attention, escape from difficult tasks). Teachers may also be asked to systematically record this information as problem behaviors occur, such as through the use of an antecedent–behavior–consequence (ABC) recording sheet. Regardless of the specific tools utilized, however, the goal is to generate a hypothesis statement regarding the most probable reason why the problem behavior is occurring (i.e., to escape peers or task, to gain attention or access to materials, or for sensory stimulation).

Step 5: Use Assessment Data to Inform Intervention Selection

The assessment data and hypothesis statement should next be used to inform intervention selection. Although a DBR-based intervention is certainly not the answer to every problem, one of the most attractive features is the broad array of uses and applications that can extend across all levels of intervention focus, settings, and populations. As highlighted in Chapter 1, DBR-like tools have been used in preschool (e.g., LeBel et al., 2013) through secondary school (e.g., Schumaker et al., 1977) to provide information about positive and negative behaviors. Such tools have also been used to change a wide range of behaviors from assignment completion (e.g., Blechman et al., 1981) to appropriate social interactions (e.g., Sainato et al., 1992).

In this book, we have discussed different ways in which DBR might be used as part of an intervention designed to increase appropriate classroom behavior. CICO, for example, may be an appropriate intervention for those students who engage in mild acting-out behavior throughout the day and for whom adult attention is reinforcing (given frequent meetings with the intervention coordinator and teachers) (e.g., Crone et al., 2010). The efficacy of DRCs has also been demonstrated across a wide range of students (Vannest et al., 2010), including those with ADHD, when incorporated as part of a comprehensive intervention package (e.g., Fabiano et al., 2007). Furthermore, there is a strong evidence base in support of the use of self-management interventions to improve classroom conduct and empower students to take greater responsibility for their own behavior (Maggin et al., 2013).

In addition to use with individual students, DBR may also be used in intervention planning when the same problem behavior has been identified for an entire group or class. That is, it is more efficient to apply the same strategy to the group rather than create multiple individualized plans that may compete for already limited resources. Although asking a classroom teacher to rate the individual behavior of every student in the classroom using DBR would quickly become unwieldy, having students complete their own self-managed DBR ratings (see Chapter 10) serves to increase the feasibility of this approach. Classwide applications of self-management interventions are often paired with reinforcement strategies that rely on group attainment of a preset goal, such as found in group contingencies. For example, all students in a class might be organized into smaller groups and taught to raise their hands (Connell, Carta, Lutz, et al., 1993) or give a thumbs-up sign (e.g., Briesch et al., 2013) to indicate performance of a skill or behavior. Rewards may be determined based on individual performance (i.e., independent group contingency; Miller, Strain, Boyd, Jarzynka, & McFetridge, 1993), overall team performance (i.e., interdependent group contingency; Chafouleas, Sanetti, Jaffery, et al., 2012), or the performance of a select group of team members (Briesch et al., 2013).

Although interventions involving DBR have been shown to positively influence a wide range of common school-based concerns, use of DBR is not appropriate in every case. First, DBR interventions have been used predominantly to address externalizing behaviors to date. Meta-analyses of both DRC (Vannest et al., 2010) and self-management interventions (e.g., Briesch & Briesch, 2015) have identified on-task and disruptive behavior as the most common behavioral targets. Preliminary evidence has emerged recently in support of the use of a CICO intervention to address internalizing concerns such as social withdrawal or anxiety (e.g., Dart et al., 2015; Hunter, Chenier, & Gresham, 2014); however, more work is needed in this area before concrete recommendations can be made. Second, use of a DBR-based intervention is not appropriate for addressing dangerous or infrequent behaviors. The extent and type of behavioral feedback provided through a DBR intervention would likely not be sufficient for those students engaging in behavior that threatens to harm either themselves or others. On the other hand, engaging in daily monitoring and feedback may be too much for those behaviors that occur very infrequently (e.g., tantrums that occur once every 2 weeks). Although DBR may be used as part of an individualized, multicomponent intervention for those students with intensive behavioral needs, most research thus far has focused on the use of DBR at either the universal or targeted level of intervention.

Plan Implementation

Although intervention or strategy implementation is central to the third stage of the problem-solving model, the work does not end when the plan is put into place. This is because effective consultation involves not only identifying an intervention for which there is a high probability of success, but also providing adequate supports to ensure that the intervention is implemented properly (Noell, 2008). Furthermore, it is essential that student performance be reviewed periodically during implementation to ensure that any necessary modifications can be made in a timely fashion.

Step 6: Implement Intervention and Monitor Integrity

Treatment integrity can be measured using a variety of methods, including direct observation, review of permanent products, and self-report. As is true of most assessment methods, what one gains in accuracy often comes at the cost of feasibility (and vice versa!). Use of direct observation, for example, reduces the influence of bias, but requires a greater commitment of resources. Because an external observer must enter the room to conduct integrity checks, these will likely be made irregularly. As a result, the limited number of integrity checks may not adequately represent actual implementation behavior. Furthermore, there may be an increased likelihood of observer-related reactivity, such that the plan is implemented with greater fidelity when an external observer is present.

Integrity can also be monitored using self-report. Typically, teachers are asked to complete a checklist indicating which intervention components were implemented (e.g., "Did I review the behavioral expectations with the student?"; "Did I provide verbal reinforcement for meeting behavioral expectations?"). However, it has also been suggested that DBR can be used to assess multiple dimensions of treatment integrity (e.g., participant responsiveness, implementation quality) beyond component integrity alone (Sanetti, Chafouleas, Christ, & Gritter, 2009). For example, a classroom teacher might be asked to rate the degree to which students were actively engaged in a group intervention, using an 11-point scale (see Figure 13.2). Despite requiring minimal resources (e.g., time for summarization of data, external raters), it should be noted that there is greater potential for bias with the use of self-report. For example, studies have shown that teachers tend to report higher levels of treatment integrity than suggested by direct observation (Wickstrom, Jones, LaFleur, & Witt, 1998) or permanent product data (Noell et al., 2005).

Finally, treatment integrity can be monitored through the use of permanent products. *Permanent products* are those data that are already available in the school environment. If a student is involved in a manualized social skills intervention, for example, worksheets could be reviewed to ensure that they are being completed consistently. Although not all interventions result in permanent product data, this

To what degree were the intervention components implemented as planned?

0 1 2 3 4 5 6 7 8 9 10

0% Not at all — 50% Somewhat — 100% Fully

To what extent did you feel confident in implementing the intervention?

0 1 2 3 4 5 6 7 8 9 10

0% Not at all — 50% Somewhat — 100% Fully

To what extent were the students engaged in the intervention?

0 1 2 3 4 5 6 7 8 9 10

0% Not at all — 50% Somewhat — 100% Fully

FIGURE 13.2. Sample of DBR for monitoring intervention implementation.

is yet another advantage of an intervention that involves DBR. In addition to serving as an intervention and assessment tool, the DBR rating form can be considered a record of implementation. That is, forms can be reviewed to ensure that ratings were completed at the appropriate date and time. If tangible or activity rewards are used as part of the intervention, it may also be helpful to record when these rewards were administered on the form so that this information can be reviewed as well. An example of how a self-management DBR could be used to assess implementation integrity is provided in Figure 13.3.

Step 7: Monitor Progress in Response to Intervention

During intervention implementation, ongoing data collection should take place using the system that was initiated during baseline. Progress monitoring can be seen as a way of providing all involved parties with continuous feedback regarding the student's behavior. As reviewed in Chapter 3, DBR contains features that can facilitate proactive and ongoing communication about a student's behavior across settings (e.g., home, school, community). An important first step is to identify which parties (e.g., parent, teacher, community agency, student) should be included in the

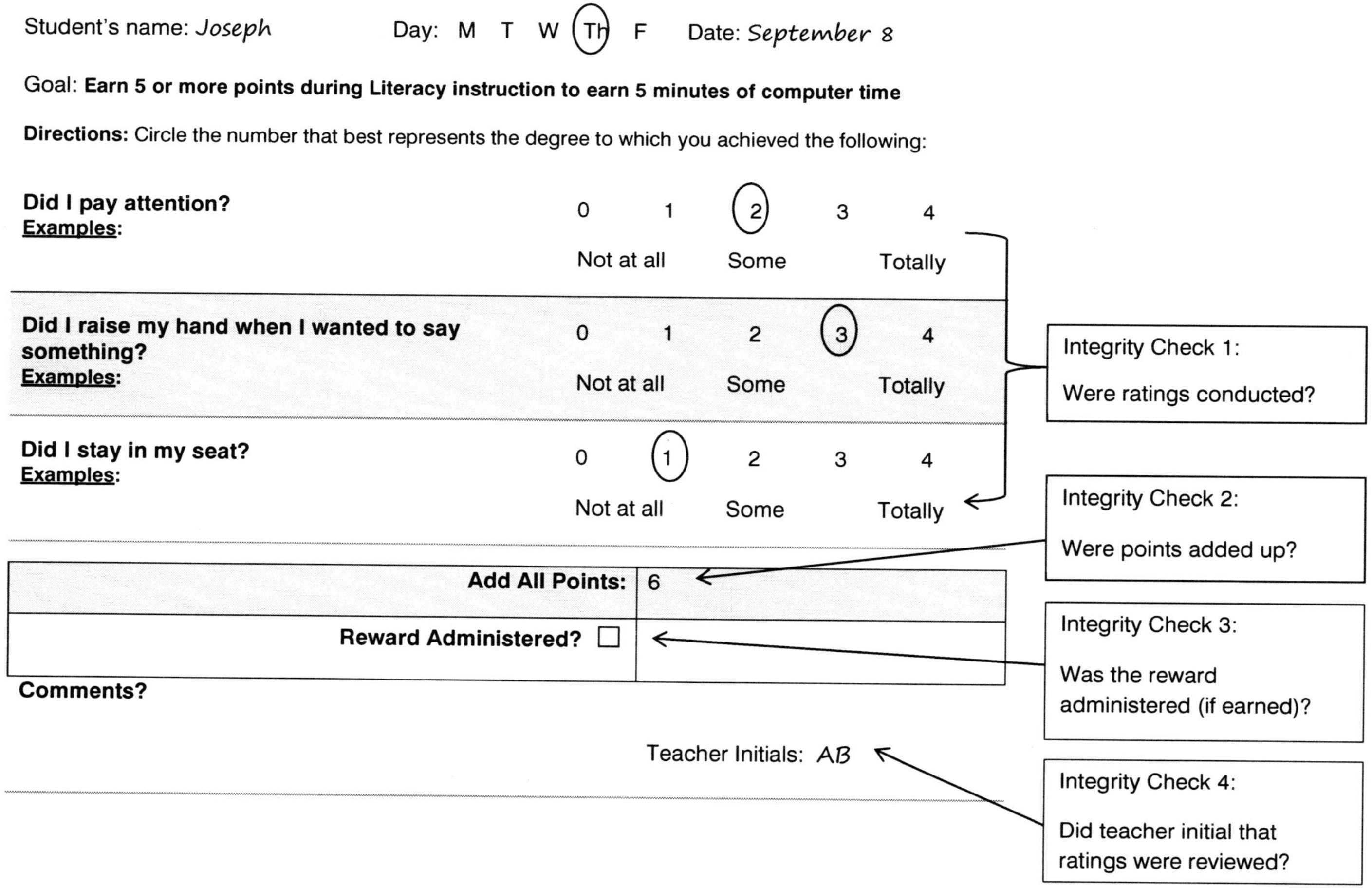

FIGURE 13.3. Treatment integrity example for a self-management intervention.

routine communication about progress. Depending on the intensity of student need, progress monitoring data can be collected and shared more or less frequently. That is, weekly monitoring may be necessary for a student with more intensive behavioral needs, whereas monthly monitoring may be appropriate for students receiving targeted intervention. Although it is important to regularly review progress monitoring data to understand whether the student is progressing toward a goal, it is also important to allow sufficient time for the intervention to have an effect before making changes to the plan. Decisions regarding the appropriate "wait time" should be made in relation to the type of intervention being implemented and how quickly one might expect to see change. For example, we would expect an intervention involving reinforcement of appropriate behavior and planned ignoring of problem behavior to result in more immediate effects than a skills-based intervention in which students are instructed according to a 10-week curriculum.

Plan Evaluation

Step 8: Determine Plan Effectiveness

In the final stage of plan evaluation we wish to determine whether the plan was effective in changing student behavior. Determining effectiveness involves consideration of both formative (as discussed above) and summative data (Tilly et al., 2009). Whereas formative data are used to determine whether progress has been made over time, summative data are used to assess where performance falls in relation to the expectation established during problem identification. That is, we are interested in knowing whether the gap between current and expected performance has been narrowed.

As discussed in Chapter 11, one of two conclusions can be drawn from analyzing the data: Either the intervention was effective or no effect has been demonstrated. In the case of positive effects, the intervention may be kept intact, modifications may be made to enhance feasibility, or strategies may be implemented in order to promote generalization. If implementing a DRC or CICO intervention, for example, one might begin to transition from adult-completed ratings to the use of self-monitoring. If no effect is seen, however, the first issue is to determine whether the plan was implemented as intended. This can be determined through review of treatment integrity data (e.g., checklists, permanent product data) as well as by talking with the implementer. If integrity is found to be low, strategies should be put into place for enhancing integrity, such as the use of performance feedback (e.g., Sanetti, Fallon, & Collier-Meek, 2012).

If the plan was implemented with fidelity but positive effects were not seen, it may be necessary to intensify the intervention. An intervention can be intensified by increasing the dosage (e.g., increasing the minutes per day that self-monitoring takes place, increasing the length/number of adult–student check-ins), changing conditions of implementation (e.g., selecting a different CICO coordinator), or further individualizing the plan (National Center on Intensive Intervention, 2013). As discussed in Chapter 9, individualized interventions should incorporate functionally based data. The Prevent–Teach–Reinforce (PTR; Iovannone et al., 2009) intervention model, for example, incorporates individualized evidence-based strategies to modify relevant antecedents, teach replacement behaviors, and arrange consequences such that appropriate behaviors are reinforced and problem behaviors are less likely to occur.

One point to keep in mind during this final stage of plan evaluation is Kazdin's (2005) argument that it is important not only to assess the reliability of change (i.e., "Is there observed change above and beyond what would be expected given random fluctuations?"), but also the clinical significance of change. That is, it is important to know whether the observed changes are believed to be important to stakeholders and whether they equate to meaningful differences in the student's life. One of the important advantages of DBR is the ability to judge this clinical significance. That is, because DBR involves asking important stakeholders about their perceptions of student behavior, any changes noted over time may be the result of (1) actual behavior change, (2) changed perceptions of behavior, or (3) a combination of the two. Although it is difficult to tease these apart, it has been argued that changed perceptions of behavior may be just as important in assessing plan effectiveness if positive perceptions ultimately result in an improved classroom climate (Chafouleas et al., 2002). This is particularly true given that changes in a teacher's attitude toward a particular target student can mean "the difference between willingness to modify a classroom to accommodate special learners and refusal to tolerate such students" (Fuchs & Fuchs, 1989, p. 275).

Problem Solving within a Comprehensive, Multi-Tiered Model

In a comprehensive model, this four-stage process is not reserved only for those cases demonstrating the highest needs; rather, problem solving takes place across all tiers of service delivery (i.e., universal, targeted, intensive). What differs from one level to the next, however, is the rigor of the process. That is, as the intensity of the problem and the stakes of decision making become higher, our assessment procedures must also become more rigorous (Heartland Area Education Agency, 2008). One way in which to think about *rigor* is with regard to the measures used. That is, those assessments that demonstrate stronger psychometric properties (i.e., reliability, validity), are conducted in closer proximity to actual behavior (i.e., directness) and require a lesser degree of inference (i.e., objectivity) are considered to be more rigorous. Another aspect of *rigor* concerns the amount of data that are collected. As emphasized by Whitcomb and Merrell (2012), comprehensive assessment involves the use of multiple methods (e.g., interviews, ratings), sources (e.g., teacher, parent, self), and settings (e.g., school, home, community). Therefore, as the stakes of decision making increase, so, too, should the number of data points. Finally, we may also think about *rigor* in terms of the formality of the process and the individuals who are involved in it. The higher the stakes of decision making, the more specialized knowledge is needed and the more formal the process becomes (Tilly et al., 2009; see Figure 13.4). We wish here to highlight Heartland Area Education Agency's problem solving framework, in which three levels of response are delineated before eligibility for special education is considered. Although these levels of support can be considered sequential, students need not move through each level. Rather, teams

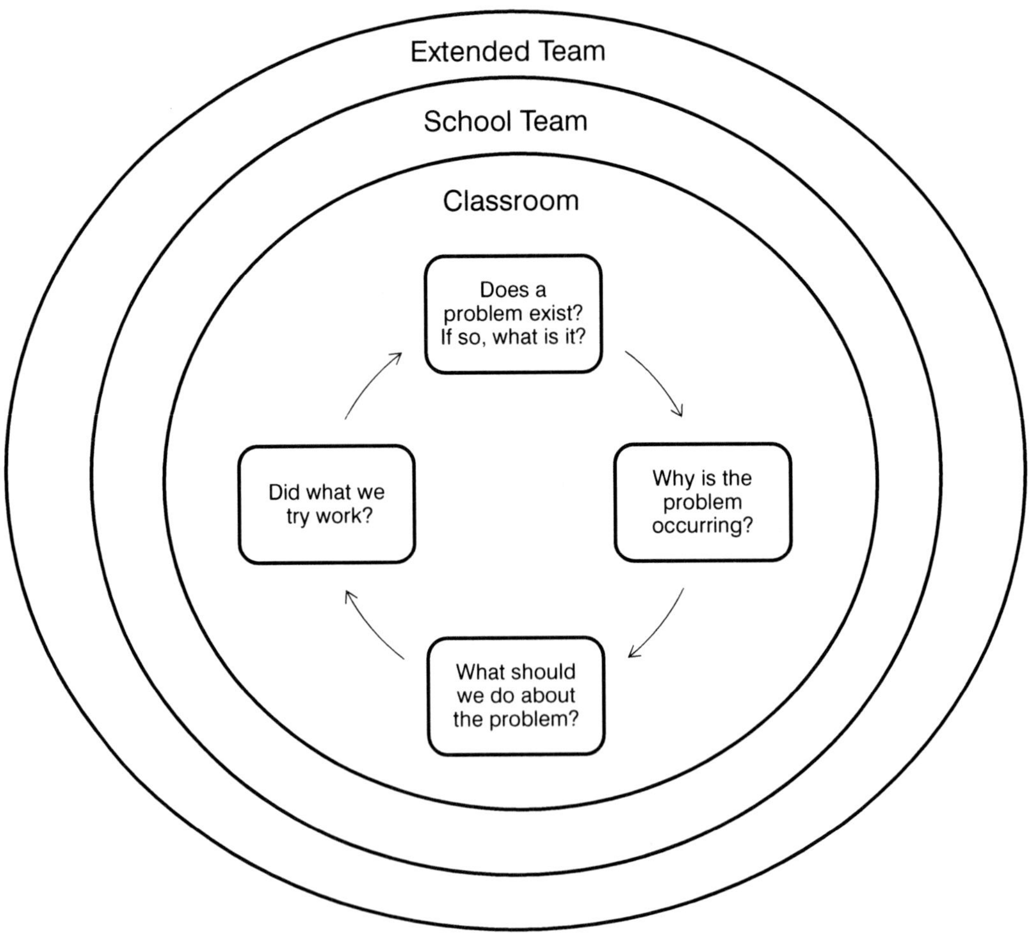

FIGURE 13.4. The rigor of problem-solving activities varies across levels of response.

are encouraged to consider the needs of each individual case and make decisions accordingly with regard to the level of support needed (Tilly et al., 2009).

Classroom-Level Problem Solving

At the first level, when problems first arise, classroom teachers and families work together to support student behavior without the involvement of external personnel. The goal at this stage is to open up the lines of communication between school and home and to design and implement interventions that are feasible within the general education setting. Although a problem must be identified in order to begin the problem-solving process, it may not be defined as formally as has been described in this chapter (e.g., defining the discrepancy between current and expected performance based on obtained data). Furthermore, intervention selection decisions can be made without collecting additional data. Interventions such as the DRC can be implemented at this level if the classroom teacher has received training in the procedure and feels confident to implement it independently; however, less formalized strategies can also be tested at this stage. Although the effectiveness of the plan should be monitored, documentation at this stage is relatively informal and decisions are often made based on individual perceptions (Heartland Area Education Agency, 2008; Tilly et al., 2009).

Team-Based Problem Solving

When informal problem solving between the teacher and family does not prove successful, the next level involves consultation with building colleagues. Although building assistance teams go by many different names (e.g., *Student Support Team*, *Building Assistance Team*), the common function of these teams is to assist teachers in analyzing problems and developing appropriate interventions (Lane et al., 2003). The composition of these teams may vary from one building to the next; however, they most typically include some mix of classroom teachers, administrators, and support personnel (e.g., special education teachers, school social workers). One clear advantage at this stage is that the classroom teacher is able to draw from the collective wisdom of several team members, some of who may have dealt with similar problems previously. Interventions should be selected from among those that have a sufficient evidence base and effectiveness should be monitored using standardized, yet feasible, methods of data collection (Heartland Area Education Agency, 2008; Tilly et al., 2009).

Formal Problem Solving Involving an Extended Team

At the third level, specialists (e.g., mental health professionals) are brought in to consult and collaborate with classroom teachers. It is at this level that the full four-stage problem-solving model is formally carried out. Sufficient data should be collected in order to inform the development of a formally documented intervention plan. Those data sources that are based on rater perception, including DBR, should likely be supplemented with other sources of more direct data. At this stage, treatment integrity is more formally evaluated and progress monitoring data more frequently reviewed (Heartland Area Education Agency, 2008; Tilly et al., 2009).

Conclusions

DBR may be a fairly new term; however, the history behind this type of tool is clearly rich and complex. When DRC interventions first emerged in the literature nearly half a century ago, the benefits of such an intervention approach with regard to efficiency (i.e., time and resource requirements) and defensibility (i.e., treatment effectiveness) were quickly recognized. In recent years, however, researchers have begun to take advantage of the flexibility of DBR to explore its full potential within a multi-tiered system of supports. As we have outlined both in this chapter and throughout the book, one of the greatest benefits of DBR to school-based professionals is that one tool can be adapted to serve a variety of problem-solving purposes. DBR has demonstrated utility not only within varied assessment (e.g., screening, progress monitoring) and intervention (e.g., universal, targeted, individualized) contexts, but also beyond. Recent work has suggested the potential for DBR to be used to explore behavioral function and to monitor treatment integrity as well. Ongoing research is still needed, however, in order to better understand the parameters of DBR usage, such as which target behaviors may be reliably measured and addressed through intervention using a DBR approach. As this evidence base continues to grow, we expect the role of DBR in linking assessment, intervention, and communication to further solidify, thereby maximizing the capacity for DBR to promote student success.

References

Achenbach, T. M., McConaughy, S. H., & Howell, C. T. (1987). Child/adolescent behavioral and emotional problems: Implications of cross-informant correlations for situational specificity. *Psychological Bulletin, 101*, 213–232.

Achenbach, T. M., & Rescorla, L. A. (2001). *Manual for the ASEBA School-Age Forms and Profiles*. Burlington, VT: University of Vermont, Research Center for Children, Youth, & Families.

AIMSweb. (n.d.). Academic Improvement Measurement System. Retrieved from *www.aimsweb.com*.

Allday, R. A., & Pakurar, K. (2007). Effects of teacher greetings on student on-task behavior. *Journal of Applied Behavior Analysis, 40*, 317–320.

Amato-Zech, N. A., Hoff, K. E., & Doepke, K. J. (2006). Increasing on-task behavior in the classroom: Extension of self-monitoring strategies. *Psychology in the Schools, 43*, 211–221.

American Educational Research Association, American Psychological Association, & National Council on Measurement in Education. (1999). *Standards for educational and psychological testing*. Washington, DC: American Psychological Association.

Angkaw, A. C., Tran, G. Q., & Haaga, D. A. F. (2006). Effects of training intensity on observers' ratings of anxiety, social skills, and alcohol-specific coping skills. *Behaviour Research and Therapy, 44*, 533–544.

Appleton, J. J., Christenson, S. L., Kim, D., & Reschly, A. L. (2006). Measuring cognitive and psychological engagement: Validation of the Student Engagement Instrument. *Journal of School Psychology, 44*, 427–445.

Ardoin, S. P., & Martens, B. K. (2004). Training children to make accurate self-evaluations: Effects on behavior and the quality of self-ratings. *Journal of Behavioral Education, 13*, 1–23.

Arthur, M. W., Hawkins, J. D., Pollard, J. A., Catalano, R. F., & Baglioni, A. J. (2002). Measuring risk and protective factors for substance abuse, delinquency, and other adolescent problem behaviors: The Communities That Care Youth Survey. *Evaluation Review, 26*, 575–601.

Autry, L. B., & Langenbach, M. (1985). Locus of control and self-responsibility for behavior. *Journal of Educational Research, 79*, 76–84.

Axelrod, M. I., Zhe, E. J., Haugen, K. A., & Klein, J. A. (2009). Self-management of on-task homework behavior: A promising strategy for adolescents with attention and behavior problems. *School Psychology Review, 38*, 325–333.

Ayllon, T., Garber, S., & Pisor, K. (1975). The elimination of discipline problems through a combined school–home motivational system. *Behavior Therapy, 6*, 616–626.

Azevedo, R., & Bernard, R. M. (1995). A meta-analysis of the effects of feedback in computer-based instruction. *Journal of Educational Computing Research, 13*, 111–127.

Bailey, J. S., Wolf, M. M., & Phillips, E. L. (1970). Home-based reinforcement and the modification of pre-delinquents' classroom behavior. *Journal of Applied Behavior Analysis, 3*, 223–233.

Barnett, D. W., Bauer, A. M., Ehrhardt, K. E., Lentz, F. E., & Stollar, S. A. (1996). Keystone targets for change: Planning for widespread positive consequences. *School Psychology Quarterly, 11*, 95–117.

Barriga, A. Q., Doran, J. W., Newell, S. B., Morrison, E. M., Barbetti, V., & Robbins, B. D. (2002). Relationships between problem behaviors and academic achievement in adolescents: The unique role of attention problems. *Journal of Emotional and Behavioral Disorders, 10*, 233–240.

Barry, L. M., & Messer, J. J. (2003). A practical application of self-management for students diagnosed with attention-deficit/hyperactivity disorder. *Journal of Positive Behavior Interventions, 5*, 238–248.

Barth, R. (1979). Home-based reinforcement of school behavior: A review and analysis. *Review of Educational Research, 49*(3), 436–458.

Batsche, G. M., Castillo, J. M., Dixon, D. N., & Forde, S. (2008). Linking assessment to intervention. In A. Thomas & J. Grimes (Eds.), *Best practices in school psychology V* (pp. 177–194). Bethesda, MD: National Association of School Psychologists.

Begeny, J. C., & Martens, B. K. (2006). Assessing pre-service teachers' training in empirically-validated behavioral instruction practices. *School Psychology Quarterly, 21*, 262–285.

Bennett, K. J., Lipman, E. L., Racine, Y., & Offord, D. R. (2003). Annotation: Do measures of externalising behavior in normal populations predict later outcome?: Implications for targeted interventions to prevent conduct disorder. *Journal of Child Psychology and Psychiatry, 39*, 1059–1070.

Bergan, J. R., & Tombari, M. L. (1976). Consultant skill and efficiency and the implementation and outcomes of consultation. *Journal of School Psychology, 14*, 3–14.

Bermudez, A. B., & Marquez, J. A. (1996). An examination of a four-way collaborative to increase parental involvement in schools. *Journal of Educational Issues of Language Minority Students, 16*(6), 1–16.

Birnbrauer, J. S., & Lawler, J. (1964). Token reinforcement for learning. *Mental Retardation, 2*, 275–279.

Blair, K. C., Umbreit, J., & Bos, C. S. (1999). Using functional assessment and children's preferences to improve the behavior of young children with behavioral disorders. *Behavioral Disorders, 24*, 151–166.

Blechman, E. A., Schrader, S. M., & Taylor, C. J. (1981). Family problem solving versus home notes as early intervention with high-risk children. *Journal of Counseling and Clinical Psychology, 49*, 919–926.

Bolstad, O., & Johnson, S. (1972). Self-regulation in the modification of disruptive classroom behavior. *Journal of Applied Behavior Analysis, 5*, 443–454.

Bongers, I. L., Koot, H. M., van der Ende, J., & Verhulst, F. C. (2004). Developmental trajectories of externalizing behaviors in childhood and adolescence. *Child Development, 75*, 1523–1537.

Borman, W. C. (1977). Consistency of rating accuracy and rater errors in the judgment of human performance. *Organizational Behavior and Human Performance, 20*, 238–252.

Bradley, R., Doolittle, J., & Bartolotta, R. (2008). Building on the data and adding to the discussion: The experiences and outcomes of students with emotional disturbance. *Journal of Behavioral Education, 17*, 4–23.

Bramlett, R. K., Murphy, J. J., Johnson, J., Wallingsford, L., & Hall, J. D. (2002). Contemporary practices in school psychology: A national survey of roles and referral problems. *Psychology in the Schools, 39*, 327–335.

Brennan, R. L. (2001). *Generalizability theory*. New York: Springer-Verlag.

Breslau, J., Miller, E., Breslau, N., Bohnert, K., Lucia, V., & Schweitzer, J. (2009). The impact of early behavior disturbances on academic achievement in high school. *Pediatrics, 123*, 1472–1476.

Briesch, A. M., & Briesch, J. M. (2015). A meta-analysis of behavioral self-management interventions in single-case research. *School Psychology Review, 44*.

Briesch, A. M., Briesch, J. M., & Mahoney, C. (2014). Reported use and acceptability of self-management interventions to target behavioral outcomes. *Contemporary School Psychology, 18*, 222–231.

Briesch, A. M., & Chafouleas, S. M. (2009). Defining behavioral self-management: A review and analysis of the literature 1988–2008. *School Psychology Quarterly, 24*, 106–118.

Briesch, A. M., Chafouleas, S. M., & Riley-Tillman, T. C. (2010). Generalizability and dependability of behavioral assessment methods to estimate academic engagement: A comparison of systematic direct observation and Direct Behavior Rating. *School Psychology Review, 3*, 408–421.

Briesch, A. M., Ferguson, T. D., Volpe, R. J., & Briesch, J. M. (2013). Examining teachers' perceptions of social–emotional and behavioral referral concerns. *Remedial and Special Education, 34*, 249–256.

Briesch, A. M., Hemphill, E., & Daniels, B. (2013). Check your SLANT: Adapting self-management for use as a class-wide intervention. *School Psychology Research Forum: Research in Practice, 7*, 29–39.

Briesch, A. M., Kilgus, S. P., Chafouleas, S. M., Riley-Tillman, T. C., & Christ, T. J. (2012). The influence of alternative scale formats on the generalizability of data obtained from Direct Behavior Rating Single Item Scales (DBR-SIS). *Assessment for Effective Intervention, 38*, 127–133.

Briesch, A. M., & Volpe, R. J. (2007). Important considerations in the selection of progress monitoring measures for classroom behaviors. *School Psychology Forum, 1*, 59–74.

Briesch, A. M., Volpe, R. J., & Ferguson, T. D. (2013). The influence of student characteristics on the dependability of behavioral observation data. *School Psychology Quarterly, 29*, 171–181.

Broden, M., Hall, R. V., & Mitts, B. (1971). The effect of self-recording on the classroom behavior of two eighth-grade students. *Journal of Applied Behavior Analysis, 4*, 191–199.

Bronfenbrenner, U. (1979). *The ecology of human development: Experiments by nature and design*. Cambridge, MA: Harvard University Press.

Bronfenbrenner, U. (1992). Ecological systems theory. In R. Vasta (Ed.), *Six theories of child development: Revised formulations and current issues* (pp. 187–249). London: Jessica Kingsley.

Brophy, J. E., & Evertson, C. M. (1974). *Process–product correlations in the Texas teacher effectiveness study: Final report*. Austin: Texas Research and Development Center for Teacher Education.

Brown, A., & Green, T. (2003). Showing up to class in pajamas (or less!): The fantasies and realities of on-line professional development course for teachers. *The Clearing House, 76*, 148–151.

Bruhn, A. L., Lane, K. L., & Hirsch, S. E. (2014). A review of Tier 2 interventions conducted within multitiered models of behavioral prevention. *Journal of Emotional and Behavioral Disorders, 22*, 171–189.

Bruhn, A. L., Woods-Groves, S., & Huddle, S. (2014). A preliminary investigation of emotional and behavioral screening practices in K–12 schools. *Education and Treatment of Children, 37*, 611–634.

Bryk, A. S., & Schneider, B. (2002). *Trust in schools: A core resource for improvement*. New York: Sage Foundation.

Burke, M. D., Hagan-Burke, S., & Sugai, G. (2003). The efficacy of function-based interventions for students with learning disabilities who exhibit escape-maintained problem behaviors: Preliminary results from a single-case experiment. *Learning Disability Quarterly, 26*, 15–25.

Burkwist, B. J., Mabee, W. S., & McLaughlin, T. F. (1987). The effect of a daily report card system on inappropriate classroom verbalizations with a junior high school learning-disabled student. *Techniques: A Journal for Remedial Education and Counseling, 3*, 265–272.

Bush, R. N. (1984). *Effective staff development in making our schools more effective: Proceedings of three state conferences*. San Francisco: Far West Laboratory.

Cain-Smith, P., & Kendall, L. M. (1973). Retranslation of expectations: An approach to the construction of unambiguous anchors for rating scales. *Journal of Applied Psychology, 47,* 149–155.

Caprara, G. V., Barbaranelli, C., Pastorelli, C., Bandura, A., & Zimbardo, P. G. (2000). Prosocial foundations of children's academic achievement. *Psychological Science, 11,* 302–306.

Carlson, C., & Christenson, S. L. (Eds.). (2005). Evidence-based parent and family interventions in school psychology [Special issue]. *School Psychology Quarterly, 20*(4).

Carr, E. G., Dunlap, G., Horner, R. H., Koegel, R. L., Turnbull, A. P., Sailor, W., et al. (2002). Positive behavior support: Evolution of an applied science. *Journal of Positive Behavior Interventions, 4,* 4–16.

Carr, E. G., Langdon, N. A., & Yarbrough, S. C. (1999). Hypothesis-based intervention for severe problem behavior. In A. C. Repp & R. Horner (Eds.), *Functional assessment of problem behavior: From effective assessment to effective support* (pp. 9–31). Belmont, CA: Wadsworth.

Carr, S. C., & Punzo, R. P. (1993). The effects of self-monitoring of academic accuracy and productivity on the performance of students with behavioral disorders. *Behavioral Disorders, 18*(4), 241–250.

Carroll, J. (1963). A model for school learning. *Teachers College Record, 64,* 723–733.

Center for Children & Families. (n.d.). How to establish a school–home daily report card. Retrieved from *http://ccf.fiu.edu/for-families/resources-for-parents/printable-information/how_to_establish_a_school_drc.pdf.*

Centers for Disease Control and Prevention. (2000). *Measuring healthy days.* Atlanta: Author.

Chafouleas, S. M. (2011). Direct Behavior Rating: A review of the issues and research in its development. *Education and Treatment of Children, 34,* 575–591.

Chafouleas, S. M., Briesch, A. M., Riley-Tillman, T. C., Christ, T. J., Black, A., & Kilgus, S. P. (2010). An investigation of the generalizability and dependability of Direct Behavior Rating Single Item Scales (DBR-SIS) to measure academic engagement and disruptive behavior of middle school students. *Journal of School Psychology, 48,* 219–246.

Chafouleas, S. M., Christ, T. J., & Riley-Tillman, T. C. (2009). Generalizability and dependability of scaling gradients on direct behavior ratings. *Educational and Psychological Measurement, 69,* 157–173.

Chafouleas, S. M., Christ, T. J., Riley-Tillman, T. C., Briesch, A. M., & Chanese, J. M. (2007). Generalizability and dependability of daily behavior report cards to measure social behavior of preschoolers. *School Psychology Review, 36,* 63–79.

Chafouleas, S. M., Jaffery, R., Riley-Tillman, T. C., Christ, T. J., & Sen, R. (2013). The impact of target, wording, and duration in rating accuracy for Direct Behavior Rating. *Assessment for Effective Intervention, 39,* 39–53.

Chafouleas, S. M., Kilgus, S. P., & Hernandez, P. (2009). Using Direct Behavior Rating (DBR) to screen for school social risk: A preliminary comparison of methods in a kindergarten sample. *Assessment for Effective Intervention, 34,* 224–230.

Chafouleas, S. M., Kilgus, S. P., Jaffery, R., Riley-Tillman, T. C., Welsh, M., & Christ, T. J. (2013). Direct behavior rating as a school-based behavior screener for elementary and middle grades. *Journal of School Psychology, 51,* 367–385.

Chafouleas, S. M., Kilgus, S. P., Riley-Tillman, T. C., Jaffery, R., & Harrison, S. (2012). Preliminary evaluation of various training components on accuracy of Direct Behavior Ratings. *Journal of School Psychology, 50,* 317–334.

Chafouleas, S. M., Kilgus, S. P., & Wallach, N. (2010). Ethical dilemmas in school-based behavioral screening. *Assessment for Effective Intervention, 35,* 245–252.

Chafouleas, S. M., McDougal, J. L., Riley-Tillman, T. C., Panahon, C. J., & Hilt, A. M. (2005). What do daily behavior report cards (DBRCs) measure?: An initial comparison of DBRCs with direct observation for off-task behavior. *Psychology in the Schools, 42,* 669–676.

Chafouleas, S. M., Riley-Tillman, T. C., & Christ, T. J. (2009). Direct Behavior Rating (DBR): An emerging method for assessing social behavior within a tiered intervention system. *Assessment for Effective Intervention, 34,* 195–200.

Chafouleas, S. M., Riley-Tillman, R. W., Christ, T. J., & Briesch, A. M. (2008). *Direct Behavior Ratings (DBRs): The impact of alternate scale formats on accuracy and generalizability*. Unpublished manuscript.

Chafouleas, S. M., Riley-Tillman, R. W., Christ, T. J., & Sugai, G. (2009). DBR Standard Form. Retrieved from *www.directbehaviorratings.org*.

Chafouleas, S. M., Riley-Tillman, T. C., Jaffery, R., Miller, F. G., & Harrison, S. E. (2015). Preliminary investigation of the impact of a web-based module on Direct Behavior Rating accuracy. *School Mental Health, 7*(2), 92–104.

Chafouleas, S. M., Riley-Tillman, R. W., Fabiano, G. A., Welsh, M. E., & Swaminathan (2011). *Project VIABLE-II: Unified validation of Direct Behavior Rating (DBR) in a problem-solving model*. Washington, DC: Institute of Education Sciences.

Chafouleas, S. M., Riley-Tillman, T. C., & McDougal, J. (2002). Good, bad, or in-between: How does the daily behavior report card rate? *Psychology in the Schools, 39*, 157–169.

Chafouleas, S. M., Riley-Tillman, T. C., & Sassu, K. A. (2006). Acceptability and reported use of daily behavior report cards in a sample of teachers. *Journal of Positive Behavior Interventions, 8*, 174–182.

Chafouleas, S. M., Riley-Tillman, T. C., Sassu, K. A., LaFrance, M. J., & Patwa, S. S. (2007). Daily behavior report cards (DBRCs): An investigation of consistency of on-task data across raters and method. *Journal of Positive Behavior Interventions, 9*, 30–37.

Chafouleas, S. M., Riley-Tillman, T. C., & Sugai, G. (2007). *School-based behavioral assessment: Informing intervention and instruction*. New York: Guilford Press.

Chafouleas, S. M., Sanetti, L. M. H., Jaffery, R., & Fallon, L. M. (2012). Research to practice: An evaluation of a class-wide intervention package involving self-management and a group contingency on behavior of middle school students. *Journal of Behavioral Education, 21*, 34–57.

Chafouleas, S. M., Sanetti, L. M. H., Kilgus, S. P., & Maggin, D. M. (2012). Evaluating sensitivity to behavioral change across consultation cases using Direct Behavior Rating Single-Item Scales (DBR-SIS). *Exceptional Children, 78*, 491–505.

Chafouleas, S. M., Volpe, R. J., Gresham, F. M., & Cook, C. R. (2010). School-based behavioral assessment within problem-solving models: Current status and future directions. *School Psychology Review, 39*, 343–349.

Cheney, D., Flower, A., & Templeton, T. (2008). Applying response to intervention metrics in the social domain for students at risk of developing emotional or behavioral disorders. *Journal of Special Education, 42*, 108–126.

Christ, T. J., & Boice, C. (2009). Rating scale items: A brief review of nomenclature, components, and formatting to inform the development of Direct Behavior Rating (DBR). *Assessment for Effective Intervention, 34*, 242–250.

Christ, T. J., Chafouleas, S. M., & Riley-Tillman, T. C. (2007). *Direct Behavior Ratings Scale (DBR-S): How many points on a scale do we need?* Unpublished manuscript, University of Minnesota, Minneapolis.

Christ, T. J., Riley-Tillman, T. C., & Chafouleas, S. M. (2009). Foundation for the development and use of Direct Behavior Rating (DBR) to assess and evaluate student behavior. *Assessment for Effective Intervention, 34*, 201–213.

Christ, T. J., Riley-Tillman, T. C., Chafouleas, S. M., & Boice, C. H. (2010). Generalizability and dependability of Direct Behavior Ratings (DBR) across raters and observations. *Educational and Psychological Measurement, 70*, 825–843.

Christ, T. J., Riley-Tillman, T. C., Chafouleas, S. M., & Jaffery, R. (2011). Direct Behavior Rating (DBR): An evaluation of alternate definitions to assess classroom behaviors. *School Psychology Review, 40*, 181–199.

Christenson, S. L., & Reschly, A. L. (Eds.). (2010). *Handbook of school–family partnerships*. New York: Routledge/Taylor & Francis Group.

Christenson, S. L., & Sheridan, S. M. (2001). *Schools and families: Creating essential connections for learning*. New York: Guilford Press.

Clarke, B. L., Sheridan, S. M., & Woods, K. E. (2010). Elements of healthy family–school relationships. In S. L. Christenson & A. L. Reschly (Eds.), *Handbook of school–family partnerships* (pp. 61–79). New York: Routledge.

Clemens, N. H., Shapiro, E. S., & Thoemmes, F. (2011). Improving the efficacy of first grade reading screening: An investigation of word identification fluency with other early literacy indicators. *School Psychology Quarterly, 26*, 231–244.

Coie, J. D., Watt, N. F., West, S. G., Hawkins, J. D., Asarnow, J. R., Markman, H. J., et al. (1993). The science of prevention: A conceptual framework and some directions for a national research program. *American Psychologist, 48*, 1013–1022.

Cole, C. L., & Bambara, L. M. (1992). Issues surrounding the use of self-management interventions in the schools. *School Psychology Review, 21*, 193–201.

Cole, C. L., & Bambara, L. M. (2000). Self-monitoring: Theory and practice. In E. S. Shapiro & T. R. Kratochwill (Eds.), *Behavioral assessment in schools* (2nd ed., pp. 202–232). New York: Guilford Press.

Compton, D. L., Fuchs, D., Fuchs, L. S., & Bryant, J. D. (2006). Selecting at-risk readers in first grade for early intervention: A two-year longitudinal study of decision rules and procedures. *Journal of Educational Psychology, 98*, 394–409.

Cone, J. D. (1978). The Behavioral Assessment Grid (BAG): A conceptual framework and taxonomy. *Behavior Therapy, 9*, 882–888.

Connecticut State Department of Education. (1999). *Connecticut's preschool curriculum framework and benchmarks for children in preschool programs*. Hartford, CT: Author.

Connell, M. C., Carta, J. J., & Baer, D. M. (1993). Programming generalization of in-class transition skills: Teaching preschoolers with developmental delays to self-assess and recruit contingent teacher praise. *Journal of Applied Behavior Analysis, 26*, 345–352.

Connell, M. C., Carta, J. J., Lutz, S., Randall, C., Wilson, J., & Lamb, D. R. (1993). Building independence during in-class transitions: Teaching in-class transition skills to preschoolers with developmental delays through choral-response-based self-assessment and contingent praise. *Education and Treatment of Children, 16*, 160–174.

Cook, C. R., Rasetshwane, K. B., Truelson, E., Grant, S., Dart, E. H., Collins, T. A., et al. (2011). Development and validation of the Student Internalizing Behavior Screener: Examination of reliability, validity, and classification accuracy. *Assessment for Effective Intervention, 36*, 71–79.

Cook, C. R., Volpe, R. J., & Livanis, A. (2010). Constructing a roadmap for future universal screening research beyond academics. *Assessment for Effective Intervention, 35*, 197–205.

Cooper, J. O., Heron, T. F., & Heward, W. L. (2007). *Applied behavior analysis* (2nd ed.). Upper Saddle River, NJ: Pearson.

Copeland, A. P. (1982). Individual difference factors in children's self-management: Toward individualized treatments. In P. Karoly & F. H. Kanfer (Eds.), *Self-management and behavior change: From theory to practice* (pp. 207–239). Oxford, UK: Pergamon Press.

Cox, D. D. (2005). Evidence-based interventions using home–school collaboration. *School Psychology Quarterly, 20*, 473–497.

Crews, S. D., Bender, H., Cook, C. R., Gresham, F. M., Kern, L., & Vanderwood, M. (2007). Risk and protective factors of emotional and/or behavioral disorders in children and adolescents: A mega-analytic synthesis. *Behavioral Disorders, 32*, 64–77.

Crick, N. R. (1996). The role of overt aggression, relational aggression, and prosocial behavior in the prediction of children's future social adjustment. *Child Development, 67*, 2317–2327.

Cronbach, L. J., Gleser, G. C., Nanda, H., & Rajaratnam, N. (1972). *The dependability of behavioral measurements: Theory of generalizability for scores and profiles*. New York: Wiley.

Crone, D. A., Hawken, L. S., & Horner, R. H. (2010). *Responding to problem behavior in schools: The Behavior Education Program* (2nd ed.). New York: Guilford Press.

Dalton, T. D., Martella, R. C., & Marchand-Martella, N. E. (1999). The effects of a self-management program in reducing off-task behavior. *Journal of Behavioral Education, 9*, 157–176.

Dart, E. H., Furlow, C. M., Collins, T. A., Brewer, E., Gresham, F. M., & Chenier, K. H. (2015). Peer-mediated check-in/check-out for students at-risk for internalizing disorders. *School Psychology Quarterly, 30*(2), 229–243.

Davies, D. E., & McLaughlin, T. F. (1989). Effects of a daily report card on disruptive behavior in primary students. *BC Journal of Special Education, 13*, 173–181.

DeHaas-Warner, S. (1991). Effects of self-monitoring on preschoolers' on-task behavior: A pilot study. *Topics in Early Childhood Special Education, 11*, 59–73.

DeHaas-Warner, S. (1992). The utility of self-monitoring for preschool on-task behavior. *Topics in Early Childhood Special Education, 12*, 478–495.

Donohue, B. C., Van Hasselt, V. B., & Hersen, M. (1994). Behavioral assessment and treatment of social phobia: An evaluative review. *Behavior Modification, 18*, 262–288.

Dougherty, E. H., & Dougherty, A. (1977). The daily report card: A simplified and flexible package for classroom behavior management. In L. A. Hersov & M. Berger (Eds.), *Aggression and anit-social behavior in childhood and adolescence* (pp. 73–93). London: Pergamon Press.

Dowdy, E., Doane, K., Eklund, K., & Dever, B. V. (2013). A comparison of teacher nomination and screening to identify behavioral and emotional risk within a sample of underrepresented students. *Journal of Emotional and Behavioral Disorders, 21*(2), 127–137.

Drummond, T. (1994). *The Student Risk Screening Scale (SRSS)*. Grants Pass, OR: Josephine County Mental Health Program.

Ducharme, J. M., & Schecter, C. (2011). Bridging the gap between clinical and classroom intervention: Keystone approaches for students with challenging behavior. *School Psychology Review, 40*, 257–274.

Duchesne, S., Vitaro, F., Larose, S., & Tremblay, R. E. (2008). Trajectories of anxiety during elementary-school years and the prediction of high school noncompletion. *Journal of Youth and Adolescence, 37*, 1134–1146.

Duda, M. A., Dunlap, G., Fox, L., Lentini, R., & Clarke, S. (2004). An experimental evaluation of positive behavior support in a community preschool program. *Topics in Early Childhood Special Education, 24*, 143–155.

Dunlap, G., & Carr, E. G. (2007). Positive behavior support and developmental disabilities: A summary and analysis of research. In S. L. Odom, R. H. Horner, M. Snell, & J. Blacher (Eds.), *Handbook of developmental disabilities* (pp. 469–482). New York: Guilford Press.

Dunlap, G., Clarke, S., Jackson, M., Wright, S., Ramos, E., & Brinson, S. (1995). Self-monitoring of classroom behaviors with students exhibiting emotional and behavioral challenges. *School Psychology Quarterly, 10*, 165–177.

Dunlap, G., Iovannone, R., Kincaid, D., Wilson, K., Christiansen, K., Strain, P., et al. (2010). *Prevent–Teach–Reinforce: A school-based model of individualized positive behavior support*. Baltimore: Brookes.

Dunlap, G., Iovannone, R., Wilson, K., Strain, P., & Kincaid, D. (2010). Prevent–Teach–Reinforce: A standardized model of school-based behavioral intervention. *Journal of Positive Behavior Interventions, 12*, 9–22.

DuPaul, G. J., & Eckert, T. L. (1997). The effects of school-based interventions for attention deficit hyperactivity disorder: A meta-analysis. *School Psychology Review, 26*, 5–27.

Durand, M., & Crimmins, D. B. (1992). *The Motivation Assessment Scale administration guide*. Topeka, KS: Monaco.

Durlak, J. A., Weissberg, R. P., Dymnicki, A. B., Taylor, R. D., & Schellinger, K. B. (2011). The impact of enhancing students' social and emotional learning: A meta-analysis of school-based universal interventions. *Child Development, 82*, 405–432.

Dusenbury, L., Weissberg, R. P., Goren, P., & Domitrovich, C. (2014). *State standards to advance social and emotional learning*. Chicago: Collaborative for Academic, Social, and Emotional Learning.

Eagly, A. H. (2009). The his and hers of prosocial behavior: Examination of the social psychology of gender. *American Psychologist, 64*, 645–658.

Eckert, T. L., Hintze, J. M., & Shapiro, E. S. (1999). Development and refinement of a measure for assessing the acceptability of assessment methods: The Assessment Rating Profile—Revised. *Canadian Journal of School Psychology, 15*, 21–42.

Eckert, T. L., Martens, B. K., & DiGennaro, F. D. (2005). Describing antecedent–behavior–consequence relations using conditional probabilities and the general operant contingency space: A preliminary investigation. *School Psychology Review, 34*, 520–528.

Edelbrock, C. (1983). Problems and issues in using rating scales to assess child personality and psychopathology. *School Psychology Review, 12*, 293–299.

Edlund, C. V. (1969). Rewards at home to promote desirable behavior. *Teaching Exceptional Children, 1*, 121–127.

Edwards, L., Salant, V., Howard, V. F., Brougher, J., & McLaughlin, T. F. (1995). Effectiveness of self-management on attentional behavior and reading comprehension for children with Attention Deficit Disorder. *Child and Family Behavior Therapy, 17*, 1–17.

Eklund, K., & Dowdy, E. (2014). Screening for behavioral and emotional risk versus traditional school identification methods. *School Mental Health, 5*, 40–49.

Elliott, S. N., & Gresham, F. M. (2008). *SSIS: Social Skills Improvement System*. Minneapolis: Pearson.

Epstein, M. H., Atkins, M., Cullinan, D., Kutash, K., & Weaver, R. (2008). *Reducing behavior problems in the elementary school classroom: A practice guide* (NCEE #2008-012). Washington, DC: National Center for Education Evaluation and Regional Assistance, Institute of Education Sciences, U.S. Department of Education. Retrieved from *http://ies.ed.gov/ncee/wwc/publications/practiceguides*.

Epstein, M. H., Nordness, P. D., Gallagher, K., Nelson, J. R., Lewis, L., & Schrepf, S. (2005). School as the entry point: Assessing adherence to the basic tenets of the wraparound approach. *Behavioral Disorders, 30*, 85–93.

Erchul, W. P., & Martens, B. K. (2010). *School consultation: Conceptual and empirical bases of practice* (3rd ed.). New York: Springer.

Esler, A. N., Godber, Y., & Christenson, S. L. (2008). Best practices in supporting home–school collaboration. In A. Thomas & J. Grimes (Eds.), *Best practices in school psychology V* (pp. 917–936). Bethesda, MD: National Association of School Psychologists.

Evans, S. W., & Youngstrom, E. (2006). Evidence-based assessment of attention-deficit hyperactivity disorder. *Journal of the American Academy of Child and Adolescent Psychiatry, 45*, 1132–1137.

Fabiano, G. A., Pelham, W. E., Gnagy, E. M., Burrows-MacLean, L., Coles, E. K., Chacko, A., et al. (2007). The single and combined effects of multiple intensities of behavior modification and methylphenidate for children with attention deficit hyperactivity disorder in a classroom setting. *School Psychology Review, 36*, 195–216.

Fabiano, G. A., Vujnovic, R., Naylor, J., Pariseau, M., & Robins, M. (2009). An investigation of the technical adequacy of a daily behavior report card (DBRC) for monitoring progress of students with attention-deficit/hyperactivity disorder in special education placements. *Assessment for Effective Intervention, 34*, 231–241.

Fabiano, G. A., Vujnovic, R. K., Pelham, W. E., Waschbusch, D. A., Massetti, G. M., Pariseau, M. E., et al. (2010). Enhancing the effectiveness of special education programming for children with attention deficit hyperactivity disorder using a daily report card. *School Psychology Review, 39*, 219–239.

Fairbanks, S., Sugai, G., Guardino, D., & Lathrop, M. (2007). Response to intervention: An evaluation of a classroom system of behavior support for second grade students. *Exceptional Children, 73*, 288–310.

Family Educational Rights and Privacy Act of 1974, 20 U.S.C. § 1232g (1974).

Fantuzzo, J. W., Rohrbeck, C. A., & Azar, S. T. (1987). A component analysis of behavioral self-management interventions with elementary school students. *Child and Family Behavior Therapy, 9*, 33–43.

Fantuzzo, J. W., Tighe, E., & Childs, S. (2000). Family Involvement Questionnaire: A multivariate assessment of family participation in early childhood education. *Journal of Educational Psychology, 92*, 367–376.

Felixbrod, J. J., & O'Leary, K. D. (1973). Effects of reinforcement on children's academic behavior as a function of self-determined and externally imposed contingencies. *Journal of Applied Behavior Analysis, 6*, 241–250.

Finn, J. D., Pannozzo, G. M., & Voelkl, K. E. (1995). Disruptive and inattentive-withdrawn behavior and achievement among fourth graders. *Elementary School Journal, 95*, 421–434.

Frick, P., Kamphaus, R. W., Lahey, B. B., Loeber, R., Christ, M. G., Hart, E., et al. (1991). Academic underachievement and the disruptive behavior disorders. *Journal of Counseling and Clinical Psychology, 57*, 275–280.

Fuchs, D., & Fuchs, L. S. (1989). Exploring effective and efficient prereferral interventions: A component analysis of behavioral consultation. *School Psychology Review, 18*, 260–283.

Fuchs, D., & Fuchs, L. S. (2006). Introduction to response to intervention: What, why, and how valid is it? *Reading Research Quarterly, 41*, 93–99.

Fuchs, L. S., & Fuchs, D. (1986). Effects of systematic formative evaluation: A meta-analysis. *Exceptional Children, 53*, 199–208.

Fuchs, L. S., & Fuchs, D. (1987). The relation between methods of graphing student performance data and achievement: A meta-analysis. *Journal of Special Education Technology, 8*, 5–13.

Fuchs, L. S., Fuchs, D., Hamlett, C. L., Walz, L., & Germann, G. (1993). Formative evaluation of academic progress: How much growth can we expect? *School Psychology Review, 22*, 27–48.

Gansle, K. A., & McMahon, C. M. (1997). Component integrity of teacher intervention management behavior using a student self-monitoring treatment: An experimental analysis. *Journal of Behavioral Education, 7*, 405–419.

Gettinger, M., & Ball, C. (2008). Best practices in increasing academic engaged time. In A. Thomas & J. Grimes (Eds.), *Best practices in school psychology V* (pp. 1043–1058). Bethesda, MD: National Association of School Psychologists.

Gettinger, M., & Callan Stoiber, K. (1999). Excellence in teaching: Review of instructional and environmental variables. In C. Reynolds & T. Gutkin (Eds.), *The handbook of school psychology* (Vol. 3, pp. 383–409). New York: Wiley.

Gini, G., Albiero, P., Benelli, B., & Altoe, G. (2007). Does empathy predict adolescents' bullying and defending behavior? *Aggressive Behavior, 33*, 467–476.

Glover, T. A., & Albers, C. A. (2007). Considerations for evaluation universal screening instruments. *Journal of School Psychology, 45*, 117–135.

Goh, A. E., & Bambara, L. M. (2012). Individualized positive behavior support in school settings: A meta-analysis. *Remedial and Special Education, 33*, 271–286.

Goldfried, M. R., & Kent, R. N. (1972). Traditional versus behavioral personality assessment: A comparison of methodological and theoretical assumptions. *Psychological Bulletin, 77*, 409–420.

Good, R. H., III, & Kaminski, R. A. (n.d.). Dynamic Indicators of Basic Early Literacy Skills. Retrieved from *www.dynamicmeasurement.org/dibels.html.*

Goodman, R. (1997). The Strengths and Difficulties Questionnaire: A research note. *Journal of Child Psychology and Psychiatry, 38*, 581–586.

Greenwood, C. R., Terry, B., Marquis, J., & Walker, D. (1994). Confirming a performance-based instructional model. *School Psychology Review, 23*, 652–668.

Gresham, F. M. (1989). Assessment of treatment integrity in school consultation and prereferral intervention. *School Psychology Review, 18*, 37–50.

Gresham, F. M. (2005). Response to intervention: An alternative means of identifying students as emotionally disturbed. *Education and Treatment of Children, 28*, 328–344.

Gresham, F. M., Cook, C. R., Collins, T., Dart, E., Rasetshwane, K., Truelson, E., et al. (2010). Developing a change-sensitive brief behavior rating scale as a progress monitoring tool for social behavior: An example using the Social Skills Rating System—Teacher Form. *School Psychology Review, 39*, 364–379.

Gresham, F. M., & Elliott, S. N. (1990). *Social Skills Rating System.* Bloomington, MN: Pearson.

Gresham, F. M., & Elliott, S. N. (2008). *Social Skills Improvement System*. Minneapolis: Pearson.

Gross, A. M., & Wojnilower, D. A. (1984). Self-directed behavior change in children: Is it self-directed? *Behavior Therapy, 15*, 501–514.

Guerasko-Moore, S., DuPaul, G. J., & White, G. P. (2006). The effects of self-management in general education classrooms on the organizational skills of adolescents with ADHD. *Behavior Modification, 30*, 159–183.

Guerasko-Moore, S., DuPaul, G. J., & White, G. P. (2007). Self-management of classroom preparedness and homework: Effects on school functioning of adolescents with attention deficit hyperactivity disorder. *School Psychology Review, 36*, 647–664.

Guion, R. M. (1965). *Personnel testing*. New York: McGraw-Hill.

Gutkin, T. B. (2009). Ecological school psychology: A personal opinion and a plea for change. In T. B. Gutkin & C. R. Reynolds (Eds.), *The handbook of school psychology* (4th ed., pp. 463–496). Hoboken, NJ: Wiley.

Gutkin, T. B. (Ed.). (2012). Ecological approaches to mental health and educational services for children and adolescents [Special issue]. *Journal of Educational and Psychological Consultation, 22*(1–2).

Harrison, J. R., Vannest, K., Davis, J., & Reynolds, C. (2012). Common problem behaviors of children and adolescents in general education classrooms in the United States. *Journal of Emotional and Behavioral Disorders, 20*, 55–64.

Harrison, S. E., Riley-Tillman, T. C., & Chafouleas, S. M. (2014). Practice with feedback and base rates of target behavior: Implications for rater accuracy using Direct Behavior Ratings. *Canadian Journal of School Psychology, 29*, 3–20.

Harrop, A., & Swinson, J. (2000). Natural rates of approval and disapproval in British infant, junior and secondary classrooms. *British Journal of Educational Psychology, 70*, 473– 483.

Hawken, L. S., Adolphson, S. L., MacLeod, K. S., & Schumann, J. M. (2009). Secondary tier interventions and supports. In G. Sugai, R. H. Horner, G. Dunlap, & W. Sailor (Eds.), *Handbook of positive behavior support* (pp. 395–420). New York: Springer.

Hawken, L. S., Bundock, K., Kladis, K., O'Keeffe, B., & Barrett, C. A. (2014). Systematic review of the check-in, check-out intervention for students at risk for emotional and behavioral disorders. *Education and Treatment of Children, 37*, 635–658.

Hawken, L. S., MacLeod, K. S., & Rawlings, L. (2007). Effects of the Behavior Education Program (BEP) on office discipline referrals of elementary school students. *Journal of Positive Behavior Interventions, 9*, 94–101.

Hawkins, R. O., Barnett, B. W., Morrison, J. Q., & Musti-Rao, S. (2009). Choosing targets for assessment and intervention: Improving important student outcomes. In G. Peacock, R. Ervin, E. Daly, & K. Merrell (Eds.), *Practical handbook of school psychology: Effective practices for the 21st century* (pp. 13–32). New York: Guilford Press.

Heartland Area Education Agency. (2008). *Heartland special education procedures manual: Decision making practices*. Johnston, IA: Author.

Henderson, A. T., & Mapp, K. L. (2002). *A new wave of evidence: The impact of school, family, and community connections on student achievement*. Austin, TX: Southwest Educational Development Laboratory.

Herrero, J., Estevez, E., & Musitu, G. (2006). The relationships of adolescent school-related deviant behaviour and victimization with psychological distress: Testing a general model of the mediational role of parents and teachers across groups of gender and age. *Journal of Adolescence, 29*, 671–690.

Hertz, V., & McLaughlin, T. F. (1990). Self-recording: Effects for on-task behavior of mildly handicapped adolescents. *Child and Family Behavior Therapy, 12*, 1–11.

Hintze, J. M. (2005). Psychometrics of direct observation. *School Psychology Review, 34*, 507–519.

Hintze, J. M., & Silberglitt, B. (2005). A longitudinal examination of the diagnostic accuracy and predictive validity of R-CBM and high-stakes testing. *School Psychology Review, 34*, 372–386.

Hoagwood, K., & Erwin, H. (1997). Effectiveness of school-based mental health services for children: A 10-year research review. *Journal of Child and Family Studies, 6*, 435–451.

Hoff, K. E., & DuPaul, G. J. (1998). Reducing disruptive behavior in general education classrooms: The use of self-management strategies. *School Psychology Review, 27*, 290–303.

Holdaway, A. S., & Owens, J. S. (2015). The effect of training and consultation condition on teachers' self-reported likelihood of adoption of a daily report card. *Journal of Educational Psychology, 107*(1), 222–223.

Hoover-Dempsey, K. V., Whitaker, M. C., & Ice, C. L. (2010). Motivation and commitment to family–school partnerships. In S. L. Christenson & A. L. Reschly (Eds.), *Handbook of school–family partnerships* (pp. 30–60). New York: Routledge/Taylor & Francis Group.

Hops, H., & Walker, H. M. (1988). *CLASS: Contingencies for learning academic and social skills—A classroom behavior management program for children with acting-out behaviors*. Delray Beach, FL: Educational Achievement Systems.

Horner, S. B., Fireman, G. D., & Wang, E. W. (2010). The relation of student behavior, peer status, race, and gender to decisions about school discipline using CHAID decision trees and regression modeling. *Journal of School Psychology, 48*, 135–161.

Hosp, J. L., Howell, K. W., & Hosp, M. K. (2003). Characteristics of behavior rating scales: Implications for practice in assessment and behavioral support. *Journal of Positive Behavior Interventions, 5*, 201–208.

Hosp, M. K., Hosp, J. L., & Howell, K. W. (2016). *The ABCs of CBM: A practical guide to curriculum-based measurement* (2nd ed.). New York: Guilford Press.

Hunter, K. K., Chenier, J. S., & Gresham, F. M. (2014). Evaluation of check in/check out for students with internalizing behavior problems. *Journal of Emotional and Behavioral Disorders, 22*, 135–148.

Illinois State Board of Education. (2004). Illinois learning standards: Social/emotional learning (SEL). Retrieved March 26, 2014, from *www.isbe.net/ils/social_emotional/standards.htm*.

Imber, S. C., Imber, R. B., & Rothstein, C. (1979). Modifying independent work habits: An effective teacher–parent communication program. *Exceptional Children, 46*, 219–221.

Individuals with Disabilities Education Improvement Act of 2004, 20 U.S.C. § 1400 et seq. (2004). (Reauthorization of the Individuals with Disabilities Education Act of 1990)

Iovannone, R., Greenbaum, P. E., Wang, W., Kincaid, D., & Dunlap, G. (2009). Inter-rater agreement of the Individualized Behavior Rating Scale Tool (IBRS-T). *Effective Assessment for Intervention, 39*, 195–207.

Iovannone, R., Greenbaum, P. E., Wang, W., Kincaid, D., Dunlap, G., & Strain, P. (2014). Randomized controlled trial of the Prevent–Teach–Reinforce (PTR) tertiary intervention for students with problem behaviors: Preliminary outcomes. *Journal of Emotional and Behavioral Disorders, 17*, 213–225.

Irvin, L. K., Horner, R. H., Ingram, K., Todd, A. W., Sugai, G., Sampson, N. K., et al. (2006). Using office discipline referral data for decision making about student behavior in elementary and middle schools: An empirical evaluation of validity. *Journal of Positive Behavior Interventions, 8*, 10–23.

Irvin, L. K., Tobin, T. J., Sprague, J. R., Sugai, G., & Vincent, C. G. (2004). Validity of office discipline referral measures as indices of school-wide behavioral status and effects of school-wide behavioral interventions. *Journal of Positive Behavior Interventions, 6*, 131–147.

Jacob, S., Decker, D. M., & Hartshorne, T. S. (2011). *Ethics and law for school psychologists, Sixth Edition*. Hoboken, NJ: Wiley.

Jacobson, N. S., Follette, W. C., & Revenstorf, D. (1984). Psychotherapy outcome research: Methods for reporting variability and evaluating clinical significance. *Behavior Therapy, 15*, 336–352.

Jenson, W. R., Clark, E., Kircher, J. C., & Kristjansson, S. D. (2007). Statistical reform: Evidence-based practice, meta-analyses, and single subject designs. *Psychology in the Schools, 44*, 483–493.

Johnson, A. H., Miller, F. G., Chafouleas, S. M., Riley-Tillman, T. C., Fabiano, G. A., & Welsh, M. E. (2016). Evaluating the technical adequacy of DBR-SIS in triannual behavioral screening: A multisite investigation. *Journal of School Psychology, 54*, 39–57.

Joyce, B., & Showers, B. (1980). Improving inservice training: The messages of research. *Educational Leadership, 37*, 379–385.

Jurbergs, N., Palcic, J., & Kelley, M. L. (2007). School–home notes with and without response cost: Increasing attention and academic performance in low-income children with attention deficit hyperactivity disorder. *School Psychology Quarterly, 22*, 358–379.

Kahng, S., Iwata, B. A., & Lewin, A. B. (2002). Behavioral treatment of self-injury, 1964–2000. *American Journal of Mental Retardation, 107*, 212–221.

Kamphaus, R. W. (2012). Screening for behavioral and emotional risk: Constructs and practicalities. *School Psychology Forum, 6*, 89–97.

Kamphaus, R. W., & Reynolds, C. R. (2007). *Behavior assessment system for children—Second edition (BASC–2): Behavioral and Emotional Screening System (BESS)*. Bloomington, MN: Pearson.

Kamphaus, R. W., & Reynolds, C. R. (2008). *BASC-2 Behavioral and Emotional Screening System*. Minneapolis: Pearson.

Kanfer, F. H. (1970). Self-monitoring: Methodological considerations and clinical applications. *Journal of Consulting and Clinical Psychology, 35*, 148–152.

Kanfer, F. H., & Gaelick-Buys, L. (1991). Self-management methods. In F. H. Kanfer & A. P. Goldstein (Eds.), *Helping people change: A textbook of methods* (4th ed., pp. 305–360). New York: Pergamon Press.

Kansas State Board of Education. (2012). Kansas social, emotional, and character development model standards. Retrieved March 26, 2014, from *www.ksde.org/Agency/DivisionofLearningServices/CareerStandardsandAssessmentServices/ContentAreaMZ/SchoolCounseling/SocialEmotionalandCharacterDevelopment.aspx*

Karraker, R. (1972). Increasing academic performance through home managed contingency programs. *Journal of School Psychology, 10*, 173–179.

Kaufman, J. S., Jaser, S. S., Vaughan, E. L., Reynolds, J. S., Di Donato, J., Bernard, S. N., et al. (2010). Patterns in office referral data by grade, race/ethnicity, and gender. *Journal of Positive Behavior Interventions, 12*, 44–54.

Kauffman, J. M., Lloyd, J. W., & McGee, K. A. (1989). Adaptive and maladaptive behavior: Teachers' attitudes and their technical assistance needs. *Journal of Special Education, 23*, 185–200.

Kazdin, A. E. (2005). Evidence-based assessment for children and adolescents: Issues in measurement development and clinical application. *Journal of Clinical Child and Adolescent Psychology, 34*, 548–558.

Kellam, S. G., Rebok, G. W., Ialongo, N., & Mayer, L. S. (1994). The course and malleability of aggressive behavior from early first grade into middle school: Results of a developmental epidemiologically-based preventive trial. *Journal of Child Psychology and Psychiatry, 35*, 259–281.

Keller-Margulis, M. A., Shapiro, E. S., & Hintze, J. M. (2008). Long-term diagnostic accuracy of curriculum-based measures in reading and mathematics. *School Psychology Review, 37*, 374–390.

Kelley, M. L. (1990). *School–home notes: Promoting children's classroom success*. New York: Guilford Press.

Kelley, M. L., & McCain, A. P. (1995). Promoting academic performance in inattentive children: The relative efficacy of school–home notes with and without response cost. *Behavior Modification, 19*, 357–375.

Kennedy, C. (2005). *Single-case designs for educational research*. Boston: Allyn & Bacon.

Kilgus, S. P., Chafouleas, S. M., & Riley-Tillman, T. C. (2013). Development and initial validation of the Social and Academic Behavior Risk Screener for elementary grades. *School Psychology Quarterly, 28*, 210–226.

Kilgus, S. P., Chafouleas, S. M., Riley-Tillman, T. C., & Welsh, M. E. (2012). Diagnostic accuracy of

Direct Behavior Rating Single Item Scales as a screener of elementary school students. *School Psychology Quarterly, 27,* 41–50.

Kilgus, S. P., Riley-Tillman, T. C., Chafouleas, S. M., Christ, T. J., & Welsh, M. (2014). Direct Behavior Rating as a school-based behavior universal screener: Replication across sites. *Journal of School Psychology, 52,* 63–82.

Kilgus, S. P., Taylor, C., Kazmerski, J. S., & von der Embse, N. P. (2015). *Use of Direct Behavior Rating (DBR) to collect functional assessment data.* Manuscript submitted for publication.

Kincaid, D. (2007, March). *Response to intervention and PBS.* Paper presented at the International Positive Behavior Support Conference, Boston.

Kiresuk, T. J., Smith, A., & Cardillo, J. E. (1994). *Goal attainment scaling: Applications, theory, and measurement.* Hillsdale, NJ: Erlbaum.

Koegel, L. K., Koegel, R. L., & Dunlap, G. (1996). *Positive behavioral support: Including people with difficult behavior in the community.* Baltimore: Brookes.

Kratochwill, T. R., & Bergan, J. R. (1990). *Behavioral consultation in applied settings: An individual guide.* New York: Plenum.

Kratochwill, T. R., Hitchcock, J., Horner, R. H., Levin, J. R., Odom, S. L., Rindskopf, D. M., et al. (2010). What Works Clearinghouse: Single-case design technical documentation (Version 1.0). Retrieved from *http://ies.ed.gov/ncee/wwc/pdf/wwc_scd.pdf.*

Kulik, J. A., & Kulik, C. C. (1988). Timing of feedback and verbal learning. *Review of Educational Research, 58,* 79–97.

LaGreca, A. M. (1990). Issues and perspective on the child assessment process. In A. M. LaGreca (Ed.), *Through the eyes of the child: Obtaining self reports from children and adolescents* (pp. 3–17). Boston: Allyn & Bacon.

Lahey, B. B., Gendrich, J. G., Gendrich, S. I., Schnelle, J. F., Gant, D. S., & McNees, M. P. (1977). An evaluation of daily behavior report cards with minimal teacher and parent contacts as an efficient method of classroom intervention. *Behavior Modification, 1,* 381–394.

Lane, K. L., Bruhn, A. L., Eisner, S. L., & Kalberg, J. R. (2010). Score reliability and validity of the Student Risk Screening Scale: A psychometrically sound, feasible tool for use in urban middle schools. *Journal of Emotional and Behavioral Disorders, 18,* 211–224.

Lane, K. L., Kalberg, J. R., Bruhn, A. L., Mahoney, M. E., & Driscoll, S. A. (2008). Primary prevention programs at the elementary level: Issues of treatment integrity, systematic screening, and reinforcement. *Education and Treatment of Children, 31,* 465–494.

Lane, K. L., Kalberg, J. R., Parks, R. J., & Carter, E. W. (2008). Student Risk Screening Scale: Initial evidence for score reliability and validity at the high school level. *Journal of Emotional and Behavioral Disorders, 16,* 178–190.

Lane, K. L., Mahdavi, J. N., & Borthwick-Duffy, S. (2003). Teacher perceptions of the prereferral process: A call for assistance with school-based interventions. *Preventing School Failure, 47,* 148–155.

Lane, K. L., Oakes, W., & Menzies, H. (2010). Systematic screenings to prevent the development of learning and behavior problems: Considerations for practitioners, researchers, and policy makers. *Journal of Disability Policy Studies, 21,* 160–172.

Lane, K. L., Weisenbach, J. L., Phillips, A., & Wehby, J. (2007). Designing, implementing, and evaluating function-based interventions using a systematic, feasible approach. *Behavioral Disorders, 32,* 122–139.

Lareau, A., & McNamara-Horvat, E. (1999). Moments of social inclusion and exclusion: Race, class and cultural capital in family–school relationships. *Sociology of Education, 71,* 37–53.

LeBel, T. J., Chafouleas, S. M., Britner, P. A., & Simonsen, B. (2013). Use of a daily behavior report card in an intervention package involving home–school communication to reduce disruptive behavior in preschoolers. *Journal of Positive Behavior Interventions, 15,* 103–112.

LeBel, T. J., Kilgus, S. P., Briesch, A. M., & Chafouleas, S. M. (2010). The impact of training on the accuracy of teacher-completed Direct Behavior Ratings (DBRs). *Journal of Positive Behavioral Interventions, 12,* 55–63.

LeBuffe, P. A., Shapiro, V. B., & Naglieri, J. A. (2009). *The Devereux Student Strengths Assessment (DESSA)*. Lewisville, NC: Kaplan Press.

Lee, Y., Sugai, G., & Horner, R. H. (1999). Effect of component skill instruction on math performance and on-task, problem, and off-task behavior of students with emotional and behavioral disorders. *Journal of Positive Behavioral Interventions, 1*, 195–204.

Levendoski, L. S., & Cartledge, G. (2000). Self-monitoring for elementary school children with serious emotional disturbances: Classroom applications for increased academic responding. *Behavioral Disorders, 25*, 211–224.

Levitt, J. M., Saka, N., Romanelli, L. H., & Hoagwood, K. (2007). Early identification of mental health problems in schools: The status of instrumentation. *Journal of School Psychology, 45*, 163–191.

Levitt, V. H., & Merrell, K. W. (2009). Linking assessment to intervention for internalizing problems of children and adolescents. *School Psychology Forum, 3*, 13–26.

Lewis, T. J., & Sugai, G. (1999). Effective behavior support: A systems approach to proactive schoolwide management. *Effective School Practices, 17*, 47–53.

Lipinski, D., & Nelson, R. (1974). The reactivity and unreliability of self-recording. *Journal of Consulting and Clinical Psychology, 42*, 118–123.

Lochman, J. E. (1995). Screening of child behavior problems for prevention programs at school entry. *Journal of Consulting and Clinical Psychology, 63*, 549–559.

Loeber, R. (1982). The stability of antisocial and delinquent child behavior: A review. *Child Development, 53*, 1431–1446.

Loeber, R. (1990). Development and risk factors of juvenile antisocial behavior and delinquency. *Clinical Psychology Review, 10*, 1–41.

Loeber, R., & Dishion, T. J. (1983). Early predictors of male delinquency: A review. *Psychological Bulletin, 94*, 68–98.

Lonigan, C. J., Carey, M. P., & Finch, A. J. (1994). Anxiety and depression in children and adolescents: Negative affectivity and the utility of self-reports. *Journal of Consulting and Clinical Psychology, 62*, 1000–1008.

Luthar, S. S., Cicchetti, D., & Becker, B. (2000). The construct of resilience: A critical evaluation and guidelines for future work. *Child Development, 71*, 543–562.

Maag, J. W., Rutherford, R. B., & DiGangi, S. A. (1992). Effects of self-monitoring and contingent reinforcement on on-task behavior and academic productivity of learning-disabled students: A social validation study. *Psychology in the Schools, 29*, 157–172.

Macklem, G. L. (2014). *Preventive mental health at school: Evidence-based services for students*. New York: Springer.

Madle, R. A., Neisworth, J. T., & Kurtz, P. D. (1980). Biasing of hyperkinetic behavior ratings by diagnostic reports: Effects of observer training and assessment method. *Journal of Learning Disabilities, 13*, 30–38.

Maggin, D. M., Briesch, A. M., & Chafouleas, S. M. (2013). An application of the What Works Clearinghouse Standards for Evaluating Single-Subject Research: Synthesis of the self-management literature base. *Remedial and Special Education, 34*, 44–58.

Maggin, D. M., O'Keeffe, B. V., & Johnson, A. H. (2011). A quantitative synthesis of single-subject meta-analyses in special education, 1985–2009. *Exceptionality, 19*, 109–135.

Malecki, C. K., & Demaray, M. K. (2007). Social behavior assessment and response to intervention. In S. R. Jimerson, M. K. Burns, & A. M. VanDerHeyden (Eds.), *The handbook of response to intervention: The science and practice of assessment and intervention* (pp. 161–171). New York: Springer.

March, R. E., Horner, R. H., Lewis-Palmer, T., Brown, D., Crone, D., Todd, A. W., et al. (2000). *Functional Assessment Checklist—Teachers and Staff (FACTS)*. Eugene, OR: Educational and Community Supports.

Masten, A. S., & Reed, M. G. (2002). Resilience in development. In S. R. Snyder & S. J. Lopez (Eds.), *The handbook of positive psychology* (pp. 74–88). New York: Oxford University Press.

Matheson, A. S., & Shriver, M. D. (2005). Training teachers to give effective commands: Effects on student compliance and academic behaviors. *School Psychology Review, 34*, 202–219.

McCain, A. P., & Kelley, M. L. (1993). Managing the classroom behavior of an ADHD preschooler: The efficacy of a school–home note intervention. *Child and Family Behavior Therapy, 15*, 33–44.

McCurdy, B. L., Kunsch, C., & Reibstein, S. (2007). Secondary prevention in the urban school: Implementing the Behavior Education Program. *Preventing School Failure, 51*, 12–19.

McCurdy, B. L., & Shapiro, E. S. (1992). A comparison of teacher-, peer-, and self-monitoring with curriculum-based measurement in reading among students with learning disabilities. *Journal of Special Education, 26*, 162–180.

McDougall, D., & Brady, M. P. (1995). Using audio-cued self-monitoring for students with severe behavior disorders. *Journal of Educational Research, 88*, 309–317.

McIntosh, K., Campbell, A. L., Carter, D. R., & Zumbo, B. D. (2009). Concurrent validity of office discipline referrals and cut points used in school-wide positive behavior support. *Behavioral Disorders, 34*, 100–113.

McIntosh, K., Frank, J. L., & Spaulding, S. A. (2010). Establishing research-based trajectories of office discipline referrals for individual students. *School Psychology Review, 39*, 380–394.

McIntosh, K., Horner, R. H., Chard, D. J., Boland, J. B., & Good, R. H. (2006). The use of reading and behavior screening measures to predict nonresponse to school-wide positive behavior support: A longitudinal analysis. *School Psychology Review, 35*, 275–291.

McIntosh, K., Reinke, W. M., & Herman, K. C. (2009). Schoolwide analysis of data for social behavior problems. In G. Peacock, R. Ervin, E. Daly, & K. Merrell (Eds.), *Practical handbook of school psychology: Effective practices for the 21st century* (pp. 135–156). New York: Guilford Press.

McIntyre, R. M., Smith, D. E., & Hassett, C. E. (1984). Accuracy of performance ratings as affected by rater training and perceived purpose of rating. *Journal of Applied Psychology, 69*, 147–156.

Meier, S. T., McDougal, J. L., & Bardos, A. (2008). Development of a change-sensitive outcome measure for children receiving counseling. *Canadian Journal of School Psychology, 23*, 148–160.

Merrell, K. W. (2011). *SEARS professional manual.* Lutz, FL: Psychological Assessment Resources.

Merrell, K. W., McClun, L. A., Kempf, K. K. G., & Lund, J. (2002). Self-report assessment to identify children with internalizing problems: Validity of the Internalizing Symptoms Scale for Children. *Journal of Psychoeducational Assessment, 20*, 223–239.

Merrell, K. W., & Gimpel, G. A. (1998). *Social skills of children and adolescents: Conceptualization, assessment and treatment.* Mahwah, NJ: Erlbaum.

Merrett, F., & Wheldall, K. (1992). Teachers' use of praise and reprimands to boys and girls. *Educational Review, 44*, 73–79.

Messick, S. (1995). Validity of psychological assessment: Validation of inferences from persons' responses and performances as scientific inquiry into score meaning. *American Psychologist, 50*, 741–749.

Miller, F. G., Cohen, D., Chafouleas, S. M., Riley-Tillman, T. C., Welsh, M. E., & Fabiano, G. A. (2015). A comparison of measures to screen for social, emotional, and behavioral risk. *School Psychology Quarterly, 30*, 184–196.

Miller, F. G., Riley-Tillman, T. C., & Chafouleas, S. M., & Schardt, A. A. (in press). Direct behavior rating instrumentation: Evaluating impact of scale formats. *Assessment for Effective Intervention.*

Miller, F. G., Welsh, M. E., Chafouleas, S. M., Riley-Tillman, T. C., & Fabiano, G. A. (2015). *A question of frequency: An evaluation of annual, biannual, and triannual screenings for social, emotional, and behavioral difficulties.* Manuscript submitted for publication.

Miller, L. J., Strain, P. S., Boyd, K., Jarzynka, J., & McFetridge, M. (1993). The effects of classwide self-assessment on preschool children's engagement in transition, free play, and small group instruction. *Early Education and Development, 4*, 162–181.

Miller, P. A., & Eisenberg, N. (1988). The relation of empathy to aggressive and externalizing/antisocial behavior. *Psychological Bulletin, 103*, 324–344.

Miller, P. W. (1988). *Nonverbal communication* (3rd ed.) Washington, DC: National Education Association.

Minke, K. M. (2006). Parent–teacher relationships. In G. G. Bear & K. M. Minke (Eds.), *Children's needs III: Development, prevention, and intervention* (pp. 73–85). Bethesda, MD: National Association of School Psychologists.

Moffitt, T. E. (1993). Adolescent-limited and life-course-persistent antisocial behavior: A developmental taxonomy. *Psychological Review, 100,* 674–701.

Moore, D. W., Prebble, S., Robertson, J., Waetford, R., & Anderson, A. (2001). Self-recording with goal setting: A self-management programme for the classroom. *Educational Psychology, 21,* 255–265.

More, A. J. (1969). Delay of feedback and the acquisition and retention of verbal materials in the classroom. *Journal of Educational Psychology, 60,* 339–342.

Morrison, G. M., Robertson, L., Laurie, B., & Kelly, J. (2002). Protective factors related to antisocial behavior trajectories. *Journal of Clinical Psychology, 58,* 277–290.

Moxley, R. A. (2007). Graphing in the classroom for improving instruction: From lesson plans to research. *Education and Treatment of Children, 30,* 111–126.

Nahum-Shani, I., Qian, M., Almirall, D., Pelham, W. E., Gnagy, E. M., Fabiano, G. A., et al. (2012). Q-learning: A data analysis method for constructing adaptive interventions. *Psychological Methods, 17,* 478–494.

National Association of School Psychologists. (2002). *Position statement on students with emotional and behavioral disorders.* Bethesda, MD: Author.

National Center for Education Statistics. (2014). *Enrollment and percentage distribution of enrollment in public elementary and secondary schools, by race/ethnicity and region: Selected years, fall 1995 through fall 2023* (NCES 203.50). Washington, DC: U.S. Department of Education.

National Center on Intensive Intervention. (2013). *Data-based individualization: A framework for intensive intervention.* Washington, DC: Office of Special Education, U.S. Department of Education.

National Center on Intensive Intervention. (2014). Tools charts. Retrieved from *www.intensiveintervention.org/resources/tools-charts.*

National Center on Intensive Intervention. (n.d.). Behavioral progress monitoring tools. Retrieved from *www.intensiveintervention.org/chart/behavioral-progress-monitoring-tools.*

National Center on Progress Monitoring. (n.d.). What are the benefits of progress monitoring? Retrieved from *http://www.studentprogress.org/progresmon.asp#3.*

National Center on Response to Intervention. (2010). *Essential components of RTI: A closer look at response to intervention.* Washington, DC: U.S. Department of Education, Office of Special Education Programs, National Center on Response to Intervention.

National Center on Student Progress Monitoring. (n.d.).

National Research Council & Institute of Medicine. (2009). *Preventing mental, emotional, and behavioral disorders among young people: Progress and possibilities* (M. E. O'Connell, T. Boat, & K. E. Warner, Eds.). Washington, DC: National Academies Press.

Nelson, J. R., Benner, G. J., Reid, R. C., Epstein, M. H., & Currin, D. (2002). The convergent validity of office discipline referrals with the CBCL-TRF. *Journal of Emotional and Behavioral Disorders, 10,* 181–188.

Nelson, J. R., Colvin, G., & Smith, D. J. (1996). The effects of setting clear standards on students' social behavior in common areas of the school. *Journal of At-Risk Issues, 3,* 10–18.

No Child Left Behind Act of 2001, 20 U.S.C. § 6301 *et seq.* (2002).

Noell, G. H. (2008). Research examining the relationships among consultation process, treatment integrity, and outcomes. In W. P. Erchul & S. M. Sheridan (Eds.), *Handbook of research in school consultation* (pp. 323–341). New York: Erlbaum.

Noell, G. H. (2009). Empirical and pragmatic issues in assessing and supporting intervention implementation in schools. In G. Peacock, R. Ervin, E. Daly, & K. Merrell (Eds.), *Practical handbook of school psychology: Effective practices for the 21st century* (pp. 513–537). New York: Guilford Press.

Noell, G. H., Witt, J. C., Slider, N. J., Connell, J. E., Gatti, S. L., Williams, K. L., et al. (2005). Treatment implementation following behavioral consultation in schools: A comparison of three follow-up strategies. *School Psychology Review, 34,* 87–106.

O'Leary, S. G., & Pelham, W. E. (1978). Behavior therapy and withdrawal of stimulant medication in hyperactive children. *Pediatrics, 61,* 211–217.

O'Neill, R. E., Horner, R. H., Albin, R. W., Sprague, J. R., Storey, K., & Newton, J. S. (1997). *Functional assessment and program development for problem behavior: A practical handbook* (2nd ed.). Pacific Grove, CA: Brooks/Cole.

OSEP Technical Assistance Center on Positive Behavioral Interventions and Supports. (n.d.) Schoolwide PBS: Secondary prevention. Retrieved on December 14, 2011, from *www.pbis.org/secondaryprevention.*

Palcic, J. L., Jurbergs, N., & Kelley, M. L. (2009). A comparison of teacher and parent delivered consequences: Improving classroom behavior in low-income children with ADHD. *Child and Family Behavior Therapy, 31,* 117–133.

Parker, F. L., Boak, A. Y., Griffin, K. W., Ripple, C., & Peay, L. (1999). Parent–child relationship, home learning environment, and school readiness. *School Psychology Review, 28,* 413–425.

Parker, R. I., Vannest, K. J., & Brown, L. (2009). The improvement rate difference for single-case research. *Exceptional Children, 75,* 135–150.

Parker, R. I., Vannest, K. J., & Davis, J. L. (2011). Effect size in single-case research: A review of nine nonoverlap techniques. *Behavior Modification, 35,* 303–322.

Pas, E. T., Bradshaw, C. P., & Mitchell, M. M. (2011). Examining the validity of office discipline referrals as an indicator of student behavior problems. *Psychology in the Schools, 48,* 541–555.

Payton, J., Weissberg, R. P., Durlak, J. A., Dymnicki, A. B., Taylor, R. D., Schellinger, K. B., et al. (2008). *The positive impact of social and emotional learning for kindergarten to eighth-grade students: Findings from three scientific reviews.* Chicago: Collaborative for Academic, Social, and Emotional Learning.

PBIS Apps. (2014a). *CICO-SWIS user's manual* (Version 5.2). Eugene, OR: Authors.

PBIS Apps. (2014b). *ISIS-SWIS user's manual* (Version 5.3). Eugene, OR: Authors.

PBIS Apps. (2014c). *SWIS user's manual* (Version 5.2). Eugene, OR: Authors.

Pearcy, M. T., Clopton, J. R., & Pope, A. W. (1993). Influences on teacher referral of children to mental health services: Gender, severity, and internalizing versus externalizing problems. *Journal of Emotional and Behavioral Disorders, 1,* 165–169.

Pearson. (2010). *AIMSweb behavior administration and technical manual.* Bloomington, MN: Author.

Pelham, W. E. (1993). Pharmacotherapy for children with attention deficit hyperactivity disorder. *School Psychology Review, 22,* 199–227.

Pelham, W. E., Calrson, C., Sams, S. E., Vallano, G., Dixon, M. J., & Hoza, B. (1993). Separate and combined effects of methylphenidate and behavior modification on boys with attention deficit-hyperactivity disorder in the classroom. *Journal of Consulting and Clinical Psychology, 61,* 506–515.

Pelham, W. E., & Fabiano, G. A. (2008). Evidence-based psychosocial treatments for attention-deficit hyperactivity disorder. *Journal of Clinical Child and Adolescent Psychology, 37,* 184–214.

Pelham, W. E., Fabiano, G. A., & Massetti, G. M. (2005). Evidence-based assessment of attention deficit hyperactivity disorder in children and adolescents. *Journal of Clinical Child and Adolescent Psychology, 34,* 449–476.

Pelham, W. E., Gnagy, E. M., Burrtows-Maclean, L., Williams, A., Fabiano, G. A., Morrissey, S. M., et al. (2001). Once-a-day Concerta™ methylphenidate versus t.i.d. methylphenidate in laboratory and natural settings. *Pediatrics, 107.* Retrieved from *www.pediatrics.org/cgi/content/full/107/6/e105.*

Pelham, W. E., Wheeler, T., & Chronis, A. (1998). Empirically supported psychosocial treatments for attention deficit hyperactivity disorder. *Journal of Clinical Child Psychology, 27,* 190–205.

Pelios, L., Morren, J., Tesch, D., & Axelrod, S. (1999). The impact of functional analysis methodology on treatment choice for self-injurious and aggressive behavior. *Journal of Applied Behavior Analysis, 32*, 185–195.

Pennsylvania Department of Education. (2012). *Standards for student interpersonal skills*. Retrieved March 26, 2014, from *www.pdesas.org/Main/News/431368*.

Peterson, L. D., Young, K. R., Salzberg, C. L., West, R. P., & Hill, M. (2006). Using self-management procedures to improve classroom social skills in multiple general education settings. *Education and Treatment of Children, 29*, 1–21.

Pianta, R. C., & Walsh, D. B. (1996). *High-risk children in schools: Constructing sustaining relationships*. New York: Routledge.

Prater, M., Hogan, S., & Miller, S. (1992). Using self-monitoring to improve on-task behavior and academic skills of an adolescent with mild handicaps across special and regular education settings. *Education and Treatment of Children, 15*, 43–55.

Rabiner, D., & Coie, J. D. (2000). Early attention problems and children's reading achievement: A longitudinal investigation. *Journal of the American Academy of Child and Adolescent Psychiatry, 39*, 859–867.

Rapport, M. D., Denney, C. B., Chung, K., & Hustace, K. (2001). Internalizing behavior problems and scholastic achievement in children: Cognitive and behavioral pathways as mediators of outcome. *Journal of Clinical Child Psychology, 30*, 536–551.

Raudenbush, S. W. (1984). Magnitude of teacher expectancy effects on pupil IQ as a function of the credibility of expectancy induction: A synthesis of findings from 18 experiments. *Journal of Educational Psychology, 76*, 85–97.

Reid, R., Maag, J. W., Vasa, S. F., & Wright, G. (1994). Who are the children with attention deficit-hyperactivity disorder?: A school-based survey. *Journal of Special Education, 28*, 117–137.

Reid, R., Trout, A. L., & Schartz, M. (2005). Self-regulation interventions for children with attention deficit/hyperactivity disorder. *Exceptional Children, 71*, 361–377.

Reimers, T. M., Wacker, D. P., & Koeppl, G. (1987). Acceptability of behavioral treatments: A review of the literature. *School Psychology Review, 16*, 212–227.

Renshaw, T. L., Eklund, K., Dowdy, E., Jimerson, S. R., Hart, S. R., Earhart, J., et al. (2009). Examining the relationship between scores on the "Behavioral and Emotional Screening System" and student academic, behavioral, and engagement outcomes: An investigation of concurrent validity in elementary school. *California School Psychologist, 14*, 81–88.

Reschly, A. L., & Christenson, S. L. (2009). Parents as essential partners for fostering students' learning outcomes. In M. J. Furlong, R. Gilman, & E. S. Huebner (Eds.), *Handbook of positive psychology in schools* (pp. 257–272). New York: Routledge.

Reschly, A. L. & Christenson, S. L. (2012). Moving from "context matters" to engaged partnerships with families. *Journal of Educational and Psychological Consultation, 22*, 62–78.

Reynolds, C. R., & Kamphaus, R. W. (2015). *Behavior Assessment System for Children* (3rd ed.). Bloomington, MN: Pearson.

Reynolds, C. R., & Richmond, B. O. (2008). *Revised Children's Manifest Anxiety Scale, second edition (RCMAS-2): Manual*. Los Angeles: Western Psychological Services.

Reynolds, W. M., & Stark, K. D. (1987). School-based intervention strategies for the treatment of depression in children and adolescents. *Special Services in the Schools, 3*, 69–88.

Riley-Tillman, T. C., & Burns, M. K. (2009). *Evaluating educational interventions: Single-case design for measuring response to intervention*. New York: Guilford Press.

Riley-Tillman, T. C., Burns, M. K., & Gibbons, K. (2013). *RTI applications: Vol. 2. Assessment, analysis, and decision making*. New York: Guilford Press.

Riley-Tillman, T. C., Chafouleas, S. M., & Briesch, A. M. (2007). A school practitioner's guide to using daily behavior report cards to monitor student behavior. *Psychology in the Schools, 44*, 77–90.

Riley-Tillman, T. C., Chafouleas, S. M., Briesch, A. M., & Eckert, T. L. (2008). Daily behavior report cards and systematic direct observation: An investigation of the acceptability, reported training and use, and decision reliability among school psychologists. *Journal of Behavioral Education, 17*, 313–327.

Riley-Tillman, T. C., Chafouleas, S. M., Christ, T. J., Briesch, A. M., & LeBel, T. J. (2009). The impact of item wording and behavioral specificity on the accuracy of Direct Behavior Rating (DBR). *School Psychology Quarterly, 24*, 1–12.

Riley-Tillman, T. C., Chafouleas, S. M., Sassu, K. A., Chanese, J. A. M., & Glazer, A. D. (2008). Examining the agreement of Direct Behavior Ratings and systematic direct observation for on-task and disruptive behavior. *Journal of Positive Behavior Interventions, 10*, 136–143.

Riley-Tillman, T. C., Christ, T. J., Chafouleas, S. M., Boice, C. H. & Briesch, A. M. (2010). The impact of observation duration on the accuracy of data obtained from Direct Behavior Rating (DBR). *Journal of Positive Behavior Interventions, 13*, 119–128.

Riley-Tillman, T. C., Methe, S. A., & Weegar, K. (2009). Examining the use of Direct Behavior Rating methodology on classwide formative assessment: A case study. *Assessment for Effective Intervention, 34*, 242–250.

Riley-Tillman, T. C., Stichter, J. P., Kilgus, S. P., Schoemann, A., & Owens, S. (2015). *Agreement between Direct Behavior Rating Single Item Scales and systematic direct observation within an Asperger's sample.* Manuscript submitted for publication.

Rock, M. L. (2005). Use of strategic self-monitoring to enhance academic engagement, productivity, and accuracy of students with and without exceptionalities. *Journal of Positive Behavior Interventions, 7*, 3–17.

Romer, D., & McIntosh, M. (2005). The roles and perspectives of school mental health professionals in promoting adolescent mental health. In D. Evans et al. (Eds.), *Treating and preventing adolescent mental health disorders: What we know and what we don't know* (pp. 598–615). New York: Oxford University Press.

Rosen, L. A., Gabardi, L., Miller, D., & Miller, L. (1990). Home-based treatment of disruptive junior high school students: An analysis of the differential effects of positive and negative consequences. *Behavioral Disorders, 15*, 227–232.

Rosenshine, R. (1976). Recent research on teacher behaviors and student achievement. *Journal of Teacher Education, 27*, 61–64.

Rothstein, R. (2004). *Class and schools: Using social, economic, and educational reform to close the black–white achievement gap.* New York: Teachers College Press.

Rudasill, K. M., Reio, T. G., Stipanovic, N., & Taylor, J. E. (2010). A longitudinal study of student–teacher relationship quality, difficult temperament, and risky behavior from childhood to early adolescence. *Journal of School Psychology, 48*, 389–412.

Russell, A., Pettit, G. G., & Mize, J. (1998). Horizontal qualities in parent–child relationships: Parallels with and possible consequences for children's peer relationships. *Developmental Review, 18*, 313–352.

Russell, M., Carey, R., Kleiman, G., & Venable, J. D. (2009). Face-to-face and online professional development for mathematics teachers: A comparative study. *Journal of Asynchronous Learning Networks, 13*, 71–87.

Safran, S. P., & Safran, J. S. (1985). Classroom context and teachers' perceptions of problem behaviors. *Journal of Educational Psychology, 77*, 20–28.

Sainato, D. M., Goldstein, H., & Strain, P. S. (1992). Effects of self-evaluation on preschool children's use of social interaction strategies with their classmates with Autism. *Journal of Applied Behavior Analysis, 25*, 127–141.

Sainato, D. M., Strain, P. S., Lefebvre, D., & Rapp, N. (1990). Effects of self-evaluation on the independent work skills of preschool children with disabilities. *Exceptional Children, 56*, 540–549.

Salvia, J., Ysselydke, J. E., & Bolt, S. (2010). *Assessment in special and inclusive education* (11th ed.). Boston: Houghton Mifflin.

Sanetti, L. M. H., Chafouleas, S. M., Christ, T. J., & Gritter, K. L. (2009). Extending use of Direct

Behavior Rating beyond student assessment: Applications to treatment integrity within a multi-tiered model of school-based intervention delivery. *Assessment for Effective Intervention, 34,* 251–258.

Sanetti, L. M. H., Fallon, L. M., & Collier-Meek, M. A. (2012). Increasing teacher treatment integrity through performance feedback provided by school personnel. *Psychology in the Schools, 50,* 134–150.

Schlientz, M. D., Riley-Tillman, T. C., Briesch, A. M., Walcott, C. M., & Chafouleas, S. M. (2009). The impact of training on the accuracy of Direct Behavior Ratings (DBRs). *School Psychology Quarterly, 24,* 73–83.

Schnoes, C., Reid, R., Wagner, M., & Marder, C. (2006). ADHD among students receiving special education services: A national study. *Exceptional Children, 72,* 483–496.

Schrank, F. A., Mather, N., & McGrew, K. S. (2015). *Woodcock–Johnson IV Tests of Cognitive Abilities.* Itasca, IL: Riverside.

Schumaker, J. B., Hovell, M. F., & Sherman, J. A. (1977). An analysis of daily report cards and parent-managed privileges in the improvement of adolescents' classroom performance. *Journal of Applied Behavior Analysis, 10,* 449–464.

Scott, T. M., Alter, P. J., Rosenberg, M., & Borgmeier, C. (2010). Decision-making in secondary and tertiary interventions of school-wide systems of positive behavior support. *Education and Treatment of Children, 33,* 513–535.

Scruggs, T. E., & Mastropieri, M. A. (1998). Synthesizing single subject research: Issues and applications. *Behavior Modification, 22,* 221–242.

Scruggs, T. E., & Mastropieri, M. A. (2013). PND at 25: Past, present, and future trends in summarizing single-subject research. *Remedial and Special Education, 34,* 9–19.

Severson, H. H., Walker, H. M., Hope-Doolittle, J., Kratochwill, T. R., & Gresham, F. M. (2007). Proactive early screening to detect behaviorally at-risk students: Issues, approaches, emerging innovations, and professional practices. *Journal of School Psychology, 45,* 193–223.

Shapiro, E. S., & Cole, C. L. (1994). *Behavior change in the classroom: Self-management interventions.* New York: Guilford Press.

Shavelson, R. J., & Webb, N. M. (1991). *Generalizability theory: A primer.* Thousand Oaks, CA: Sage.

Shearer, D. D., Kohler, F. W., Buchan, K. A., & McCullough, K. M. (1996). Promoting independent interactions between preschoolers with autism and their nondisabled peers: An analysis of self-monitoring. *Early Education and Development, 7,* 205–220.

Sheridan, S. M., & Gutkin, T. B. (2000). The ecology of school psychology: Examining and changing our paradigm for the 21st century. *School Psychology Review, 29,* 485–502.

Shimabukuro, S. M., Prater, M. A., Jenkins, A., & Edelen-Smith, P. (1999). The effects of self-monitoring of academic performance on students with learning disabilities and ADD/ADHD. *Education and Treatment of Children, 22,* 397–414.

Shinn, M. R. (2010). Building a scientifically based data system for progress monitoring and universal screening across three tiers including RTI using curriculum-based measurement. In M. R. Shinn & H. M. Walker (Eds.), *Interventions for achievement and behavior problems in a three-tier model, including RTI.* Bethesda, MD: National Association of School Psychologists.

Skiba, R. J., Horner, R. H., Chung, C. G., Rausch, M. K., May, S. L., & Tobin, T. (2011). Race is not neutral: A national investigation of African American and Latino disproportionality in school discipline. *School Psychology Review, 40,* 85–107.

Skiba, R. J., Michael, R. S., Nardo, A. C., & Peterson, R. (2002). The color of discipline: Sources of racial and gender disproportionality in school punishment. *Urban Review, 34,* 317–342.

Skinner, B. F. (1953). *Science and human behavior.* New York: MacMillan.

Sluyter, D. J., & Hawkins, R. P. (1972). Delayed reinforcement of classroom behavior by parents. *Journal of Learning Disabilities, 5,* 20–28.

Smith, L. D., Best, L. A., Stubbs, D. A., & Archibald, A. B. (2002). Constructing knowledge: The role of graphs and tables in hard and soft psychology. *American Psychologist, 57,* 749–761.

Spaulding, S. A., Irvin, L. K., Horner, R. H., May, S. L., Emeldi, M., Tobin, T. J., et al. (2010).

Schoolwide social-behavioral climate, student problem behavior, and related administrative decisions. *Journal of Positive Behavior Interventions, 12*, 69–85.

Spectrum K12. (2011). Response to Intervention Adoption Survey. Retrieved from *www.spectrumk12.com/uploads/file/RTI Report2011 v5.pdf.*

Spool, M. D. (1978). Training programs for observers or behavior: A review. *Personnel Psychology, 31*, 853–888.

Stahmer, A. C., & Schreibman, L. (1992). Teaching children with autism appropriate play in unsupervised environments using a self-management treatment package. *Journal of Applied Behavior Analysis, 25*, 447–459.

Stanger, C., & Lewis, M. (1993). Agreement among parents, teachers, and children on internalizing and externalizing behavior problems. *Journal of Clinical Child Psychology, 22*, 107–115.

Steege, M. W., Davin, T., & Hathaway, M. (2001). Reliability and accuracy of a performance-based behavioral recording procedure. *School Psychology Review, 30*, 252–261.

Steege, M. W., & Watson, T. S. (2009). *Conducting school-based functional behavioral assessments: A practitioner's guide* (2nd ed.). New York: Guilford Press.

Sterling-Turner, H. E., Watson, T. S., & Moore, J. W. (2002). The effects of direct training and treatment integrity on treatment outcomes in school consultation. *School Psychology Quarterly, 17*, 47–77.

Sterling-Turner, H. E., Watson, T. S., Wildmon, M., Watkins, C., & Little, E. (2001). Investigating the relationship between training type and treatment integrity. *School Psychology Quarterly, 16*, 56–67.

Stewart, L., & Silberglitt, B. (2008). Best practices in developing academic local norms. *Best practices in school psychology V* (Vol. 2, pp. 225–242). Washington, DC: National Association of School Psychologists.

Stoner, G., & Green, S. K. (1992). Reconsidering the scientist–practitioner model for school psychology practice. *School Psychology Review, 21*, 155–166.

Strain, P. S., Kohler, F. K., Storey, K., & Danko, C. D. (1994). Teaching preschoolers with autism to self-monitor their social interactions: An analysis of results in home and school settings. *Journal of Emotional and Behavioral Disorders, 2*, 78–88.

Stranger, C., & Lewis, M. (1993). Agreement among parents, teachers, and children on internalizing and externalizing behavior problems. *Journal of Clinical Child Psychology, 22*, 107–115.

Sugai, G., & Horner, R. H. (2002). The evolution of discipline practices: School-wide positive behavior support. *Child and Family Behavior Therapy, 24*, 23–50.

Sugai, G., Sprague, J., Horner, R. R., & Walker, H. (2000). Preventing school violence: The use of office referral to assess and monitor school-wide discipline interventions. *Journal of Emotional and Behavioral Disorders, 8*, 94–101.

Sulsky, L. M., & Balzer, W. K. (1988). Meaning and measurement of performance rating accuracy: Some methodological and theoretical concerns. *Journal of Applied Psychology, 73*, 497–506.

Swift, M. S., & Spivack, G. (1968). The assessment of achievement-related classroom behavior. *Journal of Special Education, 2*, 137–149.

Tawney, J. W., & Gast, D. L. (1984). *Single-subject research in special education*. Columbus, OH: Merrill.

Thorndike, R. M. (2005). *Measurement and evaluation in psychology and educ*ation (7th ed.). Upper Saddle River, NJ: Pearson.

Tilly, W. D., Niebling, B. C., & Rahn-Blakeslee, A. (2010). Making problem solving school psychology work in schools. In G. Peacock, R. Ervin, E. Daly, & K. W. Merrell (Eds.), *Practical handbook of school psychology* (pp. 579–596). New York: Guilford Press.

Tilly, W. D. (2008). The evolution of school psychology to science-based practice: Problem solving and the three-tiered model. In A. Thomas & J. Grimes (Eds.), *Best practices in school psychology V* (pp. 17–36). Bethesda, MD: National Association of School Psychologists.

Todd, A. W., & Horner, R. H. (2007). SWIS readiness checklist. Retrieved August 19, 2014, from *www.pbis.org/common/cms/files/NewTeam/Data/SWISReadinessChecklist.pdf.*

Todd, A. W., Horner, R., & Tobin, T. (2005). *SWIS documentation project: Referral form definitions*. Eugene, OR: PBIS Apps.

Tolan, P. H., & Woo, S. C. (2010). Moving forward in school–family partnerships in promoting student competence: From potential to full impact. In S. L. Christenson & A. L. Reschly (Eds.), *Handbook of school–family partnerships* (pp. 473–501). New York: Routledge.

Tremblay, R. E., Nagin, D. S., Seguin, J. R., Zoccolillo, M., Zelazo, P. D., Boivin, M., et al. (2004). Physical aggression during early childhood: Trajectories and predictors. *Pediatrics, 114*, 43–50.

Tudge, J. R. H. (2008). *The everyday lives of young children: Culture, class, and child rearing in diverse societies*. New York: Cambridge University Press.

U.S. Department of Education, National Center for Education Statistics. (2010). *Teacher attrition and mobility: Results from the 2008–09 Teacher Follow-up Survey* (NCES 2010-353). Retrieved from *http://nces.ed.gov/pubs2010/2010353.pdf*.

U.S. Public Health Service. (2000). *Report of the Surgeon General's Conference on Children's Mental Health: A national action agenda*. Washington, DC: Department of Health and Human Services.

Vance, J. E., Bowen, N. K., Fernandez, G., & Thompson, S. (2002). Risk and protective factors as predictors of outcome in adolescents with psychiatric disorder and aggression. *Journal of the American Academy of Child and Adolescent Psychiatry, 41*, 36–43.

Vannest, K. J., Davis, J. L., Davis, C. R., Mason, B. A., & Burke, M. D. (2010). Effective intervention for behavior with a daily behavior report card: A meta-analysis. *School Psychology Review, 39*, 654–672.

Vannest, K. J., Reynolds, C., & Kamphaus, R. (2008). *BASC-2 intervention guide for learning and behavior problems*. Bloomington, MN: Pearson.

Vitaro, F., Brendgen, M., Larose, S., & Tremblay, R. E. (2005). Kindergarten disruptive behaviors, protective factors, and educational achievement by early adulthood. *Journal of Educational Psychology, 97*, 617–629.

Volpe, R. J., & Briesch, A. M. (2012). Generalizability and dependability of single-item and multiple-item Direct Behavior Rating scales for engagement and disruptive behavior. *School Psychology Review, 41*, 246–261.

Volpe, R. J., & Briesch, A. M. (2015). Multi-item Direct Behavior Ratings: Dependability of two levels of assessment specificity. *School Psychology Quarterly, 30*, 431–442.

Volpe, R. J., Briesch, A. M., & Chafouleas, S. M. (2010). Linking screening for emotional and behavioral problems to problem-solving efforts: An adaptive model of behavioral assessment. *Assessment for Effective Intervention, 35*, 240–244.

Volpe, R. J., & Fabiano, G. A. (2013). *Daily behavior report cards: An evidence-based system of assessment and intervention*. New York: Guilford Press.

Volpe, R. J., & Gadow, K. D. (2010). Creating abbreviated rating scales to monitor classroom inattention-overactivity, aggression, and peer conflict: Reliability, validity, and treatment sensitivity. *School Psychology Review, 39*, 350–363.

Volpe, R. J., Gadow, K. D., Blom-Hoffman, J., & Feinberg, A. B. (2009). Factor analytic and individualized approaches to constructing brief measures of ADHD behaviors. *Journal of Emotional and Behavioral Disorders, 17*, 118–128.

Walker, B., Cheney, D., Stage, S., & Blum, C. (2005). Schoolwide screening and positive behavior supports: Identifying and supporting students as risk for school failure. *Journal of Positive Behavior Interventions, 7*, 194–204.

Walker, H. M. (1985). *Teacher social behavior standards and expectations as determinants of classroom ecology, teacher behavior and child outcomes: Final report*. Eugene, OR: CEPM Publications, College of Education, University of Oregon.

Walker, H. M., Irvin, L. K., Noell, J., & Singer, G. H. S. (1992). A construct score approach to the assessment of social competence: Rationale, technological considerations, and anticipated outcomes. *Behavior Modification, 16*, 448–474.

Walker, H. M., Ramsey, E., & Gresham, F. M. (2003–2004). Heading off disruptive behavior: How early intervention can reduce defiant behavior and win back teaching time. Retrieved from *http://www.aft.org/periodical/american-educator/winter-2003-2004/heading-disruptive-behavior.*

Walker, H. M., & Rankin, R. (1983). Assessing the behavioral expectations and demands of less restrictive settings. *School Psychology Review, 12*, 274–284.

Walker, H. M., & Severson, H. (1992). *Systematic Screening of Behavior Disorders (SSBD): A multiple gating procedure*. Longmont, CO: Sopris West.

Walker, H. M., & Shinn, M. R. (2002). Structuring school-based interventions to achieve integrated primary, secondary, and tertiary prevention goals for safe and effective schools. In M. R. Shinn, H. M. Walker, & G. Stoner (Eds.), *Interventions for academic and behavior problems II: Preventive and remedial approaches* (pp. 1–25). Bethesda, MD: National Association of School Psychologists

Wang, M. C., Haertel, G. D., & Walberg, H. J. (1993). Toward a knowledge base for school learning. *Review of Educational Research, 63*, 249–294.

Watson, T. S., & Kramer, J. J. (1995). Teaching problem solving skills to teachers-in-training: An analogue experimental analysis of three methods. *Journal of Behavioral Education, 5*, 281–293.

Weissberg, R. P., & Cascarino, J. (2013). Academic learning + social-emotional learning = national priority. *Kappan, 95*(2), 8–13.

Wentzel, K. R., & Erdley, C. A. (1993). Strategies for making friends: Relations to social behavior and peer acceptance in early adolescence. *Developmental Psychology, 29*, 819–826.

Werner, E. E. (2005). What can we learn about resilience from large-scale longitudinal studies? In S. Goldstein & R. B. Brooks (Eds.), *Handbook of resilience in children* (pp. 91–105). New York: Springer.

Whitcomb, S., & Merrell, K. W. (2012). *Behavioral, social, and emotional assessment of children and adolescents* (4th edition). Mahwah, NJ: Erlbaum.

Wickstrom, K. F., Jones, K. M., LaFleur, L. H., & Witt, J. C. (1998). An analysis of treatment integrity in school-based consultation. *School Psychology Quarterly, 13*, 141–154.

Wilkinson, L. A. (2005). Bridging the research-to-practice gap in school-based consultation: An example using case studies. *Journal of Educational and Psychological Consultation, 16*, 175–200.

Wilson, F. E., & Evans, I. M. (1983). The reliability of target-behavior selection in behavioral assessment. *Behavioral Assessment, 5*, 15–32.

Wittlieb, E., Eifert, G., Wilson, F. E., & Evans I. M. (1978). Target behaviour selection in recent child case reports in behavior therapy. *The Behavior Therapist, 1*, 15–16.

Wolery, M., Bailey, D. B., & Sugai, G. M. (1988). *Effective teaching: Principles and procedures of applied behavior analysis with exceptional students*. Boston: Allyn & Bacon.

Wood, S. J., Murdock, J. Y., Cronin, M. E., Dawson, N. M., & Kirby, P. C. (1998). Effects of self-monitoring on on-task behaviors of at-risk middle school students. *Journal of Behavioral Education, 8*, 263–279.

Zimmer-Gembeck, M. J., Chipuer, H. M., Hanisch, M., Creed, P. A., & McGregor, L. (2006). Relationships at school and stage–environment fit as resources for adolescent engagement and achievement. *Journal of Adolescence, 29*, 911–933.

Zins, J. E., & Elias, M. J. (2007). Social and emotional learning. In G. G. Bear & K. M. Minke (Eds.), *Children's needs III: Development, prevention, and intervention* (pp. 1–13). Bethesda, MD: National Association of School Psychologists.

Index

Note: *f* following a page number indicates a figure; *t* indicates a table.

CPSIA information can be obtained at www.ICGtesting.com
Printed in the USA
BVOW03*0746270416

444996BV00005B/2/P

9 781462 525843